How Children Learn to Read

How Children Learn to Read

Current Issues and New Directions
in the Integration of Cognition,
Neurobiology and Genetics of Reading
and Dyslexia Research and Practice

Edited by

Ken Pugh and Peggy McCardle

Psychology Press
Taylor & Francis Group

New York   London

Psychology Press
Taylor & Francis Group
270 Madison Avenue
New York, NY 10016

Psychology Press
Taylor & Francis Group
27 Church Road
Hove, East Sussex BN3 2FA

© 2009 by Taylor and Francis Group, LLC
Psychology Press is an imprint of Taylor & Francis Group, an Informa business

Printed in the United States of America on acid-free paper
10 9 8 7 6 5 4 3 2 1

International Standard Book Number: 978-1-84872-843-1 (Hardback)

Library of Congress Cataloging-in-Publication Data

How children learn to read : current issues and new directions in the integration
of cognition, neurobiology, and genetics of reading and dyslexia research and
practice / editors, Ken Pugh, Peggy McCardle.
p. cm. -- (The extraordinary brain series)
Includes bibliographical references and index.
ISBN 978-1-84872-843-1 (hardcover : alk. paper)
1. Reading, Psychology of. 2. Reading--Physiological aspects. 3. Cognition in
children. 4. Dyslexia. I. Pugh, Ken. II. McCardle, Peggy D.

BF456.R2H67 2009
418'.4019--dc22   2009013220

Visit the Taylor & Francis Web site at
http://www.taylorandfrancis.com

and the Psychology Press Web site at
http://www.psypress.com

Contents

SECTION I   Major Themes in the Study of the Neurobiology of Dyslexia

SECTION II   Methods and Tools

SECTION III   Neurobiological, Genetic, and Cognitive Aspects

Chapter 10

*Laurie E. Cutting, Sarah H. Eason, Katherine M. Young,
and Audrey L. Alberstadt*

Chapter 11

Richard Olson, Brian Byrne, and Stefan Samuelsson

SECTION IV   Intervention

Chapter 14 Remediation of Reading Difficulties in English-Language

Linda S. Siegel

Chapter 15 How the Origins of the Reading Brain Instruct Our

*Maryanne Wolf, Stephanie Gottwald, Wendy Galante,
Elizabeth Norton, and Lynne Miller*

**Conclusion: Integration of Methodologies in Cognitive
Neuroscience—Research, Planning, and Policy** 301

Kenneth R. Pugh and Peggy McCardle

Preface

THE DYSLEXIA FOUNDATION—A BRIEF HISTORY

The Dyslexia Foundation, or TDF, was begun in the late 1980s, although the idea was conceived long before that, through conversations and interactions between TDF founder William H. "Will" Baker and notable researchers in dyslexia, including Norman Geschwind, Al Galaburda, Roger Saunders, Drake Duane, Margaret Rawson, and Thomas Kemper. Under the mentorship of Geschwind, Galaburda and Kemper were studying the brain of postmortem dyslexics, looking for differences in brain structure that might lend insight into this puzzling disability. They wanted to establish a brain bank and enlisted Baker's help. Through the generosity of the Underwood Company and the efforts of the Baker family, funds were given to help establish the first Dyslexia Research Laboratory at Beth Israel Hospital, Harvard Medical School, Boston, to investigate the neural foundations of dyslexia. The laboratory officially opened in 1982. Following the untimely death of Geschwind in 1984, Baker met with those at the lab to discuss how to maintain the momentum and enthusiasm that had been generated by this visionary scientist. Galaburda suggested that the field needed researchers from cognition, neuroscience, and education to work together to address the challenge of dyslexia. Baker became the director of research for the Orton Dyslexia Society, and under its auspices Galaburda and Baker—with the help of Caryl Frankenberger and with funding by Emily Fisher Landau—organized a symposium in 1987 in Florence, Italy, and the concept of the symposium series was born.

That 1987 scientific meeting brought internationally renowned researchers together to share research findings and new ideas, and to critique one another's work, spurring new and innovative approaches to the study of dyslexia. New research questions were raised, and the field began to expand—the synergy the organizers had sought became real. By 1989 it was apparent that if the research field was to advance, it would have to work concurrently with, yet independently from, the Orton Dyslexia Society. The society focused primarily on treatment and education; researchers sought a parallel group that would focus more exclusively on foundational research that could inform that treatment and education. In the spring of 1989, the National Dyslexia Research Foundation (later renamed The Dyslexia Foundation, or TDF) was formed. The foundation board members included leaders from the scientific and business community who were committed to the motto: "Research is the mother of knowledge." Baker served as the founding president and Drake Duane served as founding chairman of the Scientific Advisory Board.

In 1990, the new foundation sponsored the next symposium in Barcelona, Spain. The topic was "Dyslexia and Development: Neurobiological Aspects of Extraordinary Brains," again with Galaburda serving as the conference director.

With this second symposium, the Extraordinary Brain Series was born. After the third symposium, research collaborations among the participants and a growing synergy became apparent. The number of researchers investigating various aspects of dyslexia was growing and the aspects of reading disability being investigated broadened, deepened, and increased in innovation and productivity. Some questions were being answered and even more were being raised. Having reached the 10th symposium of this series in the summer of 2007, it is clear that there is always more work to be done, but it is equally clear that the Extraordinary Brain Series is an important forum for researchers and those keenly interested in dyslexia and the brain to build important collaborations and share ideas, methods, and concerns. And so, having reached the milestone of the 10th symposium, the series—and the foundation—will continue.

THE EXTRAORDINARY BRAIN SERIES

This volume marks the 10th symposium in the Extraordinary Brain Series; eight of the nine previous symposia have resulted in books. Each one has addressed a particular facet of the brain-based learning disability, dyslexia. The series has served as an update on the neurobiology of dyslexia, providing a window on cutting-edge research in both animal models and humans. Three symposia have addressed primarily the educational aspects of dyslexia and reading intervention or the implications for early intervention. The 10th symposium marks a culmination, in that it brings together the various aspects of how we approach the study of dyslexia, the underlying possible etiologies, the neurobiology (from animal models of neuronal development through neuroimaging of brains during the performance of reading tasks), the genetics (both quantitative and behavioral), and behavioral–educational interventions. Just as the series has examined the state of the science in various particular aspects of dyslexia, so too this symposium addresses current research in each of these areas, but importantly seeks to encourage the integration of that information, and of future research efforts across the various disciplines to allow greater linkages among the varied levels of analysis represented at the symposium. In that sense, it is an update and integration of all the previous symposia, building upon them in a way that seems fitting for the 10th anniversary symposium. Below is a listing of the 10 symposia, with their locations and the citation for each of the resulting publications:

I. June 1987, Florence, Italy
   Symposium director: Albert M. Galaburda
   Galaburda, A. M. (Ed.). (1989). *From reading to neurons*. Cambridge, MA: Bradford Books/MIT Press.

II. June 1990, Barcelona, Spain
    Symposium director: Albert M. Galaburda

Galaburda, A. M. (Ed.). (1992). *Dyslexia and development: Neurobiological aspects of extraordinary brains.* Cambridge, MA: Harvard University Press.

III. June 1992, Santa Fe, New Mexico
Symposium director: Paula Tallal
Chase, C., Rosen, G. D., & Sherman, G. F. (Eds.). (1996). *Developmental dyslexia: Neural, cognitive, and genetic mechanisms.* Baltimore: York Press.

IV. June 1994, Kauai, Hawaii
Symposium director: Benita Blachman
Blachman, B. A. (Ed.). (1997). *Foundations of reading acquisition and dyslexia: Implications for early intervention.* Mahwah, NJ: Lawrence Erlbaum Associates.

V. June 1996, Kona, Hawaii
Symposium director: Drake Duane
Duane, D. (Ed.). (1998). *Reading and attention disorders: Neurobiological correlates.* Baltimore: York Press.

VI. June 1998, Kona, Hawaii
Symposium director: Barbara Foorman
Foorman, B. R. (Ed.). (2003). *Preventing and remediating reading difficulties: Bringing science to scale.* Baltimore: York Press.

VII. June 2000, Crete, Greece
Symposium director: Maryanne Wolf
Wolf, M. (Ed.). (2001). *Time, fluency, and dyslexia.* Baltimore: York Press.

VIII. October 2002, Johannesburg, South Africa
Symposium director: Frank Wood
Multilingualism and dyslexia. No publication.

IX. June 2004, Como, Italy
Symposium director: Glenn Rosen
Rosen, G. D. (Ed.). (2005). *The dyslexic brain: New pathways in neuroscience discovery.* Mahwah, NJ: Lawrence Erlbaum Associates.

X. June 2007, Campos do Jordão, Brazil
Symposium directors: Ken Pugh and Peggy McCardle
Pugh, K., & McCardle, P. (Eds.). 2009. *How children learn to read: Current issues and new directions in the integration of cognition, neurobiology and genetics of reading and dyslexia research and practice.*

William Baker

Acknowledgments

There are specific organizations and many individuals who have helped to make this book possible. First, we must acknowledge the generous support of The Dyslexia Foundation (TDF) and the National Yang Ming University (Taiwan) and Haskins Laboratories. TDF supports biennial symposia and the writing of books that document the excellent science presented and discussed at the symposia, and thereby offers scientific support to the practices that enable dyslexic children and adults to receive the help they need learning to read. In addition, generous contributions from Keith Johnson and from individual anonymous donors helped to support the symposia and this book, and we wish to thank them heartily as well. The authors of the chapters in this volume clearly deserve a resounding thanks for their openness in the symposium discussions and for their excellent work in preparing chapters that convey the impact of those discussions. Thanks, too, to Cathleen Petree, our patient and vigilant acquisitions editor at LEA/Taylor & Francis.

Contributors

Stephanie Al Otaiba is Associate Professor of Special Education at Florida State University and a Faculty Associate of the Florida Center of Reading Research (FCRR). She received her PhD in human development in 2000 from Vanderbilt University specializing in special education and early literacy. Prior to that, she was a special education teacher for 14 years. Al Otaiba's research interests include early literacy interventions, response to intervention, and teacher training. She is currently conducting studies examining the effectiveness of early literacy interventions.

Audrey L. Alberstadt is a Research Assistant in the Department of Developmental Cognitive Neurology at the Kennedy Krieger Institute. Her primary responsibilities include recruiting, consenting, and intake screening of research participants. Her research interests include learning disabilities, ADHD, and other cognitive impairments.

Brian Byrne is Professor of Psychology at the University of New England in Australia. His research interests include the early stage of literacy acquisition in normal children and those at risk for reading disability. His group has developed and field tested teaching materials designed to foster children's phonemic sensitivity, and has shown them to be successful in supporting literacy development. Bryne codirects the International Longitudinal Twin Study (ILTS) of literacy, language, and attention.

Piers L. Cornelissen is a Reader in Psychology at the University of York, United Kingdom. As an undergraduate he studied medicine at Worcester College Oxford, continuing his clinical training at St. Thomas's Hospital in London. He studied for a DPhil with Professor John Stein at the University Laboratory of Physiology, Oxford, funded by the Wellcome Trust. After 3 years as a McDonnell-Pew postdoctoral fellow, he moved to Newcastle upon Tyne to take up a lectureship. He worked for 10 years as a lecturer, then Reader in Psychology at the University of Newcastle before moving to York in 2006. The main thrust of his research is to understand the neural basis of reading using a combination of psychophysical and neuroimaging techniques (MEG and fMRI).

Carolyn D. Cowen is Executive Director of Carroll School's Center for Innovative Learning. Prior to that, she was executive director of The Learning Disabilities Network—a nonprofit she helped found that operated for 20 years providing services to individuals with learning disabilities, their families, and professionals working on their behalf. Cowen received a master's degree in reading education and learning disabilities from Harvard University and was the recipient of the Alice H. Garside Award from the New England Branch of the International Dyslexia Association. She has been an architect of collaborative change initiatives and innovative program designs, a leader of organizations working within the community of people and groups focused on learning disabilities. She has worked within the area of learning disabilities as a teacher, consultant, reading therapist, speaker, author, editor, professional development planner, and executive director.

Laurie E. Cutting is in the Department of Developmental Cognitive Neurology at the Kennedy Krieger Institute and is Associate Professor of Neurology at Johns Hopkins School of Medicine and Associate Professor of Education at Johns Hopkins University. Her research interests are focused on brain–behavior relationships in the areas of reading and reading disabilities, particularly with regard to reading comprehension. She also has research interests in ADHD and neurofibromatosis type 1.

Sarah H. Eason is a Research Psychology Associate in the Department of Developmental Cognitive Neurology at the Kennedy Krieger Institute. Her primary responsibilities include the cognitive and neuropsychological assessment of research participants. Her current research focuses on reading disabilities and cognitive development. Other areas of interest include personality assessment and mood and anxiety disorders in children and adolescents.

Christopher G. Fiondella received his bachelor's degree from the University of Connecticut at Storrs in 2003, where he is currently enrolled as a PhD candidate in cellular biology. His research interests include the genetic mechanisms that underlie cortical development and their application to transplant therapy.

Jack M. Fletcher is Distinguished University Professor in the Department of Psychology at the University of Houston. He is a board certified clinical neuropsychologist and current President of the International Neuropsychological Society. He is an internationally renowned researcher in the area of developmental disabilities, including reading disability, ADHD, and spina bifida. Dr. Fletcher served as a member of the NICHD National Advisory Council and of the President's Commission on Excellence in Special Education. Dr. Fletcher was the recipient of the Samuel T. Orton award from the International Dyslexia Association in 2003.

Barbara Foorman, PhD, is the Francis Eppes Professor of Education and Director of the Florida Center for Reading Research at Florida State University. During 2005, Foorman served as the commissioner of Education Research in the Institute of Education Sciences in the U.S. Department of Education. Before that Foorman was professor of pediatrics and director of the Center for Academic and Reading Skills at the University of Texas Health Science Center at Houston and professor of educational psychology at the University of Houston. Foorman edits a new journal and serves on many national advisory and consensus committees. She has been principal investigator on many early reading grants and her centers have provided professional development and technical assistance to Reading First schools. Foorman has authored spelling and vocabulary curricula and developed early reading assessments used in several states.

David J. Francis is the Hugh Roy and Lillie Cranz Cullen Distinguished Professor of Quantitative Methods and Chairman of the Department of Psychology at the University of Houston, where he also serves as Director of the Texas Institute for Measurement, Evaluation, and Statistics, and Codirector of the Texas Learning and Computation Center. Francis obtained a doctoral degree in clinical neuropsychology from the University of Houston in 1985 with a specialization in quantitative methods. He is a Fellow of Division 5 (Measurement, Evaluation, and Statistics) of the American Psychology Association, chair of the Executive Board of the Council of Graduate Departments of Psychology, and a member the Independent Review Panel for the National Assessment of Title I and the National Research Council's (NRC) Board on Testing and Assessment. He was a recipient of the 2006 Albert J. Harris Award from the International Reading Association and has received the University of Houston's Teaching Excellence and Excellence in Research and Scholarship Awards. Francis' areas of interest include the modeling of individual growth and development in the study of reading and reading disabilities, and the language and literacy development of students at risk for academic failure, in particular students who are English-language learners.

Ram Frost is Professor of Psychology, Department of Psychology, Hebrew University of Jerusalem. His research focuses on the cognitive processes involved in visual word recognition, investigating what is universal in the reading process across diverse languages, and what aspects of reading are unique to each language's orthographic and morphological system. His previous work focused on the orthographic depth hypothesis, and the computation of phonological information. This latter work was the basis for the strong phonological theory of reading. Presently, he is involved in comprehensive research on morphological processing in Hebrew, which takes advantage of the characteristics of Hebrew Semitic morphology to examine lexical representation and lexical access of morphologically complex words. This ongoing investigation employs various research paradigms such as masked priming paradigm, parafoveal presentation, and brain imaging. Most of Frost's research work is pursued in collaboration with Haskins Laboratories in New Haven, Connecticut, where he is affiliated as a research scientist.

Stephen J. Frost, PhD, is Senior Scientist at Haskins Laboratories, a private, nonprofit research institute with a primary focus on speech, reading, and language, and their biological bases. Frost's research focuses primarily on examining correlations between behavioral measures of reading skill and patterns of brain activation during reading measured using functional MRI. His other research interests include exploring the extent to which spoken and written language access either modality-independent or modality-dependent phonological, orthographic, and semantic information.

Wendy Galante is the Program Coordinator at the Center for Reading and Language Research at Tufts University. She holds a master's degree in early childhood education.

Stephanie Gottwald is the Research Coordinator at the Center for Reading and Language Research at Tufts University. She conducts intervention studies for elementary-aged struggling readers. In addition, she trains educators in fluency intervention methods and reading fluency assessment. She received her master's degree in linguistics from Boston College in the Slavic and Eastern Languages Department and was a Fulbright fellow in Germany.

Elena L. Grigorenko received a PhD in general psychology from Moscow State University, Russia, in 1990, and a PhD in developmental psychology and genetics from Yale University in 1996. Currently, she is Associate Professor of Child Studies, Psychology, and Epidemiology and Public Health at Yale; and Adjunct Professor of Psychology at Columbia University and Moscow State University (Russia). Grigorenko has received awards for her work from five divisions of the American Psychological Association (APA); in 2004, she won the APA Distinguished Award for an Early Career Contribution to Developmental Psychology.

Leonard Katz, PhD, is Senior Scientist at Haskins Laboratories and Professor Emeritus in Psychology at the University of Connecticut. He has studied the reading process in the writing systems of several European, Middle Eastern, and Asian languages. Katz's recent work concerns the design and analysis of studies that combine brain activation and behavioral data.

Nicole Landi, PhD, is Assistant Professor of Educational Psychology at the University of Minnesota and Research Scientist at Haskins Laboratories. Her research uses electrophysiological and functional MRI techniques to study reading development and reading disability.

Joseph J. LoTurco received an MS in psychology from Yale University, New Haven, Connecticut, in 1987, and a PhD in neuroscience from Stanford University, Palo Alto, California, in 1991. He conducted postdoctoral research in the Department of Genetics, Harvard Medical School, from 1992 to 1994, and he has been on the faculty at the University of Connecticut, Storrs, in the Department of Physiology and Neurobiology since 1994.

Peggy McCardle, PhD, MPH, is Chief of the Child Development and Behavior Branch at the Eunice Kennedy Shriver National Institute for Child Health and Human Development (NICHD) of the National Institutes of Health in Bethesda,

Maryland. In addition to her oversight of the branch, she directs the research program on language, bilingual, and biliteracy, which includes research on monolingual, bilingual, and cross-linguistic studies of language development and bilingual/language minority reading. McCardle also developed the branch programs in adolescent and adult literacy. McCardle is lead editor of the volumes *The Voice of Evidence in Reading Research* (Brookes, 2004); *Childhood Bilingualism* (Multilingual Matters, 2006); and *Infant Pathways to Language: Methods, Models, and Research Directions* (Erlbaum/Taylor & Francis, 2008) and has served as guest editor of thematic journal issues on reading, bilingualism, and English-language learner research.

W. Einar Mencl, PhD, is Senior Scientist and Director of Neuroimaging Research at Haskins Laboratories. His research applies functional MRI to the study of reading, reading disability, and childhood development of the skilled reading system. He plays an integrative role across all the neuroimaging projects at Haskins and is active in the development of new statistical analysis techniques to identify neural systems engaged in language processing.

Lynne Miller is Assistant Director of the Center for Reading and Language Research at Tufts University. She conducts intervention studies for children with dyslexia, as well as English-language learners, and helped to create the versions of the RAVE-O program.

Robin Morris is Vice President for Research and Regent's Professor of Psychology at Georgia State University where he holds appointments in the Department of Psychology in the College of Arts and Sciences and the Department of Educational Psychology and Special Education in the College of Education. Dr. Morris is a licensed Clinical Neuropsychologist and an internationally renowned expert in the area of reading and developmental disabilities. He is widely cited for his contributions to the literature on identification, classification, and subtypes in neuropsychology and developmental psychology. He has served as a member of the NICHD National Advisory Council and as a Presidential Appointee to the National Advisory Board for the National Institute for Literacy.

Adam J. Naples is a doctoral student in the Department of Psychology at Yale University. He is currently completing his doctoral research and transitioning into a postdoctoral fellow position at the Yale Child Study Center.

Elizabeth Norton is a doctoral student in child development and a member of the Center for Reading and Language Research at Tufts University. She is a National Science Foundation Graduate Research Fellow.

Richard Olson is Professor of Psychology at the University of Colorado, Boulder, and Director of the Colorado Learning Disabilities Research Center (CLDRC). His research has focused on the genetic and environmental etiology of deficits and individual differences in the components of reading and related skills in school-age children and young adults. Other research with coinvestigators in the CLDRC has focused on specific genes associated with reading disabilities (RD), comorbidity between RD and ADHD, and on the development and application of computer-based interventions for RD. His research team is exploring genetic and environmental influences on individual differences in pre-reading skills and reading development through the early grades.

Kenneth R. Pugh is President and Director of Research, Haskins Laboratories, New Haven, Connecticut; and Associate Professor, Department of Pediatrics, Yale University School of Medicine, where he is also Director of the Yale Reading Center. His primary research interests are in the areas of cognitive neuroscience and psycholinguistics. His research program examines the neurobiology of language development with a particular emphasis on reading and reading disability, and employs combined behavioral and functional neuroimaging techniques.

Franck Ramus is a CNRS researcher at Laboratoire de Sciences Cognitives et Psycholinguistique, Département d'Etudes Cognitives, Ecole Normale Supérieure, Paris. His research focuses on language acquisition and its disorders (dyslexia, specific-language impairment, as well as autism).

Glenn D. Rosen earned a PhD in developmental psychobiology from the University of Connecticut, Storrs, in 1982. For the past 26 years, he has been associated with the Dyslexia Research Laboratory at Beth Israel Deaconess Medical Center in Boston, of which he is currently director. He also holds an academic appointment at Harvard Medical School as Associate Professor of Neurology (neuroscience). His research interests include the anatomic substrates of developmental dyslexia and the genetic investigation of complex traits of the nervous system.

Jay G. Rueckl is Associate Professor of Psychology at the University of Connecticut and a Senior Scientist at Haskins Laboratories. He earned his PhD at the University of Wisconsin. Before moving to Connecticut, he taught at Harvard University. He served as Director of the Cognitive Science Program at the University of Connecticut from 2000 to 2007 and was an associate editor for *Memory and Cognition*.

Stefan Samuelsson is a Professor in special education at Linköping University, Sweden. He also works as a professor at the National Centre for Reading Education and Reading Research at Stavanger University, Norway. He received his PhD in education from Linköping University in 1994. Besides his more recent interest in behavioral genetics, Samuelsson has focused on reading and writing difficulties among children and adolescents as well as adults. In his research, Samuelsson has also focused on aspects of reading in particular samples, such as children with very low birth weights, prison inmates, and single cases with brain lesions.

Rebecca Sandak, Senior Scientist at Haskins Laboratories, passed away on October 9, 2006, in a car accident. Her research focused on understanding the cognitive processes underlying skilled and impaired reading, reading acquisition, and successful reading instruction and remediation. Her functional MRI research examined how learning conditions, reading expertise, and reading strategies influence the areas of the brain recruited for reading.

Mark S. Seidenberg is Hilldale Professor and Donald O. Hebb Professor in the Department of Psychology at the University of Wisconsin-Madison. He is presently also a visiting professor at the University of Provence, Aix-en-Provence, France. He holds a PhD in psychology from Columbia University, where he studied psycholinguistics and helped raise the cute but linguistically deficient chimpanzee Nim Chimpsky. Seidenberg is known for his research on reading and language, particularly the development of computational models of reading acquisition and skilled performance, which emphasize the role of phonological information in learning to read and in dyslexia, and the division of labor among visual and phonological processes in skilled reading. In recent work, he has used the same computational concepts in studies of infant language learning and critical period effects in learning first and second languages. He is also investigating the achievement gap, the relatively low levels of reading achievement among minority children, and specifically how language background affects learning. He views computational models as the interface between behavior (such as reading) and its brain bases.

Gordon F. Sherman received his PhD in developmental psychobiology from the University of Connecticut, Storrs, in 1980 and has more than 25 years of research experience related to the development of the brain and the understanding of developmental dyslexia. He is Executive Director of The Newgrange School and Education Center located in Mercer County, New Jersey. Before joining Newgrange he was director of the Dyslexia Research Laboratory at Beth Israel Deaconess Medical Center, Boston, and a faculty member in neurology (neurosciences) at Harvard Medical School. Sherman is a former president of the International Dyslexia Association, and recipient of the association's Samuel T. Orton Award, which is presented annually to a person who has made a dramatic impact in the field of dyslexia. Sherman speaks nationally and internationally to parents, teachers, and scientists about cerebrodiversity, learning differences, brain development, and the enlightened classroom.

Linda S. Siegel holds the Dorothy C. Lam Chair in Special Education and is Professor of Educational and Counselling Psychology and Special Education at the University of British Columbia. She has a BA from Queens College of the City University of New York and an MS and PhD from Yale University. She has published articles on cognitive and language development, reading, spelling, and dyslexia. Siegel has been the associate editor of *Child Development* and the editor of the *International Journal of Behavioral Development,* and has served on the editorial boards of a number of journals.

Gayaneh Szenkovits completed her PhD on the phonological deficit in dyslexia at Laboratoire de Sciences Cognitives et Psycholinguistique, Paris. She is currently a postdoctoral fellow at the MRC Cognition and Brain Sciences Unit, Cambridge, United Kingdom.

Yu Wang received a bachelor of medicine from Central South University Xiangya School of Medicine, China, in 2000. He is now a PhD candidate in physiology and neurobiology at the University of Connecticut, Storrs. His research interests include the genetics, cellular, and molecular biology of the nervous system.

Maryanne Wolf is the John DiBiaggio Professor of Citizenship and Public Service in the Eliot-Pearson Department of Child Development at Tufts University, where she is also Director of the Center for Reading and Language Development. She is the recipient of the American Psychological Association's Teacher of the Year Award, the Distinguished Teacher Award from the Massachusetts Psychological Association, and the Geschwind Lecture Award from the International Dyslexia Association. She is the author of *Proust and the Squid: The Story and Science of the Reading Brain.*

Katherine M. Young is a Research Assistant in the Department of Developmental Cognitive Neurology at the Kennedy Krieger Institute. Her primary responsibilities include institutional review board correspondence, database maintenance, and recruitment and tutoring of children with reading disabilities and other pediatric disorders. Her research interests include learning disabilities, education, and child development.

Introduction: How Children Learn to Read—Current Issues and New Directions in the Integration of Cognition, Neurobiology, and Genetics of Reading and Dyslexia Research and Practice

In recent years, research on assessment and treatment of specific reading disability (dyslexia) has become a magnet for the application of new techniques and technologies from neuroscience, cognitive psychology, behavioral and quantitative genetics, and cognitive neuroscience. This interdisciplinary fusion has yielded numerous and diverse findings regarding the brain bases of this syndrome. This book seeks to bring together information about dyslexia intervention research as it relates to genetic and neurobiological research, critically reviewing extant methodologies and findings in basic research and treatment studies. It seeks to set the stage for new approaches and ideas that will move the field forward scientifically, and that will ultimately inform what happens in the classroom, and why and how what happens in the classroom succeeds when it does. We hope that it will stimulate work on variation in etiology, subtypes of reading disorders, cross-linguistic comparisons, and the impact of multilingual experience in typical and atypical reading development. Information is presented on analytic methods, gene–brain–behavior integration methods, early detection (biomarkers), the development of computational models, and optimization of design in treatment research (taking into account special talents, subtypes and individual variation, and the demands of translational research).

At the level of genetics, it has been established with careful observation and behavioral studies that dyslexia is a highly heritable disorder, but the contributions of environment, including instruction, are important. In the search for etiology, a number of candidate genes have been proposed. Research has demonstrated possible early "miswiring" guided by genes that may explain at least part of why some individuals have difficulty learning to read (Rosen et al., 2007; Threlkeld et al., 2007; Wang et al., 2006; for a review, see Galaburda, LoTurco, Ramus, Fitch, & Rosen, 2006). Despite a few breakthrough studies, the area of the genetics of reading and reading disability remains a challenging field, and one that clearly must be studied in conjunction with neurobiology.

At the level of brain systems, brain activation anomalies at key left hemisphere (LH) posterior regions have been observed with surprising consistency in different languages and across different developmental stages. Moreover, a growing number of recent studies have reported that intensive remediation/intervention is associated with increased responsivity of LH posterior systems. These seminal findings on brain plasticity in dyslexia are highly promising, but need to be expanded to include a deeper focus on individual differences, subtypes, and the accompanying differential responses to intervention. As we take stock of existing knowledge and directions in which to build on that knowledge with increased use and integration of recent and emerging technologies, several pressing research needs can be identified.

At present, there are limited but growing numbers of cross-linguistic neuroimaging studies on reading development, disability, and the effects of intervention. Although the initial evidence has provided support for a common neurobiological signature of both skilled and impaired reading (Fiebach, Friederici, Mueller, & von Cramon, 2002; Kuo et al., 2003, 2004; Paulesu et al., 2001; Pugh, Sandak, Frost, Moore, & Mencl, 2005), some differences have been observed (Siok, Perfetti, Jin, & Tan, 2004). Given the significant variability in orthographic form, orthographic-to-phonological mappings, methods of reading instruction, and manifestations of reading disability across languages and cultures, more work needs to be done in the area of cross-linguistic and bilingual studies of reading to identify the neurobiological universals of dyslexia and to understand how the functional organization of reading varies with language-specific features. Such knowledge is crucial to a full theoretical and practical account of reading acquisition and dyslexia. Related to this, and of considerable practical importance to public health and education leaders in this country, is how reading difficulties might manifest and differ in multilingual children (particularly those bilingual children with limited English proficiency in environments where English is the societal language). Research that examines all this in different writing systems and in different languages promises to deepen our general understanding of dyslexia and to address relevant public health goals.

In June 2007, The Dyslexia Foundation (TDF), with generous contributions from the Yang Ming University Taiwan and Haskins Laboratories as well as individual donors, sponsored a symposium that brought together leading researchers from multiple disciplines across various countries to address several crucial, cutting-edge, interrelated topics, and to share their work and their thoughts on how best to integrate these disciplines to move the research to new frontiers. An overarching goal of this meeting was to engage all of the participants in developing recommendations for new directions in dyslexia-related research. On the last 2 days of the meeting, participants convened to develop consensus recommendations for new research directions and priorities; methodological developments necessary to support these new directions; best approaches to extending the work to diverse written languages and to strengthening links between research and practice; and policy and funding implications. The speakers present for that meeting provided both depth and breadth of expertise in the areas that underlie how children learn to read, that is, cognition, neurobiology, and genetics, as well as the areas of instruction and intervention.

Like the symposium, this volume begins with a brief historical overview of the symposium's main sponsor, The Dyslexia Foundation. After this introduction, the book is laid out in four major sections: major themes in the study of dyslexia; methods and tools used in the study of reading and dyslexia; the neurobiological, genetic, and cognitive aspects; and intervention. The conclusion serves to lay out next steps for the field, as developed by the participants of the symposium, pulling together all the areas covered in the sections of the volume, and offers a call to interdisciplinary, innovative research action.

One major question that symposium participants were asked to consider was: Are there multiple neurobiological etiologies in dyslexia? Brain imaging and genetics studies often tacitly assume a unitary neurobiological mechanism in dyslexia. Although individual differences in brain and behavior profiles are always evident, whether this implies different brain causal pathways is an understudied question. In Section 1 of this book, "Major Themes in the Study of the Neurobiology of Dyslexia," the authors provide overviews of major areas of research that set the stage to consider this question: developmental cognitive neuroscience; genes, brain anatomy and behavior; and translation to the classroom. In Chapter 1, Frost et al. discuss the behavioral and neurobiological circuitry mapping of skilled and disabled readers, as a foundation for understanding the sections that follow in terms of ongoing work on the neurobiological bases of reading and reading difficulties. In Chapter 2, Rosen, Wang, Fiondella, and LoTurco discuss animal models and the links among anatomic, genetic, and behavioral studies that bear on our understanding of dyslexia. Chapter 3 completes the overview by addressing the transfer of research to actual practice. Sherman and Cowen lay out the challenges in bringing research findings to bear in teaching and intervening, one of which is the individual differences students bring to education.

Section 2, "Methods and Tools," addresses methods and tools used in the study of reading and dyslexia (methodological/analytic tools, neuroimaging, computational modeling, and genetics). In Chapter 4, Francis addresses advances in methodology that can be used to analyze the behavioral data that will need to be integrated with neurobiological and genetic data to move the field forward. Chapter 5, by Mencl, Frost, and Pugh, carries this theme forward by covering tools for multimodal imaging. The authors outline the challenges that must be met to examine data consistently across functional magnetic resonance imaging (fMRI), magnetoencephalography (MEG), and diffusion tensor imaging (DTI).

The kinds of complex data acquired at brain or behavioral levels of analysis in the study of dyslexia need to be better integrated. Sophisticated computational models have been proposed to account for behavioral deficits, but these computational frameworks have not yet been extended to brain–behavior relations. Such work will be of high priority in making clinically meaningful links between (a) variation in brain development and individual differences in reading and cognitive profiles, (b) why certain types of remediation might be optimal for certain neurobiological subtypes, and (c) how differences in language or bilingualism might interact with neurobiological risk factors in dyslexia. Rueckl and Seidenberg, in Chapter 6, relate computational modeling of reading and reading disability behavioral data to the neurobiological data. The integration of genetic data is also crucial, and Grigorenko and Naples present information on genetics as a tool for understanding reading and reading disability in Chapter 7.

Are there legitimate neurobiological subtypes? Answering this question will not only improve our ability to interpret brain and genetics findings, it will also have direct implications on how we go about testing for effective treatments. To do so, we must study in an integrated way the neurobiological, genetic, and cognitive aspects of reading and dyslexia (phonological abilities, visual word recognition and neuroimaging, reading comprehension and neuroimaging, genetic and environmental influences on reading and reading difficulties, and morphological differences between languages that impact learning to read). The chapters in Section 3, "Neurobiological, Genetic, and Cognitive Aspects," collectively address this area. Ramus and Szenkovits, in Chapter 8, address the nature of the phonological deficit. Cornelissen, in Chapter 9, relates MEG data on visual word recognition to developmental dyslexia. In Chapter 10, Cutting, Eason, Young, and Alberstadt also use neuroimaging (this time fMRI) data in conjunction with careful behavioral assessment to examine reading comprehension abilities. Olson, Byrne, and Samuelsson bring behavioral genetic techniques to bear on the issues of heritability and individual differences in reading deficits in Chapter 11. In Chapter 12, Ram Frost examines differences in reading in Hebrew and English.

Intervention is also a key theme in the dialogue about reading and dyslexia, and Section 4 is dedicated to this topic. There is a growing body of evidence that successful reading interventions in at-risk children result in increased response in functionally anomalous left hemisphere brain systems (Shaywitz et al., 2004; Simos et al., 2002; Temple et al., 2003; see also Frost et al., and Cutting et al., this volume). A number of recently published studies have utilized training programs that emphasize phonological training to differing degrees. However, several pressing questions remain: Are neurobiological responses to decoding interventions that improve the early skills foundational to reading similar to responses to interventions at more cognitively complex levels of reading (e.g., those who are accurate decoders but exhibit difficulties in reading comprehension)? Are there specific etiological factors that distinguish children who demonstrate only minimal gains with such treatments from responders? And do these factors also differ by type/level of reading deficit? If so, might alternative instructional approaches be more effective for these children? Are there qualitative differences in response to treatment given different language experiences/ linguistic systems, and how does bilingual experience impact response to intervention and its neurobiological pattern? These are complex issues that often demand large-scale studies to compare and contrast various interventions and examine interactions with individual difference or subtype dimensions. Such contrastive research will greatly extend the utility of brain-based developmental research. Intervention, including large-scale reading remediation, intervention with English-learning students, and targeted fluency and comprehension intervention, therefore, must be part of this overall discussion. Section 4 of this volume presents three chapters that address intervention. In Chapter 13, Foorman and Al Otaiba address some of the challenges of intervention research and offer a state-of-the-art overview. Siegel describes intervention with English-language learning students (Chapter 14), and Wolf, Gottwald, Galante, Norton, and Miller (Chapter 15) present information on an intervention drawn from knowledge of the origins of the "reading brain."

As we point out in some detail in the book's conclusion, there is a clear need to find better markers of abnormal trajectories in very young (preschool age) children, as well as to develop appropriate early interventions. Whereas it is known that the development of phonemic awareness is strongly and causally related to the development of reading skill (e.g., Bradley & Bryant, 1985; Wagner & Torgesen, 1987; see also Ramus & Szenkovits, this volume), little is known about the cognitive primitives underlying the development of phonemic awareness. The puzzle of reading comprehension and its neurobiological correlates (Cutting et al., this volume) present measurement challenges and remain understudied. Exciting studies from several longitudinal cohorts (Molfese, Molfese, & Espy, 1999; Molfese, Molfese, Modglin, Kelly, & Terrell, 2002; Lyytinen et al., 2005) have suggested that early brain responses to speech stimuli might constitute a crucial biomarker of risk for dyslexia. However, studies of this sort are few and far between (and full examination of neurobiological measures such as genetics, neuroanatomy, and neurochemistry have yet to be examined). Future behavioral and neuroimaging work needs to continue to examine the development of early language competence and later reading achievement to better understand the etiology of reading disabilities at multiple levels of analysis.

All of these issues—neurobiology, genetics, behavior, and how individuals learn—and the tools we use to study them and to develop and test interventions for reading problems are related; none of them can be examined in a vacuum. Accordingly, in the TDF symposium on which this book is based, sessions examined these topics in depth and included integrative discussion, with a goal of gauging where we need to go as a research community in the coming years to advance our ability to improve quality of life for children and adults with dyslexia. These chapters have benefited from the formal and informal discussions that took place at the symposium and include thoughts for future work that will contribute additional information to the puzzle of how children learn to read.

Peggy McCardle, Nicole Landi, and Kenneth R. Pugh

REFERENCES

Bradley, L., & Bryant, P. (1985). *Rhyme and reason in reading and spelling.* Ann Arbor, MI: University of Michigan Press.

Fiebach, C. J., Friederici, A. D., Mueller, K., & von Cramon, D. Y. (2002). fMRI evidence for dual routes to the mental lexicon in visual word recognition. *Journal of Cognitive Neuroscience, 14,* 11–23.

Galaburda, A. M., LoTurco, J., Ramus, F., Fitch, R. H., & Rosen, G. D. (2006). From genes to behavior in developmental dyslexia. *Nature Neuroscience, 9*(10), 1213–1217.

Kuo, W.-J., Yeh, T.-C., Lee, C.-Y., Wu, Y.-T., Chou, C.-C., Ho, L.-T., et al. (2003). Frequency effects of Chinese character processing in the brain: An event-related fMRI study. *NeuroImage, 18,* 720–730.

Kuo, W.-J., Yeh, T.-C., Lee, J.-R., Chen, L.-F., Lee, P.-L., Chen, S.-S., et al. (2004). Orthographic and phonological processing of Chinese characters: An fMRI study. *NeuroImage, 21,* 1721–1731.

Lyytinen, H., Guttorm, T., Huttunen, T., Hämäläinen, J., Leppänen, P. H. T., & Vesterinen, M. (2005). Psychophysiology of developmental dyslexia: A review of findings including studies of children at risk for dyslexia. *Journal of Neurolinguistics, 18,* 167–195.

Molfese, D., Molfese, V., Modglin, A., Kelly, S., & Terrell, S. (2002). Reading and cognitive abilities: Longitudinal studies of brain and behavior changes in young children. *Annals of Dyslexia, 52,* 99–119.

Molfese, D. L., Molfese, V. J., & Espy, K. A. (1999). The predictive use of event-related potentials in language development and the treatment of language disorders. *Developmental Neuropsychology, 16,* 373–377.

Paulesu, E., Demonet, J.-F., Fazio, F., McCrory, E., Chanoine, V., Brunswick, N., et al. (2001). Dyslexia: Cultural diversity and biological unity. *Science, 291,* 2165–2167.

Pugh, K. R., Sandak, R., Frost, S. J., Moore, D., & Mencl, W. E. (2005). Examining reading development and reading disability in English language learners: Potential contributions from functional neuroimaging. *Learning Disabilities Research & Practice, 20,* 24–30.

Rosen, G. D., Bai, J., Wang, Y., Fiondella, C. G., Threlkeld, S. W., LoTurco, J. J., et al. (2007). Disruption of neuronal migration by RNAi of Dyx1c1 results in neocortical and hippocampal malformations. *Cerebral Cortex, 17*(11), 2562–2572.

Shaywitz, B. A., Shaywitz, S. E., Blachman, B. A., Pugh, K. R., Fulbright, R. K., Skudlarski, P., et al. (2004). Development of left occipitotemporal systems for skilled reading in children after a phonologically-based intervention. *Biological Psychiatry, 55,* 926–933.

Simos, P. G., Fletcher, J. M., Bergman, E., Breier, J. I., Foorman, B. R., Castillo, E. M., et al. (2002). Dyslexia-specific brain activation profile becomes normal following successful remedial training. *Neurology, 58,* 1203–1213.

Siok, W. T., Perfetti, C. A., Jin, Z., & Tan, L. H. (2004). Biological abnormality of impaired reading is constrained by culture. *Nature, 431,* 70–76.

Temple, E., Deutsch, G. K., Poldrack, R. A., Miller, S. L., Tallal, P., Merzenich, M. M., et al. (2003). Neural deficits in children with dyslexia ameliorated by behavioral remediation: Evidence from functional MRI. *Proceedings of the National Academy of Sciences, 100,* 2860–2865.

Threlkeld, S. W., McClure, M. M., Bai, J., Wang, Y., LoTurco, J. J., Rosen, G. D., et al. (2007). Developmental disruptions and behavioral impairments in rats following in utero RNAi of Dyx1c1. *Brain Research Bulletin, 71*(5), 508–514.

Wagner, R., & Torgesen, J. (1987). The nature of phonological processing and its causal role in the acquisition of reading skills. *Psychological Bulletin, 101*, 192–212.

Wang, Y., Paramasivam, M., Thomas, A., Bai, J., Kaminen-Ahola, N., Kere, J., et al. (2006). DYX1C1 functions in neuronal migration in developing neocortex. *Neuroscience, 143*(2), 515–522.

Section I

Major Themes in the Study of the Neurobiology of Dyslexia

1 Mapping the Word Reading Circuitry in Skilled and Disabled Readers[1]

Stephen J. Frost, Rebecca Sandak,
W. Einar Mencl, Nicole Landi, Jay G. Rueckl,
Leonard Katz, and Kenneth R. Pugh

Research on the neurocognitive foundations of reading in typically and atypically developing readers has benefited in recent years from advances in several neuroimaging technologies (see Papanicolaou, Pugh, Simos, & Mencl, 2004, for a review). In this chapter we describe recent studies from our lab, and from others, that were designed to generate data, not only on localization of reading-related brain activation, but also to examine patterns of interactions and trade-offs among these distributed reading-related systems. Acquiring data of this sort is necessary, in our view, if we are to begin to construct neurobiological models of word identification that can speak to the complexities and dynamics of reading performance. Indeed, computational models of reading stand or fall, not by their capacity to account for simple group differences on behavioral measures of reading performance or main effects of isolated variables, but rather by whether they can account for complex interactions among them (Harm & Seidenberg, 1999). Ultimately, the same criteria must be applied to neurobiologically grounded models as well. Thus, it is critical that we begin to look beyond simply more fine-tuned localization and consider also a systems-level approach. Research on systems appears to be a realistic possibility at this stage in the development of these new technologies, given the evidence that extant neurophysiologic measures are amenable to sophisticated psycholinguistic designs (Dehaene et al., 2004; Frost et al., 2005; Sandak, Mencl, Frost, Mason, Rueckl, et al., 2004). When we add to all this the clinically oriented goal of better understanding what differences in activation patterns between skilled and struggling readers imply about core deficits and optimal remediation, it becomes all the more pressing to develop a more comprehensive neurobiological account of how component processes interact and change with learning and development (Pugh et al., 2006). We focus here primarily on studies of phonological processing in reading, given that this stage is typically the

3

most sensitive in discriminating nonimpaired (NI) from reading disabled (RD) cohorts (Pugh, Mencl, Shaywitz, et al., 2000).

We begin with a short review of relevant behavioral studies of component processing in fluent word identification, focusing on the role of sublexical phonology, which studies have shown to be compromised in RD cohorts. We then discuss the current literature on the neurobiology of skilled and disabled reading, along with consideration of a series of recent studies from our lab that aim to capture brain correlates of component processes, again with an emphasis on how the findings help to better understand the cooperative–competitive dynamics of the neurocircuitry supporting word identification. Finally, we take stock of what we consider to be crucial next steps (both technical and theoretical) in the emerging cognitive neuroscience of reading and its disorders.

BEHAVIORAL STUDIES OF SKILLED READING

A central issue in studies of skilled readers concerns the question of whether phonological information mediates access to the mental lexicon visual word identification. As indicated earlier, given that measures of the ability to map from spelling to pronunciation are typically the most sensitive in discriminating nonimpaired from RD cohorts (Pugh, Mencl, Jenner, et al., 2000), acquiring behavioral data on this question is crucial if we are to correctly interpret reader group differences in patterns of activation across the reading circuitry. Many studies have now demonstrated that phonological access in visual word recognition is early and automatic for skilled readers (see R. Frost, 1998, for review). For example, Van Orden and his colleagues showed that participants in a semantic categorization task produced more false-positive responses to words that are homophones or pseudohomophones of category exemplars than for spelling foils (e.g., categorizing ROWS/ROZE as a flower more often than the control foil ROBS/REEZ; Van Orden, 1987; Van Orden et al., 1988). Moreover, this effect persisted, even at brief exposure durations, indicating that phonological recoding occurred early in processing and, because pseudohomophones are not represented lexically, Van Orden et al. (1988) concluded that the effect must occur before lexical access.

Findings from studies using brief exposure paradigms, such as backward masking and priming, also point to an early and robust influence of phonology on lexical access (Lesch & Pollatsek, 1993; Lukatela, Frost, & Turvey, 1999; Lukatela & Turvey, 1994a, 1994b; Perfetti & Bell, 1991; Perfetti, Bell, & Delaney, 1988). For example, Perfetti and colleagues (1988) found significantly better identification rates when briefly presented target words were followed by pseudoword masks that were phonemically similar than when they were graphemically similar, suggesting that phonological information was automatically extracted from the pseudoword mask and contributed to the identification of the target (Perfetti & Bell, 1991; Perfetti et al., 1988). Lukatela and Turvey (1994a; see also Lesch & Pollatsek, 1993) observed priming of a target word (e.g., FROG) at a short prime-target interval for a semantic associate (TOAD), a homophone of the associate

(TOWED), and a pseudohomophone of the associate (TODE) relative to matched controls. At a long interval, both TOAD and TODE effects were observed, but TOWED effects were eliminated. The authors concluded that the initial access code must be phonological in nature, with orthographic constraints coming into play relatively late.

BEHAVIORAL STUDIES OF READING DISABILITY

Significant progress has been made in understanding the cognitive and linguistic skills that must be in place to ensure adequate reading development in children (Bruck, 1992; Liberman, Shankweiler, Fischer, & Carter, 1974; Shankweiler et al., 1995; Stanovich & Siegel, 1994). With regard to reading disability, deficits in behavioral performance are most evident at the level of single word and pseudo-word reading; RD individuals are both slow and inaccurate relative to NI readers. A number of explanations have been proposed to account for these reading difficulties, including processing speed deficits (Wolf & Bowers, 1999), rapid auditory processing (Tallal, 1980), general language deficits (Scarborough & Dobrich, 1990), or visual deficits (Cornelissen & Hansen, 1998). However, there is growing consensus that for the majority of struggling readers, a core difficulty in reading manifests itself as a specific deficiency within the language system at the level of phonological representation and processing (Ziegler & Goswami, 2005; Liberman, 1992).

Many lines of evidence converge on the conclusion that the word and pseudo-word reading difficulties in RD individuals are, to a large extent, manifestations of more basic deficits at the level of assembling the phonological code represented by a given letter string (Bradley & Bryant, 1983). The failure to develop efficient (both accurate and rapid) phonological assembly skill in word and pseudoword reading, in turn, appears to stem from difficulties—at the earliest stages of literacy training—in the development of phonological awareness. Phonological awareness, in general, is defined as the metalinguistic understanding of the segmental nature of speech; that spoken words are composed of segments including the smallest of these segments, phonemes, which in turn can be represented by alphabetic characters (Bruck, 1992; Liberman et al., 1974; Shankweiler et al., 1995; Stanovich & Siegel, 1994).

As for why RD readers should have exceptional difficulty developing phonological awareness, the etiological underpinnings of this difficulty are still actively being investigated and the question of whether such language-level challenges might, in some children at least, be linked to more basic deficits in one or more of the above-mentioned domains is much debated. Nonetheless, a large body of evidence directly relates deficits in phonological awareness, and fine-grained phonemic awareness in particular, to difficulties in learning to read: phonological awareness measures predict later reading achievement (Bradley & Bryant, 1983; Stanovich et al., 1984; Torgesen et al., 1994); deficits in phonological awareness consistently separate RD and nonimpaired children (Fletcher et al., 1994; Stanovich & Siegel, 1994); phonological deficits persist into adulthood (Bruck, 1992; Shaywitz et al., 1998); and instruction in phonological awareness promotes the acquisition of reading skills (Ball & Blachman, 1991; Foorman, Francis, Fletcher, Schatschneider, & Mehta, 1998; Torgesen, Morgan, & Davis, 1992). For children with adequate phonological skills, the process of phonological assembly in word and pseudoword reading becomes highly automated, efficient, and, as the evidence here suggests, continues to serve as an important component in rapid word identification even for mature skilled readers (R. Frost, 1998).

FUNCTIONAL IMAGING STUDIES OF SKILLED READING AND READING DEVELOPMENT

Given the importance of phonological information evidenced from behavioral studies of skilled and impaired reading, identifying the neuroanatomical correlates of phonology and their interactions with regions that support orthographic, morphological, and lexico-semantic component processes represents an important step toward understanding the functional architecture of reading and reading failure. Evidence from functional imaging studies indicates that skilled word recognition involves a left hemisphere (LH) cortical reading circuit with ventral, dorsal, and anterior components (see Pugh, Mencl, Jenner, et al., 2000; Sarkari et al., 2002, for reviews). This circuit broadly includes an anterior subsystem and two posterior subsystems: a ventral (occipitotemporal) and a dorsal (temporoparietal) system.

The anterior system, centered in and near Broca's area in the inferior frontal gyrus (IFG), is associated with phonological coding during reading, among other functions (e.g., phonological memory, syntactic processing); more anterior aspects of IFG seem to play a role in semantic retrieval (Poldrack et al., 1999). The phonologically relevant components of this multifunctional system are more strongly engaged by low-frequency words (particularly, words with irregular/inconsistent spelling-to-sound mappings) and pseudowords than by high-frequency words (Fiebach, Friederici, Mueller, & von Cramon, 2002; Fiez & Peterson, 1998). The temporoparietal system, which includes the angular gyrus (AG) and supramarginal gyrus (SMG) in the inferior parietal lobule, and the posterior aspect of the superior temporal gyrus (Wernicke's area), seems to be involved in mapping visual percepts of print onto the phonological and semantic structures of language (Black & Behrmann, 1994; Price, Winterburn, Giraud, Moore, & Noppeney, 2003). Similar to the IFG, regions within the LH temporoparietal system (particularly the SMG) respond with greater activity to pseudowords than to familiar words, and to print more than pictures (Price, Wise, & Frackowiak, 1996; Sandak, Mencl, Frost, Mason, Rueckl, et al., 2004; Simos, Breier, et al., 2002). We have speculated that this temporoparietal system operates in close conjunction with the anterior system to decode new words during normal reading development (Pugh, Mencl et al., 2000).

The ventral system includes extrastriate areas, a left inferior occipitotemporal/ fusiform gyrus, and appears to extend anteriorly into the middle and inferior temporal gyri (MTG, ITG). Whereas the more anterior foci within the ventral system extending into the MTG to ITG appear to be semantically tuned (Fiebach et al., 2002; Simos, Breier, et al., 2002a), it has been suggested by some researchers that the occipitotemporal (OT) region functions as a presemantic visual word form area (VWFA; c.f. Cohen et al., 2002, but see Price et al., 2003 for an alternative conceptualization). Importantly, the functional specificity of sites along the ventral pathway for reading appears to be late developing and critically related to the acquisition of reading skill (Booth et al., 2001; see Shaywitz et al., 2002, discussed later), leading us to refer to this region more neutrally as the ventral "skill zone." The ventral system, particularly the posterior aspects thought to be prelexical and presemantic, is also fast acting in response to print stimuli in skilled readers but not in RD individuals (Salmelin et al., 1996). Although there is disagreement in the literature about the precise taxonomy of critical subregions comprising the ventral system (Dehaene et al., 2004; Price et al., 2003), recent studies examining both timing and stimulus-type effects suggest that subregions respond to word and word-like stimuli in a progressively abstracted and linguistic manner as one moves anteriorly along the ventral pathways (Dehaene et al., 2004; Tagamets, Novick, Chalmers, & Friedman, 2000; Tarkiainen, Cornelissen, & Salmelin, 2003).

Of these three systems, the dorsal and anterior systems appear to dominate during initial reading acquisition in normally developing beginning readers with an increased ventral response to print stimuli as proficiency in word recognition increases. Shaywitz et al. (1998) observed that in normally developing children younger than 10.5 years of age, activation during pseudoword and real-word reading tasks is largely limited to the temporoparietal and anterior systems; in contrast, children older than 10.5 years of age showed increased engagement of the ventral system, which in turn was positively correlated with reading skill. Indeed, when multiple regression analyses examined both age and reading skill (measured by performance on standard reading tests) the critical predictor was reading skill level: the higher the reading skill, the stronger the response in the LH ventral cortex (with several other areas including right hemisphere [RH] and frontal lobe sites showing age- and skill-related reductions). RD readers, by contrast, showed age-related increases in a widely distributed set of regions across both the LH and RH. Based on these cross-sectional developmental findings, we suggest that a beginning reader on a successful trajectory employs a widely distributed cortical system for print processing including temporoparietal, frontal, and RH posterior areas. As reading skill increases, LH ventral sites become more active, and presumably more central to the rapid recognition of printed (word) stimuli (see Turkeltaub, Gareau, Flowers, Zeffiro, & Eden, 2003, for similar arguments).

REFINING OUR ACCOUNT OF NEUROBIOLOGY OF SKILLED WORD RECOGNITION

As outlined earlier, we have speculated that the temporoparietal and anterior systems are critical in learning to integrate orthographic, phonological, and semantic features of words, whereas the ventral system develops, as a consequence of adequate learning during reading acquisition, to support fluent word identification in normally developing, but not reading disabled, individuals. This general tax-onomy, however, is both coarse grained and underspecified. To explore functional subspecialization further we have recently conducted a series of experiments with skilled readers (Frost et al., 2005; Katz et al., 2005; Sandak, Mencl, Frost, Mason, & Rueckl, et al., 2004; summarized in depth by Sandak, Mencl, Frost, Mason, & Pugh, 2004). We examined phonological/semantic trade-offs (Frost et al., 2005) and critical factors associated with repetition effects (Katz et al., 2005) and adaptive learning (Sandak, Mencl, Frost, Mason, & Rueckl, et al., 2004). This line of research is aimed at providing more information on both subspecialization with the major LH regions and how different component systems modulate process-ing in relation to one another in response to varied stimuli and at different stages during learning. Given the importance of the ventral pathway in the development of fluent reading, we are particularly interested in assessing the tuning character-istics of the skilled-correlated OT region (along with remote areas most closely linked to processing within this ventral area).

TRADE-OFFS BETWEEN PHONOLOGY AND SEMANTICS

RD readers have acute problems in mapping from orthography to phonology and appear to rely on semantic information to supplement deficient decoding skills (Plaut & Booth, 2000; Strain & Herdman, 1999). NI readers too appear to show a trade-off between these component processes. Strain, Patterson, and Seidenberg (1995) provided behavioral confirmation of this, demonstrating that the standard consistency effect on low-frequency words (longer naming latencies for words with inconsistent spelling-to-sound mappings such as PINT relative to words with consistent mappings such as MILL) is attenuated for words that are highly imageable. Importantly, this interaction reveals that semantics can attenuate the difficulties associated with reading words that have inconsistent orthographic-to-phonological mappings.

Using functional magnetic resonance imaging (fMRI), we sought to identify the neurobiological correlates of this trade-off between semantics and phonology (Frost et al., 2005). A go/no-go naming paradigm was employed in an event-related fMRI protocol with word stimuli representing the crossing of frequency, imageability, and spelling-to-sound consistency. High-imageable words reduced consistency-related activation in the IFG, SMG, and OT, but increased posterior parietal (AG) and middle temporal activation. This appears to be the principal neural signature of the behavioral trade-off between semantics and phonology revealed by Strain and colleagues (1995). These findings provide evidence that skilled performance results from cooperative–competitive processing involving different components of the reading circuitry.

ADAPTIVE LEARNING

Increased familiarity with specific words and increased reading skill are asso-ciated with a shift in the relative activation of the cortical systems involved in reading, from predominantly dorsal to predominantly ventral (Turkeltaub et al., 2003). We are carrying out functional neuroimaging experiments to provide a more precise characterization of the means by which practice with unfamiliar words results in this shift and to gain insights into how these systems learn to read new words. In one study from our group (Katz et al., 2005) we examined repetition effects (comparing activation for thrice repeated words relative to unrepeated words) in both lexical decision and overt naming. Across tasks, repetition was associated with facilitated processing as measured by reduced response latencies and errors. Many sites, including the IFG, SMG, supplementary motor area, and cerebellum, showed reduced activation for highly practiced tokens. Critically, we observed a dissociation within the ventral system: the OT skill zone showed repetition-related reduction (like the SMG and IFG sites), whereas more anterior ventral sites, particularly the MTG, were stable or even showed increased activation with repetition. Thus, we concluded that a neural signature of increased efficiency in word recognition has more efficient processing in dorsal, anterior, and posterior ventral sites, with stable or increased engagement of more anterior middle and inferior temporal sites.

In another study from our group, Sandak, Mencl, Frost, Mason, Rueckl, et al. (2004) examined whether the type of processing engaged in during learning would modulate the repetition-related patterns of activation observed by Katz et al. (2005). That is, we hypothesized that repetition alone is not sufficient to optimize learning; rather, we predicted that the type of processing engaged in during learning would affect the quality of the lexical representations established when new words are learned and the cortical regions engaged when that word is subsequently read. To address this question, participants completed a behavioral session prior to MRI scanning, acquiring familiarity for three sets of pronounceable pseudowords while making orthographic (consonant–vowel pattern), phonological (rhyme), or semantic (category) judgments. (Note that in the semantic condition, participants learned a novel semantic association for each pseudoword.) Following training, participants completed an event-related fMRI session in which they overtly named the trained pseudowords, untrained pseudowords, and real words.

Behaviorally, phonological and semantic training resulted in faster naming times relative to orthographic training. Of the three training conditions, we found that only phonological training was associated with both facilitated naming and the pattern of cortical activations previously implicated as characteristic of increased efficiency for word recognition (Katz et al., 2005). We suggest that for phonologically trained items, engaging in phonological processing during training facilitated learning, which, in turn, resulted in efficient phonological processing (instantiated cortically as relatively reduced activation in IFG and SMG) and efficient retrieval of presemantic lexical representations during subsequent naming (instantiated cortically as relatively reduced activation in the OT skill zone). Emphasizing semantic processing during training also facilitated learning but was associated with increased activation in areas previously implicated in semantic processing, suggesting that the establishment and retrieval of semantic representations compensated for less efficient phonological processing for these items.

Our recent experiments examining phonological–semantic trade-offs and critical factors associated with adaptive learning in reading have yielded findings that allow for the development of a more fine-grained picture of the functional neuroanatomy and subspecializations within these systems, and begin to provide information on learning-related modulation and trade-offs among component regions. Across these studies, identical sites in the SMG (within the temporoparietal system), IFG (within the anterior system), and the OT skill zone (within the ventral system) showed increased activation for spelling-to-sound-inconsistent relative to consistent words, and repetition-related reductions that were most salient in the phonologically analytic training condition. This pattern with regard to phonological variables suggests a phonological "tuning" in these subregions. (It is particularly noteworthy that the developmentally critical OT skill zone—the putative VWFA—appears to be phonologically tuned. It makes good sense that this region should be so structured given the failure to develop this system in reading disability when phonological deficits are one of the core features of this population.) By contrast, the angular gyrus (within the temporoparietal system) and the middle/inferior temporal gyri (within the ventral system) appear to have more abstract lexico-semantic functions across our studies (see Price, Moore, Humphreys, & Wise, 1997, for similar claims).

From these findings, we speculate that subregions within the SMG and IFG operate in a yoked fashion to bind orthographic and phonological features of words during learning; these systems also operate in conjunction with the AG where these features are further yoked to semantic knowledge systems distributed across several cortical regions. Adequate binding, specifically adequate orthographic/phonological integration, enables the development of the presemantic OT skill zone into a functional pattern identification system. As words become better learned, this area becomes capable of efficiently activating lexico-semantic subsystems in the MTG/ITG, further enabling the development of a rapid ventral word identification system.

FUNCTIONAL IMAGING STUDIES OF READING DISABILITY

EVIDENCE FOR ALTERED CIRCUITS IN READING DISABILITY

There are clear functional differences between NI and RD readers with regard to activation patterns in dorsal, ventral, and anterior sites during reading tasks. In disabled readers, a number of functional imaging studies have observed LH posterior functional disruption, at both dorsal and ventral sites during phonological processing tasks (Brunswick, McCrory, Price, Frith, & Frith, 1999; Paulesu et al., 2001; Pugh, Mencl, Shaywitz, et al., 2000; Salmelin et al., 1996; Shaywitz et al., 1998, 2002; Temple et al., 2001). This disruption is instantiated as a relative underengagement of these regions specifically when processing linguistic stimuli (words and pseudowords), particularly during tasks that require decoding. This functional anomaly in posterior LH regions has been observed consistently in children (Shaywitz et al., 2002) and adults (Salmelin et al., 1996; Shaywitz et al., 1998) and is evident in measures of activation and in analysis of functional connectivity (Horwitz et al., 1998; Pugh, Mencl, Shaywitz, et al., 2000). Moreover, hypoactivation in three key dorsal and ventral sites—the cortex within the temporoparietal region, the angular gyrus, and the ventral OT skill zone—is detectable as early as the end of kindergarten in children who have not reached important milestones in learning to read (Simos, Fletcher, et al., 2002).

POTENTIALLY COMPENSATORY PROCESSING IN READING DISABILITY

A number of studies have shown that on tasks that make explicit demands on phonological processing (pseudoword- and word-reading tasks), RD readers show a disproportionately greater engagement of IFG and prefrontal dorsolateral sites than NI readers (Shaywitz et al., 1998, 2002; see also Brunswick et al., 1999; Salmelin et al., 1996, for similar findings). In addition, several studies provide evidence of increased activity in posterior RH regions. Using MEG, Sarkari et al. (2002) found an increase in the engagement of the RH temporoparietal region in RD children. More detailed examination of this trend, using hemodynamic measures, indicates that hemispheric asymmetries in activity in posterior temporal and temporoparietal regions (MTG and AG) vary significantly among reading groups (Shaywitz et al., 1998): There was greater RH than LH activation in RD readers but greater LH than RH activation in NI readers. Rumsey et al. (1999) examined the relationship between RH activation and reading performance in their adult RD and NI participants and found that RH temporoparietal activation was correlated with standard measures of reading performance only for RD readers (see also Shaywitz et al., 2002).

In summary, adult and cross-sectional developmental studies have identified reading group differences in both functional neuroanatomical and behavioral trajectories. NI children develop a left hemisphere posterior (ventral) reading system capable of supporting fluent word identification, whereas RD readers, with demonstrable anomalies in temporoparietal and frontal activation (and associated difficulties with phonologically analytic processing on behavioral tests), fail to adequately "train" the ventral subsystem. We hypothesize that RD readers tend to strongly engage inferior frontal sites due to increased reliance on covert pronunciation (articulatory recoding) in an attempt to cope with their inefficient phonological analysis of the printed word. In addition, heightened activation of the posterior RH regions with reduced LH posterior activation may reflect the fact that, behaviorally, poor readers compensate for their inadequate phonological awareness and knowledge of letter–sound correspondences by overrelying on contextual cues to read individual words; their word reading errors tend to be visual or semantic rather than phonetic (see Perfetti, 1985, for review). That is, the heightened posterior RH activation suggests a process of word recognition that relies on letter-by-letter processing in accessing RH localized visuo-semantic representations rather than relying on phonologically structured word-recognition strategies.

NEUROBIOLOGICAL EFFECTS OF READING REMEDIATION WITH CHILDREN

Converging evidence from other studies supports the notion that gains in reading skill resulting from reading intervention are associated with a more "normalized" localization of reading processes in the brain. In a recent MEG study, eight young children with severe reading difficulties underwent a brief but intensive phonics-based remediation program (Simos, Fletcher, et al., 2002). After intervention, the most salient change observed on a case-by-case basis was an increase in the engagement of the LH temporoparietal region, accompanied by a moderate reduction in the activation of the RH temporoparietal areas. Similarly, Temple et al. (2003) used fMRI to examine the effects of an intervention (FastForword) on the pattern of reading-related activation of a group of 8- to 12-year-old children with reading difficulties. After intervention, increased LH temporoparietal and inferior frontal activation were observed. Moreover, the LH increases correlated significantly with increased reading scores. In a study by Blachman, Tangel, Ball, Black, and McGraw (1999) a treatment RD group of young children received 9 months of an intensive phonologically analytic intervention. The treatment group was matched with two control groups: a typically developing and an untreated RD group (average age was 6.5 years at Time 1 for all groups). Relative to RD controls, RD treatment participants showed reliable gains on reading measures (particularly on fluency-related measures). In addition to behavioral indices, children received a pre- and posttreatment fMRI employing a simple cross modal (auditory/visual) forced-choice letter-match task (Shaywitz et al., 2004). When RD groups were compared at posttreatment (Time 2), reliably greater activation increases in LH reading-related sites were seen in the treatment group. When Time 2 and Time 1 activation profiles were directly contrasted for each group, both RD treatment and typically developing, but not RD controls, showed reliable increases in LH reading-related sites. Prominent differences were seen in the LH IFG and, importantly, in the LH ventral skill zone. These changes were quite similar to those found in the NI controls as they also learned to read. Importantly, a follow-up fMRI scan for the treatment group revealed progressive LH ventral increases along with decreasing RH activation patterns even 1 year after treatment was concluded. These initial neuroimaging treatment studies suggest that a critical neurobiological signature of successful intervention, at least in younger children, appears to be increased engagement of major LH reading-related circuits and reduced compensatory reliance on RH homologues.

NEUROBIOLOGICAL EVIDENCE FOR PLASTICITY IN ADOLESCENT READERS

Although the evidence from intervention studies suggests that compromised LH systems in young RD populations are responsive to intensive training (Simos, Fletcher, et al., 2002; Shaywitz et al., 2004; Temple et al., 2003), it is not clear whether the same holds true for older children with persistent reading difficulties (Pugh, Mencl, Shaywitz, et al., 2000). We decided to explore the degree of plasticity in the cortical circuitry for reading of adolescent RD readers, focused on whether factors that alleviate processing demands on the neurocircuitry for reading might reveal latent functionality in LH systems and potentially reduce RH compensatory activation (Pugh et al., 2008). Experiment 1 examined phonological–semantic trade-offs in printed word naming as described earlier (Frost et al., 2005). Given behavioral findings indicating heightened top-down facilitative effects in RD readers (Plaut & Booth, 2000; Strain & Herdman, 1999), we compared the reader groups on difficult-to-decode (inconsistent) words that differ with regard to top-down support from frequency and imageability. Behaviorally, both groups were faster and more accurate for high-frequency, high-imageable, inconsistent words relative to low-frequency, low-imageable, inconsistent words with a larger effect on accuracy for RD readers. Neurobiologically, a dissociation was observed such that inconsistent words with top-down support produced decreases in activation levels across the major LH reading areas for NI readers; however, RD readers showed the opposite pattern—increases in activation levels in LH reading areas, particularly SMG and STG. We interpret these finding to indicate that the reading subsystems in adolescent RD readers are weak but not fundamentally disrupted.

To further examine the limits on normalization of function, Experiment 2 measured behavioral and activation patterns NI and RD adolescents for high-frequency words presented six times over the course of each functional imaging run while performing a semantic categorization task (animacy judgment). Behaviorally, both groups showed reliable decreases in latency and increases in accuracy with repetition. Activation results were quite different. Consistent with our previous results with adults (Katz et al., 2005), we observed a reliable decrease in activation in adolescent NI readers as words were repeated in LH reading-related regions, including the OT, MTG, STG, SMG, and IFG; in contrast, RD readers (with low signal in LH regions on the first exposure) showed activation increases in these brain regions across repetitions. Moreover, activation differences between reader groups in several reading-related sites such as the STG and IFG were no longer apparent on late trials. We proposed that for NI readers, decreases in activation with word repetitions reflect increases in processing efficiency; for RD readers, increases in activation with repetitions ameliorate phonological processing difficulties such that RD readers begin to engage canonical LH reading-related regions that are not normally activated for this population. One important question that the data raise is why the initial activation response in the LH is so low given that RD readers have certainly seen the words used in this experiment hundreds of times. The most straightforward hypothesis, and one that would, coupled with clinical observations, point to a very specific learning problem in RD readers, is that these readers fail to consolidate the learning experience into longer term neural changes in processing and organization. Thus, the system might be available for processing but fails to demonstrate savings with longer term modulation of connections. We suggest that future studies will need to address this possibility by shifting from the more narrow focus on simple orthographic-to-phonological mapping deficits toward a broader, systematic investigation of the mechanisms of memory and learning.

FUTURE DIRECTIONS

Although functional imaging studies have established important signatures of reader group differences in developmental trajectories, they are nonetheless merely descriptive. That is, functional neuroimaging measures are not intrinsically explanatory; they describe brain organization at a given point in development. Links between multiple indices of reading (dis)ability, including genetic polymorphisms, brain structure and function, and cognitive deficits, promise to constitute the core scientific foundation for our understanding of neurodevelopmental disorders in the coming years, with the goal of progressing from descriptive neurobiological findings to potentially explanatory models. By establishing meaningful links between the behavioral–cognitive skills that must be in place to read and neuroanatomical, neurochemical, and genetic measures, we can begin to develop an explanatory account of neurocognitive divergences in typically developing and RD children (Grigorenko, 2001; Pugh, Mencl, Jenner, et al., 2000). That is, we believe that multilevel designs will allow specifications of the biological *pathways* predisposing for risk for the development of a reading disability and explorations of elements of these pathways that might be most suitable for pharmacological and behavioral intervention.

Finally, a large body of behavioral research supports the notion that word recognition engages common processes across languages and orthographies (despite some differences in behavioral manifestations of reading disability) that, we suggest, reflect the degree of transparency in the mapping between written and spoken forms. Functional neuroimaging studies have also provided support for a common neurobiological signature of skilled reading in which language-specific differences appear to be mainly a matter of degree, not of kind (Paulesu et al., 2001); however, some qualitative differences between alphabetic and nonalphabetic writing systems have been observed (Siok et al., 2004). Given the significant variability in orthographic form, orthographic-to-phonological mappings, methods of reading instruction, and manifestations of reading disability across languages and cultures, more work needs to be done in the area of cross-linguistic studies of reading, both in order to identify the neurobiological universals of reading and to understand how the functional organization of reading and reading development varies with language-specific features. For example, we might anticipate that the initial neurocircuitry for reading will be somewhat different across languages, reflecting the different challenges that writing systems place on orthography, phonology, morphology, visual memory, and the like. This would imply that whereas a common ventral reading specialization should eventually develop for each language, the computational organization of this common neural pathway will differ somewhat as a function of the language-specific challenges during early reading development. An adequate neurobiologically grounded reading theory must be able to account for both language variance (with respect to both properties of the spoken and written forms) and language invariance (with respect to common neural pathways) over the course of development. Cross-language studies, along with studies of interactions among component processing during adaptive learning, will continue to drive the conceptual and computational development of neurobiological theories in the next phase of our research.

ACKNOWLEDGMENTS

This research was funded by National Institute of Child Health and Human Development (NICHD) grants F32-HD42391, R01-HD40411, and P01-HD01994.

NOTE

1. Portions of this chapter have appeared in: Pugh, K. Sandak, R., Frost, S. J., Moore, D., Rueckl, J. G., & Mencl, W. E. (2006). Neurobiological studies of skilled and impaired reading: A work in progress. In G. D. Rosen (Ed.), *The dyslexic brain: New pathways in neuroscience discovery* (pp. 21–47). Mahwah, NJ: Lawrence Erlbaum; and Frost, S. J., Sandak, R., Mencl, W. E., Landi, N., Moore, D., Porta, G. D., et al., (2008). Neurobiological and behavioral studies of skilled and impaired word reading. In E. L. Grigorenko & A. J. Naples (Eds.), *Single-word reading behavioral and biological perspectives* (pp. 355–376). Mahwah, NJ: Lawrence Erlbaum.

REFERENCES

Ball, E. W., & Blachman, B. A. (1991). Does phoneme awareness training in kindergarten make a difference in early word recognition and developmental spelling? *Reading Research Quarterly, 26*, 49–66.

Blachman, B. A., Tangel, D. M., Ball, E. W., Black, R., & McGraw, C. K. (1999). Developing phonological awareness and word recognition skills: A two-year intervention with low-income, inner-city children. *Reading and Writing, 11*, 239–273.

Black, S. E., & Behrmann, M. (1994). Localization in alexia. In A. Kertesz (Ed.), *Localization and neuroimaging in neuropsychology* (pp. 331–376). New York: Academic Press.

Booth, J. R., Burman, D. D., Van Santen, F. W., Harasaki, Y., Gitelman, D. R., Parrish, T. B., et al. (2001). The development of specialized brain systems in reading and oral-language. *Child Neuropsychology (Neuropsychology Development Cognition, Section C), 7*(3), 119–141.

Bradley, L., & Bryant, P. (1983). *Rhyme and reason in reading and spelling.* Ann Arbor, MI: University of Michigan Press.

Bruck, M. (1992). Persistence of dyslexics' phonological deficits. *Developmental Psychology, 28*, 874–886.

Brunswick, N., McCrory, E., Price C., Frith, C. D., & Frith, U. (1999). Explicit and implicit processing of words and pseudowords by adult developmental dyslexics: A search for Wernicke's Wortschatz. *Brain, 122*, 1901–1917.

Cohen, L., Lehericy, S., Chochon, F., Lemer, C., Rivaud, S., & Dehaene, S. (2002). Language-specific tuning of visual cortex? Functional properties of the visual word form area. *Brain, 125*, 1054–1069.

Cornelissen, P. L., & Hansen, P. C. (1998). Motion detection, letter position encoding, and single word reading. *Annals of Dyslexia, 48*, 155–188.

Dehaene, S., Jobert, A., Naccache, L., Ciuciu, P., Poline, J.-B., Le Bihan, D., et al. (2004). Letter binding and invariant recognition of masked words: Behavioral and neuroimaging evidence. *Psychological Science, 15,* 307–313.

Eden, G. F., & Zeffiro, T. A. (1998). Neural systems affected in developmental dyslexia revealed by functional neuroimaging. *Neuron 21,* 279–282.

Fiebach, C. J., Friederici, A. D., Mueller, K., & von Cramon, D. Y. (2002). fMRI evidence for dual routes to the mental lexicon in visual word recognition. *Journal of Cognitive Neuroscience, 14,* 11–23.

Fiez, J. A., Balota, D. A., Raichle, M. E., & Petersen, S. E. (1999). Effects of lexicality, frequency, and spelling-to-sound consistency on the functional anatomy of reading. *Neuron, 24,* 205–218.

Fiez, J. A., & Peterson, S. E. (1998). Neuroimaging studies of word reading. *Proceedings of the National Academy of Sciences, 95,* 914–921.

Fletcher, J., Shaywitz, S. E., Shankweiler, D. P., Katz, L., Liberman, I. Y., Stuebing, K. K., et al. (1994). Cognitive profiles of reading disability: Comparisons of discrepancy and low achievement definitions. *Journal of Educational Psychology, 86,* 6–23.

Foorman, B. R., Francis, D., Fletcher, J. K., Schatschneider, C., & Mehta, P. (1998). The role of instruction in learning to reading: Preventing reading failure in at-risk children. *Journal of Educational Psychology, 90,* 37–55.

Frost, R. (1998). Toward a strong phonological theory of visual word recognition: True issues and false trails. *Psychological Bulletin, 123,* 71–99.

Frost, S. J., Mencl, W. E., Sandak, R., Moore, D. L., Rueckl, J., Katz, L., et al. (2005). An fMRI study of the trade-off between semantics and phonology in reading aloud. *NeuroReport, 16,* 621–624.

Grigorenko, E. L. (2001). Developmental dyslexia: An update on genes, brain, and environments. *Journal of Child Psychology and Psychiatry, 42,* 91–125.

Harm, M. W., & Seidenberg, M. S. (1999). Computing the meanings of words in reading: Cooperative division of labor between visual and phonological processes. *Psychological Review, 106,* 491–528.

Horwitz, B., Rumsey, J. M., & Donohue, B. C. (1998). Functional connectivity of the angular gyrus in normal reading and dyslexia. *Proceedings of the National Academy Sciences, 95,* 8939–8944.

Katz, L., Lee, C. H., Tabor, W., Frost, S. J., Mencl, W. E., Sandak, R., et al. (2005). Behavioral and neurobiological effects of printed word repetition in lexical decision and naming. *Neuropsychologia, 43,* 2068–2083.

Lesch, M. F. & Pollatsek, A. (1993). Automatic access of semantic information by phonological codes in visual word recognition. *Journal of Experimental Psychology: Learning, Memory and Cognition, 19,* 285–294.

Liberman, A. M. (1992). The relation of speech to reading and writing. In R. Frost & L. Katz (Eds.), *Orthography, phonology, morphology, and meaning* (pp. 167–178). Amsterdam: Elsevier.

Liberman, I. Y., Shankweiler, D., Fischer, W., & Carter, B. (1974). Explicit syllable and phoneme segmentation in the young child. *Journal of Child Psychology, 18,* 201–212.

Lukatela, G., Frost, S. J., & Turvey, M. T. (1999). Identity priming in English is compromised by phonological ambiguity. *Journal of Experimental Psychology: Human Perception and Performance, 25,* 775–790.

Lukatela, G., & Turvey, M. T. (1994). Visual lexical access is initially phonological: 1. Evidence from associative priming by words, homophones, and pseudohomophones. *Journal of Experimental Psychology: General, 123,* 107–128.

Papanicolaou, A. C., Pugh, K. R., Simos, P. G., & Mencl, W. E. (2004). Functional brain imaging: An introduction to concepts and applications. In P. McCardle & V. Chhabra (Eds.), *The voice of evidence in reading research* (pp. 385–416). Baltimore: Paul H. Brookes.

Paulesu, E., Demonet, J.-F., Fazio, F., McCrory, E., Chanoine, V., Brunswick, N., et al. (2001). Dyslexia: Cultural diversity and biological unity. *Science, 291*, 2165–2167.

Perfetti, C. A. (1985). *Reading ability*. New York: Oxford University Press.

Perfetti, C. A., & Bell, L. (1991). Phonemic activation during the first 40 ms of word identification: Evidence from backward masking and priming. *Journal of Memory & Language, 30*, 473–485.

Perfetti, C. A., Bell, L., & Delaney, S. (1988). Automatic phonetic activation in silent word reading: Evidence from backward masking. *Journal of Memory and Language, 27*, 59–70.

Plaut, D. C., & Booth, J. R. (2000). Individual and developmental differences in semantic priming: Empirical and computational support for a single-mechanism account of lexical processing. *Psychological Review, 107*, 786–823.

Poldrack, R. A., Wagner, A. D., Prull, M. W., Desmond, J. E., Glover, G. H., & Gabrieli, J. D. (1999). Functional specialization for semantic and phonological processing in the left inferior prefrontal cortex. *NeuroImage, 10*, 15–35.

Price, C. J., Moore, C. J., Humphreys, G. W., & Wise, R. J. S. (1997). Segregating semantic from phonological processes during reading. *Journal of Cognitive Neuroscience, 9*, 727–733.

Price, C. J., Winterburn, D., Giraud, A. L., Moore, C. J., & Noppeney, U. (2003). Cortical localization of the visual and auditory word form areas: A reconsideration of the evidence. *Brain and Language, 86*, 272–286.

Price, C. J., Wise, R. J. S., & Frackowiak, R. S. J. (1996). Demonstrating the implicit processing of visually presented words and pseudowords. *Cerebral Cortex, 6*, 62–70.

Pugh, K. R., Frost, S. J., Sandak, R., Landi, N., Rueckl, J. G., Constable, R. T., et al. (2008). Effects of stimulus difficulty and repetition on printed word identification: A functional magnetic resonance imaging comparison of nonimpaired and reading disabled adolescent cohorts. *Journal of Cognitive Neuroscience, 20*, 1–15.

Pugh, K. R., Mencl, W. E., Jenner, A. R., Katz, L., Frost, S. J., Lee, J. R., et al. (2000). Functional neuroimaging studies of reading and reading disability (developmental dyslexia). *Mental Retardation & Developmental Disabilities Research Reviews, 6*, 207–213.

Pugh, K. R., Mencl, W. E., Shaywitz, B. A., Shaywitz, S. E., Fulbright, R. K., Skudlarski, P., et al. (2000). The angular gyrus in developmental dyslexia: Task-specific differences in functional connectivity in posterior cortex. *Psychological Science, 11*, 51–56.

Pugh, K. R., Sandak, R., Frost, S. J., Moore, D., Rueckl, J. G., & Mencl, W. E. (2006). Neurobiological studies of skilled and impaired reading: A work in progress. In G. D. Rosen (Ed.), *The dyslexic brain: New pathways in neuroscience discovery* (pp. 21–47). Mahwah, NJ: Lawrence Erlbaum

Rumsey, J. M., Horwitz, B., Donohue, B. C., Nace, K. L., Maisog, J. M., & Andreason, P. A. (1999). Functional lesion in developmental dyslexia: Left angular gyral blood flow predicts severity. *Brain & Language, 70*, 187–204.

Salmelin, R., Service, E., Kiesila, P., Uutela, K., & Salonen, O. (1996). Impaired visual word processing in dyslexia revealed with magnetoencephalography. *Annals of Neurology, 40*, 157–162.

Sandak, R., Mencl, W. E., Frost, S. J., Mason, S. A., & Pugh, K. R. (2004). The neurobiological basis of skilled and impaired reading: Recent findings and new directions. *Scientific Studies of Reading, 8*(3), 273–292.

Sandak, R., Mencl, W. E., Frost, S. J., Mason, S. A., Rueckl, J. G., Katz, L., et al. (2004). The neurobiology of adaptive learning in reading: A contrast of different training conditions. *Cognitive Affective and Behavioral Neuroscience, 4*, 67–88.

Sarkari, S., Simos, P. G., Fletcher, J. M., Castillo, E. M., Breier, J. I., & Papanicolaou, A. C. (2002). The emergence and treatment of developmental reading disability: Contributions of functional brain imaging. *Seminars in Pediatric Neurology, 9*, 227–236.

Scarborough, H., & Dobrich, W. (1990). Development of children with early language delay. *Journal of Speech and Hearing Research, 33*, 70–83.

Shankweiler, D., Crain, S., Katz, L., Fowler, A. E., Liberman, A. M., Brady, S. A., et al. (1995). Cognitive profiles of reading-disabled children: Comparison of language skills in phonology, morphology, and syntax. *Psychological Science, 6*, 149–156.

Shaywitz, B. A., Shaywitz, S. E., Blachman, B. A., Pugh, K. R., Fulbright, R. K., Skudlarski, P., et al. (2004). Development of left occipitotemporal systems for skilled reading in children after a phonologically-based intervention. *Biological Psychiatry, 55*, 926–933.

Shaywitz, S. E., Shaywitz, B. A., Fulbright, R. K., Skudlarski, P., Mencl, W. E., Constable, R. T., et al. (2002). Disruption of posterior brain systems for reading in children with developmental dyslexia. *Biological Psychiatry, 52*, 101–110.

Shaywitz, S. E., Shaywitz, B. A., Pugh, K. R., Fulbright, R. K., Constable, R. T., Mencl, W. E., et al. (1998). Functional disruption in the organization of the brain for reading in dyslexia. *Proceedings of the National Academy of Sciences, 95*, 2636–2641.

Simos, P. G., Breier, J. I., Fletcher, J. M., Foorman, B. R., Castillo, E. M., & Papanicolaou, A. C. (2002). Brain mechanisms for reading words and pseudowords: An integrated approach. *Cerebral Cortex, 12*, 297–305.

Simos, P. G., Fletcher, J. M., Bergman, E., Breier, J. I., Foorman, B. R., Castillo, E. M., et al. (2002). Dyslexia-specific brain activation profile becomes normal following successful remedial training. *Neurology, 58*, 1203–1213.

Siok, W. T., Perfetti, C. A., Jin, Z., & Tan, L. H. (2004). Biological abnormality of impaired reading is constrained by culture. *Nature, 431*, 70–76.

Stanovich, K. E., & Siegel, L. S. (1994). Phenotypic performance profile of children with reading disabilities: A regression-based test of the phonological-core variable-difference model. *Journal of Educational Psychology, 86*, 24–53.

Strain, E., & Herdman, C. M. (1999). Imageability effects in word naming: An individual differences analysis. *Canadian Journal of Experimental Psychology, 53*, 347–359.

Strain, E., Patterson, K., & Seidenberg, M. S. (1995). Semantic effects in single-word naming. *Journal of Experimental Psychology: Learning, Memory, and Cognition, 21*, 1140–1154.

Tagamets, M. A., Novick, J. M., Chalmers, M. L., & Friedman, R. B. (2000). A parametric approach of orthographic processing in the brain: An fMRI study. *Journal of Cognitive Neuroscience, 1*, 281–297.

Tallal, P. (1980). Auditory temporal perception, phonics, and reading disabilities in children. *Brain and Language, 9*, 182–198.

Tarkiainen, A., Cornelissen, P. L., & Salmelin, R. (2003). Dynamics of visual feature analysis and object-level processing in face versus letter-string perception. *Brain, 125*, 1125–1136.

Temple, E., Deutsch, G. K., Poldrack, R. A., Miller, S. L., Tallal, P., Merzenich, M. M., et al. (2003). Neural deficits in children with dyslexia ameliorated by behavioral remediation: Evidence from functional MRI. *Proceedings of the National Academy of Sciences, 100*, 2860–2865.

Temple, E., Poldrack, R. A., Salidis, J., Deutsch, G. K., Tallal, P., Merzenich, M. M., et al. (2001). Disrupted neural responses to phonological and orthographic processing in dyslexic children: An fMRI study. *NeuroReport, 12*, 299–307.

Torgesen, J. K., Morgan, S. T., & Davis, C. (1992). Effects of two types of phonological awareness training on word learning in kindergarten children. *Journal of Educational Psychology, 84*, 364–370.

Turkeltaub, P. E., Gareau, L., Flowers, D. L., Zeffiro, T. A., & Eden, G. F. (2003). Development of neural mechanisms for reading. *Nature Neuroscience, 6*, 767–773.

Van Orden, G. C. (1987). A ROWS is a ROSE: Spelling, sound, and reading. *Memory and Cognition, 10*, 434–442.

Van Orden, G. C., Johnston, J. C., & Hale, B. L. (1988). Word identification in reading proceeds from the spelling to sound to meaning. *Journal of Experimental Psychology: Memory, Language and Cognition, 14*, 371–386.

Wolf, M., & Bowers, G. P. (1999). The double-deficit hypothesis for the developmental dyslexias. *Journal of Educational Psychology, 91*, 415–438.

Ziegler, J. C. & Goswami, U. (2005). Reading acquisition, developmental dyslexia, and skilled reading across languages: A psycholinguistic grain size theory. *Psychological Bullitein, 131 (1)*, 3–29.

2 The Brain and Developmental Dyslexia
Genes, Anatomy, and Behavior

Glenn D. Rosen, Yu Wang,
Christopher G. Fiondella, and
Joseph J. LoTurco

INTRODUCTION

Dyslexia is a common reading disability, affecting 5%–10% of the population. The disorder is diagnosed usually during early school age through specialized test batteries that uncover specific behavioral profiles centered on reading, writing, and phonological awareness. The defining symptom of developmental dyslexia is a severe and specific difficulty in reading acquisition that is unexpected in relation to other cognitive abilities and educational circumstances (Lyon, Shaywitz, & Shaywitz, 2003). At the cognitive level, there is widespread agreement that a large majority of dyslexic children suffer from what is commonly termed a *phonological deficit*—a problem with some aspects of the mental representation and processing of speech sounds (Snowling, 2000). Evidence for this phonological deficit comes from three main behavioral symptoms: (a) poor phonological awareness, (b) poor verbal short-term memory, and (c) slow lexical retrieval (Ramus, 2004; Wagner & Torgesen, 1987). In addition to phonological awareness, dyslexics may also have difficulties in the speed of processing as diagnosed by their performance on tests of rapid naming (see Wolf & Bowers, 2000; Wolf, Gottwald, Galante, Norton, & Miller, this volume).

Other behavioral symptoms are often associated with dyslexia, including various types of auditory, visual, and motor deficits. Purely visual processing problems may explain reading disability in some dyslexic children, although the various theories of visual dyslexia need to be reconciled (Stein, 2001a, 2001b; Valdois, Bosse, & Tainturier, 2004). Auditory and motor disorders are often submitted to be the underlying cause of the phonological deficit (Eckert, 2004; Fitch & Tallal, 2003; Nagarajan et al., 1999; Nicolson et al., 2001; Stein & Walsh, 1997), a possibility that has not been altogether excluded. However, critics argue that their prevalence is too low to explain the phonological deficits, and that they are not specific to dyslexia (Nicolson et al., 2001; White et al., 2006). However, studies also show highly significant predictive relationships between early auditory indices, obtained both behaviorally and by magnetoencephalography (MEG), for later language performance (Benasich et al., 2006). It remains to be determined to what extent sensorimotor disorders are causes for the reading disability or to what extent they comprise only comorbid symptoms. It is likely that some of the difficulty comes from the possibility that there are several subtypes of developmental dyslexia that are confounded by our inability to classify them according to biological underpinnings.

For past two decades, our laboratory has concentrated its efforts on an attempt to understand the biological substrates underlying developmental dyslexia. Initial examination of postmortem dyslexic brains revealed abnormalities in cerebral asymmetry, abnormalities of cortical development in the perisylvian cortex, and abnormalities in the thalamus and cerebellum (Galaburda & Kemper, 1979; Galaburda, Sherman, Rosen, Aboitiz, & Geschwind, 1985; Humphreys, Kaufmann, & Galaburda, 1990). More recent findings on living dyslexic participants studied in vivo using imaging approaches such as structural and functional MRI (see Cornelissen, this volume; Frost, et al., this volume) have served to strengthen the validity of the postmortem findings. They too have underscored anomalies of cerebral asymmetry and of morphometric measurements in perisylvian cerebral cortex (Chang et al., 2005; de Oliveira et al., 2005; Eckert, 2004; Eckert et al., 2003, 2005; Silani et al., 2005; Sokol, Golomb, Carvahlo, & Edwards-Brown, 2006). The main focus of our laboratory, however, has been on the presence of small, but abundant, malformations of the cerebral cortex in the brains of dyslexics. These malformations share their origin with disturbances traceable to fetal life, specifically during the period when neurons are migrating from their proliferative zones to the cerebral cortex. These "neuronal migration disorders" are not limited, of course, to dyslexia, but what appears to make them unique is their distribution (predominantly in perisylvian cortices of the left hemisphere) and their relative focal nature. The cortical malformations affect both low-level and high-level cortical processors, for example, primary and early association auditory and premotor cortices, as well as prefrontal and anterior and posterior middle temporal cortices (Figure 2.1).

The location of the ectopias and laminar dysplasias in the human dyslexic brain suggests that they could produce dysfunction in low- and high-level cortical processors, affecting perceptual, cognitive, and even metacognitive functions. Thus, for instance, involvement of the primary auditory cortex (and probably also nearby association cortical areas) could be responsible for the difficulties with rapid sound processing, whereas involvement of prefrontal, anterior temporal, temporo-occipital (the word form area), or inferior parietal cortices could explain problems with memory and phonological awareness, as well as other aspects of phonological processing such as mapping phonemes to graphemes. Mechanisms for functional deficits could result from the additional spread of anatomical disruption from the areas of microgyria, ectopias, and laminar dysplasias to regions connected to

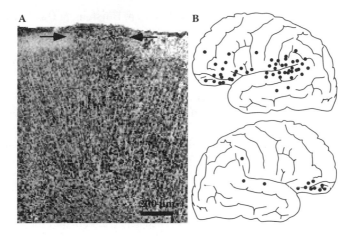

FIGURE 2.1 Malformations of the cerebral cortex in dyslexic brains. (a) Photomicrograph illustrating typical "molecular layer ectopia" in a dyslexic brains (arrows). These ectopias are neurons that have migrated to unexpected locations. (b) Schematic illustrating location of ectopias in the brains of dyslexics. These ectopias are located predominantly in the left hemisphere (top) surrounding regions of the brain important for language processing.

them. Thus, other parts of the cortex or subcortical areas connected to the areas of malformation could be affected in their growth and development. Toward that end, there are abnormalities in visual and auditory nuclei of the thalamus—the lateral and medial geniculate nuclei, respectively. In the lateral geniculate nucleus, neurons of the magnocellular layers were approximately 30% smaller in dyslexics than in control brains (Livingstone, Rosen, Drislane, & Galaburda, 1991). In the medial geniculate nucleus (MGN) there was no difference in the average neuronal size, but there was a significant shift of neuronal sizes toward smaller neurons in the dyslexic left hemisphere (Galaburda, Menard, & Rosen, 1994).

In sum, there are a variety of cortical malformations and thalamic changes seen in the brains of postmortem dyslexics. The functional and behavioral effects of these malformations are difficult to gauge in humans; we have, therefore, concentrated our efforts on the use of animal models to dissect the link between development, anatomy, and behavior.

ANIMAL MODELS

Animal experiments have aimed at modeling the anatomical findings made in postmortem dyslexic brains. Principally, they have mimicked specific types of neuronal migration disorders, including spontaneously occurring molecular layer ectopias (Sherman, Galaburda, & Geschwind, 1985; Sherman, Morrison, Rosen, Behan, & Galaburda, 1990b; Sherman, Rosen, & Galaburda, 1988; Sherman, Rosen, Stone, Press, & Galaburda, 1992; Sherman, Stone, Press, Rosen, & Galaburda, 1990; Sherman, Stone, Rosen, & Galaburda, 1990a) and induced focal microgyria (Herman, Galaburda, Fitch, Carter, & Rosen, 1997; Humphreys,

Rosen, Press, Sherman, & Galaburda, 1991; Rosen, Burstein, & Galaburda, 2000; Rosen & Galaburda, 2000; Rosen, Herman, & Galaburda, 1999; Rosen, Sherman, Richman, Stone, & Galaburda, 1992; Rosen, Windzio, & Galaburda, 2001). We had assumed from observations in fetal human tissue, as well as in developmental animal models, that ectopias and laminar dysplasias arose as a result of injury (Sarnat, 1992) some time near the end of the first half of pregnancy. We know specifically that ectopias can arise in animal models when the external glial limiting membrane/basal lamina, which limits migration of neurons up to but no farther than layer 2 of the developing cortical plate, is experimentally ruptured (Rosen et al., 1992).

The study of induced microgyria has provided important insights into possible mechanisms by which a dyslexic individual could have deficits in phonological processing. The induction of microgyria (by freeze injury of the developing cerebral cortex) in rodents caused striking plasticity-mediated changes in the architecture and connectivity of the cortex (Rosen et al., 2000). In comparison to controls, animals with microgyria showed a decrease in efferent projections from the microgyric cortex to the opposite hemisphere. Microgyria in the primary sensory cortex had abnormal efferent connections to the secondary somatosensory cortex of the opposite hemisphere. Injection of tracer into the homologous area of the undamaged hemisphere highlighted aberrant projections into frontal and secondary somatosensory cortices of the affected hemisphere. There were almost no thalamocortical or corticothalamic projections between the ventrobasal complex and the microgyrus itself. Interestingly, a dense plexus of thalamocortical fibers was often noted at the border between the malformed and normal cortex.

This reorganization, particularly that having to do with corticothalamic circuits, leads to deficits in auditory processing similar to those seen in dyslexic individuals and is potentially related to phonological deficits. Thus, a series of studies performed by Fitch and colleagues revealed that focal microgyria are associated with rapid auditory processing deficits in rodent models (Clark, Rosen, Tallal, & Fitch, 2000a, 2000b; Clark, Sherman, Bimonte, & Fitch, 2000; Fitch, Brown, Tallal, & Rosen, 1997; Fitch, Tallal, Brown, Galaburda, & Rosen, 1994; Peiffer et al., 2001; Peiffer, Rosen, & Fitch, 2002a, 2002b; Peiffer, Fitch, Thomas, Yurkovic, & Rosen, 2003; Peiffer, McClure, Threlkeld, Rosen, & Fitch, 2004; Peiffer, Rosen, & Fitch, 2004). Male rats with induced focal microgyria were unable to perform a two-tone discrimination task when the stimulus duration was relatively short. In contrast, sham animals and microgyric females performed well at all stimulus durations (Fitch et al., 1994, 1997). Exposure of perinatal female rats with induced microgyria to the androgen testosterone propionate is capable of inducing thalamic changes comparable to those seen in the males (Rosen et al., 1999). After a thorough analysis of the cortical malformations induced during the newborn period in male and female rats, no sex differences were found in the malformations themselves, only in the secondary thalamic changes (Rosen et al., 1999). This suggested a maladaptive outcome of plasticity following early cortical insult in the males and the establishment of anomalous corticothalamic circuits. These thalamic changes in male rats turn out to be relevant to the behavior, since only males develop auditory processing deficits and thalamic changes.

These animal models demonstrate that developmental, physiological, behavioral, and anatomical abnormalities vary according to sex, and that some of the behaviors correlate with changes in the thalamus while others correlate with corticocortical changes. Although the link between these animal models and developmental dyslexia is potentially important, there are a number of uncertainties that remain. For one, it is not certain what percentage of developmental dyslexics exhibit malformations of the brain—these malformations are not yet visible using noninvasive techniques such as magnetic resonance imaging (MRI) or computer topography (CT), and the number of documented postmortem cases is relatively small. In addition, the link between the animal models that we have employed and the human disorder is not direct; there is limited evidence of shared underlying biology. The explosion of knowledge of the human and animal genome in recent years, however, suggests another pathway by which we can begin to understand the biological substrates of developmental dyslexia. In the following section, we review some of the recent evidence of the role of genes in neuronal migration and in developmental dyslexia.

THE GENETICS OF DYSLEXIA AND NEOCORTICAL MALFORMATIONS

The causes of human cortical malformations have been reviewed elsewhere (Barkovich et al., 1996; Mischel, Nguyen, & Vinters, 1995; Sarnat, 1991), and it is clear that they can result from genetic or environmental events occurring during the period of neuronal migration. In the past, neuronal migration disorders of genetic etiology were thought to be more diffuse and more severe (leading to epilepsy and mental retardation, for instance), whereas those associated with focal injury or other nongenetic events produce milder clinical syndromes (including dyslexia). For example, about 90% of individuals with Miller–Dieker syndrome, who have microdeletions in a critical 350-kilobase region in chromosome 17p13.3 (Reiner et al., 1993, 1995), show diffuse anatomical and clinical effects. Additional gene mutations have been associated with the relatively diffuse pathology seen in X-linked lissencephaly and double cortex (doublecortin; des Portes, Francis, et al., 1998; des Portes, Pinard, et al., 1998; Gleeson et al., 1998; Gleeson, Minnerath, et al., 1999). In contrast, it is generally accepted that microgyria and other focal disorders of neuronal migration, including focal glioneuronal heterotopia, are the indirect results of focal injury occurring during neuronal migration (Levine, Fisher, & Caviness, 1974; Lyon & Robain, 1967; Marin-Padilla, 1996, 1999; McBride & Kemper, 1982). However, recent advances in genetics have begun to disclose milder syndromes relating to mutations or changes in function. Developmental dyslexia may be an example of a milder genetic effect on brain development, anatomy, and behavior.

Familial occurrence and twin studies have long suggested a genetic basis for dyslexia, and details concerning the search for this genetic basis are elaborated in more detail in the chapters by Olson, Byrne, and Samuelsson, and Grigorenko and Naples in this volume. For the purposes of our discussion here, we will quickly mention that linkage analysis points to dyslexic susceptibility loci on chromosomes (Chr) 1 (Tzenova, Kaplan, Petryshen, & Field, 2004), 2 (Kaminen et al., 2003; Fagerheim et al., 1999; Francks et al., 2002; Raskind et al., 2005), 3 (Nopola-Hemmi et al., 2001), 6 (Cardon et al., 1994; Deffenbacher et al., 2004; Gayán et al., 1999; Grigorenko et al., 1997; Grigorenko, Wood, Meyer, & Pauls, 2000), 7 (Kaminen et al., 2003), 11 (Hsiung, Kaplan, Petryshen, Lu, & Field, 2004), 15 (Grigorenko et al., 1997; Morris et al., 2000; Nopola-Hemmi et al., 2000; Nothen et al., 1999; Schulte-Korne et al., 1998; Smith, Kimberling, Pennington, & Lubs, 1983), 18 (Fisher et al., 2002; Schumacher, Konig, et al., 2006), and Xq27.3 (de Kovel et al., 2004). These "loci" represent an interval of a chromosome that may contain hundreds of genes, so it has been particularly exciting that candidate dyslexia susceptibility genes have recently been proposed at some of these intervals. *ROBO1*, an axon guidance and neuronal migration gene located on Chr 3, has been reported to be a candidate dyslexia susceptibility gene (Hannula-Jouppi et al., 2005), and two genes, *DCDC2* and *KIAA0319,* have been identified on Chr 6 (Cope et al., 2005; Francks et al., 2004; Meng, Smith, et al., 2005; Paracchini et al., 2006; Schumacher, Anthoni, et al., 2006). *DYX1C1* (also known as *EKN1*), a candidate dyslexia susceptibility gene located on Chr 15 has been identified (Brkanac et al., 2007; Chapman et al., 2004; Taipale et al., 2003; Wigg et al., 2004), and although there is controversy regarding its generalizability outside of Finnish populations (Bellini et al., 2005; Marino et al., 2005; Scerri et al., 2004), the suspect alleles have been associated with working memory deficits in dyslexic populations (Marino et al., 2007).

What has been most exciting about the identification of these candidate dyslexia susceptibility genes is that there is evidence that the proteins encoded by these genes, although diverse, may be functionally linked, either directly or by virtue of their similarity to other proteins, in pathways involved in neuronal migration and axon growth. In the following section, we briefly summarize some of the evidence in the literature that supports this link between candidate dyslexia susceptibility gene function and brain development, specifically neuronal migration. We will then discuss some specific experimental evidence that our colleagues and ourselves have gathered that directly supports the role of these genes in neuronal migration.

CANDIDATE DYSLEXIA SUSCEPTIBILITY GENES AND NEOCORTICAL MIGRATION

Neurodevelopmental processes such as neuronal migration and axon growth share several features and requirements, including dependence upon coordinated changes in cell adhesion, process outgrowth, and cytoskeletal restructuring. *DCDC2*, on chromosome 6p22, is one of an 11-member group of proteins whose function is beginning to be understood. The first characterized gene of this family, *DCX*, was identified after the discovery of mutations in a gene that causes severe neuronal migration abnormalities (double cortex syndrome and lissencephaly) in humans (des Portes, Pinard, et al., 1998; Gleeson et al., 1998). The protein appears critical for binding to and stabilizing microtubules, functions that are critical to neuronal migration.

KIAA0319 is the second of the two candidate dyslexia susceptibility genes on chromosome 6 (Cope et al., 2005; Paracchini et al., 2006). The gene codes for an integral membrane protein that is purported to have a role in the ability of cells to interact directly with other cells. This is particularly important in neuronal migration, as these molecules are needed to help guide neurons to their proper location. More definitive and direct tests are now required to identify the specific molecular and cell-to-cell interactions that are potentially mediated by *KIAA0319*.

ROBO1 and *DYX1C1* were both identified as candidate dyslexia susceptibility genes from either chromosomal translocations in small pedigrees or by linkage disequilibrium association studies (Hannula-Jouppi et al., 2005; Taipale et al., 2003; Wigg et al., 2004). The domain structure of *DYX1C1* does not clearly link it to cell adhesion (like *KIAA0319*) or to cytoskeletal dynamics (like *DCDC2*), but the role of invertebrate and vertebrate homologs of *ROBO1* in neuronal development has been thoroughly studied and is well understood. Initially found in a genetic screen in drosophila, this gene plays an important role in axon growth across the midline of the brain and in the spinal cord (Erskine et al., 2000; Yuan et al., 1999). The ligands of robo proteins—slits—have been implicated in both axon growth and cell migration. For example, slits have been shown to direct the migration of neurons to neocortex by acting to repel cells away from the proliferative zones—the ventricular zone and ganglionic eminence—of the developing forebrain (Zhu, Li, Zhou, Wu, & Rao, 1999).

EXPERIMENTAL TESTS OF CANDIDATE SUSCEPTIBILITY GENE FUNCTION IN RODENTS

Many of the proteins that control neuronal migration of the cortex have been identified through genetic studies in humans and mice. Included among these are the products of the lissencephaly genes *LIS1* and *DCX* (Gleeson, Lin, Flanagan, & Walsh, 1999; Guerrini, 2005; Leventer, Cardoso, Ledbetter, & Dobyns, 2001), and components of the reelin signaling pathway: reelin, dab-1, VLDLR, and ApoER2 (D'Arcangelo et al., 1995, 1999; Rice et al., 1998). RNA interference (RNAi) is now an accepted complement to standard genetic methodologies for the identification and functional characterization of new genes serving diverse cellular functions. Specifically, RNAi permits one to experimentally knock down gene function in a spatially and temporally specific manner. We have adopted an RNAi strategy using in utero electroporation of plasmids encoding short hairpin RNAs (shRNA). In this specific case, shRNA plasmids targeted against dyslexia susceptibility genes are injected into the cerebral ventricles of embryonic rats and subsequently electroporated into the progenitor cells of the cerebral cortex that lie above the ventricles. In other words, we can selectively knock down the function of specific genes in specific neurons at specific times during development. Subsequent examination of these transfected cells allows for the assessment of the effect of these genes on neuronal development.

LoTurco's laboratory used this technique to examine the effects of Dcdc2, Kiaa0319, and Dyx1c1 on migrating cortical neurons (Meng, Smith, et al., 2005; Paracchini et al., 2006; Wang et al., 2006). There was substantial evidence that all three of these genes play a role in neuronal migration. When examined 4–7 days after transfection, the majority of shRNA-transfected neurons were still in the ventricular zone; very few, if any, had migrated. In contrast, neurons that were transfected with control plasmids migrated normally (see Figure 2.2). Importantly, in all three cases the ability of shRNA-transfected neurons to migrate was rescued by the presence of exogenous protein. In other words, the migratory function of a neuron that was transfected with shRNA targeted against, for example, *Dyx1c1*, could be restored by introducing the Dyx1c1 protein to the cells. This is essential for confirming that the effects of the shRNA were specific to the genes being targeted and were not the consequence of off-target effects.

Thus, this evidence strongly suggested that knock down of these candidate dyslexia susceptibility genes disrupts neuronal migration. What was not known, however, was the effect of these disruptions on the eventual organization of the brain of these animals. To address this issue, we have examined the brains of adult rats that were embryonically transfected with shRNA targeted against dyslexia susceptibility genes. We summarize our results in the following.

Dyx1c1

We have found that after the initial migration arrest (as assessed 4–7 days posttransfection) many transfected neurons go on to migrate to the cortex, although there is significant curtailment in the total number of labeled neurons in the cortex (Rosen et al., 2007). Because relatively equal numbers of neurons are transfected in shRNA and control conditions, the smaller numbers of labeled cells in the former are most likely the result of increased cell death among transfected neurons. Interestingly, there were clusters of unmigrated cells in Dyx1c1 shRNA-transfected animals that were located either at or below the border of the cerebral cortex (see Figure 2.3). Special stains revealed that only some of these neurons were transfected, which suggested that at least some of the neurons did not migrate because of secondary, noncell autonomous effects, rather than a direct effect of *Dyx1c1* RNAi transfection.

In all the control cases examined, neurons migrated mostly to layer 3 of the neocortex, with relatively few remaining in lower layers. In contrast, there were far more neurons scattered in the lower layers in Dyx1c1 shRNA-transfected animals, and those that did migrate were found superficial to layer 3. This was confirmed quantitatively by migration distance analysis. The distribution of labeled cells through the thickness of the neocortex in controls was significantly different from that in *Dyx1c1* shRNA brains—there was a lack of migration in one group of transfected cells and abnormal (excessive) migration in another (Figure 2.4).

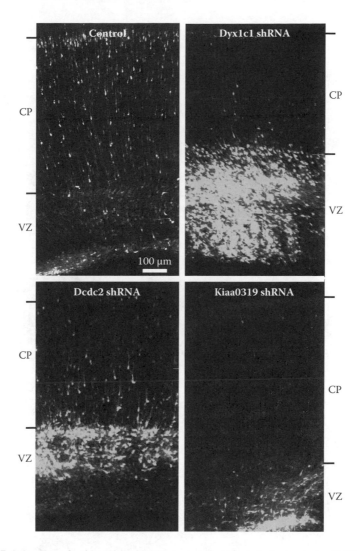

FIGURE 2.2 Transfection with shRNA targeted against dyslexia susceptibility genes disrupts neuronal migration when examined 4 days after transfection. Photomicrographs of developing rat cerebral cortex illustrating the migration of neurons with green fluorescent protein (GFP) as a control marker of neurons, compared with those cotransfected with GFP and shRNA targeted against *Dyx1c1*, *Dcdc2*, and *Kiaa0319*. In the GFP condition, neurons have migrated out of the ventricular zone (VZ) and have taken their normal position in the cortical plate (CP). In contrast, the overwhelming majority of neurons transfected with shRNA remain in the ventricular zone and do not migrate.

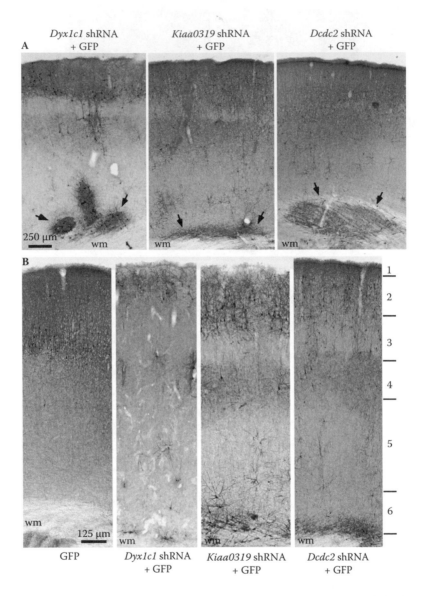

FIGURE 2.3 Immunohistochemically stained neurons in adult rat cortex following in utero electroporation of shRNA targeted against candidate dyslexia susceptibility genes. (a) Photomicrographs illustrating collections of unmigrated neurons (periventricular nodular heterotopias) around the junction between the white matter (wm) and the cerebral cortex. (b) Photomicrographs of cerebral cortex illustrating the position of transfected neurons. In the control condition (GFP) neurons tend to cluster around layer 3 (layers denoted on right margin). In contrast, neurons transfected with candidate dyslexia susceptibility genes tend to be distributed in lower cortical layers and in layer 2.

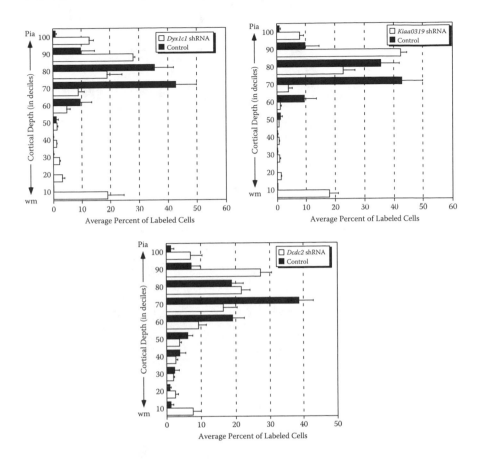

FIGURE 2.4 The laminar position of neurons is disrupted by transfection with shRNA targeted against dyslexia susceptibility genes. Histograms of mean (±SEM) average percentage of neurons in each decile of the cerebral cortex ranging from the white matter (wm) to the pial surface. These histograms demonstrate that shRNA transfected neurons tend to migrate in a bimodal distribution, with some neurons remaining near the white matter and the remaining peak past their expected locations.

Approximately 25% of the 21 *Dyx1c1* shRNA-transfected brains had ectopias in layer 1 of the cortex that were not related to the injection site. These were remarkably similar to those seen in the brains of postmortem dyslexics. There were few, if any, labeled neurons in the malformation itself, suggesting that at least some of the displaced neurons were not likely to have been transfected with Dyx1c1 shRNA and arrived in the ectopia by a secondary mechanism (Figure 2.5).

The evidence suggests that *Dyx1c1* disrupts neuronal migration in such a way that malformations similar to those seen in dyslexic brains are visible. That said, the viability of *DYX1C1* as a candidate gene for dyslexia has been called into question for the general world population and may instead only apply to a genetically distinct population. Thus, the locus described in the initial

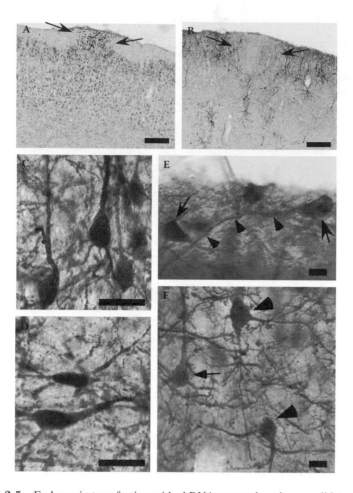

FIGURE 2.5   Embryonic transfection with shRNA targeted against candidate dyslexia susceptibility genes is associated with malformations and misorientation of neurons in the cerebral cortex in adulthood. (a) Photomicrograph of ectopia (arrows) in the brain of a rat transfected with shRNA targeted against *Dyx1c1*. This ectopia is remarkably similar to those seen in the brains of dyslexics (see Figure 2.1). (b) Photomicrograph of section adjacent to panel A stained for transfected neurons. Note that the area of the ectopia (arrows) does not contain transfected neurons, suggesting the creation of these ectopias is likely due to secondary effects of the shRNA transfection. (c and d) High-power photomicrograph of neurons embryonically transfected with *Kiaa0319*. In panel c these layer 3 neurons are normally oriented, whereas those in layer 5 (panel d) are misoriented. Bar = 25 μm. (e) High-power photomicrograph of neurons embryonically transfected with shRNA targeted against *Dcdc2* located in layer 1 of the neocortex (arrows). These neurons were misoriented, with apical dendrite running parallel to the pial surface (arrowheads). (f) High-power photomicrograph of 3 neurons embryonically transfected with shRNA directed against *Dcdc2*. Two neurons (arrowheads) are misoriented, while another is normally oriented (arrow).

report (Taipale et al., 2003) was replicated in a U.S. (Brkanac et al., 2007) and Canadian sample (Wigg et al., 2004). Chapman et al. (2004) found linkage to the same region of Chr 15 in a U.S. population, but did not directly replicate the role of *DYX1C1*. Other studies have failed to provide support for the *DYX1C1* locus in Italian (Bellini et al., 2005; Marino et al., 2003, 2005) and English (Scerri et al., 2004) populations. Recent evidence from the Italian population, however, supports the linkage of *DYX1C1* variants initially reported by Taipale et al. (2003) to working memory deficits in their population of developmental dyslexics (Marino et al., 2007).

Kiaa0319

In utero RNAi targeted against *Kiaa0319* disrupts neuronal migration (Paracchini et al., 2006), but as with the case of *Dyx1c1*, the adult neocortical phenotype has not been fully described. We have examined a series of adult brains from embryos transfected with shRNA targeted against *Kiaa0319*. As with *Dyx1c1* (and *Dcdc2*, see following subsection), there were essentially two populations of labeled cells in the neocortex. One population of cells was clustered around the white matter border, and another group of neurons had migrated to upper cortical layers (Figure 2.3). We quantified the migration distance of immunopositive neurons embryonically transfected with RNAi targeted against *Kiaa0319* in an identical manner as that described earlier for *Dyx1c1*. The results demonstrate that the neurons migrate to the upper neocortical levels past the expected lamina (Figure 2.4). In the upper layers of the *Kiaa0319* transfection, all immunopositive cells exhibited neuronal morphology and were radially oriented with respect to the pial surface. Of the deeper cells with neuronal morphology, there were large numbers that were not radially oriented as expected, but instead showed apical dendrites that were aligned in seemingly random orientations (see Figure 2.5).

Dcdc2

Meng, Hager, et al. (2005) previously demonstrated that in utero RNAi targeted against *Dcdc2* disrupts neuronal migration. As with the case of *Dyx1c1*, the adult neocortical phenotype had not been described. We have examined a series of postnatal brains that had been embryonically transfected with RNAi targeted against *Dcdc2* and their controls transfected at the same age (Burbridge et al., 2008). As with *Dyx1c1* and *Kiaa0319*, there was one population of cells clustered around the white matter border with the neocortex, and another group of neurons that migrated to upper cortical layers. We quantified the migration distances of transfected neurons from *Dcdc2* RNAi and control brains. The results showed the mainly bimodal distribution of labeled cells, with neurons that migrated to the upper neocortical levels ending past the laminar location of control neurons (Figure 2.4). Some of the neurons terminated their migration in layer 1, which is a unique feature of this dyslexia susceptibility gene knockdown experiment (Figure 2.5). Unlike the case with *Kiaa0319* transfection, there was abnormal orientation of labeled neurons in both the lower and upper cortical layers. In both upper and lower layers, there were also normally oriented labeled cells. Many of the abnormal cells had the morphology of pyramidal neurons, but their apical dendrites were not radially aligned with the neocortical surface (Figure 2.5).

Summary

Using in utero electroporation of shRNA targeted against genes *Dcdc2*, *Kiaa0319*, and *Dyx1c1*, we showed that knock down of these genes disrupts neuronal migration and causes anatomical malformations that are similar to those seen in developmental dyslexia (Chang et al., 2005; Galaburda et al., 1985). We hypothesize that knock down of *Kiaa0319* function affects migration by altering cell adhesion, *Dcdc2* affects migration by disrupting cell polarity and process extension, and *Dyx1c1* affects migration by altering the transition to the multipolar stage of neuronal migration (LoTurco & Bai, 2006). Despite these suggested differences, there are some remarkable similarities in the postnatal phenotypes, the most striking of which is the comparable bimodal distribution of the labeled neurons in the cortex.

Preliminary examination of the morphology of the labeled neurons reveals differences between *Dyx1c1*, *Kiaa0319*, and *Dcdc2*. Whereas the morphology of neurons transfected with *Dyx1c1* shRNA appears relatively normal in the cerebral cortex, the unmigrated neurons are grossly misoriented. *Kiaa0319* RNAi disrupts the orientation and morphology of transfected neurons in lower neocortical layers. In contrast, there are abnormally oriented neurons in both the upper and lower layers in *Dcdc2* RNAi brains. The morphology of these neurons is quite variable, with some neurons having typical pyramidal morphology and others having no clear apical dendrite. In addition, there are labeled, abnormally oriented neurons in layer 1—something that has not been seen in other experiments.

CONCLUSIONS

We have obviously just begun to scratch the surface in the investigation of the function of dyslexia susceptibility genes. Although we have good evidence that the genes examined thus far have roles in neural development, it is not at all known whether they may also serve different functions in adulthood. Moreover, as linkage analysis proceeds (see chapters by Grigorenko & Naples, this volume, and Olson et al., this volume), more candidate dyslexia susceptibility genes are likely to be identified, and there is no way of knowing whether these genes will have similar functions to those already investigated. Yet, these newly discovered genetic substrates may provide us with the ability to carry out proper classification, and we may yet discover that different genes predispose to different relationships between sound processing and phonological skills.

It is also important to emphasize the complex nature of developmental dyslexia. There are potentially many ways that a person's brain can be organized that would result in that person being dyslexic. Frost et al., in this volume, for example, suggests that a disruption of the "skill pathway" might disrupt the ability to learn to read following standard instruction. This reading circuit is composed of many different regions of the brain that are interconnected in many complex and intricate ways. The construction of these "information highways" during brain development is an enormously complicated endeavor, and any misstep along the way might render one's brain susceptible to developmental dyslexia. Consequently, it is reasonable to suppose that the genetic underpinnings of developmental dyslexia are going to be equally complex. Not only is it unlikely that there will be a single gene that explains all of dyslexia, it is a distinct possibility that gene–gene interaction—that is, the effect of one's gene function on another, separate gene—will play an important role. Even more likely is the possibility that the complex phenotype we know as developmental dyslexia is regulated by a large and complex gene network comprised of scores of genes that interact in ways not yet amenable to easy dissection.

No matter what holds in the future, the focus of both clinical research and animal modeling in dyslexia research is now apt to change with the introduction of candidate dyslexia susceptibility genes into the research armamentarium. In the case of animal models, many of the findings in the injury-based cortical malformations—cortical and thalamic changes, changes in connectivity, associated temporal auditory processing deficits, sex effects—will need to be rediscovered using the gene disruption model. Future experiments will need to answer questions that were not relevant in the injury models, but are important for the genetic theory of dyslexia. For instance, a challenge will be to show how variant gene function affecting a brain development gene can result in exquisitely focal anatomical and behavioral phenotypes to explain the anatomical anomalies and behavioral deficits in dyslexia. Is the effect in fact as focal as we think, or is it more widespread at the initial state before plasticity remodels the brain from the initial event?

Because of our long interest in the role of neuronal migration disorders and dyslexia, we have naturally focused our research interests there. But the use of genetic models certainly raises the possibility that other types of brain or cognitive phenotypes may be associated with dyslexia candidate gene function. An intriguing possibility is that discovery of these other associations with gene function in animals might lead to interesting biological or cognitive markers that could be investigated in human populations.

Future research on the cognitive phenotype of dyslexia will undoubtedly focus on trying to differentiate the various dyslexia phenotypes (with and without sound processing problems, or with and without motor findings, for instance) with respect to genotype, gene function, and brain characteristics. This could be further enhanced as genetic research begins to tease apart the specific biologic consequences of dyslexia gene variants. This will be helped along if early detection of dyslexia risk by genetic testing can lead to early description of behavioral and brain phenotypes, before environmentally and genetically mediated plasticity confounds the picture, and also by findings in the animal models described earlier.

REFERENCES

Barkovich, A. J., Kuzniecky, R. I., Dobyns, W. B., Jackson, G. D., Becker, L. E., & Evrard, P. (1996). A classification scheme for malformations of cortical development. *Neuropediatrics, 27,* 59–63.

Bellini, G., Bravaccio, C., Calamoneri, F., Donatella Cocuzza, M., Fiorillo, P., Gagliano, A., et al. (2005). No evidence for association between dyslexia and DYX1C1 functional variants in a group of children and adolescents from Southern Italy. *Journal of Molecular Neuroscience, 27,* 311–314.

Benasich, A. A., Choudhury, N., Friedman, J. T., Realpe-Bonilla, T., Chojnowska, C., & Gou, Z. (2006). The infant as a prelinguistic model for language learning impairments: Predicting from event-related potentials to behavior. *Neuropsychologia, 44*(3), 396–411.

Brkanac, Z., Chapman, N. H., Matsushita, M. M., Chun, L., Nielsen, K., Cochrane, E., et al. (2007). Evaluation of candidate genes for DYX1 and DYX2 in families with dyslexia. *American Journal of Medical Genetics Part B: Neuropsychiatric Genetics, 144B*(4), 556–560.

Burbridge, T. J., Wang, Y., Volz, A. J., Peschansky, V. J., Lissan, L., Galaburda, A. M., et al. (2008). Postnatal analysis of the effect of embryonic knockdown and overexpression of candidate dyslexia susceptibility gene Dcdc2. *Neuroscience, 152*(3), 723–733.

Cardon, L. R., Smith, S. D., Fulker, D. W., Kimberling, W. J., Pennington, B. F., & DeFries, J. C. (1994). Quantitative trait locus for reading disability on chromosome 6. *Science, 266,* 276–279.

Chang, B. S., Ly, J., Appignani, B., Bodell, A., Apse, K. A., Ravenscroft, R. S., et al. (2005). Reading impairment in the neuronal migration disorder of periventricular nodular heterotopia. *Neurology, 64,* 799–803.

Chapman, N. H., Igo, R. P., Thomson, J. B., Matsushita, M., Brkanac, Z., Holzman, T., et al. (2004). Linkage analyses of four regions previously implicated in dyslexia: Confirmation of a locus on chromosome 15q. *American Journal of Medical Genetics Part B: Neuropsychiatric Genetics, 131,* 67–75.

Clark, M. G., Rosen, G. D., Tallal, P., & Fitch, R. H. (2000a). Impaired two-tone processing at rapid rates in male rats with induced microgyria. *Brain Research, 871,* 94–97.

Clark, M. G., Rosen, G. D., Tallal, P., & Fitch, R. H. (2000b). Impaired processing of complex auditory stimuli in rats with induced cerebrocortical microgyria: An animal model of developmental language disabilities. *Journal of Cognitive Neuroscience, 12,* 828–839.

Clark, M. G., Sherman, G. F., Bimonte, H. A., & Fitch, R. H. (2000). Perceptual auditory gap detection deficits in male BXSB mice with cerebrocortical ectopias. *NeuroReport, 11,* 693–696.

Cope, N., Harold, D., Hill, G., Moskvina, V., Stevenson, J., Holmans, P., et al. (2005). Strong evidence that KIAA0319 on chromosome 6p is a susceptibility gene for developmental dyslexia. *American Journal of Human Genetics, 76,* 581–591.

D'Arcangelo, G., Homayouni, R., Keshvara, L., Rice, D. S., Sheldon, M., & Curran, T. (1999). Reelin is a ligand for lipoprotein receptors. *Neuron, 24,* 471–479.

D'Arcangelo, G., Miao, G. G., Chen, S. C., Soares, H. D., Morgan, J. I., & Curran, T. (1995). A protein related to extracellular matrix proteins deleted in the mouse mutant reeler. *Nature, 374,* 719–723.

de Kovel, C. G., Hol, F. A., Heister, J. G., Willemen, J. J., Sandkuijl, L. A., Franke, B., et al. (2004). Genomewide scan identifies susceptibility locus for dyslexia on Xq27 in an extended Dutch family. *Journal of Medical Genetics, 41,* 652–657.

de Oliveira, E. P., Guerreiro, M. M., Guimaraes, C. A., Brandao-Almeida, I. L., Montenegro, M. A., Cendes, F., et al. (2005). Characterization of the linguistic profile of a family with Perisylvian Syndrome. *Pro Fono, 17*, 393–402.

Deffenbacher, K. E., Kenyon, J. B., Hoover, D. M., Olson, R. K., Pennington, B. F., DeFries, J. C., et al. (2004). Refinement of the 6p21.3 quantitative trait locus influencing dyslexia: Linkage and association analyses. *Human Genetics, 115*, 128–138.

des Portes, V., Francis, F., Pinard, J. M., Desguerre, I., Moutard, M. L., Snoeck, I., et al. (1998). Doublecortin is the major gene causing X-linked subcortical laminar heterotopia (SCLH). *Human Molecular Genetics, 7*, 1063–1070.

des Portes, V., Pinard, J. M., Billuart, P., Vinet, M. C., Koulakoff, A., Carrie, A., et al. (1998). A novel CNS gene required for neuronal migration and involved in X- linked subcortical laminar heterotopia and lissencephaly syndrome. *Cell, 92*, 51–61.

Eckert, M. (2004). Neuroanatomical markers for dyslexia: A review of dyslexia structural imaging studies. *Neuroscientist, 10*, 362–371.

Eckert, M. A., Leonard, C. M., Richards, T. L., Aylward, E. H., Thomson, J., & Berninger, V. W. (2003). Anatomical correlates of dyslexia: Frontal and cerebellar findings. *Brain, 126*, 482–494.

Eckert, M. A., Leonard, C. M., Wilke, M., Eckert, M., Richards, T., Richards, A., et al. (2005). Anatomical signatures of dyslexia in children: Unique information from manual and voxel based morphometry brain measures. *Cortex, 41*, 304–315.

Erskine, L., Williams, S. E., Brose, K., Kidd, T., Rachel, R. A., Goodman, C. S., et al. (2000). Retinal ganglion cell axon guidance in the mouse optic chiasm: Expression and function of robos and slits. *Journal of Neuroscience, 20*, 4975–4982.

Fagerheim, T., Raeymaekers, P., Tonnessen, F. E., Pedersen, M., Tranebjaerg, L., & Lubs, H. A. (1999). A new gene (DYX3) for dyslexia is located on chromosome 2. *Journal of Medical Genetics, 36*, 664–669.

Fisher, S. E., Francks, C., Marlow, A. J., MacPhie, I. L., Newbury, D. F., Cardon, L. R., et al. (2002). Independent genome-wide scans identify a chromosome 18 quantitative-trait locus influencing dyslexia. *Nature Genetics, 30*, 86–91.

Fitch, R. H., Brown, C. P., Tallal, P., & Rosen, G. D. (1997). Effects of sex and MK-801 on auditory-processing deficits associated with developmental microgyric lesions in rats. *Behavioral Neuroscience, 111*, 404–412.

Fitch, R. H., & Tallal, P. (2003). Neural mechanisms of language-based learning impairments: Insights from human populations and animal models. *Behavioral and Cognitive Neuroscience Reviews, 2*, 155–178.

Fitch, R. H., Tallal, P., Brown, C., Galaburda, A. M., & Rosen, G. D. (1994). Induced microgyria and auditory temporal processing in rats: A model for language impairment? *Cerebral Cortex, 4*, 260–270.

Francks, C., Fisher, S. E., Olson, R. K., Pennington, B. F., Smith, S. D., DeFries, J. C., et al. (2002). Fine mapping of the chromosome 2p12-16 dyslexia susceptibility locus: Quantitative association analysis and positional candidate genes SEMA4F and OTX1. *Psychiatric Genetics, 12*, 35–41.

Francks, C., Paracchini, S., Smith, S. D., Richardson, A. J., Scerri, T. S., Cardon, L. R., et al. (2004). A 77-kilobase region of chromosome 6p22.2 is associated with dyslexia in families from the United Kingdom and from the United States. *American Journal of Human Genetics, 75*, 1046–1058.

Galaburda, A. M., & Kemper, T. L. (1979). Cytoarchitectonic abnormalities in developmental dyslexia: A case study. *Annals of Neurology, 6*, 94–100.

Galaburda A. M., Menard, M. T., & Rosen, G. D. (1994). *Evidence for aberrant auditory anatomy in developmental dyslexia*. Proceedings of the National Academy of Sciences USA, 91, 8010–8013.

Galaburda, A. M., Sherman, G. F., Rosen, G. D., Aboitiz, F., & Geschwind N. (1985). Developmental dyslexia: Four consecutive cases with cortical anomalies. *Annals of Neurology, 18*, 222–233.

Gayán, J., Smith, S. D., Cherny, S. S., Cardon, L. R., Fulker, D. W., Brower, A. M., et al. (1999). Quantitative-trait locus for specific language and reading deficits on chromosome 6p. *American Journal of Human Genetics, 64*, 157–164.

Gleeson, J. G., Allen, K. M., Fox, J. W., Lamperti, E. D., Berkovic, S., Scheffer, I., et al. (1998). Doublecortin, a brain-specific gene mutated in human X-linked lissencephaly and double cortex syndrome, encodes a putative signaling protein. *Cell, 92*, 63–72.

Gleeson, J. G., Lin, P. T., Flanagan, L. A., & Walsh, C. A. (1999). Doublecortin is a microtubule-associated protein and is expressed widely by migrating neurons. *Neuron, 23*, 257–271.

Gleeson, J. G., Minnerath, S. R., Fox, J. W., Allen, K. M., Luo, R. F., Hong, S. E., et al. (1999). Characterization of mutations in the gene doublecortin in patients with double cortex syndrome [see comments]. *Annals of Neurology, 45*, 146–153.

Grigorenko, E. L., Wood, F. B., Meyer, M. S., Hart, L. A., Speed, W. C., Shuster, A., et al. (1997). Susceptibility loci for distinct components of developmental dyslexia on chromosomes 6 and 15. *American Journal of Human Genetics, 60*, 27–39.

Grigorenko, E. L., Wood, F. B., Meyer, M. S., & Pauls, D. L. (2000). Chromosome 6p influences on different dyslexia-related cognitive processes: Further confirmation. *American Journal of Human Genetics, 66*, 715–723.

Guerrini, R. (2005) Genetic malformations of the cerebral cortex and epilepsy. *Epilepsia, 46*(Suppl. 1), 32–37.

Hannula-Jouppi, K., Kaminen-Ahola, N., Taipale, M., Eklund, R., Nopola-Hemmi, J., Kaariainen, H., et al. (2005). The axon guidance receptor gene ROBO1 is a candidate gene for developmental dyslexia. *PLoS Genetics, 1*, e50.

Herman, A. E., Galaburda, A. M., Fitch, H. R., Carter, A. R., & Rosen, G. D. (1997). Cerebral microgyria, thalamic cell size and auditory temporal processing in male and female rats. *Cerebral Cortex, 7*, 453–464.

Hsiung, G. Y., Kaplan, B. J., Petryshen, T. L., Lu, S., & Field, L. L. (2004). A dyslexia susceptibility locus (DYX7) linked to dopamine D4 receptor (DRD4) region on chromosome 11p15.5. *American Journal of Medical Genetics, 125B*, 112–119.

Humphreys, P., Kaufmann, W. E., & Galaburda, A. M. (1990). Developmental dyslexia in women: Neuropathological findings in three cases. *Annals of Neurology, 28*, 727–738.

Humphreys, P., Rosen, G. D., Press, D. M., Sherman, G. F., & Galaburda, A. M. (1991). Freezing lesions of the newborn rat brain: A model for cerebrocortical microgyria. *Journal of Neuropathology & Experimental Neurology, 50*, 145–160.

Kaminen, N., Hannula-Jouppi, K., Kestila, M., Lahermo, P., Muller, K., Kaaranen, M., et al. (2003). A genome scan for developmental dyslexia confirms linkage to chromosome 2p11 and suggests a new locus on 7q32. *Journal of Medical Genetics, 40*, 340–345.

Leventer, R. J., Cardoso, C., Ledbetter, D. H., & Dobyns, W. B. (2001). LIS1: From cortical malformation to essential protein of cellular dynamics. *Trends in Neuroscience, 24*, 489–492.

Levine, D. N., Fisher, M. A., & Caviness, V. S. (1974). Porencephaly with microgyria: A pathologic study. *Acta Neuropathologica, 29*, 99–113.

Livingstone, M., Rosen, G., Drislane, F., & Galaburda, A. (1991). Physiological and anatomical evidence for a magnocellular defect in developmental dyslexia. *Proceedings of the National Academy of Sciences USA, 88*, 7943–7947.

LoTurco, J. J., & Bai, J. (2006). The multipolar stage and disruptions in neuronal migration. *Trends in Neuroscience, 29*, 407–413.

Lyon, G., & Robain, O. (1967). Etude comparative des encéphalopathies circulatoires prénatales et para-natales (hydranencéphalies, porencéphalies et encéphalomalacies kystiques de la substance blanche). *Acta Neuropathologica, 9*, 79–98.

Lyon, G. R., Shaywitz, S. E., & Shaywitz, B. A. (2003). A definition of dyslexia. *Annals of Dyslexia, 53*, 1–14.

Marin-Padilla, M. (1996) Developmental neuropathology and impact of perinatal brain damage. I: Hemorrhagic lesions of neocortex. *Journal of Neuropathology & Experimental Neurology, 55*, 758–773.

Marin-Padilla, M. (1999). Developmental neuropathology and impact of perinatal brain damage. III: Gray matter lesions of the neocortex. *Journal of Neuropathology & Experimental Neurology, 58*, 407–429.

Marino, C., Citterio, A., Giorda, R., Facoett, A., Menozzi, G., Vanzin, L., et al. (2007). Association of short-term memory with a variant within DYX1C1 in developmental dyslexia. *Genes, Brain, and Behavior, 6*(7), 640–646.

Marino, C., Giorda, R., Luisa Lorusso, M., Vanzin, L., Salandi, N., Nobile, M., et al. (2005). A family-based association study does not support DYX1C1 on 15q21.3 as a candidate gene in developmental dyslexia. *European Journal of Human Genetics, 13*, 491–499.

Marino, C., Giorda, R., Vanzin, L., Molteni, M., Lorusso, M. L., Nobile, M., et al. (2003). No evidence for association and linkage disequilibrium between dyslexia and markers of four dopamine-related genes. *European Child & Adolescent Psychiatry, 12*, 198–202.

McBride, M. C., & Kemper, T. L. (1982). Pathogenesis of four-layered microgyric cortex in man. *Acta Neuropathologica, 57*, 93–98.

Meng, H., Hager, K., Held, M., Page, G. P., Olson, R. K., Pennington, B. F., et al. (2005). TDT-association analysis of EKN1 and dyslexia in a Colorado twin cohort. *Human Genetics, 118*, 87–90.

Meng, H., Smith, S. D., Hager, K., Held, M., Liu, J., Olson, R. K., et al. (2005). DCDC2 is associated with reading disability and modulates neuronal development in the brain. *Proceedings of the National Academy of Sciences USA, 102*, 17053–17058.

Mischel, P. S., Nguyen, L. P., & Vinters, H. V. (1995). Cerebral cortical dysplasia associated with pediatric epilepsy. Review of neuropathologic features and proposal for a grading system. *Journal of Neuropathology & Experimental Neurology, 54*, 137–153.

Morris, D. W., Robinson, L., Turic, D., Duke, M., Webb, V., Milham, C., et al. (2000). Family-based association mapping provides evidence for a gene for reading disability on chromosome 15q. *Human Molecular Genetics, 9*, 843–848.

Nagarajan, S., Mahncke, H., Salz, T., Tallal, P., Roberts, T., & Merzenich, M. M. (1999). Cortical auditory signal processing in poor readers. *Proceedings of the National Academy of Sciences USA, 96*, 6483–6488.

Nicolson, R., Fawcett, A. J., & Dean, P. (2001). Dyslexia, development and the cerebellum. *Trends in Neuroscience, 24*, 515–516.

Nopola-Hemmi, J., Myllyluoma, B., Haltia, T., Taipale, M., Ollikainen, V., Ahonen, T., et al. (2001). A dominant gene for developmental dyslexia on chromosome 3. *Journal of Medical Genetics, 38*, 658–664.

Nopola-Hemmi, J., Taipale, M., Haltia, T., Lehesjoki, A. E., Voutilainen, A., & Kere, J. (2000). Two translocations of chromosome 15q associated with dyslexia. *Journal of Medical Genetics, 37*, 771–775.

Nothen, M. M., Schulte-Korne, G., Grimm, T., Cichon, S., Vogt, I. R., Muller-Myhsok, B., et al. (1999). Genetic linkage analysis with dyslexia: Evidence for linkage of spelling disability to chromosome 15. *European Child & Adolescent Psychiatry, 8*(Suppl. 3), 56–59.

Paracchini, S., Thomas, A., Castro, S., Lai, C., Paramasivam, M., Wang, Y., et al. (2006). The chromosome 6p22 haplotype associated with dyslexia reduces the expression of KIAA0319, a novel gene involved in neuronal migration. *Human Molecular Genetics, 15*, 1659–1666.

Peiffer, A. M., Dunleavy, C. K., Frenkel, M., Gabel, L. A., LoTurco, J. J., Rosen, G. D., et al. (2001). Impaired detection of variable duration embedded tones in ectopic NZB/BINJ mice. *NeuroReport, 12*, 2875–2879.

Peiffer, A. M., Fitch, R. H., Thomas, J. J., Yurkovic, A. N., & Rosen G. D. (2003). Brain weight differences associated with induced focal microgyria. *BMC Neuroscience, 4*, 12.

Peiffer, A. M., McClure, M. M., Threlkeld, S. W., Rosen, G. D., & Fitch, R. H. (2004). Severity of focal microgyria and associated rapid auditory processing deficits. *NeuroReport, 15*, 1923–1926.

Peiffer, A. M., Rosen, G. D., & Fitch, R. H. (2002a). Rapid auditory processing and MGN morphology in microgyric rats reared in varied acoustic environments. *Developmental Brain Research, 138*, 187–193.

Peiffer, A. M., Rosen, G. D., & Fitch, R. H. (2002b). Sex differences in rapid auditory processing deficits in ectopic BXSB/MpJ mice. *NeuroReport, 13*, 2277–2280.

Peiffer, A. M., Rosen, G. D., & Fitch, R. H. (2004). Sex differences in rapid auditory processing deficits in microgyric rats. *Developmental Brain Research, 148*, 53–57.

Ramus, F. (2004). The neural basis of reading acquisition. In M. S. Gazzaniga (Ed.), *The cognitive neurosciences III* (pp. 815–824). Cambridge, MA: MIT Press.

Raskind, W. H., Igo, R. P., Chapman, N. H., Berninger, V. W., Thomson, J. B., Matsushita, M., et al. (2005). A genome scan in multigenerational families with dyslexia: Identification of a novel locus on chromosome 2q that contributes to phonological decoding efficiency. *Molecular Psychiatry, 10*, 699–711.

Reiner, O., Baram, I., Sapir, T., Shmueli, O., Carrozzo, R., Lindsay, E. A., et al. (1995). LIS2, gene and pseudogene, homologous to lIS1 (Lissencephaly 1), located on the short and long arms of chromosome 2. *Genomics, 30,* 251–256.

Reiner, O., Carrozzo, R., Shen, Y., Wehnert, M., Faustinella, F., Dobyns, W. B., et al. (1993). Isolation of a Miller-Dieker lissencephaly gene containing G protein beta-subunit-like repeats. *Nature, 364*, 717–721.

Rice, D. S., Sheldon, M., D'Arcangelo, G., Nakajima, K., Goldowitz, D., & Curran, T. (1998). Disabled-1 acts downstream of Reelin in a signaling pathway that controls laminar organization in the mammalian brain. *Development, 125*, 3719–3729.

Rosen, G. D., Bai, J., Wang, Y., Fiondella, C. G., Threlkeld, S. W., LoTurco, J. J., et al. (2007). Disruption of neuronal migration by targeted RNAi knockdown of Dyx1c1 results in neocortical and hippocampal malformations. *Cerebral Cortex, 17*(11), 2562–2572.

Rosen, G. D., Burstein, D., & Galaburda, A. M. (2000). Changes in efferent and afferent connectivity in rats with cerebrocortical microgyria. *Journal of Comparative Neurology, 418*, 423–440.

Rosen, G. D., & Galaburda, A. M. (2000). Single cause, polymorphic neuronal migration disorders: An animal model. *Developmental Medicine & Child Neurology, 42*, 652–662.

Rosen, G. D., Herman, A. E., & Galaburda, A. M. (1999). Sex differences in the effects of early neocortical injury on neuronal size distribution of the medial geniculate nucleus in the rat are mediated by perinatal gonadal steroids. *Cerebral Cortex, 9,* 27–34.

Rosen, G. D., Sherman, G. F., Richman, J. M., Stone, L. V., & Galaburda, A. M. (1992). Induction of molecular layer ectopias by puncture wounds in newborn rats and mice. *Developmental Brain Research, 67,* 285–291.

Rosen, G. D., Windzio, H., & Galaburda, A. M. (2001). Unilateral induced neocortical malformation and the formation of ipsilateral and contralateral barrel fields. *Neuroscience, 103,* 931–939.

Sarnat, H. B. (1991). Cerebral dysplasias as expressions of altered maturational processes. *Canadian Journal of Neurological Science, 8,* 196–204.

Sarnat, H. B. (1992). Disturbances of neuroblast migrations after 20 weeks gestation in the human fetus and neonate. In Y. Fukuyama, Y. Suzuki, S. Kamashita, & P. Casaer (Eds.), *Fetal and perinatal neurology* (pp. 108–117). Basel, Switzerland: Karger.

Scerri, T. S., Fisher, S. E., Francks, C., MacPhie, I. L., Paracchini, S., Richardson, A. J., et al. (2004). Putative functional alleles of DYX1C1 are not associated with dyslexia susceptibility in a large sample of sibling pairs from the UK. *Journal of Medical Genetics, 41,* 853–857.

Schulte-Korne, G., Grimm, T., Nothen, M. M., Muller-Myhsok, B., Cichon, S., Vogt, I. R., et al. (1998). Evidence for linkage of spelling disability to chromosome 15. *American Journal of Human Genetics, 63,* 279–282.

Schumacher, J., Anthoni, H., Dahdouh, F., Konig, I. R., Hillmer, A. M., Kluck, N., et al. (2006). Strong genetic evidence of DCDC2 as a susceptibility gene for dyslexia. *American Journal of Human Genetics, 78,* 52–62.

Schumacher, J., Konig, I. R., Plume, E., Propping, P., Warnke, A., Manthey, M., et al. (2006). Linkage analyses of chromosomal region 18p11-q12 in dyslexia. *Journal of Neural Transmission, 113,* 417–423.

Sherman, G. F., Galaburda, A. M., & Geschwind, N. (1985). Cortical anomalies in brains of New Zealand mice: A neuropathologic model of dyslexia? *Proceedings of the National Academy of Sciences USA, 82,* 8072–8074.

Sherman, G. F., Morrison, L., Rosen, G. D., Behan, P. O., & Galaburda, A. M. (1990b). Brain abnormalities in immune defective mice. *Brain Research, 532,* 25–33.

Sherman, G. F., Rosen, G. D., & Galaburda, A. M. (1988). Neocortical anomalies in autoimmune mice: A model for the developmental neuropathology seen in the dyslexic brain. *Drug Development Research, 15,* 307–314.

Sherman, G. F., Rosen, G. D., Stone, L. V., Press, D. M., & Galaburda, A. M. (1992). The organization of radial glial fibers in spontaneous neocortical ectopias of newborn New-Zealand black mice. *Developmental Brain Research, 67,* 279–283.

Sherman G. F., Stone, J. S., Press, D. M., Rosen, G. D., & Galaburda, A. M. (1990c). Abnormal architecture and connections disclosed by neurofilament staining in the cerebral cortex of autoimmune mice. *Brain Research, 529,* 202–207.

Sherman, G. F., Stone, J. S., Rosen G. D., & Galaburda, A. M. (1990a). Neocortical VIP neurons are increased in the hemisphere containing focal cerebrocortical microdysgenesis in New Zealand Black Mice. *Brain Research, 532,* 232–236.

Silani, G., Frith, U., Demonet, J. F., Fazio, F., Perani, D., Price, C., et al. (2005). Brain abnormalities underlying altered activation in dyslexia: A voxel based morphometry study. *Brain, 128,* 2453–2461.

Smith, S. D., Kimberling, W. J., Pennington, B. F., & Lubs, H. A. (1983). Specific reading disability: Identification of an inherited form through linkage analysis. *Science, 219,* 1345–1347.

Snowling, M. J. (2000). *Dyslexia* (2nd ed.). Oxford, UK: Blackwell.

Sokol, D. K., Golomb, M. R., Carvahlo, K. S., & Edwards-Brown, M. (2006). Reading impairment in the neuronal migration disorder of periventricular nodular heterotopia. *Neurology, 66*, 294 (author reply).

Stein, J. (2001a). The sensory basis of reading problems. *Developmental Neuropsychology, 20*, 509–534.

Stein, J. (2001b). The magnocellular theory of developmental dyslexia. *Dyslexia, 7*, 12–36.

Stein, J., & Walsh, V. (1997). To see but not to read; the magnocellular theory of dyslexia. *Trends in Neuroscience, 20*,147–152.

Taipale, M., Kaminen, N., Nopola-Hemmi, J., Haltia, T., Myllyluoma, B., Lyytinen, H., et al. (2003). A candidate gene for developmental dyslexia encodes a nuclear tetratricopeptide repeat domain protein dynamically regulated in brain. *Proceedings of the National Academy of Sciences USA, 100*,11553–11558.

Tzenova, J., Kaplan, B. J., Petryshen, T. L., & Field, L. L. (2004). Confirmation of a dyslexia susceptibility locus on chromosome 1p34-p36 in a set of 100 Canadian families. *American Journal of Medical Genetics, 127B*, 117–124.

Valdois, S., Bosse, M.-L., & Tainturier, M.-J. (2004). The cognitive deficits responsible for developmental dyslexia: Review of evidence for a selective visual attentional disorder. *Dyslexia, 10*, 339–363.

Wagner, R. K., & Torgesen, J. K. (1987) The nature of phonological processing and its causal role in the acquisition of reading skills. *Psychological Bulletin, 101*, 192–212.

Wang, Y., Paramasivam, M., Thomas, A., Bai, J., Kaminen, N., Kere, J., et al. (2006). Dyx1c1 functions in neuronal migration in developing neocortex. *Neuroscience, 143*, 515–522.

White, S., Frith, U., Milne, E., Rosen, S., Swettenham, J., & Ramus, F. (2006). A double dissociation between sensorimotor impairments and reading disability: A comparison of autistic and dyslexic children. *Cognitive Neuropsychology, 23*(5), 748–761.

Wigg, K. G., Couto, J. M., Feng, Y., Anderson, B., Cate-Carter, T. D., Macciardi, F., et al. (2004). Support for EKN1 as the susceptibility locus for dyslexia on 15q21. *Molecular Psychiatry, 9*, 1111–1121.

Wolf, M., & Bowers, P. G. (2000). Naming-speed processes and developmental reading disabilities: An introduction to the special issue on the double-deficit hypothesis. *Journal of Learning Disabilities, 33*, 322–324.

Yuan, W., Zhou, L., Chen, J. H., Wu, J. Y., Rao, Y., & Ornitz, D. M. (1999). The mouse SLIT family: Secreted ligands for ROBO expressed in patterns that suggest a role in morphogenesis and axon guidance. *Developmental Biology, 212*, 290–306.

Zhu, Y., Li, H., Zhou, L., Wu, J. Y., & Rao, Y. (1999). Cellular and molecular guidance of GABAergic neuronal migration from an extracortical origin to the neocortex. *Neuron, 23*, 473–485.

3 A Road Less Traveled

From Dyslexia Research Lab to School Front Lines; How Bridging the Researcher–Educator Chasm, Applying Lessons of Cerebrodiversity, and Exploring Talent Can Advance Understanding of Dyslexia

Gordon F. Sherman with Carolyn D. Cowen

Seven years ago, a career change brought me from a research laboratory at Boston's Beth Israel Deaconess Medical Center to an independent school for children with learning disabilities (LDs) in Princeton and—via outreach—to public schools throughout New Jersey. I went from being a neuroscientist investigating the brain basis of developmental dyslexia to being executive director of both a school for children with language-based LDs and an education center providing professional development and direct service. It was a professional leap from research to practice that imparted eye-opening lessons about (a) the complex realities behind research-to-practice assumptions, (b) the limitations of existing conceptual models of dyslexia and learning disabilities, and (c) the multifaceted needs and abilities of children with dyslexia.

From vantage points along this research-to-practice path, this chapter considers the neurobiological, genetic, and cognitive bases of developmental dyslexia as well as intervention implications. This is less a report of empirical findings and more a speculative discourse informed by neuroscience and by today's school realities. As political winds fluctuate across the research–policy–practice landscape and as efforts to translate research into effective educational practices move forward, bridge building between researchers and educators and frontline reporting both are essential. Both themes weave throughout this chapter, which presents:

- Observations on translation of neuroscience research to educational practice with suggestions for spanning the chasm between researchers and educators to advance the work of both.
- The *cerebrodiversity (CD)*[1] *model*, which reframes developmental dyslexia as a by-product of cerebrodiversity and places brain variation in an evolutionary context.
- Thoughts on the hypothesis that particular talents are associated with dyslexia and their possible implications in a digital environment.

In this discourse, I follow in the traditions of Norman Geschwind, whose seminal research on the brain established relationships between its structure and function (Geschwind, 1965). His later speculations and reflections (e.g., 1984) inspire this chapter in theme and spirit. As the chapter progresses, I shift from first person as I am joined by my coauthor.

GOING FROM RESEARCH TO PRACTICE: BRIDGES NEEDED TO SPAN THE CHASM

Brain research has generated important insights about dyslexia and related LDs over the last three decades. How much of this information has filtered accurately into schools? How much has enhanced teaching and learning, particularly for children with dyslexia? To what extent is so-called brain-based teaching actually grounded in neuroscience or an evidence base?

Overreaching interpretation of the application of neuroscience research led an international group of distinguished neuroscientists and cognitive psychologists at a recent conference in Chile to draft the Santiago Declaration (2007). In an era of "translational science," this document is remarkable in its cautionary message. The declaration summarizes principles of consensus about child development and early learning,[2] but goes on to say that these principles of consensus "are based primarily on findings from social and behavioral research, not brain research," cautioning that "neuroscientific research at this stage in its development does not offer scientific guidelines for policy, practice, or parenting." The declaration concludes by saying that "current brain research offers a promissory note, however, for the future" (para. 8 and 9).

Important strides have been made in the reading research–policy–practice arena, but for the most part, exciting breakthroughs in neuroscience do not translate into equally exciting breakthroughs in education. Not yet. Nevertheless, random bits of information and misinformation have achieved urban-legend status as relevant "scientific facts" supporting so-called brain-based teaching tenets and practices (not to mention untold publications, trainings, and products) that may or may not be sound. To a neuroscientist stepping into the field of education, the pervasiveness and persistence of these myths are astonishing. Here are some:

- We use only 10% of our brain capacity.
- There are two kinds of students—left brain and right brain. Each requires a different teaching approach.
- Theory, hypothesis, and belief systems are more or less the same.
- The perfect brain exists.
- Functional neuroimaging gives an exact picture of how a brain works.
- IQ and the bell curve are infallible indices.
- We are born with fixed potential, and our cognitive development and learning proceed in an orderly linear fashion to reach this fixed potential.

It would be easy to fault educators for falling prey to these myths and misunderstandings. And it would be unfair. Educators face formidable obstacles learning from relevant research, including lack of background knowledge and technical vocabulary; inability to access scientific journals; and school demands that often focus attention on day-to-day coping. The average educator, even one with an interest in neuroscience, rarely hurdles these obstacles to access, analyze, and digest relevant brain research. Typically, educators (and parents) are at the mercy of attention-grabbing headlines and entrepreneurial ventures and products exploiting a flourishing brain-based, evidence-based market niche.

In this era of evidence-based reform, educators hardly can be blamed for seeking to apply cutting-edge brain research to their teaching. In fact, they would appear to be target consumers of brain research. Scientific papers reporting the latest findings often include a statement about educational relevance. If brain researchers cite educational implications to justify research, does that impart a responsibility not only to help translate findings into articles educators can access and understand, but also, in the spirit of the Santiago Declaration, to be mindful of the need to urge caution, when appropriate, about immediate applications?

In a related vein, do brain researchers investigating dyslexia and related LDs have an obligation to check assumptions about educational relevance and to understand the complex realities of today's school environments as well as the impact social and educational environments have on the syndromes they study? Dynamic gene–brain–environment interplay coupled with developmental variation yield much heterogeneity. Even in independent schools for students with dyslexia, "pure dyslexics" are few and far between. Dyslexia and the myriad issues influencing learning are complex. Adding to that complexity is individual variation among dyslexic students. Could deeper insights about such realities and complexities inform brain research and hasten payment on its promissory note?

To be fair, competition for funding and other practical considerations and constraints inhibit researchers from reaching out to educators. Nevertheless, all researchers who see educational relevance in their work should at least understand the obstacles educators face in learning about and comprehending research findings[3] and brain researchers (and journalists!) should be extra cautious about implying classroom applications for findings in neuroscience.

Efforts to span the chasm between researcher and educator not only can help curtail overreaching interpretations of research for classroom application, but also can inform and elevate the work of both groups. Much has been said about the value of linking research to practice. Indeed, research on reading development and dyslexia's cognitive phenotype has yielded a wealth of knowledge about reading, reading disabilities, and essential components of reading instruction, which in turn, has led to national policies and initiatives to translate this information to classroom practice. Much also has been said about the need for interdisciplinary research (e.g., neuroscience, cognitive psychology, cognitive science, genetics) to generate a coherent picture of learning and development.

What might be further gained from dynamic two-way researcher–practitioner interactions? During my 7-year journey from the research lab to school front lines, I have pondered this question and have toyed with tentative ideas, such as:

- Researcher–educator summits and think tanks
- Brain research Web sites/push pages, electronic mailing lists (e.g., the Neuroscience for Kids Web site and Nfknews, the Neuroscience for Kids Newsletter), and Real Simple Syndication (RSS) feeds for teachers
- Neuroscientists in residence (in schools), visiting educators (in labs)
- Funding of various initiatives and projects to stimulate and support researcher–educator collaborations and cross-fertilization
- Training of education-to-neuroscience and neuroscience-to-education translators
- Guidelines to help researchers prepare papers and presentations for educators

Communication, collaboration, and technology are among the powerful tools we can leverage not only to dispel myths about the brain and applications of neuroscience to education, but also to enhance interdisciplinary research, disseminate relevant findings, and develop and improve educational solutions. Although important progress in the reading research–policy–practice arena has been achieved, formidable challenges remain. Initiatives connecting educators with researchers to foster research–practice links at grassroots levels might bear fruit in various ways, including:

- Elevating work in both practice and research (integrating perspectives to foster reciprocal and synergistic advances) and hastening payment on the promissory note of neuroscience
- Applying research tools to understand and address school-based challenges in implementing evidence-based practices
- Supporting and sustaining efforts in the reading research–policy–practice arena

- Improving learning and life trajectories for all students, particularly those with LDs

Connecting educators and researchers at grassroots levels also can deepen understanding of children with dyslexia and related LDs, bringing real-life complexities and challenges as well as the talents and promise into sharper focus. This enhanced picture might inspire fresh scientific questions and new research directions. For example, ask any group of veteran educators specializing in dyslexia if they see a high incidence of certain talents among their students and if these abilities seem connected to dyslexia. Typically, the response is an emphatic yes on both counts. Another urban legend? An impression skewed by wishful thinking or lack of exposure to a control population? Perhaps. Testimonials without evidence have limitations. But there may be something to this impression and to other insights educators have—something worth investigating. To date, little research has been conducted on the talents and abilities that might be associated with dyslexia, even though they have been noted clinically since before the turn of the last century.[4]

The reasons for building bridges between educators and researchers concerned with dyslexia and reading are compelling, particularly given the goal of evidence-based teaching and the likelihood that shifting political winds are reshuffling priorities once again. Top-down evidence-based reform may be more sustainable and expandable with bottom-up grassroots involvement of educators and researchers working together. But building bridges between the two will be challenging; there are obstacles on both sides. For example, the ivory tower syndrome persists, just as the classroom cave mindset exists (a "leave me alone, let me teach my students" attitude). There are powerful and complex reasons for both that must be addressed in any effort to span the chasm between researchers and educators and, for that matter, to bring evidence-based teaching goals to fruition in schools across the country.

The difficulties in translating research to practice cannot be overstated. Oversimplifying these complexities or painting them in too optimistic a light to garner support for educational initiatives and reforms probably does more harm than good in the end. Progress falls short when measured against unrealistic expectations and disappointment sets the stage for policy and reform reversals.

Nevertheless, connecting educators and researchers, particularly those sharing a focus on reading and dyslexia, is a fertile area for creative and thoughtful planning, one that not only might yield results that outlive educational pendulum swings and political climate shifts, but also might inspire an interweaving of perspectives that elevates both practice and research. In fact, in the next section, we present a theoretical model that emerged from just such an interweaving of perspectives.

CEREBRODIVERSITY MODEL: AN EVOLUTIONARY PERSPECTIVE

Despite advances in neuroscience, cognitive psychology, genetics, and intervention research, thorny questions still confront researchers and educators alike, particularly when it comes to dyslexia. Is dyslexia dimensional, a spectrum syndrome (like hypertension) on a continuum of atypical brain development? Or, is dyslexia a specific brain abnormality with distinct boundaries? In either case, where are the cut points, where are the boundaries? Is there an appreciable difference in how so-called garden-variety poor readers respond to intervention compared to how those with dyslexia respond? In other words, is a reading problem a reading problem, *period*, regardless of its cause, or do children with developmental dyslexia require more intensive and specialized instruction than other poor readers? Do other cognitive processes, in addition to phonological awareness, factor into dyslexia? Are there subtypes of dyslexia? If so, do they derive from deficiencies in distinct but dynamically and developmentally networked cognitive processes, which, in turn derive from distinct but dynamically and developmentally networked neurobiological anomalies?

Educators have long struggled with the fact that dyslexia defies tidy definitions and clear-cut categories. How do we make sense of its heterogeneity—its diverse constellations of symptoms and their various patterns of overlap and degrees of severity? What about dyslexia's comorbidities and the frequency with which they co-occur (e.g., ADHD)? How do we account for dyslexia's different structural (neurobiological) and functional anomalies? Its multiple genetic mechanisms? What about the persistent observation that dyslexia often seems to be associated with certain talents and abilities? *Is dyslexia more than a reading problem?*

This is not the first laundry list of such questions about dyslexia. Over the years, these and similar questions have been at the root of much debate (e.g., definition of dyslexia, prevalence estimates, disability vs. difference), various intervention models (e.g., pull-out, regular education initiative, inclusion, response-to-intervention), and doubt about the validity of the LD construct or whether developmental dyslexia actually exists. Perhaps there is something important about dyslexia's variability and lack of tidiness. Perhaps these persistent questions are clues leading to a conceptual model that views learning diversity through the widest angle lens possible, one that imparts perspective about this diversity and its place in the broadest biological–sociological context (i.e., human evolution), one that brings the big implications and possibilities into focus.

A need for an expansive conceptual framework to assimilate the enigmas and complexities behind ongoing questions about dyslexia—in both research and education—inspired the cerebrodiversity model. This working model is grounded in evolution theory, influenced by observations of Geschwind (1982, 1984; Geschwind & Galaburda, 1987), and informed by contemporary researcher–educator perspectives. Cerebrodiversity refers to the collective neural heterogeneity of humans. The term captures the idea that neural differences (anatomical, cellular, and connectional) in individuals yield cognitive strengths and weaknesses that differ from person to person. Typically, these structural and functional differences are small. Sometimes they are important. Taken together, they constitute the neural heterogeneity of the human species, that is, our cerebrodiversity.

Applying what we know from neuroscience and genetics brings deeper understanding of cerebrodiversity's causes and effects. Cerebrodiversity results from the dynamic interaction between various genetic mechanisms and subsequent environmental influences, which modify, via neuroplasticity, the structure and function of the brain. (Neuroplasticity is the brain's ability to alter or form new neuronal connections and reorganize.) This dynamic interaction translates into variation in cognitive processing (strengths and weaknesses within and across individuals) and sets the stage for learning differences that in the extreme and in certain constellations and contexts become disabilities and talents.

From an evolutionary perspective, cerebrodiversity is an adaptive advantage for our species with mechanisms rooted in natural selection and its agents (diversity, adaptability, and environmental change)—the forces that produced our big-brained bipedal ancestors 150,000 years ago. Thus, cerebrodiversity is a product of chance events in evolution and of a dynamic interplay between a genetic blueprint bequeathed by natural selection and by our experiences in the environment (including our social world).

The bottom line? Cerebrodiversity is *good*. It played a key role in our species' success, as this simple but insightful poem conveys.

The Brain Thinking

If everybody was the same
And someone had a thought
And, it was wrong,
Then everybody would be wrong
So ...
Everybody needs to be different.

Abbott Cowen[5] (at 7 years of age)

Dyslexia: By-product of Cerebrodiversity

The cerebrodiversity (CD) model reframes dyslexia and other LDs as by-products of cerebrodiversity and places developmental brain variation (e.g., dyslexia) in an evolutionary context—a broader biological–sociological framework than the disability paradigm, which is limited by its assumptions and political agenda, however well meaning and useful. This evolutionary context, informed by modern neuroscience and genetics research, not only deepens understanding of the environmental (including uterine) contributions to the structural and functional brain basis of dyslexia, but also imparts perspective for seeing LDs as an environmental effect. Said another way: Neural circuitry reflects gene–brain–environment interplay, but the disabling consequences (and talents for that matter), generally, are socially defined and confined. For example, dyslexia did not exist, at least not as a disability, before the advent of the printing press 600 years ago, but the brain designs we now label as being dyslexic surely did.

Microscopic Lens

For a moment, let us change our focus to view some neural differences in dyslexia through the microscope. We might think of these microscopic structural and functional brain differences as being "ectopia-based," at least in some cases. Summarizing Galaburda and Sherman (2007), ectopias—out-of-place clusters of neurons in layer I of the cerebral cortex—alter the focal connectivity of the affected cortical areas (Galaburda, Sherman, Rosen, Aboitiz, & Geschwind, 1985). The likely mechanism for ectopias is a breach in the superficial pial membrane, which allows neuroblasts to migrate too far into the cortical plate resulting in ectopias. Multiple genetic origins are suspected. Ectopias are present mostly in perisylvian locations—the superior temporal gyrus area (containing Wernicke's area)—and the inferior premotor and prefrontal cortex (containing Broca's area). Ectopias are also seen in other cortical areas that are involved in linguistic/cognitive functions (Frenkel, Sherman, Bashan, Galaburda, & LoTurco, 2000). More ectopias appear to be in the left hemisphere,[6] especially in males.

Because ectopias occur during neuronal migration, wide-ranging and unusual connections are produced between neurons in the ectopias and other cortical and subcortical areas. Thus, ectopias may result in diverse neural systems, such as symmetry in the planum temporale (Galaburda et al., 1985; Hynd, Semrud-Clikeman, Lorys, Novey, & Eliopulos, 1990; Steinmetz, Volkmann, Jäncke, & Freund, 1991) and changes in the size of neurons in the thalamic nuclei (Galaburda, Menard, & Rosen, 1994; Livingstone, Rosen, Drislane, & Galaburda, 1991). Symmetry of the planum temporale may affect sound and phonological processing, and smaller neurons in visual and auditory relay nuclei in the thalamus may affect slower visual and auditory processing.

Ectopias represent one way to alter neural connectivity and brain organization, thereby producing the "dyslexic behavioral phenotype." Viewing dyslexia through a high magnification microscope, we might understand dyslexia's heterogeneity and comorbidities as a function of the number, location, size, and connectivity of the ectopias interacting with environmental and additional genetic influences. But other environmental–genetic interactions also might produce the dyslexic phenotype. There is much still to discover.

Evolutionary Lens

Now we back up again to view developmental dyslexia—intrinsic, brain based, but to some degree, mutable—through an evolutionary scope, as a by-product of cerebrodiversity. This wide-angle view brings some 150,000 years into view and offers a framework expansive yet grounded enough to assimilate and inform modern science's burgeoning discoveries about the brain (including ectopias) and the gene–brain–environment dynamic.

An evolutionary framework sharpens perspective on the transience of the environmental context defining today's learning assets and liabilities (seeing these as naturally occurring human variation), but does not detract from those realities or abrogate our responsibility to think and plan around current academic needs and deficits. This framework reminds us to *also* consider a future that redefines learning assets and liabilities as it makes new demands. (For example, how many of us have become afflicted with *dsytechnia* over the years, especially compared to our children or students?) The last century, even the last decade, reveals how rapidly we reconstruct our social and technological environments, exposing the shortsightedness in assuming that school success *today* necessarily predicts life success *tomorrow* and that those who do well in traditional school environments will contribute most to future societies.[7] We do not know what kind of inventive minds humankind may need in the future.[8] Certainly, we have benefited from innovative thinkers who were not successful students in the past (e.g., Winston Churchill, Thomas Edison, Pablo Picasso).

Seen within the broad sweep of human evolution and as a by-product of cerebrodiversity, dyslexia's heterogeneity and comorbidities, its various structural and functional neural differences, and its multiple genetic mechanisms begin making sense. Something else starts making sense: dyslexia's paradoxical guises. *Depending on environmental demand*, dyslexia can manifest as a reading disability and, in some cases, as a brain design with virtues.[9] This paradox drives home the adaptive advantage of cerebrodiversity—a key ingredient in the gene–brain–environment dynamic that enabled our species to adapt to environmental variables and dominate the planet. For now.

CD MODEL: PRACTICAL CONSIDERATIONS

The CD model steps outside the disability paradigm and highlights limitations of the LD construct, but the two are not antithetical. The LD lens is narrower than the CD lens and helps focus attention on the plight and rights of diverse learners in today's schools and the cascade of serious problems academic-skill deficits cause.[10] The CD lens offers a wide-angle view of learning diversity—its relationship to the mechanisms that produce structural and functional brain differences, its importance in human evolution, and the broad implications and possibilities. A wide-angle lens enables us to see the forest for the trees and to glimpse and ponder the outliers, where we may discover something important. A narrow, more finely focused lens magnifies information we might miss with a broad view. A clear picture requires both perspectives. The challenges we face demand working with the clearest picture possible.

Can a conceptual framework account for an array of clinical observations and research findings (sometimes at odds), inform intervention models and practices, and help shape coherent policy? Even falling short, efforts to articulate a unifying framework[11] can impart much-needed clarity, integration, and coherence, dovetailing with efforts to synthesize interdisciplinary perspectives from cognition, neurobiology, genetics, and education. Key unifying features of the CD model include the following:

- Applying evolution theory to reframe developmental dyslexia as a by-product of cerebrodiversity, revealing congruity in a host of seemingly

disparate phenomena (e.g., dyslexia's continua of severity, heterogeneity, comorbidity, different structural and functional anomalies, multiple genetic mechanisms, and disability–ability paradox)
- Providing a framework flexible and expansive enough to assimilate and inform modern science's burgeoning discoveries about the brain and the gene–brain–environment dynamic, particularly vis-à-vis dyslexia
- Bringing into focus the transience of the environmental context defining today's learning assets and liabilities, while offering insights into mechanisms that generate both and broaden our view of both

The strength of a conceptual model typically is the foundation it provides for developing testable hypothetical constructs leading to coherent theories. To translate for educators, such a conceptual model also must be grounded in classroom realities and offer practical utility. At this stage, the CD model is a working framework. Its foundation is untested; its utility is unclear. In fact, the variability and complexities that have made definitions of dyslexia difficult to operationalize point to an explanatory framework that may not translate readily into neat formulas and tenets for guiding researchers, practitioners, and policymakers.

Perhaps, though, the temptation to reduce complexities into artificial orderliness should be resisted, or at least tempered. Oversimplification may be at the heart of many of the difficulties encountered in bringing to scale interventions that succeed in controlled experimental settings but disappoint in the complex social systems of schools and classroom environments. Indeed, if there is a tenet embodied in the CD model, it might be best expressed this way: Pay attention to the diversity, variance, outliers, contexts, complexities, developmental change, and multifaceted needs. Therein lies the challenges, especially in translating research to practice, and, quite likely, the insights, solutions, and opportunities.

Even in its working-draft form, the cerebrodiversity hypothesis and reframing dyslexia as a by-product of cerebrodiversity seem to strike a chord with both educators and parents, perhaps because this framework explains variability and aligns with observations and insights about strengths and talents in children with dyslexia. It also might strike a chord because this framework focuses attention on current needs and realities (e.g., the need for evidence-based teaching to impart fundamental academic skills, particularly in deficit areas) as much as it focuses on future possibilities. Perhaps all this, coupled with its biological grounding, makes the CD model, even as a working-draft framework, a useful tool for building bridges between researchers and educators.

In any case, the need for coherent, dynamic, expansive, flexible, and practical models is clear. So, too, is the need to go beyond today's simplistic paradigms of disability and talent. Finally, paradoxically, as knowledge of the brain and its development (and as technology contributing to that knowledge) advance future models of learning and learning disorders, we still will need to look *back* at our origins and evolution to truly understand our enigmas, our possibilities, and ourselves. Perhaps Geschwind articulated the most cogent reason for placing developmental dyslexia in an evolutionary context: "(T)he knowledge of every aspect of dyslexia will be enriched by seeing it in its broadest biological and sociological settings" (1984, p. 327).

DYSLEXIA AND TALENTS: MANY QUESTIONS, SOME ANSWERS

"Enigmas" and "possibilities" are a good segue to a discussion about a possible link between dyslexia and talents. We start with the big question: Are certain talents[12] overrepresented within the dyslexic population? This is not the same as asking whether people with dyslexia can have profiles of strengths and weaknesses that can include talents. Although no less important, this second question is less controversial. Let us set it aside for a moment while we consider the possibility that dyslexia and certain talents might be linked, a premise that gets traction among many parents and teachers of children with dyslexia.[13]

Are people with dyslexia more variable as a group than those without and, thus, do they (and perhaps people with dyslexia in their families) have a higher representation of talents (and various comorbidities) than nondyslexics? If dyslexia and certain talents do tend to co-occur, is this because they share cerebrodiversity mechanisms of some sort? Pursuing another line of thought, perhaps a brain design that is suited poorly for one task might be suited uniquely well for another. Is the neurobiological design underlying a constellation of deficits also, in some cases, a substrate for certain talents? To follow yet another line of thinking, are some brains bestowed with talent in one area at the expense of another, yielding an area of deficiency? Turning that last question on its head, does a brain saddled with liabilities sometimes develop compensatory talents? If so, is this because some innate ability exists already or is it because other avenues are blocked?

We lack definitive answers for these and related questions. We do not even know if dyslexia and talent are linked. So far, scientific evidence for a dyslexia–talent connection has proven elusive. There are, however, a few intriguing findings.

DYSLEXIA–TALENT LINK EVIDENCE: THIN BUT INTRIGUING

In batteries of tests designed to reveal spatial strengths, young subjects with dyslexia performed no better than controls, often worse, except on one task— the "Impossible Figures Test" (von Károlyi, Winner, Gray, & Sherman, 2003). Children with dyslexia performed this task not only as accurately as controls but also faster. Did dyslexics outperform controls because people with dyslexia process information more globally than those without? In this test, global processing was a more efficient strategy for perceiving spatial relationships than a sequential linear approach. Was a global approach compensatory, a fallback strategy because a systematic approach was inaccessible or less automatic? Or does a global strategy in this task represent ability, even talent?

The central and peripheral visual fields are anatomically and functionally segregated in the brain. The central field is adept for visual search tasks, and the peripheral field is adept at rapid processing over broad regions. People differ in their ability to process information in the center versus the periphery, and individuals who excel in one tend to be less adept at the other (which the CD model predicts). The periphery-to-center ratio (PCR) indicates the degree of peripheral bias (Schneps, Rose, & Fischer, 2007). They hypothesize that some people with dyslexia favor the peripheral visual field over the center, resulting not only in search deficits but also in talents for visual comparisons. A high PCR (strong peripheral/weak center visual processing) would translate into poor processing of temporally sequential information and may contribute to initial difficulties learning to read, at least for a subset of the dyslexic population. The Impossible Figures task may be facilitated by a peripheral bias, which may underlie talents involving global visual processing abilities. The key question is whether a high PCR bias in dyslexia is responsible both for visual talents and reading difficulties.

Animal studies represent another avenue of research vis-à-vis spatial strengths in dyslexia. In a study of spatial learning and memory (Morris water maze), autoimmune mice with ectopias seemed to outperform genetically identical littermates without ectopias (Denenberg, Sherman, Schrott, Rosen, & Galaburda, 1991). This finding is interesting because the ectopias were present in layer I of the cerebral cortex, as were the ectopias seen in human postmortem studies (Galaburda et al., 1985).

Is dyslexia (or a dyslexic subgroup) linked with strengths in global visual processing? Even with these intriguing studies, evidence establishing a dyslexia–talent link is thin, largely because the topic has not been a research priority. One way to investigate the hypothesis that people with dyslexia have spatial strengths might be a functional imaging study comparing activation patterns of expert spatial processors—say, professional baseball outfielders (our preference is for players from the Boston Red Sox)—with dyslexic subjects and controls while engaged in spatial tasks. Would activation patterns between the outfielders and dyslexic subjects be more similar than between the outfielders and controls? This and the larger question of a dyslexia–talent link remain open.

WHY STUDY THE DYSLEXIA–TALENT LINK?

Why conduct research on whether dyslexia and talent are linked? Even if research does eventually demonstrate a relationship, why should we care if people with dyslexia have special talents? We have established that they have special *needs*, particularly in reading. Reading comes first, right?

Just for fun, imagine that political winds favor continued implementation of No Child Left Behind (NCLB) and Reading First. Imagine that a multitiered, response-to-intervention (RTI)[14] approach is adopted and places heroic emphasis on preventing academic skill deficits. Imagine that research-validated screening and progress monitoring as well as comprehensive and integrated instruction and intervention are conducted across all academic skill areas with fidelity by general and special educators who are highly skilled, knowledgeable, and motivated (graduates of state-of-the-art, evidence-based teacher preparation programs). Imagine that effective school administrators and cutting-edge school designs support all these efforts. Finally, imagine that we strike a balance between federal education legislation and the shifting and conflicting forces that periodically mount campaigns to reform the latest education reforms.

Imagine that we live to see all these variables align in the most utopian way possible, and we not only prevent reading skill deficits in most children but also diminish the severity and prevalence of these deficits in children whose neuro-biological designs predispose them for dyslexia. Imagine that we manage to do all this, but along the way, we neglect talents. Would it matter? Even if there is a dyslexia–talent link, does it matter much in light of other priorities—the ones being met in the utopian universe?

There are several reasons to think twice before dismissing the question of a dyslexia–talent link as some esoteric or marginal concern. Pursuing a single-minded campaign to eradicate reading skill deficits while neglecting talents and strengths might not be wise in the long run. Apart from a reasonable but predict-able argument in favor of enrichment (e.g., keeping the arts and sports in schools), there are other reasons not only to explore the hypothesis that such a link exists but also to plan around the possibility that it does.

The first reason is implicit in the previous discussion about cerebrodiversity. If dyslexia and certain talents are flip sides of the same coin or if a great per-centage of people with dyslexia also have high talents, our species may be well served by efforts to identify and nurture these abilities *as early as possible.* (This applies to all children with exceptional abilities, not only those with dyslexia.) Just as early intervention is critical in preventing and diminishing reading skill deficits, early cultivation of talents is important in maximizing their expression. Neuroplasticity—the brain's capacity to form new neuronal connections and to dynamically reorganize—continues throughout life (contrary to former beliefs). Young brains, however, are *most* plastic. Early intervention and early cultivation both capitalize on neuroplasticity at its peak, which speaks to a timeframe (as early as possible), but does not constitute a rationale.

The rationale for the study and cultivation of talent includes reasons such as:

- **Exploration/scientific discovery.** The brain and its enigmas represent a fascinating and important frontier of knowledge.
- **Indirect payoff.** Spin-off advances in knowledge and pedagogy can benefit all learners.
- **Compassion.** Talent is a "terrible thing to waste."
- **Societal concerns.** Talent enriches society via arts, technological inno-vations, creative problem solving; untapped talent, particularly among those with LDs, can cost society, for example, crime and delinquency (Winters, 1997), unproductive lives, and underemployment.

The most important argument in favor of studying and cultivating talent, however, may be this: Cerebrodiversity *already* has played a role in our species' survival. It is our most precious natural resource. A proven commodity! Even if contemporary society is none too intelligent about appreciating or nurturing the assets of cerebrodiversity, particularly across varying contexts, it is clear that diverse strengths and talents—even paradoxical talents in alternative brain designs (e.g., developmental dyslexia)—have played a role in our past and probably will bear strongly on our future.

In the grand scheme of things—evolution of life—the big issues are *diversity, adaptability*, and *environmental change*. A chance alignment of these forces enabled humans to thrive for the last several million years, which might sound like a long time, but represents only 0.0001% of Earth's 4.5-billion-year history.[15] Another fact underscores the tenuousness of life and the spectacular chance in the alignment of forces favoring the human species: Of the billions and billions of species that have ever lived, 99.99% are extinct.

Throughout human history, our behavior rarely has focused beyond ourselves, family, or tribe to abet continued survival of our species; if anything, our hubris usually inspires us in other directions. Given turbulent events on our planet and challenges such as climate change, cultivating the benefits of cerebrodiversity might be one way to improve our odds. Forging funding partnerships to invest in cutting-edge research focused on talent (including a possible dyslexia–talent link) as well as on initiatives to guide thoughtful planning (including researcher–practitioner bridge building) might be upstream strategies for generating innovative solutions downstream.

LESSON FROM INDEPENDENT LD SCHOOLS: DO NOT NEGLECT STRENGTHS AND TALENTS

As we wrap up, we return to the question set aside earlier in the chapter: Do people with dyslexia have profiles of strengths and weaknesses that can include talents? Even without research, no expert on dyslexia would assert that having this learning difference precludes having strengths and talents. Even skeptics of a dyslexia–talent link would acknowledge that at least *some* people with dyslexia have talents (sometimes referred to as being "twice exceptional"). Whether these strengths and talents occur in the dyslexic population more often or even as often as in the general population remain open questions, at least as far as research is concerned. That these strengths and talents *do* occur few would contest. Indeed, examples of highly accomplished people with dyslexia abound (Bowers, 2007; Fink, 2006).

That strengths and talents can co-occur with dyslexia has not been lost on the independent schools providing intensive evidence-based and innovative interventions for students with this learning difference. Recognition that dyslexia and strengths/talents can co-occur (and might even be linked) has led these schools to develop rich menus of programs and approaches to tap and nurture their students' abilities in order to build self-esteem and to motivate, engage, and enhance learning in academic skill areas. For decades, these independent LD schools have been champions, pioneers, models, stewards, and disseminators of evidence-based practices, particularly in reading. That these schools *also* focus on tapping and nurturing strengths and talents in their students merits attention.

In some respects, independent LD schools come close to achieving the ideals of the utopian universe described earlier in this chapter. None of these schools is perfect, of course, but most are highly adept at preventing and diminishing academic skill deficits in children with dyslexia, and most do not neglect their students' talents and strengths along the way. Even if "there is little evidence that instruction addressing strengths and weaknesses in cognitive skills is related to intervention outcomes" (Fletcher et al., 2007, p. 49), most independent LD schools enlist and nurture their students' strengths in the process of addressing academic skill deficits. And with good reason. Evidence-based instruction in academic skills is necessary, but it is not sufficient. As an article about the impact of independent LD schools on American education points out:

> (M)ost successful LD schools have come to recognize that remediating their students' academic skill deficits is not their sole purpose. They realize that helping students discover and develop their talents or "affinities" as Mel Levine calls them, is just as important. Consequently, LD schools have been leaders in developing ways of integrating effective skills teaching methods with other components of the curriculum such as the arts. (Burke-Fabrikant, 2005, pp. 22–23)

A quick review of just a handful of the leading independent LD schools[16] supports this statement. For example:

- **Assets School** in Honolulu, Hawaii, for gifted, gifted–dyslexic, and dyslexic students, focuses on acceleration, remediation, and enrichment; and its high school mentorship program enables students to explore career options, pursue passions, and capitalize on their strengths in hands-on, community-based learning experiences.
- **The Carroll School** in Lincoln, Massachusetts, so highly values integration of the arts and movement into its academics, that the 2007 faculty back-to-school orientation featured a full day of immersion in the school's programs in woodworking, art, music, performing arts, library, yoga/movement, gym, and Bounders (an adapted Outward Bound program). Goals included (a) highlighting the role of these programs in a student's school day, (b) demonstrating how these activities can be harnessed in academic classrooms and tutorials, and (c) building commitment about how Carroll educates children.
- **The Lab School** in Washington, DC, is well known for emphasizing arts-based and experiential learning in remediating academic skill deficits and teaching academic content.
- **Landmark School** in Beverly, Massachusetts, sees its extracurricular program as being integral to a student's development and not as "extra," pointing out that some students with LDs do not have the opportunity to participate in programs or lack confidence to perform, while others excel in nonacademic activities and need opportunities to continue developing or discovering their talents.

- **Marburn Academy** in Columbus, Ohio, believes that in addition to developing academic skills, a wide range of extracurricular opportunities provide the experiences of success needed to build personal confidence and self-worth.
- **The Newgrange School** in Mercer County, New Jersey, is experimenting with digital audio media and is exploring the hypothesis that "dyslexic talents" might be uniquely expressed in digital media.

Comparing independent schools to public schools is not the point here. The point is to raise questions such as these: What lessons can we learn from the schools that have become experts in dyslexia and reading? What can be learned from the schools that put reading first long before Reading First became a national initiative and educational policy tagline? One lesson might be best summed up simply as: *Do not neglect the strengths and talents.*

What would happen if we pursued a single-minded campaign to eradicate reading skill deficits while neglecting talents and strengths? The question is not rhetorical. Enrichment programs in public education are under constant threat due to funding constraints. High-stakes testing not only focuses instructional time on achieving narrow (albeit exceedingly important) outcomes—improved reading and math scores[17]—but also could be influencing the amount of time teachers devote to students at the far ends of the academic performance spectrum.[18] Many of those students probably have dyslexia. Many also may be twice exceptional.

The need to target reading skill deficits for intensive remediation in children with dyslexia is of critical importance. But we also must consider the unintended consequences of any *single-minded* effort, no matter how important, when applied to complex and dynamic multifaceted issues. We must find ways to integrate evidence-based skills teaching with other components of the curriculum, including the arts, to nourish the spirits and inspire the minds of children as we prepare them to live in a challenging future.

CONCLUSION: AN EYE-OPENING JOURNEY

This speculative discourse—inspired by an eye-opening journey from research to practice—has ranged widely over a broad landscape, focusing on (a) complex realities behind research-to-practice assumptions, (b) limitations of existing models of dyslexia, and (c) multifaceted needs and abilities of children with dyslexia. Along the way, we have presented a working-draft model for reframing dyslexia—as a by-product of cerebrodiversity. We also make the following recommendations:

- Build bridges between educators and researchers at grassroots levels; the results may outlive educational pendulum swings and political climate shifts.
- Investigate the dyslexia–talent link hypothesis; who knows what kind of inventive minds humans may need in the future?

• Identify and cultivate talents as early as possible to exploit the neuroplasticity of young brains and, in targeting academic skill deficits, particularly in children with dyslexia, do not neglect talents and strengths.

We propose that the three themes in this chapter—spanning the researcher–educator chasm, applying the lessons of cerebrodiversity, and exploring the talent–disability enigma—offer promising avenues not only for advancing understanding of dyslexia, but also for hastening payment on neuroscience's promissory note to generate insights and solutions for all learners.

To bring this wide-ranging theoretical discourse to a practical conclusion, we close with a short description of Newgrange School's innovative digital audio music program—a cutting-edge program that not only nurtures musical abilities in children with dyslexia, but also might open doors of opportunity in a rapidly developing digital environment.

Coda: Digital Audio Technologies Open Doors to Musical Composition and More

> Just as the printing press … changed how knowledge works, we have hypothesized that these new digital media will have the same effect. It's critical that we understand (digital media's) benefits and its unintended consequences. There are implications for both of those schools. —Connie Yowell, MacArthur Foundation (Borja, 2006, p. 12)

Why would an independent school for children with dyslexia pioneer using new digital audio technologies to blaze trails in student composition and performance of original music? After all, such schools have a pressing agenda: to impart the fundamental academic skills their students find so difficult to master, particularly in reading, and to do so quickly. To close achievement gaps, ongoing remedial work must be intensive, systematic, and focused explicitly on the structure of language. *Why fiddle around with digital audio technologies, especially in music?*

At the Newgrange School the rationale is both pragmatic and visionary. It is founded upon and inspired by the neurological strengths and weaknesses often noted in children with dyslexia (which include visual–spatial strengths and linguistic–linear weaknesses). Until now, their strengths may not have found many avenues of expression, never mind environments that nurture further development of these abilities. But digital audio software programs, such as Apple's GarageBand (iLife '08) and Logic Pro 8 are opening new pathways to music for Newgrange students, enabling them to bypass traditional barriers (e.g., lack of technical training, such as *reading* music) to explore and discover musical affinities and abilities. (Newgrange also is experimenting with digital video programs in filmmaking.) In fact, this technology ushers these children into the domains of original composition and accomplished performance, once the purview of the musical elite. As a result, digital audio technologies may be expanding career opportunities in music (a $40-billion-a-year industry) for students who sometimes face limited options as adults, even after aggressive intervention from highly skilled educators.

Since the brains of many children with dyslexia may be uniquely suited to respond to various demands and opportunities in a changing music industry, it makes sense for schools serving these students to explore emerging digital audio technologies to nurture and develop abilities in musical composition and performance. Certainly, not all children with dyslexia will have these abilities or even an interest. Nor is it clear precisely how the technology trends, still nascent, will play out. However, given what we already know about their trajectory and these children, neglecting to expose them to technologies and experiences that might enable them to pursue gainful employment as well as passions in areas of talent is a gamble, if not unkind. Meaningful work in areas of talent and passion ranks high in the hierarchy of human experience.

Fundamental academic skills still need to be taught aggressively; our students need to become responsible citizens and capable stewards of the world. However, our world is being transformed by technology at a singular rate, perhaps even an exponential one. Many of these "disabled students" not only might find a comfortable niche in this new world, but also may play a role in its transformation. Why should schools specializing in meeting needs of students with dyslexia explore applications of digital audio technologies to music? Again, the rationale is both pragmatic and visionary. The transformation is underway. These students may be uniquely prepared. In the new digital order, they may turn out to be the new talent.

ACKNOWLEDGMENTS

This chapter is dedicated to Nancee G. Sherman. Special thanks to Deardra Ledet-Rosenberg and Steve Wilkins for their assistance with this manuscript.

NOTES

1. Gordon F. Sherman coined the term *cerebrodiversity* in 2002 in a series of talks and articles for educators and parents and has presented the topic in numerous talks since.
2. Santiago consensus: The need to design policies, programs, and products around developmental ranges and patterns of growth rather than absolute ages, the importance of active rather than passive learning, the need for socially sensitive and responsive environments, the benefits of embedding learning in meaningful contexts, the value of developmental learning models as roadmaps, and, finally, that these principles (coupled with insights about children at cognitive risk) can improve learning among all children.
3. The What Works Clearinghouse (WWC) might be a step in the right direction, if it can provide information that is fair, meaningful, and grounded in high-quality research. Established in 2002 by the U.S. Department of Education's Institute of Education Sciences, the WWC

(http://ies.ed.gov/ncee/wwc) seeks to provide educators, policymakers, researchers, and the public with a source of scientific evidence of what works in education.

4. In his seminal report, W. Pringle Morgan (1896) described the case of 14-year-old Percy F. who could not read and wrote his own name as Precy; but he could multiply 749 by 887 *quickly* and *correctly*.

5. A young man whose extended family includes more members with dyslexia than without.

6. The original Galaburda and Kemper study (1979) found ectopias only in the left hemisphere. Subsequent examination by Sherman revealed ectopias in the right hemisphere, though fewer than in the left hemisphere.

7. In a study of 100 highly successful adult men and women with severe dyslexia (Fink, 1995), all became skilled readers despite great difficulties in integrating sight and sound. All forged eminent careers in business, science, education, and the arts.

8. Others have made similar points, including Howard Gardner (1993), Norman Geschwind (1984), Mel Levine (2002), Margaret Rawson (1988), Robert Sternberg (1987), Priscilla Vail (1994), and Thomas West (1997).

9. The following people are thought to have dyslexia (or at least struggled to learn to read): Thomas Edison, Albert Einstein, Leonardo da Vinci, Winston Churchill, Woodrow Wilson, Auguste Rodin, Pablo Picasso, Paul Orfalea, Jerry Pinkney, Stephen Cannell, David Boies, Jack Horner, Henry Winkler, and Bruce Jenner.

10. Since literacy and math skills will remain vital tools for productive lives in the immediate future, all children need evidence-based and effective instruction in these and other fundamental skills.

11. Others have offered frameworks to address variability. For example, Gilger and Kaplan (2001) propose the term *atypical brain development* (ABD) and an accompanying conceptual framework to address the nonspecific underlying mechanisms, heterogeneity, and comorbidity of developmental LDs. (The ABD model shares many themes and features with the CD model.) Fletcher, Lyon, Fuchs, and Barnes (2007) propose a framework for understanding the different sources of variability (neurobiology, core cognitive processes, behavioral/psychosocial factors, environment) that influence outcomes in children with LDs, focusing on academic skill deficits. Fischer, Rose, and Rose (2007) suggest that dynamic models hold promise for understanding learning disorders, proposing that "development is not a linear process, but a dynamic interaction between the individual's mind, brain, and social and physical environments ... children's abilities to compensate for perceptual or cognitive difficulties are constructed from the properties of this interaction" (p. 101). Fischer and colleagues' dynamic framework (which also shares themes and features with the CD model) not only contributes tools for assessing diverse developmental pathways in "all their real life

complexity," but also focuses on "recurrent growth cycles" and making connections between neurological and cognitive growth.

12. Talents sometimes associated with dyslexia include spatial analyses, mechanical/digital aptitude, creative approaches to problem solving, connecting disparate pieces of information, visualization, artistic expression, and athletics.

13. However, some point out that this premise, embedded in dyslexia's folklore for years, can set up unrealistic expectations that lead to additional disappointment.

14. To prevent academic skill deficits or close gaps, RTI models provide one or more research-validated interventions—often of increasing intensity in tiers (e.g., classroom instruction with professional development support for teachers, small-group instruction, tutoring). Failure to respond to intervention is an indication of LD. Upsides include: students do not wait for identification to receive intervention, academic skill deficits can be prevented or diminished, and costly special-education services are reserved to target the most severe LDs. Downsides include: expectations and comparison groups in very low- or high-performing schools might skew intervention decisions and successful implementation of the model is predicated on effective ongoing screening and progress monitoring as well as on skilled instruction and intervention in classrooms and tiers. Without effective monitoring and highly skilled teaching, the model suffers.

15. If a soccer field represents 4.5 billion years, human life takes up only about 2 centimeters or 0.8 inches.

16. For more information on the pioneering role of independent schools vis-à-vis dyslexia and effective reading instruction and their impact on American education, see *Perspectives* (Oremus, 2005.)

17. According to a survey of 349 districts by the Center on Education Policy (McMurrer, 2007), 44% are spending less time on science, history, art, music, physical education, lunch, and recess.

18. A recent study suggests that NCLB accountability systems might be encouraging teachers and principals to neglect the "most academically advantaged" as well as, ironically, "the least academically advantaged" in order to concentrate on students near proficiency levels (Neal & Schanzenbach, 2007).

REFERENCES

Borja, R. R. (2006). Funder seeding work in the emerging field of digital learning. *Education Week, 26*(12), 12.

Bowers, B. (2007, December 6). Tracing business acumen to dyslexia: A study reinforces how a disorder helps build careers. *New York Times*, pp. 1, 6.

Burke-Fabrikant, K. (2005). The impact of private LD schools on American education. *Perspectives, 31*(1), 21–23.

Denenberg, V. H., Sherman G. F., Schrott, L. M., Rosen, G. D., & Galaburda, A. M. (1991). Spatial learning, discrimination learning, paw preference and neocortical ectopias in two autoimmune strains of mice. *Brain Research, 18,* 98–104.

Fink, R. P. (1995). Successful dyslexics: A constructivist study of passionate interest reading. *Journal of Adolescent and Adult Literacy, 39,* 268–280.

Fink, R. P. (2006). *Why Jean and John couldn't read—and how they learned: A new look at striving readers.* Newark, DE: International Reading Association.

Fischer, K. W., Rose, L. T., & Rose, S. P. (2007). Growth cycles of mind and brain: Analyzing developmental pathways of learning disorders. In K. W. Fischer, J. Holmes Bernstein, & M. H. Immordino-Yang (Eds.), *Mind, brain, and education in reading disorders* (pp. 101–132). Cambridge, UK: Cambridge University Press.

Fletcher, J. M., Lyon, G. R., Fuchs, L. S., & Barnes, M. A. (2007). *Learning disabilities: From identification to intervention.* New York: The Guildford Press.

Frenkel, M., Sherman, G. F., Bashan, K. A., Galaburda, A. M., & LoTurco, J. J. (2000). Neocortical ectopias are associated with attenuated neurophysiological response to rapidly changing auditory stimuli. *NeuroReport, 11,* 575–579.

Galaburda, A. M., & Kemper, T. L. (1979). Cytoarchitectonic abnormalities in developmental dyslexia: A case study. *Annals of Neurology, 6*(2), 94–100.

Galaburda, A. M., Menard, M. T., & Rosen, G. D. (1994). Evidence for aberrant auditory anatomy in developmental dyslexia. *Proceedings of the National Academy of Sciences, 91,* 8010–8013.

Galaburda, A. M., & Sherman, G. F. (2007). The genetics of dyslexia: What is the phenotype? In K. W. Fischer, J. Holmes Bernstein, & M. H. Immordino-Yang (Eds.), *Mind, brain, and education in reading disorders* (pp. 37–58). Cambridge, UK: Cambridge University Press.

Galaburda, A. M., Sherman G. F., Rosen, G. D., Aboitiz, F., & Geschwind, N. (1985). Developmental dyslexia: Four consecutive patients with cortical anomalies. *Annals of Neurology, 18,* 222–233.

Gardner, H. (1993). *Multiple intelligences: The theory in practice.* New York: Basic Books.

Geschwind, N. (1965). Disconnection syndromes in animals and man. *Brain, 88,* 237–294.

Geschwind, N. (1982). Why Orton was right. *Annals of Dyslexia, 32,* 13–30.

Geschwind, N. (1984). The brain of the learning disabled individual. *Annals of Dyslexia, 34,* 319–327.

Geschwind, N., & Galaburda, A. M. (1987). *Cerebral lateralization: Biological mechanisms, associations, and pathology.* Cambridge, MA: MIT Press.

Gilger, J. W., & Kaplan, B. J. (2001). Atypical brain development: A conceptual framework for understanding developmental learning disabilities. *Developmental Neuropsychology, 21*(2), 465–481.

Hynd, G., Semrud-Clikeman, M., Lorys, A., Novey, E., & Eliopulos, R. (1990). Brain morphology in developmental dyslexia and attention deficit disorder/hyperactivity. *Archives of Neurology, 47,* 919–926.

Levine, M. (2002). *A mind at a time.* New York: Simon & Schuster.

Livingstone, M., Rosen, G., Drislane, F., & Galaburda, A. M. (1991). Physiological and anatomical evidence for a magnocellular defect in developmental dyslexia. *Proceedings of the National Academy of Sciences, 88,* 7943–7947.

McMurrer, J. (2007, July). *Choices, changes, and challenges: Curriculum and instruction in the NCLB era.* Washington, DC: Center on Education Policy.

Morgan, W. P. (1896). A case of congenital word blindness. *British Medical Journal, 2,* 1378.

Neal, D. A., & Schanzenbach, D. W. (2007, July). *Left behind by design: Proficiency counts and test-based accountability.* Chicago: Harris School of Public Policy Studies at the University of Chicago.

Oremus, E. B. (2005). Independent schools for children with learning differences. *Perspectives, 31*(1), 21–23.

Rawson, M. B. (1988). *The many faces of dyslexia.* Baltimore: International Dyslexia Association.

Santiago Declaration. (2007). Retrieved November 5, 2007, from http://www.santiagodeclaration.org.

Schneps, M. H., Rose, T. L., & Fischer, K. W. (2007). Visual learning and the brain: Implications for dyslexia. *Mind, Brain, and Education, 1*(3), 128–139.

Steinmetz, H., Volkmann, J., Jäncke, L., & Freund, H. J. (1991). Anatomical left-right asymmetry of language-related temporal cortex is different in left and right-handers. *Annals of Neurology, 29*, 315–319.

Sternberg, R. (1987). *Beyond IQ: A triarchic theory of human intelligence.* New York: Cambridge University Press.

Vail, P. L. (1994). *Emotion: The on off switch for learning.* Rosemont, NJ: Modern Learning Press.

von Károlyi, C., Winner, E., Gray, W., & Sherman, G. F. (2003). Dyslexia linked to talent: Global visual-spatial ability. *Brain and Language, 85*, 427–431.

West, T. G. (1997). *In the mind's eye* (rev. ed.). Amherst, NY: Prometheus Books.

Winters, C. A. (1997). Learning disabilities, crime, delinquency, and special education placement. *Adolescence, 32*(126), 451–462.

Section II

Methods and Tools

4 Recent Methodological Advances in the Analysis of Developmental Data
An Introduction to Growth Mixture Models

*David J. Francis, Jack M. Fletcher,
and Robin Morris*

This chapter is about methodological advances in the statistical analysis of developmental data that have specific promise for addressing questions about specific learning disabilities (SLD). These methods are especially well suited to capturing information about the nature of development and about individual differences in developmental processes, including differences of either a quantitative or qualitative nature. Although these methods are complex and can be used in quite sophisticated ways to address difficult questions, they can be explained in a conceptual way that is nonetheless rigorous and reasonably comprehensive. It is the goal of this chapter to provide such an introduction. At the same time, discussion of SLD and of these new statistical methods is made easier if readers have a firm understanding about the nature of measurement in psychology and education, and understand the central importance of both measurement theory and latent variables to psychological explanations. For that reason, this chapter is organized so as to first provide the reader some background on measurement in psychological science and on SLD. Subsequently, we will examine some specific advances in statistical modeling of developmental data, along with some examples to help the reader develop a clearer understanding of the models and their implications for research on SLD.

LATENT AND MANIFEST VARIABLES AND THE CONCEPT OF SPECIFIC LEARNING DISABILITIES

Behavioral and social scientists are acutely aware that most phenomena of interest to them are only indirectly observable. Concepts such as intelligence, motivation, achievement, language proficiency, self-efficacy, happiness, depression, and so forth are abstractions that serve the purpose of reducing to a single label what is an otherwise complex constellation of observable behaviors. In the vernacular of the social and behavioral sciences, this distinction between that which is directly observable and that which must be inferred on the basis of covariation among those observables is known as the distinction between manifest (observable) and latent (unobservable) variables. The introduction of latent variables into psychological measurement dates to the start of the last century through the work of Spearman on intelligence (Spearman, 1904, as cited in Borsboom, Mellenbergh, & van Heerden, 2003). To be clear, latent variables are not latent in the individual, but latent in the direct observations that scientists make on their subjects. Borsboom et al. (2003) distinguish two ways in which latent variables are used: The first is a formal, technical way, which at its roots is a mathematical formulation that describes the relations among directly observable variables in terms of their relations with the underlying latent variables. The second is empirical and reflects the combining of scores on observable variables into estimates of scores on the underlying latent variables. Although these two uses are inextricably connected, they are distinguishable from one another, and it is generally in the former sense that the term *latent variable* is used throughout this chapter.

Latent variables have generally been considered to fall into one of two general distributional forms. Continuous latent variables, like continuous manifest variables, imply that a dimension exists that is unobserved, but along which individuals can, nevertheless, be ordered. The marginal distribution of the latent variable is presumed to be described by a continuous probability distribution (such as the normal distribution) or the multivariate normal distribution (in the case of two or more continuous latent variables). Commonly, the continuous latent variable is posited to underlie/explain performance on continuous manifest variables, as is the case in common factor analysis of test scores, although the model can be extended to also describe the performance of individuals on binary and ordered categorical test items, such as in attitude surveys and tests of achievement. Continuous latent variables function to account for covariation among the manifest variables, and as such, they work to cluster together manifest variables on the basis of their tendency to covary.

In contrast to continuous latent variables, categorical latent variables work to cluster together individuals on the basis of the similarity in their response patterns. Categorical latent variables have their roots in the work of Meehl (1962, 1995) and his students who developed the field of taxometrics in his efforts to understand the nature of psychopathology. Categorical latent variables imply the existence of discrete, yet unobservable, categories of individuals, for example, individuals with and without hypertension. Although it is possible, there is no requirement that the categories be ordered. For example, a categorical latent variable of learning style might characterize individuals as either visual or verbal learners, in which case the latent classes would be considered unordered. In contrast, a latent variable of English language proficiency that had categories of non-English speaker, beginner, intermediate, advanced intermediate, and fluent English speaker would consist of ordered latent classes. Categorical latent variables can be posited to explain manifest variables that are nominal, ordinal, continuous, and/or counts.

The concept of SLD originated from early observations of cognitive and behavioral disorders that resulted from frank brain injuries and evolved to include inferred or presumed brain injuries on the basis of disordered cognition or unexpected underachievement. More recently, the concept has evolved to refer to disorders in the basic psychological processes underlying the use of spoken or written language in the absence of known causes (see Fletcher et al., 1998, for a review). Historically, research on learning disabilities has concentrated on identification, screening and prevention, classification and subtyping, and intervention. In the area of identification and classification, considerable focus has been placed on the use of intelligence tests, on profiling cognitive abilities, and on operationalization of the concept of unexpected underachievement as a discrepancy between academic achievement and intellectual potential, as low achievement, and most recently as a failure to respond to intervention (RTI; Fletcher, Denton, & Francis, 2005). Although this literature has not been explicitly linked to the philosophy of science literature on latent variables, this focus on identification corresponds to the empirical use of latent variables referred to by Borsboom et al. (2003).

In all of these endeavors, it is important to bear in mind that SLD is a construct, an abstraction whose utility rests in its ability to encapsulate, or represent in a single term, important features of the systematic variation in human behavior. In the language of measurement introduced earlier, SLD is a latent variable that is always imperfectly measured (Francis, Fletcher, Shaywitz, Shaywitz, & Rourke, 1996; Francis et al., 2005) and that can only be inferred on the basis of patterns of observable test performance at a single point in time (Francis, Fletcher, et al., 1996) or over the course of development (Boscardin, Muthen, Francis, & Baker, 2008; Francis, Shaywitz, Stuebing, Shaywitz, & Fletcher, 1996). Variation in the approach to measurement does not necessarily imply variation in the underlying construct being measured, nor do controversies about measurement imply that the underlying construct is not real. The major question, from the standpoint of validity of the underlying construct, is whether different approaches to the measurement of observable behavior lead to the identification of a unique group of individuals who represent the construct of unexpected underachievement, the key component of most conceptualizations of SLD (Lyon et al., 2001). If there are problems with the reliability of how unexpected underachievement is measured, such that the underlying psychometric model is not suitable for identifying a unique group of children, then the validity issue is moot. Valid classifications require that measurement first be reliable. Inferences cannot be valid without reliability in the underlying measurements (Francis et al., 2005).

Readers will recognize this statement as a variation on the often-cited phrase that reliability represents the upper limit of validity. The basic logic behind this truism is that reliability reflects the degree to which observations are free from error or random fluctuations. Fluctuations in test scores that are attributable to error must, by definition, not be influenced by systematic factors of any type. As a result, this portion of the variance in test scores is unrelated to any dimension of psychological or educational interest that is purported to underlie test scores. Because test validity reflects the degree to which inferences about test scores are true, test validity depends on the relation between test scores and the educational or psychological dimensions about which we wish to make inferences.

Consequently, reliability places a numerical upper limit on test validity since it is only the error-free variance in test scores that can relate to the dimensions of psychological or educational interest.

How SLD is defined and identified reflects a classification indicating how individuals with SLD are similar and dissimilar (i.e., unique) relative to other children and adults (Fletcher & Morris, 1986; Morris & Fletcher, 1988). This comparison can be formulated at the manifest variable level but is most compelling at the latent variable level. Although it is relatively easy to demonstrate that SLD is a valid classification when comparisons are made to children with mental retardation, to typical achievers, or across different academic types of SLD (e.g., reading versus math disability), it is harder to validate classifications that separate subgroups *within* major academic domains. For example, it has proven much more difficult to demonstrate differential validity for the IQ–achievement discrepancy model of classification over a low-achievement model (see Fletcher et al., 2002). It is not that the competing systems (by definition) do not identify distinct individuals but that the individuals so identified are not differentiated on other important dimensions relevant to the construct of interest. Different approaches simply do not identify unique subgroups, partly because of problems with the underlying measurement models (see Francis et al., 2005; Stuebing et al., 2002).

This point may seem uninteresting or merely academic, but, in fact, the implications for the nature of SLD can be profound. If the failure to identify unique subgroups of SLD within major SLD categories (e.g., reading, math, and language) is not due to limitations of methodology and measurement, then it may be that children with SLD and children without SLD are not qualitatively different from one another. That is, the differences are differences of degree not differences of type. If so, it would imply that children with SLD learn in the same way, using the same processes and skills, as children without SLD. Of course, whether SLD represents a difference of degree or kind remains an unanswered question, in part because it is unclear if the failures to answer this question in the past are the result of methodological problems and/or measurement problems.

It is possible that the measurement problems stem from the dimensional nature of SLD. Some studies of children with SLD (in reading) have suggested that the distribution of achievement test scores is not normal and have identified discontinuities that could be used as a cut point (Miles & Haslum, 1986; Rutter & Yule, 1975; Wood & Grigorenko, 2001). However, a series of epidemiological, population-based studies of reading and math disabilities in children have shown that reading (Jorm et al., 1986; Rodgers, 1983; Shaywitz et al., 1992; Silva et al., 1985; Stevenson, 1988) and math (Lewis, Hitch, & Walker, 1994; Shalev et al., 2000) skills are normally distributed in our population. There is no consistent evidence for bimodality or other forms of nonnormality in the population distributions of these skills. Even genetic studies are not consistent with the presence of qualitatively different characteristics associated with the heritability of reading and math disorders; the assumption of normal variation is pivotal for this type of research (Gilger, 2001). These observations are important because as normally distributed traits that exist on a continuum, there are no natural breaks in the distribution of IQ and achievement that serve to separate individuals with reading or math disabilities from those who are not disabled (Shaywitz et al., 1992). Consequently, it is difficult, if not impossible, in the absence of external criteria (e.g., functional outcomes), to specify boundaries on the joint distribution of IQ and achievement that accurately and reliably identify individuals with SLD. Alternatively, the problem may stem from the limited dimensionality of IQ and achievement as studied.

A dimensional nature to SLD would complicate the use of single cut points or boundaries on the continuous univariate distribution of achievement or the bivariate distribution of achievement and IQ. Identifications would be unreliable in predictable ways if they were based on static, single assessments (Francis et al., 2005; Stuebing et al., 2002). This problem with the use of such assessments in classification does not, necessarily, mean that SLD is simply underachievement. Rather, the measurement system is incapable of adequately reflecting the phenomenon of interest because the measurement model is underidentified. Put another way, the system carries insufficient information about the phenomenon of interest to allow for reliable and valid classification of individuals along the unobservable dimension(s) of interest. This problem would be partly ameliorated if SLD was a manifest concept, that is, if SLD were a phenomenon that is directly observable in the behavior of affected individuals. But SLD is not directly observable; rather SLD is a latent construct in the same sense that achievement and intelligence are latent constructs. Thus, SLD must be inferred from the observed pattern of relations among manifest operations. The more observed relations that we have at our disposal, the more information we have on which to base our inference regarding the presence of SLD, the more reliable and valid that inference becomes and the finer the distinctions that can be supported by the system.

When the measurement system is underidentified, the only solution is to expand the dimensionality of the measurement system to increase the number of observed relations. In that sense, it is the absence of a directly observable criterion that makes it difficult to identify a unique subgroup of underachieving individuals consistent with the construct of SLD when identification is based on a single assessment at a single time point. Adding external criteria increases the dimensionality of the measurement system and makes latent classification possible, even when the external criteria are themselves imperfect. At the same time, the reader should note that it is impossible to use the data to choose between dimensional and categorical representations of the underlying structure without reliance on strong theory. For example, it has been shown that any $k-1$ continuous latent variables will produce the same means, variances, and covariances as a k group latent profile solution (i.e., k unobserved groups can be used to explain any data set that requires $k-1$ continuous latent variables to explain it [Molenaar & von Eye, 1994]). In that sense, the data do not help in choosing between the $k-1$ continuous latent variable and the k unobserved groups *explanations* of the data. This mathematical equivalence implies that the debate will not be solved by simple examinations of empirical model fits, that is, it is not simply a matter of looking at how well the model captures the data. However, by increasing the dimensionality of the data structure, it becomes easier to choose between different representations based on parsimony and relevant theory about dimensions of behavior and subgroups of individuals. Only through continued development of explicit theories about that nature of learning and learning disabilities can we hope to represent these theoretical distinctions in statistical models and potentially chose between them. It is through the intersections of theory with data, models, and scientific principles of parsimony that we can resolve the debate about the nature of SLD, or at least develop a clearer understanding of the limitations of competing theories.

Hypotheses concerning subtypes of learning disabilities are sometimes confused with the fundamental distinction between categorical and dimensional representations of SLD. The debate over categorical and dimensional representations of SLD goes to the root nature of SLD, that is, to the distinction between the presence of SLD and its absence. The debate over subtypes within the population of individuals with SLD does not address this fundamental point, but asks whether individuals with SLD can be sorted into groups on the basis of strengths and weaknesses in their profiles of cognitive abilities. Even if it is possible to sort individuals with SLD in this way, these same profiles may also be found in the nondisabled population, with the primary distinction being the elevation of the SLD profiles relative to their normative counterparts and not their shape (Francis, Espy, Rourke, & Fletcher, 1991; Stevens, 1986). Consequently, the identification of subtypes within the SLD population does not imply rejection of the dimensional hypothesis of SLD, although the search for subtypes through the use of techniques like cluster analysis (Morris et al., 1998) is consistent with the notion of categorical latent classes within the population of SLD individuals.

The foregoing discussed the distinction between manifest and latent variables and introduced the notion that SLD is an example of a latent variable or construct. We also distinguished between two views of SLD as a latent variable: one that posits that SLD reflects variation on a continuum of ability; and one that posits that SLD represents a distinct class, or set of classes of learners, and in this sense represents variation in types of learners as opposed to variation in degree. In the next section, we examine different statistical models for describing the relations between manifest and latent variables. Taken together these models provide researchers with a set of tools for investigating the nature of SLD, the manifest variables that provide evidence about its existence, and the role of development in both.

ADVANCES IN LATENT VARIABLE MODELS

By now, most developmental researchers have become familiar with the language, if not the specific application, of individual growth models and their estimation through hierarchical and multilevel modeling software (Bryk & Raudenbush, 1987; Francis, Fletcher, Stuebing, Davidson, & Thompson, 1991; Francis, Shaywitz, Stuebing, Shaywitz, & Fletcher, 1992; Rogosa, Brandt, & Zimowski, 1982). This approach relies on a conceptually straightforward formulation of individual growth models as consisting of essentially two parts. The first part describes change at the individual level and captures the essential elements of change for each person in a relatively small set of *growth* parameters that describe the trajectory of the outcome with respect to time for the particular individual. The simplest description of change at this *person* level is that of a straight line, which can be captured using two individual *growth* parameters, namely, a slope and an intercept. The second part of the growth model describes interindividual differences in change and is formulated as a regression model where the *growth* parameters, which describe change at the individual level in part 1, become the dependent variables in the model of interindividual differences in change in part 2. Indeed, it is possible to fit the two parts of the model separately (Willett, 1987), although there are distinct statistical advantages to estimating the parameters of both models simultaneously as a single hierarchical or multilevel model (Bryk & Raudenbush, 1987).

Although it is somewhat easier to conceptualize the process of modeling individual growth in the hierarchical/multilevel framework, other formulations exist. Willett and Sayer (1994) showed how individual growth models could be conceptualized and estimated as latent variable structural equation models (SEM) when all individuals were measured at the same time points. Mehta and West (2000) further showed how this framework could be extended to data structures where the timing of observations varies across individuals. The differences between SEM approaches for modeling fixed versus varying time points across individuals need not concern us here. More important is what they have in common. Specifically, the individual growth parameters are represented as latent variables (i.e., unobservables) in both SEM formulations of individual growth models. More importantly, the means, variances, and covariances of these latent variables determine the means, variances, and covariances of the manifest variables, analogous to part 1 of the multilevel model framework. In addition, the means, variances, and covariances of the latent variables that represent the individual growth parameters can be modeled as a function of other measured and latent variables in an effort to describe interindividual differences in the processes of change, analogous to part 2 of the multilevel model framework.

Unification of the multilevel and SEM frameworks has significantly expanded the methodological toolbox of developmental researchers (Muthen, 2002; Muthen & Muthen, 1998). Two important extensions are the ease with which development of multiple processes can be studied simultaneously, including the examination of influences that one process might exert on another and the ability to model heterogeneity in development when the sources of that heterogeneity are unobserved. Boscardin et al. (2008) exploit these two extensions in a recent investigation of heterogeneity in the acquisition of early reading skills. Before looking at this example in somewhat greater detail, we will look more concretely at the notion of categorical latent variables and the models that employ them.

MODELS WITH CATEGORICAL LATENT VARIABLES

As an introduction to models with categorical latent variables, it is helpful to distinguish among three different models: latent class analysis, latent profile analysis/ latent class cluster analysis, and factor mixture models. Latent class analysis (LCA), pioneered by Clogg and Goodman (1984), typically involves analysis of data collected on categorical, manifest variables at a single point in time. The model seeks to estimate the number of classes and the probability of class membership in each class such that the model explains the response probabilities for each of the categorical manifest variables so that independence holds within each class. That is, the classes defined by the latent variables fully explain the covariation among item responses in the observed data. The raw data are the multidimensional contingency of response probabilities. For item responses to be independent within a class, it must be the case that within a class, the probability of any particular pattern of responses to the set of items is just the product of the marginal probabilities for the items in that class. To make this idea more concrete without introducing a specific mathematical formulation of the model, consider Figure 4.1A, which provides a graphical representation of a latent class model (for the mathematical formulation of the LCA model, see Collins, Fidler, & Wugalter, 1996; McCutcheon, 2002). In Figure 4.1A, the U_j represent individual items, such as test items that take on scores of 0 and 1. C is the latent categorical variable that explains performance on the four items. The arrow leading from C to the item indicates that class membership determines the probability of responding correctly to that item. Each arrow is associated with a factor loading that reflects the response probability for that item (i.e., probability of scoring a 1 on item j for an individual in class $= k$). Thus, the values for the loading differ across classes reflecting the different probabilities of correct responding in each class. Factor loadings close to 1 or close to 0 indicate items that are highly related to class membership.

A second model involving categorical latent variables is the latent profile analysis (LPA) model (Lazarsfeld & Henry, 1968; Vermunt & Magidson, 2002), which is depicted in Figure 4.1B. The latent profile model is quite similar to the latent class model depicted in Figure 4.1A except that the U_j in Figure 4.1A have been replaced by continuously distributed Y_j rather than categorical manifest

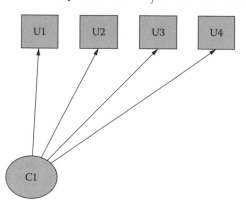

FIGURE 4.1A Latent class model. U_j are individual items (e.g., test items taking on scores of 0 and 1). C is a latent categorical variable that explains performance on the four items. Each arrow is associated with a factor loading that reflects the response probability for that item (i.e., probability of scoring a 1 on item j for an individual in class $= k$).

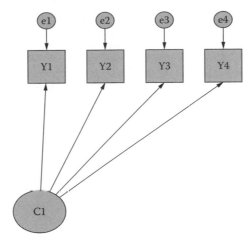

FIGURE 4.1B Latent profile model. The categorical U_j have been replaced by continuously distributed manifest variables Y_j and their associated errors of measurement, e_j.

variables. (Note that changing the distributional properties of the manifest variables requires that a series of latent variables representing errors of measurement $[e_j]$ in the manifest variables be introduced into the figure, such that each manifest variable has two causes: the categorical latent variable, C, and the unobserved variable that represents error for that manifest variable. Standard assumptions about the errors imply that they are unrelated across measures, are normally distributed, and have means of 0.) In the LPA model, the categorical latent variable is introduced to explain the variances, covariances, and means of the continuously distributed manifest variables.

In the classical LPA model, the manifest variables are considered to be independent within a class. Thus, the covariances among the manifest variables in the aggregate sample result from the differences in means between classes. In modern latent profile models, this assumption of within-class independence is often relaxed (Muthen & Muthen, 1998). By allowing the manifest variables to correlate within-class, the modern latent profile model is actually a statistical model for uncovering mixtures of distributions (Vermunt & Magidson, 2002), or latent class cluster analysis (LCCA). Thus, in modern applications of LPA/LCCA, the goal is to determine the number of classes; the probability of class membership; and the means, variances, and covariances for each class, that is, the latent profiles. As mentioned, the model may or may not place various restrictions on the parameters of the model. The increased control that the researcher is able to exert over model constraints (e.g., restricting covariances equal across groups) makes the modern version of LPA a model-based approach to cluster analysis.

The general idea behind mixtures of distributions is depicted in an overly simplified way in Figure 4.2. In Figure 4.2, the hatched histogram shows the observed distribution for a manifest variable, Y. Examination of the histogram suggests that Y is normally distributed, but, in fact, Y is comprised of two normal distributions

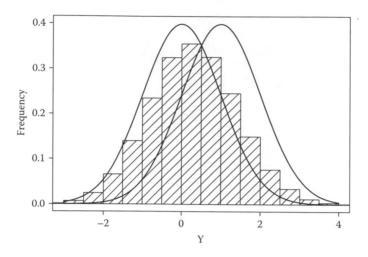

FIGURE 4.2   Hypothetical mixture distribution formed by combining two normal distributions with different means in unequal proportions.

mixed in unequal proportions.[1] The two underlying distributions are represented by the solid lines, and these distributions are in fact normal, but have unequal means and were combined in unequal proportions. The researcher has observed the single distribution of Y and has no information about individual's membership in population 1 or 2 (i.e., this information is unobserved). The objective of the analysis is to uncover the two underlying distributions that were combined to create the resultant distribution of Y.

Of course, in actual applications of LPA/LCCA, the researcher is working with more than one manifest variable. Although the problem is thus multivariate in nature, unlike the univariate problem depicted in Figure 4.2, the general objective is the same. Figure 4.3 gives a simplified view of a multivariate mixture problem. In the top panel of Figure 4.3, a scatter plot is shown depicting the relation between two hypothetical continuously distributed variables. The two variables are moderately correlated ($r = 0.28$), and there is no obvious clustering of observations into groups. However, the distribution of points in the top and bottom panels is precisely the same. In the lower panel of Figure 4.3, the observations have been displayed in such a way as to highlight the two separate populations that were combined to form the plot in the top panel. Note that in each population, there is no relation between the two variables plotted on the graph ($r = 0.00$ in each of the two subpopulations). The correlation between measures in the top panel results from combining the two populations who differ in their means.[2] This correlation is analogous to the nonindependence introduced into clustered samples in other research settings, such as studies of students within schools. The only difference is that in the current case, the cluster membership is unobserved, and the analysis is intended to uncover it.

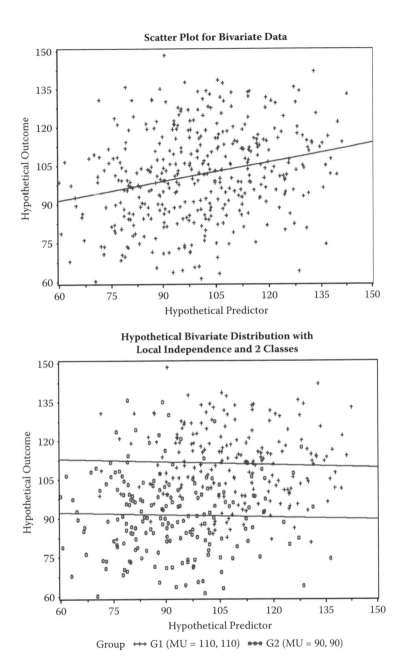

FIGURE 4.3 Hypothetical two-class distribution with local independence in both classes. The top panel shows the combined distribution ($r = 0.28$); the bottom panel shows the two separate distributions that have been combined to form the single distribution in the top panel. Note $r = 0.00$ in each of the two populations in the bottom panel.

A similar situation is depicted in Figure 4.4. However, in this case, two populations, which differ in their mean and covariance structure (Figure 4.4, bottom panel), have been combined (Figure 4.4, top panel). The means and variances in the two populations are the same as in Figure 4.3. The primary difference between Figures 4.3 and 4.4 is the covariance structure. In Figure 4.3, independence is held within each population. In Figure 4.4, independence holds for population 2, but the correlation in population 1 is .84. The resulting correlation in the combined population is .66, and the standard deviation is 18, instead of 15 as it was in the combined population depicted in Figure 4.3. Together Figures 4.3 and 4.4 are intended to show that the means, variances, and covariances in the combined population will reflect the means, variances, covariances, and mixing proportions of the populations being combined.

In the first two models that were introduced, LCA and LPA/LCCA, the categorical latent variable directly explains the properties of the manifest variables. With the expansion of structural equation modeling programs into more general latent variable modeling tools, further extensions of latent variable models have become possible. An obvious extension is to impose one or more continuously distributed latent variables as the primary determinant of the manifest variables, with the latent categorical variable explaining variation in the distribution of the continuous latent variable(s). This model, depicted in Figure 4.5, is sometimes referred to as a factor mixture model (Lubke & Muthen, 2005), because the mixture of distributions is proposed for the underlying factor structure, which in turn impacts the distribution of the manifest variables. Thus, the distribution of the manifest variables differs across classes of the latent class factor, C. However, these differences arise through the direct effects of C on F, a continuously distributed latent variable that, in turn, directly affects the continuously distributed manifest variables, Y_j. Thus, the effects of C on the manifest variables are indirect insofar as all of the effects of C on the manifest variables are explained by the effects that C exerts on the distribution of F.

COMBINING MODELS: THE GENERAL GROWTH MIXTURE MODEL

As mentioned previously, the latent variable approach to individual growth models has several advantages over other formulations of the model. These advantages are most apparent when working with multiple growth processes that influence one another either simultaneously or sequentially (Muthen & Muthen, 1998; Reise & Duan, 2003). The latent variable approach to individual growth modeling also affords some advantages when modeling growth in multiple observed populations, that is, when the group structure to the data is known or observed. However, in more recent years, advances in latent variable structural equation modeling software coupled with the development of high-speed personal computing has made possible the combination of latent variable structural equation modeling and factor mixture modeling. This model is directly analogous to the factor mixture model of Figure 4.5, except that in this instance, the continuously distributed factors are designed to capture the growth processes for individuals,

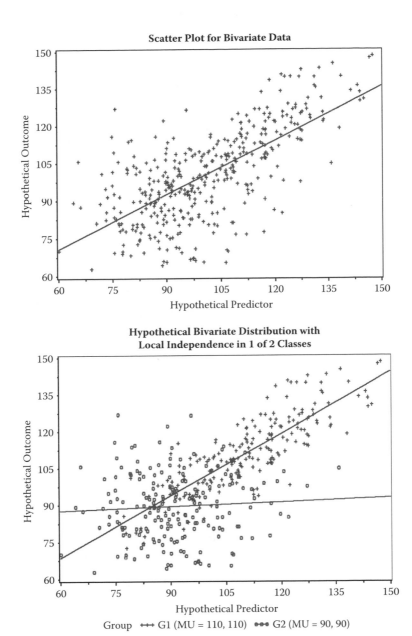

FIGURE 4.4   Hypothetical two-class distribution with local independence in one class. The top panel shows the combined distribution (mean = 100, sigma = 18, r = 0.66); the bottom panel shows the two distributions that were combined in the top panel. Note r = 0.84 in population 1 and r = 0.00 in population 2. The means and standard deviations and mixing proportions for the two populations are the same as in Figure 4.3.

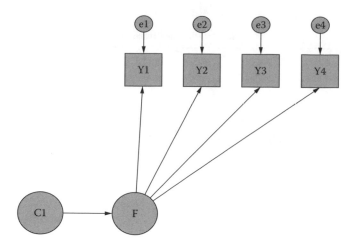

FIGURE 4.5   Simple factor mixture model.

while the categorical latent variables capture unobserved heterogeneity in the growth processes. It is possible to impose the mixture model into the more traditional individual growth modeling framework, and this approach has been used by Nagin (2005) to study trajectories of antisocial behavior, criminality, and physical aggression. The approach taken by Nagin differs from what is described here in that he does not postulate that the latent classes have any basis in reality. Rather, for Nagin the classes serve merely as useful descriptions of patterns of performance. That is, they are useful empirical characterizations of the data, but they do not otherwise possess a psychological reality. The classes are themselves independent of one another and serve to reduce the entire multivariate distribution into a minimum number of nonoverlapping and independent clusters. In this sense, they function much like principal components in other multivariate data reduction strategies. For that reason, the model employed by Nagin assumes independence of the measured variables within classes, in much the same way that classical LPA assumes independence within classes. Although this approach conflicts with the arguments put forth by Borsboom et al. (2003) regarding the realism of the latent variables, this issue is by no means resolved among social scientists. It is also not the case that the individual growth frameworks are fundamentally limited in the approaches that they can take to the problem of incorporating mixtures into the growth model. However, it is accurate to say that the greatest modeling flexibility is currently afforded by the latent variable structural equation modeling framework provided in the most recent release of the statistical modeling program MPlus (Muthen & Muthen, 2007). For that reason, we focus for the remainder of the chapter on that particular framework.

The growth mixture modeling framework combines individual growth modeling in a latent variable framework with a factor mixture model applied to the latent variables representing the individual growth parameters. This approach is discussed in detail in part I of a recent edited volume by Hancock and Samuelsen

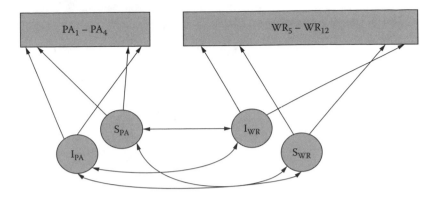

FIGURE 4.6   Traditional latent variable model of individual growth in two processes.

(2008). Figure 4.6 provides a graphical representation of a traditional individual growth model in the latent variable structural equation modeling framework. This model depicts growth in two sequentially related processes: (a) phonological awareness in kindergarten, represented by the block of measures PA_1 to PA_4, and (b) word reading in grades 1 and 2, represented by the block of measures WR_5 to WR_{12}. Growth in each of the two processes is described by a slope and intercept latent variable, S_{PA}, I_{PA}, and S_{WR}, I_{WR}, respectively. The two sets of growth parameters are allowed to correlate with one another as reflected by the series of four two-sided arrows. Although useful, this traditional individual growth model assumes that there is a single underlying population and that the growth parameters exert the same influence the observable measures in the same way for all individuals. The model is silent with regard to the possibility that the developmental relationship between growth parameters for these two sets of skills may differ for subsets of children, subsets whose relative size and whose membership may be unknown.

Whereas the model in Figure 4.6 disregards such population heterogeneity, the model depicted in Figure 4.7 attempts to directly model this possible heterogeneity in the distribution of growth parameters. In Figure 4.7, the covariation between the two sets of slopes and intercepts is accounted for on the basis of the class structure that underlies the distributions of the four latent variables. As drawn, the model stipulates that the latent class structure fully accounts for the covariation among the growth parameters. In that sense, the model of Figure 4.7 is a *classical* latent profile analysis model, with the exception being that the profile is being formed on the basis of four growth parameters, which are themselves unobserved.

The model depicted in Figure 4.7 has been fit to a large longitudinal data set (Boscardin et al., 2008) involving four assessments per year in kindergarten through grade 2. Results from these analyses showed that there is a subgroup of children who show very little growth in phonological awareness in kindergarten. This group of children similarly showed very low growth in word reading skills in grades 1 and 2. This group of students showing low growth in phonological

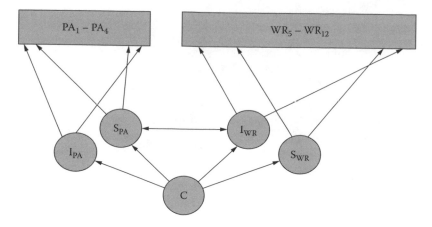

FIGURE 4.7   Growth mixture model for phonological awareness and word reading.

awareness followed by low growth in word reading represented approximately 11% of the total sample of 407 readers. These students were highly differentiated from the other classes of students on the basis of their poor performance on rapid naming of letters in kindergarten, such that children had roughly equal odds of being in this class or the next class, which showed low growth in phonological awareness, but relatively better word reading growth, if their rapid naming score was roughly one standard deviation below the mean. For children who scored between one and three standard deviations below the mean in rapid naming, the probability of being in the problematic reading class rose precipitously with increasingly lower scores on rapid naming of letters. Based on the results of this complex growth mixture model, Boscardin et al. (2008) conclude that it is possible to identify a class of individuals who are at significant risk of poor reading outcomes in grades 1 and 2 based entirely on growth in phonological awareness over the kindergarten year and automaticity with letter naming at the end of the kindergarten year.

FITTING AND EVALUATING GROWTH MIXTURE MODELS

Although growth mixture models hold significant promise for developmental researchers, the models are not without their limitations. The objective of the analysis is to first determine the number of latent classes, as well as the mixing proportions. Of course, a key question to be asked in the analysis concerns whether there is evidence of latent classes or if the data are consistent with having been derived from a single population (i.e., the number of classes, k, is 1). Several possible approaches to deciding the number of classes have been proposed, and certainly one possibility is to compare the likelihood ratio from a one-class solution to that from a two-class solution. However, this comparison is not straightforward as it is in testing nested structural equation models, and several of the proposed solutions appear not to work especially well (Nylund, Asparouhov, & Muthen, 2007).

One of the main limitations of the models is estimating the model and arriving at a stable solution. As models become increasingly complex, computing time and memory demands can become an issue. This problem is exacerbated by the proclivity for models to find local minima in the log-likelihood function. Research to date seems to indicate that the best approach for arriving at a stable solution is to use a large number of random starting points (Nylund et al., 2007) and to compute a bootstrap estimate of the likelihood ratio test by refitting the model many times based on random permutations of the best sets of starting values. Although the tedium of estimating the model many times has been addressed in the most recent release of the MPlus software (Muthen & Muthen, 2007), estimating latent class models still requires some care and potentially significant computing resources when fitting complex models. Although the Monte Carlo simulation work of Nylund et al. (2007) is promising, whether their approach to deciding on the number of classes will prove to be best across a broad class of growth mixture and latent class models awaits further research. It should be added, however, that the tools available for determining the integrity of the solutions to latent class and growth mixture models are far superior to the largely subjective tools that are available for evaluating solutions from traditional cluster analyses.

A second major component of the evaluation of model fit in growth mixture and latent class cluster models is to examine the average posterior probabilities of class membership. Unlike the approach to group-based modeling followed by Nagin (2005), where individuals are assigned unambiguously to a particular class in fitting the model, the growth mixture and latent class cluster analysis approach does not assign individuals to classes in the process of model fitting. Rather, each individual has some probability (ranging from 0 to 1.0) of belonging to each class in the resultant solution. What is desired is that individuals have a high probability of membership to one class and small or zero probability of belonging to all other classes. Thus, it is possible to compute an average posterior probability for each class by first assigning individuals to the class for which their posterior probability of membership is highest, and then averaging across individuals the respective probabilities of belonging to that class. If everyone assigned to a class has a high probability of belonging to that class, and that class only, then the average posterior probability of membership will be high (say, above .9), and the average probability for these individuals to belong to any other class will be low. What is desired is that all classes have high average posterior probabilities, and that classes are clearly differentiated such that few individuals have high probability of assignment to more than one class. In the analysis conducted by Boscardin et al. (2008), the average posterior probability of assignment to the problem class was 0.90 with an average probability of assignment to the next closest class of 0.10. There was zero probability of assignment to any of the other eight classes in the solution.

SUMMARY AND FUTURE DIRECTIONS

This chapter has provided an overview of recent advances in latent variable modeling that are useful for developmental researchers. This chapter was motivated out of questions regarding the fundamental nature of SLD and whether they reflect variation on a continuum of development or distinct classes of development. The chapter attempted to place growth mixture modeling into the broader context of latent variable models for individual growth, latent class and latent profile analysis, and factor mixture models. The development of this unified framework for latent variable models, and in particular the integration of latent class cluster analysis and growth mixture models into this framework, holds substantial promise in addressing the challenge posed by the basic question raised regarding the nature of SLD. The results of Boscardin et al. (2008) mentioned briefly here are suggestive of the possibility that atypical development can be identified early, making possible the promise of early intervention. Just how strongly these data bear on the fundamental question of continuous development versus discrete subgroups of learners awaits further research. With the tools outlined in this chapter and the advances being made every year in statistical software and computing horsepower, it is reasonable to expect that significant work on these basic questions will continue into the future with potentially new and exciting results as we work to link information on behavior, genes, and environmental influences on children's development.

Returning to the question posed at the start of this chapter concerning the very nature of SLD as qualitative or quantitative variations on normal development, these models hold specific promise for operationalizing distinctions between the two formulations of SLD. Using latent class and latent dimensional SEM models, it is possible to compare and contrast the two distinct formulations of SLD by fitting contrasting models to high-dimensional data that directly measures individual development of multiple skills where theories predict differences in the developmental trajectories and processes that influence those trajectories for children with and without SLD, or for children with different types of SLD. Although SLD has not previously been demonstrated to be a unique class of development, past approaches to addressing this question have modeled data of limited complexity. Moreover, these efforts, by necessity, have largely ignored the explicit modeling of learning and development while simultaneously seeking to answer the question of whether SLD represents a unique class of development or variation on a continuum of normative development. With the advances reviewed in this chapter and with continued improvements in statistical computing, these limitations no longer apply for developmental researchers interested in SLD. Not only is it possible to simultaneously model growth at the individual level in multiple related processes, including processes that codevelop and processes that follow one from another, it is possible to study these complex developmental processes in such a way as to explicitly test hypotheses about unobserved latent classes of development that alter the individual developmental processes, the relations between them, or the factors that affect transitions from one developmental stage to another. Incorporating data from genetics and neuroimaging studies and data capturing individual responses to treatment and/or pharmacological intervention is within the grasp of developmental researchers. Of course, the complexity of these models necessitates that the researcher draw heavily on theory in constructing and testing the models, and that the scientific community continues to rely on replication to substantiate the claims emerging from specific models. Dyslexia is surely a prime candidate for such integrated examinations of developmental, genetic, neuroimaging, and treatment-outcome data. Theories of dyslexia are more advanced and better validated than for other SLD, and there is much stronger empirical support for the different nodes that researchers might seek to incorporate into a comprehensive model of the development of reading problems and dyslexia. It is possible that the work of the new Eunice Kennedy Shriver National Institute of Child Health and Human Development (NICHD)-funded learning disabilities research centers may lead to such examinations in the very near future. The promise that such investigations hold for improving our understanding of the nature of developmental dyslexia and other SLD may soon be realized.

ACKNOWLEDGMENTS

This research was supported in part by funding from the National Institute of Child Health and Human Development, grant number HD28172 titled "Detecting Reading Problems by Modeling Individual Growth," and P50 HD052117 titled "Texas Center for Learning Disabilities." Portions of this chapter appeared in *Response to Intervention (RTI): A Conceptually and Statistically Superior Alternative to Discrepancy* by David J. Francis, Jack M. Fletcher, and Robin Morris, December 2003, paper presented at the National Research Center on Learning Disabilities Responsiveness-to-Intervention Symposium, Kansas City, MO. Available at http://www.nrcld.org/symposium2003/francis/francis.pdf.

NOTES

1. The mean of Y in the combined population is 0.3, while the standard deviation is 1.1, and the skew is 0.1. The kurtosis is 0.0. Population 1 has a mean of 0 and a standard deviation of 1.0; population 2 has a mean of 1.0 and standard deviation of 1.0. Individuals from the first population comprise 70% of the combined population, while individuals from the second population comprise 30% of the combined population.
2. The means for population 1 are 110 and 110, whereas the means for population 2 are 90 and 90. In both groups, the standard deviation for each measure is 15. In the combined population depicted in the top panel, the mean for each measure is 100 and the standard deviation is 15. The two populations were combined in equal proportions.

REFERENCES

Borsboom, D., Mellenbergh, G. J., & van Heerden, J. (2003). The theoretical status of latent variables. *Psychological Review, 110*, 203–219.

Boscardin, C., Muthen, B., Francis, D. J., & Baker, E. (2008). Early identification of reading difficulties using heterogeneous developmental trajectories. *Journal of Educational Psychology, 100*(1), 192–208.

Bryk, A. S., & Raudenbush, S. W. (1987). Application of hierarchical linear models to assessing change. *Psychological Bulletin, 101*, 147–158.

Clogg, C. C., & Goodman, L. A. (1984). Latent structure analysis of a set of multidimensional contingency tables. *Journal of the American Statistical Association, 79*, 762–771.

Collins, L. M., Fidler, P. L., & Wugalter, S. E. (1996). Some practical issues related to estimation of latent class and latent transition parameters. In A. von Eye & C. C. Clogg (Eds.), *Analysis of categorical variables in developmental research*.

Fletcher, J. M., Denton, C., & Francis, D. J. (2005). Validity of alternative approaches for the identification of LD: Operationalizing unexpected underachievement. *Journal of Learning Disabilities, 38*, 545–552.

Fletcher, J. M., Francis, D. J., Shaywitz, S. E., Lyon, G. R., Foorman, B. R., Stuebing, K. K., et al. (1998). Intelligent testing and the discrepancy model for children with learning disabilities. *Learning Disabilities: Research and Practice, 13*, 186–203.

Fletcher, J. M., Lyon, G. R., Barnes, M., Stuebing, K. K., Francis, D. J., Olson, R. K., Shaywitz, S. E., & Shaywitz, B. A. Classification of learning disabilities: An evidenced-based evaluation. In R. Bradley, L. Danielson, & D.P. Hallahan (Eds.). *Identification of learning disabilities: Research to practice* (pp. 185–250). Mahwah, NJ: Erlbaum, 2002.

Fletcher, J. M., & Morris, R. (1986). Classification of disabled learners: Beyond exclusionary definitions. In S. Ceci (Ed.), *Handbook of cognitive, social, and neuropsychological aspects of learning disabilities* (Vol. 1– pp. 55–80). New York: Lawrence Erlbaum.

Francis, D. J., Espy, K. A., Rourke, B. P., & Fletcher, J. M. (1991). Validity of intelligence test scores in the definition of learning disability: A critical analysis. In B. P. Rourke (Ed.), *Validation of learning disability subtypes* (pp. 15–44). New York: Guilford.

Francis, D. J., Fletcher, J. M., & Morris, R. (2003, December). *Response to intervention (RTI): A conceptually and statistically superior alternative to discrepancy.* Paper presented at the National Research Center on Learning Disabilities Responsiveness-to-Intervention Symposium, Kansas City, Missouri. http://www.nrcld.org/symposium2003/francis/francis.pdf.

Francis, D. J., Fletcher, J. M., Shaywitz, B. A., Shaywitz, S. E., & Rourke, B. P. (1996). Defining learning and language disabilities: Conceptual and psychometric issues with the use of IQ tests. *Language, Speech, and Hearing Services in Schools, 27*, 132–143.

Francis, D. J., Fletcher, J. M., Stuebing, K. K., Davidson, K. C. & Thompson, N. R. (1991). Analysis of change: Modeling individual growth. *Journal of Consulting and Clinical Psychology, 59*, 27–37.

Francis, D. J., Fletcher, J. M., Stuebing, K. K., Lyon, G. R., Shaywitz, B. A., & Shaywitz, S. E. (2005). Psychometric approaches to the identification of LD: IQ and achievement scores are not enough. *Journal of Learning Disabilities, 38*(2), 98–108.

Francis, D. J., Shaywitz, S. E., Stuebing, K. K., Shaywitz, B. A., & Fletcher, J. M. (1992). The measurement of change: Assessing behavior over time and within a developmental context. In G. R. Lyon (Ed.), *Frames of reference for the assessment of learning disabilities* (pp. 29–58). Baltimore: Paul H. Brookes.

Francis, D. J., Shaywitz, S. E., Stuebing, K. K., Shaywitz, B. A., & Fletcher, J. M. (1996). Developmental lag versus deficit models of reading disability: A longitudinal individual growth curves analysis. *Journal of Educational Psychology, 1*, 3–17.

Gilger, J.W. (2001). Current issues in the neurology and genetics of learning-related traits and disorders: Introduction to the Special Issue. *Journal of Learning Disabilities, 34*, 490–491.

Hancock, G. R., & Samuelsen, K. M. (Eds.). (2008). *Advances in latent variable models.* Charlotte, NC: Information Age Publishing.

Jorm, A. F., Share, D. L., Matthews, M., & Matthews, R. (1986). Cognitive factors at school entry predictive of specific reading retardation and general reading backwardness: A research note. *Journal of Child Psychology*, 45–54.

Lazarsfeld, P. F., & Henry, N. W. (1968). *Latent structure analysis.* Boston: Houghton Mifflin.

Lewis, C., Hitch, G. J., & Walker, P. (1994). The prevalence of specific arithmetic difficulties and specific reading difficulties in 9-10 year old boys and girls. *Journal of Child Psychology and Psychiatry, 35*, 283–292.

Lubke, G., & Muthen, B. O. (2005). Investigating population heterogeneity with factor mixture models. *Psychological Methods, 10*, 21–39.

Lyon, G. R., Fletcher, J. M., Shaywitz, S. E., Shaywitz, B. A., Wood, F. B., Schulte, A., & Olson, R. (2001). Rethinking learning disabilities. In C. E. Finn, Jr., RA. J. Rotherham, & C. R. O'Hokanson, Jr. (Eds.) *Rethinking special education for a new century.* Washington, DC: Thomas B. Fordham Foundation and Progressive Policy Institute.

McCutcheon, A. L. (2002). Basic concepts and procedures in single- and multiple-group latent class analysis. In J. A. Hagenaars & A. L. McCutcheon (Eds.), *Applied latent class analysis* (pp. 56–85). Cambridge, UK: Cambridge University Press.

Meehl, P. E. (1962). Schizotaxia, schizotypy, schizophrenia. *American Psychologist, 17*, 827–838.

Meehl, P. E. (1995). Bootstraps taximetrics: Solving the classification problem in psychopathology. *American Psychologist, 50*, 266–275.

Mehta, P. D., & West, S. G. (2002). Putting the individual back into individual growth curves. *Psychological Methods, 5*(1), 23–43.

Miles, T. R., & Haslum, M. N. (1986). Dyslexia: Anomaly or normal variation. *Annals of Dyslexia, 36*, 103–117.

Molenaar, P. C. M., & von Eye, A. (1994). On the arbitrary nature of latent variables. In A. von Eye & C. C. Clogg (Eds.), *Latent variables analysis: Applications for developmental research* (pp. 226–242). Thousand Oaks, CA: Sage.

Morris, R., & Fletcher, J. M. Classification in neuropsychology: A theoretical framework and research paradigm. *Journal of Clinical and Experimental Neuropsychology, 1988, 10*, 640–658.

Morris, R. D., Stuebing, K. K., Fletcher, J. M., Shaywitz, S. E., Lyon, G. R., Shankweiler, D. P., et al. (1998). Subtypes of reading disability: Variability around a phonological core. *Journal of Educational Psychology, 90*, 347–373.

Muthen, B. O. (2002). Beyond SEM: General latent variable modeling. *Behaviormetrika, 29*, 81–117.

Muthen, B. O., & Muthen, L. K. (1998). *M-Plus user's guide.* Los Angeles: Statistical Model.

Muthen, B. O., & Muthen, L. K. (2007). *M-Plus user's guide.* Los Angeles: Statistical Model.

Nagin, D. S. (2005). *Group-based modeling of development.* Cambridge, MA: Harvard University Press.

Nylund, K. L., Asparouhov, T., & Muthen, B. O. (2007). Deciding on the number of classes in latent class analysis and growth mixture modeling: A Monte Carlo simulation study. *Structural Equation Modeling, 14,* 535–569.

Reise, S. P., & Duan, N. (Eds.). (2003). *Multilevel modeling: Methodological advances, issues, and applications.* Mahwah, NJ: Lawrence Erlbaum Associates.

Rodgers, B. (1983). The identification and prevalence of specific reading retardation. *British Journal of Educational Psychology, 53,* 369–373.

Rogosa, D. R., Brandt, D., & Zimowski, M. (1982). A growth curve approach to the measurement of change. *Psychological Bulletin, 90,* 726–748.

Rutter, M., & Yule, W. (1975). The concept of specific reading retardation. *Journal of Child Psychology and Psychiatry, 16,* 181–197.

Shalev, R. S., Auerbach, J., Manor, O., & Gross-Tsur, V. (2000). Developmental dyscalculia: Prevalence and prognosis. *European Child and Adolescent Psychiatry, 9,* 58–64.

Shaywitz, S. E., Escobar, M. D., Shaywitz, B. A., & Fletcher, J. M., & Makuch, R. (1992). Distribution and temporal stability of dyslexia in an epidemiological sample of 414 children followed longitudinally. *New England Journal of Medicine, 326,* 145–150.

Silva, P. A., McGee, R., & Williams, S. (1985). Some characteristics of nine-year-old boys with general reading backwardness or specific reading retardation. *Journal of Child Psychology and Psychiatry, 20,* 407–421.

Spearman, C. (1904). General intelligence, objectively determined and measured. *American Journal of Psychology, 15,* 201–293.

Stuebing, K. K., Fletcher, J. M., LeDoux, J. M., Lyon, G. R., Shaywitz, S. E., & Shaywitz, B. A. (2002). Validity of IQ-discrepancy classifications of reading disabilities: A meta-analysis. *American Educational Research Journal, 39,* 2002, 469–518.

Stevens, J. (1986). *Applied multivariate statistics for the social sciences.* Mahwah, NJ: Lawrence Erlbaum Associates.

Stevenson, J. (1988). Which aspects of reading disability show a "hump" in their distribution? *Applied Cognitive Psychology, 2,* 77–85.

Vermunt, J. K., & Magidson, J. (2002). Latent class cluster analysis. In J. A. Hagenaars & A. L. McCutcheon (Eds.), *Applied latent class analysis* (pp. 89–106). Cambridge, UK: Cambridge University Press.

Willett, J. B. (1987). Questions and answers in the measurement of change. *Review of Research in Education, 15,* 345–422.

Willett, J. B., & Sayer, A. G. (1994). Using covariance analysis to detect correlates and predictors of individual change over time. *Psychological Bulletin, 116,* 363–381.

Wood, F. B., & Grigorenko, E. L. Emerging issues in the genetics of dyslexia: A methodological preview. *Journal of Learning Disabilities.* Vol 34(6), Nov-Dec 2001, 503–511.

5 Tools for Multimodal Imaging

W. Einar Mencl, Stephen J. Frost, and Kenneth R. Pugh

Recent years have seen an explosion in the use of functional magnetic resonance imaging (fMRI) for the investigation of the neural bases of cognitive function in general and language processing specifically. However, a broad range of techniques is in use and provides alternate ways of measuring brain activity. It would be wise to attempt to integrate knowledge gained from these myriad techniques to avoid the shortcomings of any one method and to take advantage of the strengths of each. Here, we first relate some initial work on directly combining data from two imaging modalities, fMRI and magnetoencephalography (MEG). Second, several findings of related structural and functional linkages among brain areas are reviewed, with direct implications for skilled and impaired reading.

A STUDY OF BASIC SPEECH PERCEPTION USING fMRI AND MEG

Two broad categories of neuroimaging techniques can be distinguished, each with its own advantages and disadvantages. First, the neuroelectric (EEG/ERP, electroencephalography/event-related potentials) and neuromagnetic (MEG) techniques measure at or above the surface of the scalp, electrical currents stemming from neuronal firing (EEG/ERP) and their associated magnetic fields (MEG). Because these measures are directly responsive to the firing of neurons in real time, the resultant data is time resolved, that is, temporal differences in activations on the order of milliseconds can be recorded and compared. However, since the initial signals are recorded with an array of sensors outside the brain, an integral part of analysis is to estimate which of the many possible sets of source activations is likely to have caused the data recorded at the surface sensors.

Second, whole-brain imaging methods such as positron emission tomography (PET) and fMRI measure tracers or endogenous compounds as they are transported and used throughout the brain. Most useful of these methods is tracking the oxygen levels, or the BOLD (blood-oxygen level dependent) response: Simply, when neurons in an area use oxygen to produce action potential firings, freshly oxygenated blood is rapidly reintroduced to resupply that local area. The proportion of oxygenated to deoxygenated blood can be measured by the MRI scanner across the brain at relatively precise spatial resolutions, commonly at ~3 mm cubes. However, because the signal is driven by the vascular system, and

not directly by the neurons themselves, the BOLD response is a highly temporally smoothed and lagged version of the underlying neuronal firing. The typical
response in any given area to a single event, like a brief flash of light, leaves
baseline levels at approximately 2 seconds poststimulus, reaches a peak at around
5 seconds, and slowly returns to baseline levels again by 12 to 16 seconds after
stimulation. Because of the smearing imposed by the vascular response, the time
course of fMRI data does not provide clean information about the timing of neuronal firing on the millisecond level; indeed, BOLD data are typically sampled at
very low temporal resolutions, such as every 2 seconds.

A primary inherent difference between fMRI and MEG should now be apparent as a distinction between temporal resolution and spatial resolution. MR
imaging allows measurement throughout the entire brain at millimeter spatial
resolution, but the signal is terribly temporally impoverished; MEG recording
allows millisecond temporal resolution measurement but requires strong assumptions to precisely localize the activation sources. Combining these two measures
is a logical next step, and formed the rationale for the following experiment.

In this study (Billingsley-Marshall et al., 2007), we used both fMRI and MEG
to measure cortical activations in response to simple spoken words. Researchers
in each of these domains have longstanding and routinized methods of analyzing data and localizing the source of activations. The initial approach taken here,
then, was to acquire data using each approach on the exact same task in the same
set of subjects (in separate sessions), use standard techniques within each laboratory to identify the activation sources, and then directly overlay the findings from
both on a single brain image for each subject. By examining the extent of overlap
(and differences) in the resulting images, we expected some initial insight into the
common and unique contributions of each method.

In both the fMRI and MEG sessions, subjects participated in the same simple
task. Immediately prior to imaging, subjects heard a spoken list of 30 common
words through headphones. Then during scanning, they heard a randomized
sequence of these 30 words ("old" words), mixed with 10 filler words as yet
unheard ("new" words). The subject's task was to press a button whenever an old
word is heard and not to respond to new words. This process was repeated six
times. This experiment was chosen not because it is particularly incisive about
cognitive function (although it does permit later investigation of memory function), but rather because it strongly activates the speech perception and language
systems, and had already been extensively used in MEG for presurgical planning
(Papanicolaou et al., 2004).

Results were mixed. In both the fMRI and MEG sessions, subjects generally
showed activations in response to speech tokens in and around the superior and
middle temporal gyri, areas known to support speech perception. However, the
spatial agreement between the two measures was much poorer than expected:
The mean linear distance between the strongest activated site identified with
fMRI versus MEG was 6.3 cm and 5.7 cm for the left and right hemispheres,
respectively. Examples of three subjects are shown in Figure 5.1: (a) a subject with
some agreement in both left and right temporal cortex; (b) a subject with good

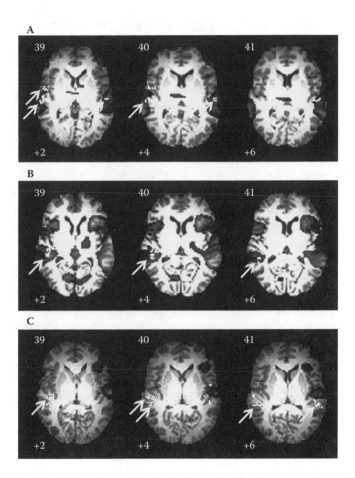

FIGURE 5.1   Results from three subjects showing activations in response to spoken words as measured by fMRI and MEG. The grayscale underlay shows the anatomy at three successive axial slice locations in MNI standard space. The number at the top is slice number within the image; the number at the bottom is the z-coordinate of the slice in MNI space. Grayscale shading shows activated areas recorded with fMRI. White points and clusters, noted by arrows, indicate activation sources as identified by MEG. Anterior is toward the top of each slice; the right hemisphere is on the left per radiological convention.

agreement in the right temporal cortex but not in the left; and (c) a subject with relatively poor agreement in both hemispheres.

Why might this be the case? Although this initial study was not designed to differentiate among potential causes, several possibilities exist, stemming from specific inherent weaknesses of each method. First, with fMRI, sensitivity varies considerably across the brain. Some areas, particularly medial frontal and inferior temporal, are particularly susceptible to reduction in signal levels caused by nearby borders of tissue, bone, and air cavities. Second, each cube ("voxel") measured with fMRI is relatively large (~3 mm cubed) and contains tens of thousands of neurons. A small subset of these neurons firing in synchrony may not be enough to produce significant average activation levels in the voxel as a whole. Similarly, the measured activation levels at each voxel are values accrued over a relatively long period of time (typically 2 seconds per image). If a group of neurons fire in a brief burst, as opposed to a sustained manner, the average activation level across the image period may not be enough to reach significance. With MEG, a different set of concerns applies. First, to be detectable with MEG, a group of neurons must fire relatively synchronously, and the cells must be oriented similarly, in a strip or patch of cortex parallel to the surface. This is because the magnetic field generated by each individual neuron's firing is extremely weak and oriented perpendicular to the cell fiber along which the electric potential travels. When a large group of neurons fire, the resulting magnetic fields sum together into a signal strong enough to be observable at the surface if the cells are aligned but can cancel out if misaligned. Similarly, MEG signals are difficult to measure from banks of neurons that are not oriented parallel to the surface (i.e., on the top of a gyrus as opposed to a sulcal wall) or that are deeper within the brain. Second, coordinated timing of the group firing is critical: Asynchronous firing will not generate a large enough magnetic field at any given time to be reliably measured.

In sum, whereas MEG is relatively more sensitive to brief, synchronous group neuronal firing, fMRI is more sensitive to asynchronous firing and also to activations from cells at any orientation. Subsequent investigations will need to specifically address these individual questions, for instance, by using higher resolution fMRI scanning (to discriminate neuronal firing on gyral peaks versus sulcal walls), and relating fMRI and MEG results back to single-unit recording studies (to discriminate group synchronous versus asynchronous activity).

RELATING ANATOMIC CONNECTIVITY AND FUNCTIONAL CONNECTIVITY

Two distinct types of connectivity are being aggressively investigated in the field. The first is *anatomic connectivity*, the locations and characteristics of white matter fiber tracts (axons) that connect cortical areas and serve as the communication conduit for action potentials between neurons. Historically, histological postmortem studies were the primary method of assessing white matter tracts in the human brain, a time-consuming process with limited applicability for looking at neural development. With the advent of MRI, however, scan sequences have been developed for indirectly imaging white matter tracts in vivo. These sequences depend on the natural random diffusion tendencies of water molecules within the brain: They tend to preferentially travel up or down longitudinally within and alongside nerve fibers and do not tend to travel crosswise across fiber tracts because they are physically impeded from doing so. The directional tendencies of water diffusion thus provide a measure that can be used to recreate the location and orientation of fiber tracts in the human brain, and MRI scans employing diffusion tensor imaging protocols (diffusion tensor imaging, or DTI) can now measure these signals.

Second is *functional connectivity*, broadly defined as correlations between remote neurophysiological events, that is, activations (Friston, 1994; Horwitz et al., 1992). The correlations measured in functional connectivity analyses are commonly assumed to reflect causal relationships among processing sites—in its most simple form, activated neurons in one area fire action potentials that travel down axons and cause activations at the remote site. Areas that participate in correlated activity are likely candidates for processing nodes performing distinct functions in a larger network; conversely, absence of correlations between two areas suggests that they are not cooperatively engaging in support of the same cognitive function. Since these analyses are correlation based, they do not prove a direct causal relationship. For instance, a third cortical area may be independently driving the activation in the two observed sites, which then show correlated responses. Still, correlational analysis remains popular because it is readily available and highly suggestive of network architecture, and true causal analyses require either acquisition of additional specific types of data or assumption-laden a priori specification of a processing model.

Linking data about anatomic connectivity and functional connectivity then, should result in a tighter picture of the neural systems underlying reading and reading disability: anatomic connectivity provides information about the underlying hardware available, and functional connectivity informs us as to the way these communication lines are being used for interregional communication. What follows is a restricted review of studies toward this goal.

A growing number of studies are converging on one particular locus for a white matter anomaly in developmental dyslexia. Initially, Klingberg et al. (2000) reported that in a sample of 12 adults (6 good readers and 6 poor readers), measures of diffusion in white matter ("anisotropy") in the left temporoparietal region were significantly correlated with reading ability. This correlation held both across the entire sample as well as within the subgroups of good and poor readers. Klingberg et al. interpreted their findings as reflecting an increased coherence in the microstructure of the white matter tracts in this area in good readers. Subsequently, two studies nearly simultaneously extended this finding to encompass children as well. Deutsch et al. (2005) showed that in 14 children (7 good readers and 7 poor readers) anisotropy in this left temporoparietal region again correlated with several measures of reading ability, spelling, and rapid naming. Beaulieu et al. (2005) reported a similar finding in a broad sample of 32 children (28 average and above average reading ability and 4 below average): Anisotropy in the left temporoparietal region again correlated with reading ability. Niogi and McCandliss (2006) reported on a larger sample of 31 children (20 good readers and 11 poor readers) and replicated the earlier results: Anisotropy within the left temporoparietal area again correlated with reading scores.

Initial interpretation of these findings (Klingberg et al., 2000) suggested the precise locus to be the arcuate fasciculus, a fiber tract that connects inferior frontal cortex (Broca's area) and posterior superior temporal cortex (Wernicke's area), and as such has long been suspected to play a role in reading and reading disability. Following studies allowed the possibility that the difference lies near the boundary of the arcuate fasciculus and the corona radiata, a tract that connects nearby cortical areas to the cerebellum, thalamus, and brain stem (Deutsch et al., 2005). Finally, Dougherty et al. (2007) proposed another possible interpretation, that "exuberant growth" of the posterior portion of the corpus callosum serves to displace fiber tracts in the arcuate fasciculus and/or corona radiata, and the intrusion of differently oriented tracts results in the decreased measures of fiber coherence in this area.

Although the exact location and nature of the white matter tract differences is not yet resolved, the replication of the general effect still invites interpretation with reference to the classic "disconnection syndrome" hypothesis (Dejerine, 1892; Galaburda, Sherman, Rosen, Aboitiz, & Geschwind, 1985; Geschwind, 1965). This approach suggests that it is impaired communication among areas, as opposed to impaired functioning of these areas themselves, that results in reading disability.

Which cortical areas are important for reading? In truth, vast portions of cortex are engaged in full sentential reading, which places demands not only on word identification but also on higher level processing of syntax, semantics, and memory. Given that the core deficit in developmental dyslexia appears to be relatively constrained to single word identification, we can restrict our attention here to a smaller set of regions, primarily in the left hemisphere, implicated by a large body of research (for a review, see Pugh et al., 2001).

1. The area at the junction of the temporal and parietal cortex, posterior to Wernicke's area and including portions of the angular gyrus and supramarginal gyrus, is suggested to employ rule-based analysis, generally enacting grapheme-to-phoneme rules. This area is hypothesized to strongly subserve early reading, when these rules are learned and practiced.
2. At the juncture of the inferior occipital and temporal lobes lies an area often referred to as the ventral word form area or VWFA. This area appears to develop with reading experience to serve as a rapid word-recognition area (Shaywitz et al., 2002), although the extent to which its internal processing is based primarily on visual/orthographic features or also incorporates other aspects of linguistic structure (i.e., phonology, morphology) is still under investigation.
3. An anterior region centered in the inferior frontal gyrus, and including Broca's area, is typically active when phonological manipulations are required; one hypothesized function is for recoding phonological representations into a form applicable for output to speech.

Next, we review the growing literature on functional connectivity among these regions (and others) in developmental dyslexia.

The earliest neuroimaging study to examine functional connectivity in dyslexia was reported by Horwitz, Rumsey, and Donohue (1998). They examined 31 adult men (14 good readers and 17 dyslexics) with positron emission tomography (PET) while they read single words and pseudowords. Importantly, PET imaging is similar to fMRI in that it relies on a vascular measure, regional cerebral blood flow (rCBF). Each subject provides a small number of images that reflect summed activity over a large period of time (i.e., minutes). For typical analysis, images are subtracted from one another to isolate areas that are more or less active in each task or group of subjects. Here, this analysis was complemented by a new method: "The main assumption of this method is that subject-to-subject differences in using a systems-level neural network result in strongly correlated neural activity. … Some subjects may find the task easier than others and thus use the network somewhat less, with the result that there is less rCBF in two functionally connected regions; other subjects use the network more, resulting in more rCBF … the net result is a large within-task, across-subject correlation in rCBF between the two regions" (Horwitz et al., 1998, p. 8939). Indeed, their results showed that across the set of good readers there were strong correlations between the left angular gyrus and several other reading-related sites, including the inferior frontal gyrus, areas of the extrastriate cortex, and temporal lobe. In contrast, the group of dyslexic subjects did show significant correlations between the angular gyrus and these target sites. This suggests that communication among these regions is impaired in the poor readers.

Pugh et al. (2000) followed up on these findings with data from a similar study of adult dyslexics (Shaywitz et al., 1998). Here, a larger sample of 61 unremediated dyslexic adults (32 good readers and 29 dyslexics) was examined with fMRI while they performed multiple different tasks designed to progressively tap the component processes of single word reading: visual-spatial processing (line orientation judgment), orthographic analysis (letter case match), simple phonological transcoding (letter name rhyme judgment), complex phonological sequencing (nonword rhyme judgment), and semantic processing (word relatedness judgment). Connectivity analysis centered on the angular gyrus showed a similar pattern of results as the earlier Horwitz et al. (1998) study. Posterior left hemisphere cortical areas, including striate, extrastriate, and the posterior temporal lobe, showed strong and significant correlations to the angular gyrus in good readers while they were rhyming nonwords—the task that places the highest demands on rule-based grapheme-to-phoneme mapping. By contrast, the dyslexic group showed weak and nonsignificant correlations among these regions. Connectivity analysis (also using the Horwitz across-subjects method) on data from the single-letter rhyme task, however, showed a different pattern: Both groups exhibited reasonable connectivity among these posterior areas. This pattern suggests that connections among these areas may be weak in dyslexics and insufficient to support proficient transcoding of grapheme strings (nonwords), yet additionally implies that they are not completely disrupted and can still support simpler phonological processes.

Hampson et al. (2006) used a different method of assessing functional connectivity with fMRI. While in the scanner, subjects simply read full sentences on the screen for repeated 4 minutes sessions, and a full functional MR image was gathered every second. For each subject separately, the image-to-image time course of activity levels in Broca's area was extracted. This time series was then correlated with the time course of other targeted areas in the brain to assess functional connectivity. The individual subject-by-subject measures were then averaged to obtain composite connectivity scores. Across subjects in general, Broca's area correlated with other areas in the reading system, including posterior aspects of the superior and middle temporal lobes, and the inferior occipitotemporal junction. Most striking, when individual reading subtest scores were compared to these connectivity scores, a clear relationship was found: subjects with lower reading scores showed lower connectivity values between Broca's and the angular gyrus; subjects with higher reading scores showed higher connectivity. This study presents the first report of network connectivity measures within single subjects predicting reading ability.

In an attempt to assess connectivity among a larger set of regions in the reading network, we employed a multivariate connectivity analysis on data gathered from a large set of children (Mencl et al., 2003; Shaywitz et al., 2002). This sample of 144 children was initially scanned while performing several reading-related tasks, including reading real words. For subsequent analysis, we split the sample into older good readers ($N = 27$; mean age, 13.5 years; mean Woodcock–Johnson Word Attack (WJWA) score, 519); younger good readers ($N = 47$; mean age, 9.4 years); older dyslexic readers ($N = 46$; mean age, 14.9 years); and younger dyslexic readers ($N = 24$; mean age, 10.1 years). This allowed us to compute across-subjects functional connectivity measures within each group separately and then compare these measures by age cohort and reading ability in order to identify region-to-region connections within the reading network that change as a function of age and skill. We first isolated primary regions of interest, including Broca's area, a medial and lateral aspect of the inferior occipitotemporal area, the temporoparietal area, and the anterior cingulate gyrus. Initial targeted univariate analyses examined the correlations between the occipitotemporal area and Broca's area in each of the groups. Although all groups showed a numerically positive correlation between these two sites, it was largest and only reached significance in the older good readers. We also observed a weak replication of findings reviewed earlier (Hampson et al., 2006; Horwitz et al., 1998; Pugh et al., 2000): Correlations between the angular gyrus and the occipitotemporal area were numerically stronger in both the younger and older good readers than in the dyslexic groups, although the direct comparisons between reader groups did not reach significance.

Clearly, analysis of this large number of possible bivariate correlations, and the group differences among them, presents analytical problems. We therefore applied a multivariate analysis (partial least squares, or PLS; McIntosh, Bookstein, Haxby, & Grady, 1996) to group these correlations into sets, or components, that change together by age or subject group. These components represent sets of linkages among areas that change together and can be interpreted as shifts in the reading network at a systems level. The first component from this analysis shows group loadings (Figure 5.2B) that reflect a connectivity pattern that increases with age in the nonimpaired readers (a negative loading for the young cohort and a positive loading for the older cohort). Group loadings for the two dyslexic age cohorts are nearer to zero, indicating that this component is not strongly expressed in those subjects. The brain loadings (Figure 5.2A) among a set of areas indicate a positive shift in connectivity in the older cohort, relative to the younger cohort, specifically including the connection between Broca's area and the left occipitotemporal area (connection between LBR and LOT; see the figure caption for full details), and between the left occipitotemporal area and the angular gyrus. This reflects the difference observed in the initial univariate analyses: an increase in functional connectivity between these two areas in the older cohort of good

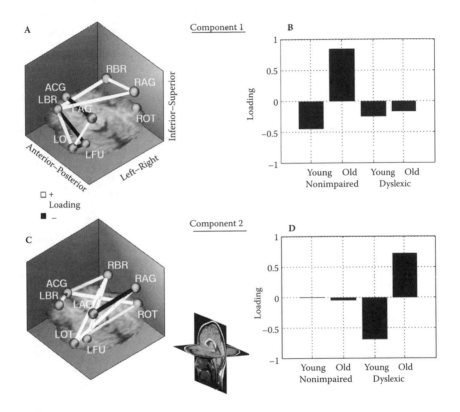

FIGURE 5.2   Results from the PLS analysis of connectivity in four groups of children. Top two panels: (a) brain loadings and (b) group loadings for the first component. Bottom two panels: (c) brain loadings and (d) group loadings for the second component. The eight regions of interest are shown as spheres. Brain loadings between areas are shown as connecting tubes: white indicates positive changes on connectivity; black indicates negative changes in connectivity. The 3-D inset at the bottom shows the orientation of the schematic brains in (a) and (c). LBR, left hemisphere (LH) Broca's area; RBR, right hemisphere (RH) Broca's area homologue; ACG, anterior cingulate gyrus; LTP, LH temporoparietal area; LOT, LH occipitotemporal area; LFU, LH fusiform area; RTP, RH temporoparietal area; ROT, RH temporoparietal area.

readers, compared to the younger cohort. One negative shift should be noted, that between the anterior cingulate gyrus and the left angular gyrus. This effect suggests a reduction in the involvement of the anterior cingulate gyrus in the older cohort. The second component shows group loadings (Figure 5.2D) that indicate a developmental shift in the dyslexic subjects, with near-zero loadings for the good readers. Brain loadings (Figure 5.2C) show a dramatically different set of changes in connectivity: Broadly, the left occipitotemporal and fusiform areas are increasing connectivity with *right hemisphere* homologues of regions in the reading system. Further, the anterior cingulate gyrus shows higher connectivity to bilateral inferior frontal gyrus and to the right hemisphere occipitotemporal area. Clearly, interpretation of these entire patterns of correlational shifts would be difficult and fraught with assumptions. However, the prominent aspects of these results make sense with reference to the theorized roles of the regions involved. First, older good readers increase the functional linkage between the occipitotemporal area and Broca's area, suggesting an increased integration of the skill-based input site with the frontal output system with age. Second, the older dyslexic readers increase linkage of the anterior cingulate gyrus into the reading network, highly suggestive of a more attentionally demanding, effortful style of reading. Further, the increased linkage of the occipitotemporal areas with right hemisphere regions is compatible with earlier observations of the engagement of the contralateral hemisphere for alternative processing strategies in dyslexics (c.f. Shaywitz et al., 2002). This analysis thus presents an initial attempt to integrate knowledge of the processing roles of cortical regions with functional connectivity analysis at the level of the reading network as a whole.

   In summary, research on white matter connectivity appears to be converging on a relatively small zone for differences in dyslexia—the left posterior temporoparietal cortex. Research on the functional connections among regions suggests more numerous differences, yet strongly implicates connections with posterior regions as well, particularly connections involving the left hemisphere angular gyrus, the occipitotemporal area, and Broca's area. One testable hypothesis for future work is that the functional connectivity differences observed in dyslexia—even between remote regions—are a result of degraded information transfer through the specific white matter tracts identified by anatomic studies. Finally, relating the hypothesized processing roles of these regions to available anatomic and functional connectivity data provides the elements for specifying more precisely a neurological basis of developmental dyslexia.

ACKNOWLEDGMENTS

Portions of this work were supported by NICHD grants HD-01994 and HD-048830.

REFERENCES

Beaulieu, C., Plewes, C., Paulson, L. A., Roy, D., Snook, L, Concha, L., & Philips, L. (2005). Imaging brain connectivity in children with diverse reading ability. *NeuroImage, 25*, 1266–1271.

Billingsley-Marshall, R., Clear, T., Mencl, W. E., Simos, P. G., Swank, P. R., Men, D., et al. (2007). A comparison of functional MRI and magnetoencephalography for receptive language mapping. *Journal of Neuroscience Methods, 161*, 306–313.

Dejerine, J. (1892). Contribution a l'etude anatomo-pathologique et clinique des differentes varietes de cecite verbale. *Memoires de la Societede Biologie, 4*, 61–90.

Deutsch, G. K., Dougherty, R. F., Bammer, R., Siok, W. T., Gabrieli, J. D. E., & Wandell, B. (2005). Children's reading performance is correlated with white matter structure measured by diffusion tensor imaging. *Cortex, 41*, 354–363.

Dougherty, R. F., Ben-Shachar, M. B., Deutsch, G. K., Hernandez, A., Fox, G. R., & Wandell, B. A. (2007). Temporal-callosal pathway diffusivity predicts phonological skills in children. *Proceedings of the National Academy of Sciences, 104*(20), 8556–8561.

Friston, K. (1994). Functional and effective connectivity in neuroimaging: A synthesis. *Human Brain Mapping, 2*, 56–78.

Galaburda, A. M., Sherman, G. F., Rosen, G. D., Aboitiz, F., & Geschwind, N. (1985). Developmental dyslexia: Four consecutive patients with cortical anomalies. *Annals of Neurology, 18*, 222–233.

Geschwind, N. (1965). Disconnexion syndromes in animals and man. *Brain, 88*, 237–294.

Hampson, M., Tokoglu, F., Sun, Z., Schafer, R., Skudlarski, P., Gore, J. C., et al. (2006). Connectivity-behaviour analysis reveals that functional connectivity between left BA39 and Broca's area varies with reading ability. *NeuroImage, 31*, 513–519.

Horwitz, B., Grady, C. L., Haxby, J. V., Schapiro, M. B., Rapoporrt, S. I., Ungerleider, L. G., et al. (1992). Functional associations among human posterior extrastriate brain regions during object and spatial vision. *Journal of Cognitive Neuroscience, 4*, 311–322.

Horwitz, B., Rumsey, J. M., & Donohue, B. C. (1998). Functional connectivity of the angular gyrus in normal reading and dyslexia. *Proceedings of the National Academy of Sciences, 95*, 8939–8944.

Klingberg, T., Hedehus, M., Temple, E., Salz, T., Gabrieli, J. D., Moseley, M. E., et al. (2000). Microstructure of temporo-parietal white matter as a basis for reading ability: Evidence from diffusion tensor magnetic resonance imaging. *Neuron, 25*, 493–500.

McIntosh, A. R., Bookstein, F. I.., Haxby, J. V., & Grady, C. L. (1996). Spatial pattern analysis of functional brain images using partial least squares. *NeuroImage, 3*, 143–157.

Mencl, W. E., Shaywitz, B., Shaywitz, S., Pugh, K., Fulbright, R., Skudlarski, P., et al. (2003). Functional connectivity of brain regions in good and poor readers. Paper presented at the ninth annual meeting of the Society for Human Brain Mapping, New York, May 2003; *NeuroImage, 19*(2), 2628–2629.

Niogi, S. N., & McCandliss, B. D. (2006). Left lateralized white matter microstructure accounts for individual differences in reading ability and disability. *Neuropsychologia, 44*, 2178–2188.

Papanicolaou, A. C., Simos, P. G., Castillo, E. M., Breier, J. I., Sarkari, S., Pataraia, E., et al. (2004). Magnetocephalography: A non-invasive alternative to the Wada procedure. *Journal of Neurosurgery, 100*(5), 867–876.

Pugh, K. R., Mencl, W. E., Jenner, A. J., Lee, J. R., Katz, L., Frost, S., et al. (2001). Neuroimaging studies of reading and reading disability. *Learning Disabilities Research and Practice, 16*(4), 240–249.

Pugh, K. R., Mencl, W. E., Shaywitz, B. A., Shaywitz, S. E., Fulbright, R. K., Skudlarski, P., et al. (2000). The angular gyrus in developmental dyslexia: Task-specific differences in functional connectivity in posterior cortex. *Psychological Science, 11*, 51–56.

Shaywitz, B. A., Shaywitz, S. E., Pugh, K. R., Mencl, W. E., Fulbright, R. K., Skudlarski, P., et al. (2002). Disruption of posterior brain systems in children with developmental dyslexia. *Biological Psychiatry, 52*(2), 101–110.

Shaywitz, S. E., Shaywitz, B. A., Pugh, K. R., Fulbright, R. K., Constable, R. T., Mencl, W. E., et al. (1988). Functional disruption in the organization of the brain for reading in dyslexia. *Proceedings of the National Academy of Sciences, 95*, 2636–2641.

6 Computational Modeling and the Neural Bases of Reading and Reading Disorders

Jay G. Rueckl and Mark S. Seidenberg

As the content of this volume reveals, considerable progress has been made in understanding basic reading processes through extensive behavioral and neuroimaging studies of normal and impaired reading. This research has led to the development of detailed models of word reading, reading acquisition, and the bases of reading impairments. As many researchers have noted, writing systems afford two ways of determining the meanings of words: by mapping from spelling to meaning (the "direct" route) or by mapping from spelling to an intermediate phonological code and then to meaning (phonologically mediated access). The origin of the term *dual-route model* is obscure, but the concept of visual and phonological procedures was discussed as early as Baron and Strawson (1976; cf. Carr & Pollatsek, 1985; Seidenberg, 1985). Research within this framework has focused on the properties of these routes, and how their use differs as a function of factors such as type of word (e.g., high or low frequency), type of writing system (deep or shallow), and reader skill (see Seidenberg, 1995, for review).[1]

One of the major theoretical approaches that has emerged from this research is a theory of normal and disordered reading based on principles of the connectionist or parallel distributed processing (PDP) framework (Harm & Seidenberg, 1999, 2004; Plaut, McClelland, Seidenberg, & Patterson, 1996; Seidenberg & McClelland, 1989). This theory has been implemented as a series of computational models that simulate different aspects of reading; they are collectively referred to as the "triangle" model. Specific principles on which the model is based (e.g., statistical learning of mappings between orthographic, phonological, and semantic codes; cooperative division of labor between components) are relevant to interpreting evidence concerning brain mechanisms. The modeling framework can be used to generate behavioral and neuroimaging predictions about different types of words, individual differences among readers, how properties of orthographies influence reading, the bases of developmental and acquired reading impairments, and other central questions. Specific predictions aside, the model provides a way of thinking about how the brain solves the computational problem of reading efficiently and a way of interpreting neuroimaging data.

The purpose of this chapter is to explain this approach and to discuss its implications for future research. Along the way, we describe how computational models are implemented, review key insights that have emerged from simulations of the triangle model, and demonstrate how these insights can be used to interpret the results of neuroimaging studies.

CONNECTIONISM AND COMPUTATIONAL MODELING

Connectionist models are sometimes called neurally inspired because they incorporate structures and processes that are meant to mirror—at a quite abstract level—those found in the brain.[2] Thus, a connectionist network is composed of many simple, neuron-like processing units called *nodes* that communicate by sending excitatory and inhibitory signals to one another. Each signal is weighted by the strength of the connection that it is sent across, and the state of each node (its *activation*) is a nonlinear function of the sum of these weighted signals. Like neural synapses, the connections in a network are plastic, and a learning algorithm is used to adjust their strengths (or *weights*) such that, over the course of learning, the flow of activation becomes tailored to the structure and task demands of the environment in which the network is embedded (for overviews, see Elman et al., 1996; Rumelhart, Hinton, & Williams, 1986).

To model a specific cognitive process, this general theoretical framework must be augmented by domain-specific facts and conditions. In the case of reading, the essential facts concern the relationships between the spellings, sounds, and meanings of words (orthography, phonology, and semantics). As is clear from the triangle representation (see Figure 6.1), each code can be computed directly from another code or indirectly via the remaining code. The semantic code, for example can be computed directly from orthography or indirectly via phonology (spelling–sound–meaning). The phonological code can be computed directly from orthography or indirectly via semantics (spelling–meaning–sound). These facts follow from the nature of spoken language (mappings between sound and meaning) and the nature of writing systems (written symbols are associated with both sounds and meanings).[3] These facts have been widely noted and incorporated in many reading models. Disagreements have focused on issues such as how these codes are represented (e.g., word-specific vs. distributed representations) and the extent to which the different pathways are involved in determining the meaning or pronunciation of a word.

In the triangle model, the relations among the codes are embodied by the architecture of the model. As depicted in Figure 6.1, the model includes distinct layers of nodes responsible for representing the orthographic, semantic, and phonological properties of written words. In each layer, the patterns of activation that represent different words are chosen so that words that are similar on the relevant linguistic dimension are represented by similar patterns of activation.

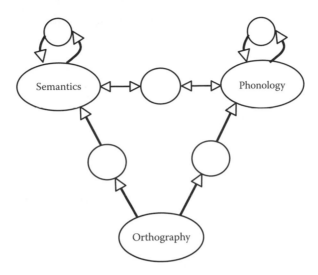

FIGURE 6.1   The triangle model (adapted from Harm & Seidenberg, 2004).

Thus, similarly spelled words are represented by similar patterns of activation over the orthographic layer, semantically similar words are represented by similar patterns of activation over the semantic layer, and so on. The nodes in these layers communicate with one another via the sets of connections (and "hidden units," which will be discussed in more detail later) depicted in the figure. Seeing a word causes its corresponding pattern of activation to be instated over the orthographic layer. Activation then propagates to the phonological and semantic layers via the connections and hidden units (which are discussed in more detail later) depicted in Figure 6.1. Note that the inclusion of the phon⇔sem pathway entails that the computation of word meaning is, in part, mediated by phonological knowledge and, conversely, that the computation of a word's pronunciation is, in part, mediated by semantic knowledge.

An important tool for connectionists in general, and for proponents of the triangle model in particular, is computational modeling. The term *computational modeling* refers to the implementation of cognitive theories as computer simulations. There are a number of motivations for implementing theories in this way. First, simulations require a far more explicit theoretical description than is typically provided by traditional box-and-arrow models. Second, the behavior of a connectionist network is a consequence of complex, nonlinear interactions among a large number of components. Simulations provide a means of verifying that the model works as advertised; they can also lead to new insights about the nature of the underlying mechanism. Finally, simulations are a form of experimentation, allowing the modeler to investigate the effects of various sorts of manipulations. In the case of dyslexia, simulations have explored both hypotheses about possible underlying causes for the deficit and the effectiveness of various remediation strategies (Harm, McCandliss, & Seidenberg, 2003).

Simulations of connectionist models involve three steps: the initial specification of the model, training, and testing and analysis. During the first step the modeler specifies the network's architecture, and activation and learning functions; the structure of the task environment; and the representational scheme for the network's input and outputs (i.e., the relationship between patterns of activation within the network and properties of its environment, including the actions it can take). The purpose of a simulation is to determine how these factors jointly determine the network's behavior. Thus, during the training phase the network is presented with a series of inputs, responds to each in turn, and adjusts its pattern of connectivity in accordance with its learning rule. At any point during the course of training, the modeler can employ a variety of behavioral and analytic tools to ask how the network is behaving and why it is behaving in the way that it is.

Over the last two decades a number of simulations of the triangle model have been conducted. Often these simulations focus on a single leg of the triangle (either orth⇒phon, e.g., Plaut et al., 1996; Seidenberg & McClelland, 1989; or orth⇒sem, e.g., Plaut & Gonnerman, 2000; Plaut & Shallice, 1993; Rueckl & Raveh, 1999), but recently several simulations of the full model have been reported (Harm & Seidenberg, 2004; Kello & Plaut, 2003). In many cases the network was trained on a set of real English words (Harm & Seidenberg, 2004; Plaut et al., 1996; Seidenberg & McClelland, 1989), but simulations involving Chinese (Yang, Zevin, Shu, McCandliss, & Li, 2006) and artificial vocabularies (Plaut & Gonnerman, 2000; Rueckl & Raveh, 1999) have also been conducted. Collectively, these simulations have been used to study a wide variety of tasks and phenomena, including word and nonword naming (Kello & Plaut, 2003; Plaut et al., 1996; Seidenberg & McClelland, 1989), reading for meaning (Harm & Seidenberg, 2004), the role of morphology in reading (Plaut & Gonnerman, 2000; Rueckl & Raveh, 1999), the effects of brain damage on reading (Plaut, 1995; Plaut & Shallice, 1993), developmental dyslexia (Harm & Seidenberg, 1999), and the effects of educational and remediational practices (Harm et al., 2003).[4]

Given the number and range of these simulations, we have chosen not to provide a comprehensive review (for this, the reader is referred to Harm & Seidenberg, 2004, and Seidenberg, 2005). Instead, our intention is to use some of the simulation results to illustrate how the network's behavior embodies the consequences of several critical computational principles. We then discuss the insights these principles provide about recent behavioral and neuroimaging results, as well as the implications of these principles for the direction of future research.

COMPUTATIONAL PRINCIPLES

THE IMPORTANCE OF STATISTICAL STRUCTURE

Learning attunes a connectionist network to the structure of its environment. In the case of reading, this structure involves the frequency and consistency of the correspondence between the orthographic, phonological, and semantic properties of written words. Simulations of the triangle model have demonstrated the close relationship between the network's behavior and the statistical structure of the task environment and highlighted the differences between the triangle model and other conceptions of the word identification process.

Many of the simulations have focused on the mapping between orthography and phonology. This mapping is "quasiregular" in the sense that correspondences between the components of written and spoken words vary in the degree to which they are correlated, and the correlations are rarely perfect. For example, -ILL is always pronounced /il/ (as in PILL), and -INT is usually pronounced /int/ (as in MINT)—except that in the context of P- it is pronounced /Int/ (PINT)—but OUGH is pronounced differently in the contexts R-, C-, D-, PL-, THR-, and coda –T. Simulations have shown that the behavior of the triangle model reflects this fact: The speed with which a word can be named depends on whether the pronunciation of its body is consistent with the pronunciation of other words containing the same body. As is the case for human readers, the effects of orth⇒phon consistency are inversely related to word frequency, decrease as reading skill increases, and occur in both word and nonword naming (see Plaut et al., 1996, and Seidenberg & McClelland, 1989, for relevant simulation results and discussions of related behavioral findings).

The mapping from orthography to semantics is less systematic than the one from orthography to phonology, but even in this mapping statistical structure exists, particularly in the form of morphological regularities. That is, while in general there is no correlation between orthographic and semantic similarity, morphologically related words tend to both look alike and overlap in meaning (contrast BAKE, TAKE, and LAKE with BAKE, BAKER, and BAKERY). Simulations (e.g., Plaut & Gonnerman, 2000; Rueckl & Raveh, 1999) have shown that the triangle model can take advantage of these regularities, sometimes in rather subtle ways. For example, Plaut and Gonnerman (2000) showed that in their model morphological priming (the influence of seeing one word on the recognition of a subsequently presented morphological relative) depends not only on the joint orthographic–semantic similarity of the prime and target, but also on the "morphological richness" of the language. Priming was more robust if the network was trained on a language that contains a great deal of morphological structure (like Hebrew) than on a language in which morphological regularities are less frequent (like English).

THE DIVISION OF LABOR

In dual-route models a central issue concerns relations between the proposed pathways. The architecture of these models entailed that the visual and phonological pathways to meaning operated independently and in parallel. However, there were different views about which pathway would dominate in normal skilled reading. Some researchers (e.g., Coltheart, 1978, and subsequently) assumed that the visual pathway was faster in virtue of being more direct; moreover, the phonological pathway was thought to be unreliable given the irregularities in English spelling–sound correspondences. Other researchers concluded that each pathway would tend to succeed for some types of words (e.g., direct: high-frequency words, words with irregular pronunciations; phonologically mediated: words with "rule-governed" pronunciations).

In the Coltheart, Rastle, Perry, Langdon, & Ziegler (2001) dual-route cascade (DRC) model, the two pathways mapping between orthography and phonology are not independent. Both pathways contribute to the activation of phonemes that are used in pronouncing a word or nonword. The routes involve different types of knowledge and processes (rules vs. an interactive-activation model). These built-in differences between the routes determine the division of labor between them, with exceptions handled lexically and nonwords nonlexically. As the 2001 model was implemented, the two routes interact very little in processing words, because the nonlexical route finishes much more slowly than the lexical route.

The triangle model incorporates a different idea: There is a cooperative division of labor such that input from all parts of the system jointly determines both what a word means and how it is pronounced. In the Harm and Seidenberg (2004) model, for example, the meaning of a word is activated by input from both orth⇒sem and orth⇒phon⇒sem parts of the triangle. This cooperative computation is possible because the same types of representations (distributed) and processing mechanisms (spread of activation) are used in all parts of the model. Thus, both orthographic and phonological units can activate semantic units. Harm and Seidenberg (2004) term this property *representational homogeneity*. The division of labor between the pathways emerges as the model learns to compute from orthography to meaning quickly and efficiently.

Harm and Seidenberg (2004) reported an extensive series of simulations exploring the division of labor in the triangle model, focusing primarily on the computation of word meaning. Using a variety of measures (including direct measures of the input the semantic units receive from other parts of the network, as well as the behavioral effects of lesions removing one or the other pathway), they confirmed that semantic activation depends on the cooperative interactions of the orth⇒sem and orth⇒phon⇒sem pathways. Their findings demonstrated that the semantic units receive significant input from both orth⇒sem and orth⇒phon⇒sem for almost all words, and that the model with both pathways intact computes meanings more efficiently than the paths do independently. Their results also revealed that the division of labor is affected by lexical properties such as frequency and spelling–sound consistency. On average, the isolated orth⇒sem and orth⇒phon⇒sem pathways were equally likely to compute the correct meaning of a low-frequency consistent word. In contrast, the orth⇒sem pathway was more accurate for high-frequency words and for low-frequency inconsistent words.

Two other findings that emerged from the Harm and Seidenberg (2004) simulations are particularly important. First, the division of labor changed over the course of learning. Early on, the model's behavior was controlled by the orth⇒phon⇒sem pathway; as learning progressed and the orth⇒sem pathway became more efficient, the model moved toward a more cooperative division of labor. Second, even at the end of training, the computation of phonology enjoys certain advantages over the computation of meaning: It occurs more rapidly, is less sensitive to visual masking, and so forth. These characteristics of the network's behavior relate well to findings concerning the primacy of phonological codes in reading acquisition (Jorm & Share, 1983; Liberman & Shankweiler, 1985), the central role of phonology in skilled reading (Frost, 1995; Van Orden, Pennington, & Stone, 1990), and the close link between phonological deficits and impairments in reading acquisition (Fletcher et al., 1994; Snowling, 1991; Stanovich & Siegel, 1994).

The prominent role of phonology in both skilled reading and reading acquisition is a reflection of the fact that spelling and pronunciation are more highly correlated than spelling and meaning (Van Orden et al., 1990). However, with sufficient practice, the model picks up on mappings between spelling and meaning. The resulting division of labor therefore reflects characteristics of all of the mappings between codes, which vary from less predictable (orth⇒sem, phon⇒sem) to more predictable (orth⇒phon). These aspects of the model's performance highlight the important role of statistical structure in determining its behavior, but statistics are not the whole story. Another crucial factor is that the triangle model employs a *compensatory learning* procedure.

COMPENSATORY LEARNING

In the triangle model, learning is error driven, that is, changes in the strengths of the connections are based on the difference between the actual response of the model to an input and the ideal response given that input. Error (the difference between the actual and ideal responses) is generated whenever the network cannot produce the correct response or does so too slowly. In a system where input converges from several sources, the response of the network depends on the joint influence of those inputs, and thus the learning that occurs in one component of the network depends on the successes and failures of other components. In the triangle model, for example, the learning that occurs within the orth⇒sem pathway will depend on how quickly and accurately the orth⇒phon⇒sem pathway can activate the meaning of a written word. If the correct meaning can be generated rapidly by the orth⇒phon⇒sem pathway alone, little learning will take place within the orth⇒sem pathway. In contrast, if the orth⇒phon⇒sem pathway is not up to the job, the orth⇒sem pathway can learn to compensate for this deficiency. This type of learning contrasts with mechanisms that are correlative rather than driven by error, the classic example being Hebbian learning (Hebb, 1949). In such systems, learning of an item by one component (e.g., orth⇒sem) would be independent of the success or failure of other components (e.g., orth⇒phon⇒sem).

Compensatory learning is what allows the triangle model to maximize the cooperative interactions among its components. To illustrate this point, consider how the model learns to compute the meaning of a homophone. Under normal presentation conditions, homophones are disambiguated through the use of both orth⇒sem and orth⇒phon⇒sem. The isolated orth⇒phon⇒sem pathway can produce correct patterns for higher frequency, dominant homophones. In the intact model, however, orth⇒sem also delivers relevant activation quickly, particularly for higher frequency words. The role of orth⇒sem is shaped by the fact that the orth⇒phon⇒sem pathway cannot accurately compute both meanings of a homophone pair. The latter pathway eventually becomes more tuned to the higher frequency member of a pair because it is trained more often; however, orth→sem also processes these words effectively and so contributes significantly.

LEARNED HIDDEN REPRESENTATIONS

The triangle model employs two kinds of representations: The representations over the visible layers (i.e., the orthographic, phonological, and semantic layers) are stipulated by the modeler and (as noted earlier) are designed to capture certain kinds of similarity. In contrast, the modeler makes no a priori assumptions about the patterns of activation over the hidden layers; instead, the organization of these representations emerges from the learning process that adjusts the pattern of connectivity to improve the network's performance. The choice of stipulated representations is nontrivial, and significant advances have been made by considering the consequences of different representational schemes (see, for example, Plaut et al.'s, 1996, discussion of the implications of different means of representing the serial position of the letters or phonemes in a word). That being said, we believe that in the long run the properties of the learned hidden representations will be of greater theoretical significance. For example, as we discuss later, these properties suggest certain hypotheses about the function of the cortical circuits that underlie skilled (and disordered) word recognition. More broadly, the principles that determine how hidden representations are organized provide a means for paying back the "loan on intelligence" that is taken out when a theory stipulates what a person knows and how that knowledge is represented (Rueckl, 2002).

Hidden representations are necessary for the computation of some input–output mappings (the exclusive-OR task being the most well known, see Rumelhart et al., 1986), but in principle hidden units can play a role in the computation of any mapping. In particular, hidden units mediate the mapping computed by each leg (orth⇒phon, orth⇒sem, and phon⇒sem) of the triangle model, and simulations of the triangle model (and other connectionist models) have begun to yield insights about characteristics of learned hidden representations. One important insight is that the hidden representations are as *componential* as the prevailing conditions allow. That is, if there are statistical regularities involving components of an input (e.g., letters, word bodies, morphemes), the patterns of activation over the hidden units representing that input will contain (more or less) subpatterns corresponding to these components. Another key insight is that the hidden representations are organized to capture both similarities among the input patterns and similarities among the responses to which these inputs must be mapped. Thus, for example, the hidden units mediating the orth⇒phon mapping are organized such that words that are similar in spelling (LAKE, TAKE) have relatively similar hidden representations, but so too do words that are similar in pronunciation (BEAR,

BARE). Taken together, these characteristics provide the network with an efficient means for dealing with quasiregularity. For example, by positioning the representation of PINT somewhere near—but not too near—the representations of MINT and HINT, the network can take advantage of the similarities among these words (namely, that NT is pronounced /nt/) while also ensuring that PINT isn't pronounced as a rhyme of MINT. Similarly, learned hidden representations also provide a means for the network to generalize its knowledge to novel situations—for example, generating a plausible pronunciation of the nonword ZINT.

A number of simulations of the triangle model have explored how factors such as phonological consistency (Plaut et al., 1996; Seidenberg & McClelland, 1989) and morphological structure (Rueckl & Raveh, 1999) influence the organization of its hidden units. One noteworthy finding was reported by Harm et al. (2003) in a simulation exploring hypotheses concerning the effectiveness of various intervention methods designed to overcome developmental reading disorders. The simulation implemented the orth⇒phon leg of the triangle model and the model was trained to pronounce English words. To instantiate the hypothesis that dyslexia is an anomaly related to the representation of phonology, half of the connections among the phonological nodes were eliminated before training began. This manipulation renders the phonological system less able to clean up noisy input, and thus puts more pressure on the orth⇒phon connections to deliver precise input to the phonological layer. A comparison of this model's behavior to that of an intact network revealed that both networks correctly pronounced a high percentage of the words from their training set, but the impaired network was much worse at reading nonwords. Analysis of the hidden representations showed why: The impaired network's hidden representations were more holistic and less clustered by phonological similarity. As a consequence, the mapping from the hidden layer to the phonological representations was more idiosyncratic in the impaired model, and although experience with familiar words allowed the network to associate the hidden patterns for these words with their correct pronunciations, this knowledge could not be effectively generalized when the network was confronted with an unfamiliar input.

One surprising aspect of these results concerns the specificity of the input the phonological units receive from the hidden layer. One might suppose that the problems associated with dyslexia arise because the orthographic processes provide relatively noisy input to the phonological system, and that the nonword reading is more impaired than word reading because top-down knowledge can compensate somewhat for this degraded bottom-up input. However, the Harm et al. (2003) simulations suggest the opposite conclusion. Harm et al. compared the pattern of hidden-layer input to the phonological layer to the pattern of activation representing the pronunciation of each word. They found that these patterns were more similar in the impaired network than in the intact model. Thus, at least in this case, the deficit in reading skill was associated with hyperspecific inputs to the phonological level, not the sort of degraded inputs one might have expected. This finding not only points to the subtle properties of the learned hidden representations, but also to the importance of the compensatory nature of the learning mechanism. The reason that the bottom-up input needed to be more exact is that the impaired network had fewer resources available (in the form of connections among the clean-up units) to compensate for any imprecision in the input to the phonological system. This result could also help explain the inconsistent evidence concerning the relationship between phonological processing and dyslexia—mild impairments in phonological processing that may be difficult to observe in commonly used tests of phonological processing could still have significant consequences on the reading acquisition process (see Harm & Seidenberg, 1999, as well as the following discussion).

THE TRIANGLE MODEL AND THE NEURAL BASES OF WRITTEN WORD RECOGNITION

The development of the triangle model has centered primarily on behavioral studies of skilled adult readers. That is, for the most part, simulation studies have examined how closely the behavior of the model mirrors that of participants in experiments studying skilled word recognition, and to a large extent the experiments that have been conducted to test the predictions of the model have focused on the behavior of skilled readers. In contrast, although there have been some simulations addressing findings concerning the neural bases of reading (e.g., Plaut et al., 1996; Plaut & Shallice, 1993), there has not yet been a serious attempt to ground the model in the wealth of recent findings concerning the brain mechanisms that support reading, nor is there a large number of brain-based experiments directly inspired by the triangle model.

In this section we discuss the relationship between the triangle model and evidence concerning the neural underpinnings of word recognition. In the last several decades, the development of neuroimaging techniques—in particular, functional magnetic resonance imaging (fMRI) and positron emission tomography (PET)—led to rapid growth in our understanding of the neural underpinnings of reading. The neuroimaging evidence points toward three major left hemisphere (LH) components, each of which contains functionally dissociable subregions: a *posterior ventral* circuit including lateral extrastriate areas and a left inferior occipitotemporal (OT) area; a *posterior dorsal* circuit including the angular gyrus and supramarginal gyrus (SMG) in the inferior parietal lobule and the posterior aspect of the superior temporal gyrus (Wernicke's area); and an *anterior* circuit centered in and around Broca's area in the inferior frontal gyrus (IFG; see S. Frost et al., this volume.)

Inferences concerning the computational role of each region are based on evidence concerning the effects of factors such as lexical status (word–pseudoword), word frequency, and task (e.g., reading aloud vs. reading for meaning). This evidence suggests that the dorsal and anterior systems support phonological processes such as spelling-to-sound decoding and overt naming. These regions are strongly activated during phonologically oriented tasks (e.g., rhyme judgments) and in beginning readers (who are thought to be strongly reliant on phonological recoding). In addition, activation in the anterior region is inversely correlated with phonological consistency (Fiez, Balota, Raichle, & Petersen, 1999; Frost et al., 2005; Herbster, Mintun, Nebes, & Becker, 1997), as would be expected of circuits underlying phonological processes in reading. Within the ventral system, the more anterior (middle temporal gyrus [MTG] and ITG) components appear to be semantically tuned: These regions tend to be strongly activated by tasks that recruit semantic processes (Price, Moore, Humphreys, & Wise, 1997; Rossell, Price, & Nobre, 2003); similarly, activation in these regions is correlated with semantic variables such as imageability (Frost et al., 2005; Sandak et al., 2004). In contrast, activation of OT is relatively unaffected by semantic variables, but is influenced by orthographic factors (Cornelissen, Tarkiainen, Helenius, & Salmelin, 2003; Dehaene, Cohen, Sigman, & Vinckier, 2005; Devlin, Jamison, Gonnerman, & Matthews, 2006; Vinckier et al., 2007) as well as variables such as frequency and lexicality (Fiebach, Friederici, Muller, & von Cramon, 2002; Kronbichler et al., 2004). Hence, this region is often described as the visual word form area (VWFA; Dehaene, Le Clec'H, Poline, Bihan, & Cohen, 2002; McCandliss, Cohen, & Dehaene, 2003).

At a broad level, then, the neuroimaging evidence suggests that the cortical reading system involves two major subsystems: a dorsal-anterior circuit that maps written words onto their phonological forms and a ventral circuit that computes the meanings of written words directly (that is, without phonological mediation). This is a comforting result in that it comports with a large body of behavioral findings and computational considerations that lead to the same conclusion. It is also suggestive of a mapping between the components of the triangle model and subcircuits of the cortical reading system. Specifically, we hypothesize that the role of the orthographic input units in the model is subserved by the occipitotemporal juncture (OT), that the orth⇒sem pathway in the model is embodied by the cortical pathway including the OT and the more anterior regions of the ventral system (MTG and ITG), and that the orth⇒phon leg of the model is instantiated by a cortical circuit that includes the OT and components of the dorsal and anterior subsystems (SMG and IFG, respectively). In light of this hypothesis, it is interesting to note that like the orth⇒phon subsystem in the triangle model, the dorsal-anterior pathway develops earlier in reading acquisition, is more strongly implicated in phonological processing, and operates less efficiently in less skilled readers (Pugh et al., 2000; Turkeltaub et al., 2003). Similarly, like orth⇒sem in the model, the ventral system develops more slowly but is more strongly implicated in skilled performance.

Thus, the hypothesized mapping between the triangle model and the cortical reading system seems like a reasonable first approximation. However, it should also be noted that others (e.g., Fiebach et al., 2002; Jobard, Crivello, Tzourio-Mazoyer, 2003) have interpreted the neuroimaging evidence in terms of more traditional dual-route models—models that are based on different computational principles, hold that the direct and phonological routes operate largely or completely independently of one another, and assume that the phonological route plays a relatively minor role in skilled word recognition, particularly when reading for meaning (e.g.,

Coltheart, 1978; Coltheart et al., 2001). To a certain extent, adjudicating between these views will be a question for future research. However, a consideration of the available evidence provides support for the triangle-model interpretation. Next, we consider evidence related to three issues: interactions between phonology and semantics in skilled word recognition, learning-related changes in brain activation, and the organization of representations in the OT/VWFA.

Interactions Between Phonology and Semantics

According to the triangle model, word recognition is achieved through coopera-tive interactions among the components of the reading system. These interactions are shaped by a compensatory learning mechanism that allows the contribu-tion of one pathway to make up for deficiencies in the other. For example, the orth⇒sem pathway plays an especially important role in computing the mean-ing of a low-frequency homophone (e.g., EWE) because the connectivity of the orth⇒phon⇒sem pathway is tuned to compute the meaning of its higher fre-quency partner (YOU).

Thus, one signature of the cooperative division of labor is that the contribution of one pathway is stronger when the contribution of the other pathways is deficient. Given the fairly large number of neuroimaging studies of reading that have now been conducted, it is noteworthy that very few have attempted to look for such a signature—perhaps because the strategy has most often been to gather evidence that might isolate the specific contribution of various key cortical regions rather than focusing on the coordination among these regions. One exception is a study by Frost et al. (2005) that used fMRI to investigate the neural underpinnings of the Strain effect—a behavioral phenomenon first reported by Strain, Patterson, and Seidenberg (1995).

Strain et al. (1995) conducted a behavioral study examining the interaction between semantic and phonological influences on spoken word naming. To do so, they varied imageability (a semantic variable associated with the richness of a word's meaning), spelling-to-sound consistency (a phonological variable), and word frequency. Strain et al. found that the effect of consistency (consistent words named faster and more accurately than inconsistent words) was largest for words that are low in both frequency and imageability, and that the effect of imageabil-ity (high-imageable words named faster and more accurately than low-imageable words) occurred for low-frequency inconsistent words but not for low-frequency consistent words. This pattern of results suggests that word naming relies on both the orth⇒phon and orth⇒sem⇒phon pathways and that the influence of each pathway is most pronounced when the other pathway is slowest and most error prone. Thus, this pattern is a manifestation of the cooperative interactions between the phonological and semantic pathways posited by the triangle model. (It is worth noting that simulations of the triangle model confirmed that its behav-ior exhibits this same pattern; Harm & Seidenberg, 2004.)

Frost et al. (2005) used fMRI to identify the neurobiological correlates of the Strain et al. (1995) findings. The stimuli included low-frequency words that varied in imageability and spelling-to-sound consistency. These critical words were presented in a sequence that also included nonword fillers, and participants were instructed to read aloud the words but not the nonwords. The behavioral results revealed the Consistency × Imageability interaction found by Strain et al. In the fMRI analyses, higher activation for high-imageable words was found in the middle temporal gyrus (MTG) and the angular gyrus (AG)—regions that are often associated with semantic effects in reading (e.g., Price et al., 1997; Rossell et al., 2003). In contrast, as had previously been reported by Fiez et al. (1999) and Herbster et al. (1997), higher activation for inconsistent relative to consistent words was found in the IFG. Critically, this consistency effect was modulated by imageability: Imageability was associated with reduced consistency-related activation in IFG. This interaction appears to be the principal neural signature of the behavioral trade-off between semantics and phonology revealed by Strain and colleagues.

In addition to illuminating the division of labor among the cortical subsystems that underlie skilled reading, the Strain effect has also proven to be a useful tool for shedding light on reading disability. In a recent study, Pugh et al. (in press) observed that compared to nonimpaired controls, reading disabled adolescents exhibited an exaggerated Strain effect: Both groups benefited from high frequency and high imageability when reading difficult-to-decode inconsistent words, but these benefits were more pronounced for the disabled readers. The neurobiological underpinnings of this difference were examined by an analysis contrasting hemodynamic responses to the easiest (high-frequency/high-imageable/inconsistent) and hardest (low-frequency/low-imageable/inconsistent) words. For nonimpaired readers, the easier words were associated with relatively reduced activation in most of the critical cortical reading circuits. In contrast, for reading-disabled individuals, easier words were associated primarily with heightened activation at key LH reading-related regions. An analogous pattern was observed in a second experiment, in which stimulus repetition was used to manipulate ease of processing. Whereas easier (i.e., repeated) words resulted in less activation of reading-related regions in nonimpaired readers, they evoked more activation in these regions for disabled readers.

One speculative interpretation of these results is that both disabled and non-impaired readers rely on the cooperative interaction of the orth⇒phon and orth⇒sem⇒phon pathways, but the division of labor between these components of the reading system differs in the two groups. In particular, a greater reliance on the orth⇒sem⇒phon pathway (perhaps compensating for deficiencies in the orth⇒phon system) would yield the more pronounced benefits of imageability and frequency exhibited by the reading disabled. What would remain an open question is why the manipulations that are associated with a decrease in activation in the nonimpaired readers are associated with an increase in activation in the reading disabled. One possibility is that there is an inverted-U-shaped relationship between learning and neural activation, and that reading-disabled and nonimpaired readers are at qualitatively different points on this learning curve (see Pugh et al., in press, and the following discussion). Although this specific interpretation is clearly speculative and requires additional experimental support, the fact that the hemodynamic responses of impaired and nonimpaired readers differ in this way will surely prove telling about the neurobiological basis of both skilled and disordered reading.

LEARNING-RELATED CHANGES IN THE DIVISION OF LABOR

A variety of findings indicate that in normally developing readers, increasing proficiency is associated with a shift in the relative contributions of the ventral and dorsal-anterior pathways. For example, in a cross-sectional study of young (7- to 17-year-old) normally developing readers, Shaywitz et al. (2002) found that during reading tasks, younger children exhibited strong engagement of the dorsal and anterior systems but showed limited engagement of the ventral system. In contrast, older children tended to show increased engagement of the ventral system, particularly the LH OT region. Importantly, this shift was related to reading proficiency and not merely chronological age: Activation in the OT was positively correlated with reading skill, such that greater activation was associated with higher reading scores. These results indicate that early in the acquisition process (when most written words are relatively unfamiliar), beginning readers rely on a more distributed system with greater right hemisphere involvement. As reading skill increases, many of these regions play relatively diminished roles, whereas LH ventral regions (especially OT) become more critical (see Booth et al., 2001, and Turkeltaub et al., 2003, for additional support for this conclusion).

The dorsal-to-ventral shift that occurs as reading skill increases is also evident in the effects of word familiarity on the brain activation in skilled adult readers. Thus, compared to familiar words, unfamiliar pseudowords tend to result in more activation in the dorsal and anterior sites associated with phonological processing, but less activation in the more anterior sites in the temporal lobe associated with word meaning (Mechelli et al., 2005; Pugh et al., 1996; Rumsey et al., 1997). Experimental manipulations of familiarity yield similar results (Katz et al., 2005; Poldrack & Gabrieli, 2001). For example, Katz et al. (2005) found that multiple repetitions of a word resulted in reduced activation in a number of regions, including, in particular, the dorsal (SMG) and anterior (IFG) phonological circuits. This pattern was found in both lexical decision and naming, and was more pronounced in the lexical decision task, presumably reflecting the greater phonological demands of the naming task. (There was weak evidence of an increase in activation in anterior ventral sites—more so in lexical decision than overt naming.)

Learning-related changes in the neurobiology of reading are accompanied by behavioral changes that also suggest a shift in the division of labor between semantic and phonological processes. For example, beginning readers exhibit strong effects of spelling-to-sound consistency on both low- and high-frequency words (Waters, Seidenberg, & Bruck, 1984). In contrast, in skilled adult readers the effects of spelling-to-sound consistency are generally limited to the processing of relatively unfamiliar low-frequency words. Experimentally increasing familiarity through repetition also diminishes or eliminates the consistency effect (Katz et al., 2005; Visser & Besner, 2001).

These learning-related changes in the magnitude of the consistency effect have often been taken as evidence the phonological route plays a secondary role—its primary contribution in skilled reading confined to the processing of relatively unfamiliar words and nonwords. According to this sort of account, the consistency effect comes about because the lexical and phonological routes yield conflicting information about the pronunciation of inconsistent words, with the phonological route assumed to operate via rules that "regularize" an inconsistent word (for example, reading PINT as a rhyme for HINT). However, this conflict only has behavioral consequences if the lexical and sublexical processes have similar time courses. Repeated encounters with a word have the effect of speeding the lexical route, and thus as a word becomes more familiar the slower sublexical route becomes increasingly irrelevant to the recognition of that word. On this view, the dorsal-to-ventral shift in brain activation reflects this learning-related marginalization of the phonological route: Increased familiarity with a word results in a reduction in dorsal and anterior activation and/or an increase in the activation of an anterior ventral area (MTG), as would be expected if learning results in both the progressive engagement of the ventral (lexical) system and a corresponding disengagement of the dorsal and anterior (sublexical/phonological) subsystems.

The triangle model offers a different interpretation of both the behavioral and the neurobiological evidence. With regard to the behavioral evidence, the triangle model shares with the independent-routes account the assumption that the interaction of consistency and familiarity (measured by frequency, repetition, or skill level) is due, in part, to the greater influence of the orth⇒sem system on the recognition of high-frequency words. In contrast, the models differ in their assumptions about the characteristics of the phonological path. Due to the kind of computations it implements, in the triangle model the orth⇒phon pathway can compute the correct pronunciation of both consistent and inconsistent words. Inconsistent words are more difficult due to their statistical properties, but with sufficient training this difference is minimized. Indeed, simulations have shown that the widely observed interaction of frequency and consistency occurs even when the orth⇒phon pathway operates in isolation (i.e., when the orth⇒sem⇒phon pathway isn't implemented). Thus, in contrast to a common interpretation of behavioral findings, the fact that under certain circumstances consistent words are read no faster than inconsistent words does not necessarily entail that the phonological pathway played an insignificant role in the reading of those words. This conclusion only follows given certain assumptions about the nature of the phonological recoding process—incorrect assumptions from our perspective.

A similar argument applies to the neurobiological evidence. Neuroimaging studies of perceptual and motor skill learning have demonstrated that although initial skill acquisition (unskilled performance) is associated with increased activation in task-specific cortical areas, continued practice of an acquired skill tends to be associated with task-specific *decreases* in activation in the same cortical regions (e.g., Poldrack & Gabrieli, 2001; Ungerleider, Doyon, & Karni, 2002;

Wang, Sereno, Jongman, & Hirsch, 2003). Thus, while one interpretation of the reduction in the activation of the dorsal-anterior circuit that occurs as a word becomes more familiar is that it reflects the disengagement of phonological recoding as the direct route (subserved by the ventral system) takes over; another explanation is that this reduction reflects the increasing efficiency of the phonological circuit that occurs over the course of learning (and that is revealed behaviorally in phenomena such as the Frequency × Consistency interaction discussed earlier).

In light of this contrast, the results of an fMRI experiment by Sandak et al. (2004) are particularly interesting. In the initial phase of that experiment participants completed a behavioral session in which they performed tasks that were designed to focus their attention on different properties of three sets of pronounceable pseudowords. Specifically, the participants made orthographic (consonant–vowel pattern) judgments about one set of pseudowords, phonological (rhyme) judgments about another set, and semantic (category) judgments about a third. (In the semantic condition, participants learned a novel semantic association for each pseudoword; these associations formed the basis for the category judgments.) Over the course of the training session, each pseudoword was presented eight times (and in the same training condition across repetitions). Following training, participants completed an event-related fMRI session in which they overtly named trained pseudowords, untrained pseudowords, and real words. The experiment yielded a wealth of results, of which the ones involving the contrast between phonological and semantic training are especially relevant here.

Behaviorally, phonological and semantic training produced comparable benefits, as indexed by faster naming times compared to the orthographic condition. Neurobiologically, however, the effects of phonological and semantic training were remarkably different. Compared to the other training conditions, phonological training resulted in a reduction in the activation of dorsal (SMG) and anterior (IFG) sites that are thought to subserve phonological recoding. In contrast, semantic training was associated with increased activation in MTG, an anterior ventral site that has been implicated in semantic processing. Note, then, that these results include both elements of the dorsal-to-ventral shift—a reduction in dorsal/anterior activation and an increase in ventral activation. However, given the strong link between the activation changes and the nature of the training tasks that gave rise to them, these results do not suggest that the behavioral consequences of semantic and phonological training were due to the same underlying mechanism (a shift from phonological to lexical processes). Rather, they reveal that semantic and phonological training differentially affected the computations performed by the ventral and dorsal-anterior pathways. Semantic training involved the establishment of new semantic representations in MTG, resulting in more activation in this region and speeding overt naming by strengthening the contribution of the orth⇒sem⇒phon mapping. Phonological training improved the efficiency of the dorsal/anterior circuit (by strengthening the pre-existing knowledge that allows readers to generate a plausible pronunciation for an unfamiliar pseudoword), resulting in faster naming times and less activation in these regions.

One other aspect of the Sandak et al. (2004) results is of particular importance here. Phonological training was not only associated with an activation reduction in SMG and IFG, but also with a reduction in the activation of the ventral OT region (the VWFA). This pattern was also observed in the Katz et al. (2005) study discussed earlier: Repetition of real words (in both lexical decision and naming) led to an activation reduction in the SMG, IFG, *and* OT. Interpreting the reduced activation in the SMG and IFG as reflecting disengagement of these systems with learning creates a paradox if the same logic is applied to the reduced activation observed in the OT, given its crucial role in skilled reading. A more plausible interpretation is that the activation reduction in the OT, like the concurrent reductions in the SMG and IFG, is a reflection of an item-specific improvement in processing efficiency.

Role of OT/VWFA

Given the critical role of the ventral OT region in skilled reading and reading acquisition, considerable effort has been dedicated to understanding its precise role. Several kinds of hypotheses have emerged from these efforts. According to some accounts (Cohen & Dehaene, 2004; Dehaene et al., 2002, 2005), the role of the OT is to store prelexical visual word forms—representations of letters and letter combinations. Other accounts (e.g., Kronbichler et al., 2004) suggest that the OT stores lexical (rather than prelexical) representations. Critically, by either account the representations stored in this region are orthographic in nature. That is, they capture information about how a word (and by the first account, a pseudoword) is spelled (in a way that abstracts over variations in font, case, and so on) independently of the word's phonological and semantic properties. An alternative account is that the OT acts as an interface between information about visual form and higher order properties such as what a word means and how it is pronounced (Devlin et al., 2006).

Earlier we posited that the OT region in the brain is the analog of the orthographic input units in the triangle model. Given the nature of the orthographic representations used in extant simulations, this mapping would seem to suggest that the triangle model embodies the prelexical/orthographic account of the role of the OT. However, it is important to distinguish between the theory and its implementation. Implementations of the model have employed stipulated orthographic representations to investigate the properties of the downstream processes that map visual inputs onto semantic and phonological representations. However, this simplification overlooks important properties of the human reading system, which are relevant to the debate about the OT. First, we assume that all representations in the reading system are learned. Orthographic representations, for example, are learned primarily by seeing (comprehending) and writing (producing) letters and letter strings. Thus the units labeled "orthographic" in the simplified models are more like hidden-layer representations that mediate between perception and production. We assume the same is true for phonology (units mediate comprehension and production of speech) and semantics (units mediate comprehending and producing messages).

Second, the properties of the orthographic units will be shaped by their participation in various mappings. Orthography is both the input to the mapping between orth⇒phon and the output of the mapping from phon⇒orth. Since the same hidden units are used in both directions, the properties of the orthographic representations will be shaped by their participation in both mappings. More generally, the "orthographic" representations can be thought of as hidden-unit representations that mediate many mappings. There is considerable evidence that phonological representations are shaped by orthographic knowledge; phonemic representations are closely tied to exposure to an alphabet (Bertelson & de Gelder, 1989). Harm and Seidenberg's (1999) simulation showed this developmental tendency. Phonology is likely to have a similar effect in shaping orthographic representations. These properties of the computational model are consistent with the idea that OT employs componential representations that are organized to capture both input (visual/orthographic) and output (phonological and semantic) similarity. In this respect, our account is similar to the interface hypothesis proposed by Devlin et al. (2006).[2]

Like other theories about the role of the OT in reading (Dehaene et al., 2005; Devlin et al., 2006; McCandliss et al., 2003), our account assumes that the visual system is organized such that at the time that a child begins to learn to read, printed words activate the OT and are represented in a manner that is relatively invariant over visual properties such as size and retinal position. Attempts to name these words or understand what they mean can generate error signals that pressure the OT to construct representations that are better suited to these tasks. Thus, while bottom-up input from the earlier parts of the visual system will tend to force the OT to represent visually similar words with similar codes, top-down feedback from phonological and semantic regions will tend to force the OT to organize its representations to capture phonological and semantic similarity.

Recent neuroimaging studies provide evidence that representations in the OT are phonologically and semantically "tuned" in this way. For example, in an fMRI study by Mencl et al. (2005), readers made lexical decisions about words that were preceded by primes that were either (a) both orthographically and phonologically similar to the targets (bribe–TRIBE), (b) orthographically similar but phonologically dissimilar (couch–TOUCH), or (c) unrelated (lunch–SCREEN). The phonologically dissimilar pairs (couch–TOUCH) evoked more activation than the phonologically similar pairs (bribe–TRIBE) in several LH cortical areas hypothesized to underlie phonological processing, including IFG, Wernicke's area, and SMG. Notably, this phonological priming effect was also obtained within the LH OT (VWFA), as would be expected if the organization of the OT is influenced by phonological similarity and not purely orthographic similarity, as other accounts (Dehaene et al., 2005; Kronbichler et al., 2004) would suggest.

Other results provide evidence that the OT is semantically tuned as well. For example, Devlin et al. (2006) contrasted the activation of this region when readers were presented with prime-target pairs such as teacher–TEACH and corner–CORN. These pairs are matched in terms of orthographic similarity, but differ in their semantic (and morphological) relatedness. Devlin et al. observed differential priming effects on the activation of the OT, again suggesting that orthographic similarity is not the sole determinant of how words are represented in this region.

It is important to note that while the triangle model predicts that the OT is both phonologically and semantically tuned, it also suggests that the influence of phonology will be more pronounced (for readers of English in particular). One reason for this difference is that the mapping between spelling and phonology is far more systematic than the mapping between spelling and meaning, and thus phonological feedback will provide a more coherent influence on the organization of the OT representations. Another relevant factor is the developmental trajectory of the reading system. As discussed earlier, the orth⇒phon⇒sem path dominates performance early in the acquisition process, and thus phonological feedback will be especially influential in the initial stages of learning (when the representations in the OT are most open to reorganization).

The differential influence of phonological feedback on the OT provides an explanation for a variety of findings. For example, we noted earlier that activation in this region during reading tasks is correlated with reading skill in children and adolescents (Paulesu et al., 2001; Shaywitz et al., 2002, 2004), and, critically, that dyslexics do not engage this region during reading (Paulesu et al., 2001; Shaywitz et al., 1998, 2002). This would be expected if the phonological system serves as a teacher that helps the OT develop representations that are appropriate for reading and if the underlying cause of dyslexia is a phonological deficit. If the phonological system fails to provide an appropriate teaching signal, the OT would not be able to learn properly and the reader would have to rely on other (less well-suited) processes.

The differential influence of phonological feedback on the OT is also relevant to the results of experiments investigating learning-related changes in skilled readers. Recall that in both the Katz et al. (2005) and Sandak et al. (2004) experiments discussed earlier, activation in the OT tracked activation in dorsal (SMG) and anterior (IFG) phonological sites. That is, manipulations that yielded activation reductions in other phonological sites (repetition in lexical decision and naming in Katz et al., phonological training in Sandak et al.) also produced activation reductions in the OT, whereas the manipulation that did not affect the phonological regions (semantic training in Sandak et al.) also failed to affect activation in OT. From our perspective, the strong coupling of OT with SMG and IFG reflects the systematic structure of the mapping from spelling to meaning and, as a consequence, the coherence of phonological feedback to OT. Given the arbitrary relation of spelling and meaning, semantic feedback will generally be less coherent, and thus more difficult to detect. (Morphological regularities provide an exception to this rule, as morphologically related words are typically similar in both form and meaning. Thus, we predict that when learning involves regularities of this sort there will be a measurable effect on activation in the OT.)

IMPLICATIONS AND FUTURE DIRECTIONS

In the preceding sections, we identified the computational principles embodied by the triangle model, described the results of simulations that illustrate how the model accounts for a wide variety of behavioral findings, and considered how the model might provide insights about the neural mechanisms that underlie reading. In this final section we look to the future, identifying some of the research questions that seem to us to be most pressing.

THE ARCHITECTURE OF THE READING SYSTEM

As indicated by both the earlier discussion and several of the other chapters in this volume, a great deal is now known about the network of cortical regions that subserve printed word recognition. That being said, there is surely much yet to be learned.

One critical issue concerns the further differentiation of the major cortical reading systems. As we noted earlier, although early neuroimaging results suggested that the reading system is comprised of three major subsystems (Pugh et al., 2000), this partitioning is rather coarse-grained and the accumulating evidence indicates that each of these regions includes several functionally distinct sites. For example, we have emphasized the contrast between the posterior and anterior components of the ventral system: The former includes the OT (the VWFA) and functions as an interface between the visual input and phonological and semantic subsystems; the latter includes areas responsible for processing word meaning, including the MTG and ITG. One important question is whether a more fine-grained differentiation of these ventral regions is needed (as suggested, for example, by the model of progressive abstraction within the fusiform region described by Dehaene et al., 2005, and Vinckier et al., 2007). Of particular interest given our hypothesis about the process that results in the specialization of the OT for reading is whether phonological and semantic feedback tunes the same region, or if instead they influence anatomically distinct sites. Similarly, within both the anterior and dorsal systems, functionally distinct sites have been identified based on their differential contribution to phonological or semantic processing (Devlin, Matthews, & Rushworth, 2003; McDermott, Petersen, Watson, & Ojemann, 2003; Roskies, Fiez, Balota, Raichle, & Petersen, 2001).

For us, getting better fine-grained characterization of these systems is a pressing concern for several reasons. One is that many of the sites in question are involved in speech perception and production as well as reading. Thus, there is the opportunity to connect reading research to the large body of findings concerning the neurobiology of speech (Hickok & Poeppel, 2004; Indefrey & Levelt, 2004; Scott & Johnsrude, 2003) and constrain our theories accordingly. Second, and relatedly, the relation between the processes involved in speech and reading is a relatively undeveloped aspect of the triangle model. It is not implausible that there are a number of "phonological" representations involved in speech perception and production, and these representations could differ in both their function and their organization (e.g., whether they better capture acoustic similarity, articulatory similarity, or more abstract phonological properties).[5] The triangle model does not differentiate among these possibilities and quite likely falls short because of this. For example, in the triangle model the phonological layer functions as the primary phonological subsystem in both "speech perception" (mapping phonology to semantics) and "speech production" (mapping semantics to phonology). Arguably, in the brain these functions are subserved by different regions (STG and IFG, respectively).

It is worth noting that the preceding discussion illustrates that the relationship between the model and brain data is a two-way street. On the one hand, we believe the model provides a useful theoretical framework for interpreting neurobiological evidence and generating hypotheses that can be tested using neurobiological methods. On the other hand, we expect that the results of neurobiological studies will motivate revisions of the computational theory, which is clearly oversimplified at present.

THE ROLE OF MORPHOLOGICAL STRUCTURE

Readers are influenced by the morphological structure of the words they read. Morphological effects on word recognition have been studied extensively using behavioral paradigms (for review, see Henderson, 1985; Rueckl, Mikolinski, Raveh, Miner, & Mars, 1997; Seidenberg & Gonnerman, 2000). In contrast, relatively little is known about the relationship between morphological structure and the cortical subsystems that support word reading, and only recently has research on this topic begun to emerge (e.g., Bick, Goelman, & Frost, 2008; Bozic, Marslen-Wilson, Stamatakis, Davis, & Tyler, 2007; Devlin et al., 2006). For a number of reasons, we believe there is a pressing need for this to change.

First, with the exception of morphological relatives, words that are similar in spelling or pronunciation are generally not similar in meaning. In other words, morphological regularities are a major source of statistical structure in the otherwise arbitrary mapping from form to meaning. From our perspective, statistical structure organizes the recognition process, and thus morphological regularities are as central to the operation of the orth⇒sem pathway as spelling-to-sound regularities are to the operation of the orth⇒phon pathway. In this light, it is interesting to note that many of the empirical and theoretical debates related to phonological recoding have parallels in the literature concerning the role of morphology in reading.

Second, and relatedly, manipulations of morphological variables could prove valuable in studying the division of labor between the phonological and semantic subsystems. It is striking that although there are many parallels between the literatures on the roles of phonology and morphology in reading, and, indeed, although many of the same scientists contribute to both literatures, relatively few studies have investigated whether morphological effects are modulated by phonological variables or vice versa, or, more generally, how the morphological and phonological properties of printed words jointly determine the process by which those words are recognized.

Finally, understanding the effects of morphological structure on word recognition will be a critical aspect of research that compares word recognition processes across languages and writings systems (e.g., see R. Frost, this volume).

CROSS-LANGUAGE RESEARCH

Our working hypotheses are that the same neural systems are implicated cross-linguistically and that the computational principles that establish the division of labor in English also apply to other writing systems. These principles imply that because languages and writing systems differ in their statistical properties (e.g., orthographic depth—the degree to which an orthographic unit is consistently mapped to the same phonological unit), learning to read in different languages will give rise to somewhat different outcomes. However, these differences will not involve qualitatively distinct organizations, but rather different weightings in the division of labor between the phonological and semantic pathways. Cross-language comparisons, therefore, provide critical tests of the neurobiological and computational generality of our theory.

There is now an extensive body of behavioral research on word recognition in numerous languages. The results of this research are generally consistent with the claim that word recognition in skilled adult readers does not differ in any fundamental manner across writing systems. That is, although there may be differences in, for example, the types of phonological units that drive word recognition (Paulesu et al., 2000; Ziegler & Goswami, 2005; Ziegler, Perry, Jacobs, & Braun, 2001), there is ample evidence that readers of all writing systems employ both direct and phonologically mediated routes, that phonology plays an early and critical role in word recognition, and so forth (R. Frost, 1998; Perfetti, 1985). Similarly, studies of the neuroanatomy of word recognition (e.g., Chee, O'Craven, Bergida, Rosen, & Savoy, 1999; Fiebach et al., 2002; Kuo et al., 2003; Paulesu et al., 2000; Salmelin, Service, Kiesilä, Uutela, & Salonen, 1996) suggest that a common set of left hemisphere cortical regions, including occipitotemporal, temporoparietal, and inferior frontal networks, are almost always engaged in reading irrespective of the specific writing system under investigation. Also consistent with behavioral evidence, the neurobiological findings suggest that language-specific differences are a matter of degree, not of kind (Kuo et al., 2003; Paulesu et al., 2000).

Two positions that contrast with the conclusions of the previous paragraph should be noted. First, R. Frost (this volume) has compiled a variety of behavioral results indicating that readers of English and Hebrew differ in their responses to a range of experimental manipulations. He attributes these differences to the greater morphological richness of the Hebrew language and questions whether these differences can be accounted for by a "universal" theory that assumes that the set of computational principles underlies word recognition in any language. Our response is twofold. First, the simulations reported by Plaut and Gonnerman (2000) (discussed earlier in the section "Computational Principles") provides some evidence that at least one finding of the sort reported by Frost falls out of the dynamics of the triangle model when it is trained on writing systems that differ in their statistical properties. Second, although we expect that the other sorts of results discussed by Frost can be understood in the same way, we agree that simulations exploring this question would be illuminating regardless of how they turned out. In our view, though, both a deep understanding of the behavioral results and the ability to conduct truly compelling simulations will require a more thorough characterization of the Hebrew language and writing system than is currently available. Differences in the morphological structure of Hebrew and English words occur against the backdrop of variation along a number of potentially relevant dimensions, including the orthographic depth of the writing systems, the number and frequency of the root morphemes in each language, the relationship between morphological structure and syllabic structure, and the size of the orthographic and phonological neighborhoods of the words in each language, to name a few. In addition to simulations that would serve to test the triangle model, corpus analyses to better characterize the languages and behavioral studies that examine the effects of these and other variables are also needed.

A second challenge to the universalist account of word recognition, this time at the neurobiological level, comes from some neuroimaging studies of reading in Chinese. In general, reading Chinese words activates many of the same cortical regions that are activated during the reading of words in English and other alphabetic languages (Kuo et al., 2003, 2004; Tan et al., 2000). However, there is some evidence that certain regions are uniquely activated by Chinese words, including both superior parietal (Kuo et al., 2003) and left middle frontal regions (Tan et al., 2000). These results, should they hold up, most likely point toward an underdeveloped aspect of our account. Namely, the theory assumes that the development of the reading system reflects the interaction of several factors: general computational principles, facts concerning the structure of the language and writing system, and initial conditions (the state of the cognitive and neural system at the time that a child begins to learn to read). At this point we have not developed a detailed account of the initial conditions (especially with regard to the properties of relevant cortical regions), nor have we developed an account of the computational processes that underlie neural specialization. These issues are not in principle problematic for our approach, but the Chinese neuroimaging results may suggest that they will need to be addressed sooner rather than later.

Dyslexia

A unique property of computational models is that they provide a way to test causal hypotheses about normal and atypical development, and the effects of brain injury. One can configure or train the models in different ways and determine if they lead to identifiable variations in behavior. For example, Harm and Seidenberg (2004) showed that a model trained with feedback on both phonology and semantics learned more rapidly than one trained with regular feedback about semantics and only occasional feedback about phonology. These results are causal: Changing the model in specific ways has specific effects. They also run counter to claims that children should learn to read visually, avoiding phonological mediation, because it is more efficient (e.g., Smith, 1978). Other experiments of this type could be conducted to determine whether there are benefits to ordering words in specific ways or teaching children about particular subword units (such as rhymes).

The models can also be used to study developmental impairments in learning to read words. A developmental disorder is simulated by introducing an anomaly in the architecture of the model, how processing occurs within the model, or in the experience the model is providing. In an early example of this type, Seidenberg and McClelland (1989) varied the number of hidden units in their model, which mapped from orthography to phonology. A model with too few hidden units could encode strong regularities between spelling and sound, but had difficulty learning irregular correspondences (as in AISLE and DONE). This pattern is seen in some dyslexic children; the pattern is sometimes termed developmental surface dyslexics (Castles & Coltheart, 1993; Manis, Seidenberg, Doi, McBride-Chang, & Peterson, 1996). However, it should be noted that most beginning readers are surface dyslexic in the sense that they perform better on words with consistent spelling–sound patterns and worse on exceptions.

The models provide tools for testing hypotheses about the causes of dyslexia, and they suggest some novel hypotheses (such as the architectural anomaly studied by Seidenberg & McClelland, 1989), but they do not make strong predictions about which anomalies actually occur in children. Most of the behavioral evidence points to the role of phonological information in developmental dyslexia. The basic hypothesis is that failures to develop segmental phonological representations (i.e., differentiate BAT into three components) interfere with learning spelling–sound correspondences, which slows the child's entry into reading and has cascading effects on comprehension, spelling, and other aspects of school performance. This deficit has little effect on spoken language because speech does not require segmental representations. Humans were using spoken language long before writing systems were invented, and the speech of illiterates is normal. Segmental representations assume importance in the context of alphabetic writing systems, which represent phonemes. Similarly, other types of writing systems require other phonological representations, for example, subsyllabic (onset-rhyme) or syllabic (Ziegler & Goswami, 2005). Thus, the impairment in dyslexia is thought to be an anomaly related to the representation of phonology that has little effect on speech but greatly interferes with learning to read.

Harm and Seidenberg (1999) reported a simulation of this pattern. There are several ways to introduce phonological anomalies in the triangle model: for example, the representations themselves can be degraded (e.g., by deleting units), or the representations can be intact but the passing of activation along the pathway can be made imprecise (e.g., by deleting connections or adding noise to the activation function). Harm and Seidenberg examined the effects of mild and strong phonological impairments on two aspects of model performance: the acquisition of spelling–sound knowledge and an analogue of a common speech-perception task—the categorical perception of phonemes. A mild impairment interfered with learning spelling–sound correspondences, producing a particularly strong deficit in nonword generalization, consistent with observations about dyslexic children. Performance on the speech-perception task remained normal, however. With a stronger phonological impairment, both reading and speech tasks were affected. Thus, the simulation results are consistent with the idea that a mild impairment could affect learning to read while having no discernable effect on spoken language processing. The results were also consistent with the observation that children with impairments in the use of spoken language (often termed *specific language impairment*) are both dyslexic and exhibit impaired speech perception (Bishop, North, & Donlan, 1996; Joanisse, Manis, Keating, & Seidenberg, 2000).

There is a strong consensus that dyslexia is associated with a phonological deficit; dyslexics consistently perform poorly on tests that require knowledge of phonemic structure. However, the basis for this impairment, and whether it is a cause or an effect of poor reading, is still unclear. Many researchers have examined whether dyslexics exhibit subtle impairments in auditory or speech processing. The literature here is highly inconsistent. Deficits have been observed in some studies (e.g., Ziegler, Pech-Georgel, George, Alario, & Lorenzi, 2005), but in others the effects have been limited to a subset of dyslexics who are also more broadly language impaired (Manis et al., 1996). There are also reports of failures to observe speech or auditory deficits in dyslexics who are not language impaired (e.g., Ramus & Szenkovits, this volume). Other failures to observe such effects may have occurred but would not be published because they are negative results. It is also possible that differences between dyslexics and nondyslexics are more prominent when they are young; such differences may resolve by the time the children reach ages at which they are identified as dyslexic. At this point, the hypothesis that dyslexia derives from a milder form of the speech-related processing impairment that is observed in children with specific language impairment (SLI) remains a viable hypothesis. Further studies, coupled with modeling of the sort described earlier, will be critical in addressing this debate and the related question of whether dyslexia is best viewed as a single phenotype or a condition comprised of several subtypes.

CONCLUSION

From the connectionist perspective, a reader's behavior is the manifestation of the interaction of a number of neural subsystems that cooperate to map a word's written form onto representations of its phonological and semantic properties. The division of labor among these subsystems is determined by a number of factors, including fundamental computational principles, neural constraints, and initial conditions related to the knowledge available to the beginning reader. Critically, the division of labor is also shaped by a learning process that attunes the reader to the statistical structure of the mappings among orthography, phonology, and semantics. Through the learning process, regularities in the task environment shape the reading network's pattern of connectivity, which in turn organizes the flow of activation that gives rise to behavior.

One purpose of this book (and the meeting from which it stems) is to identify the most promising directions for future research that would help us understand and address reading disability. Given the perspective articulated in this chapter, these directions might be organized around (a) identifying the environmental regularities that shape the reading process (for better or worse), (b) understanding the learning process that attunes a reader to the task environment (and that, perhaps, goes astray in dyslexia), and (c) characterizing the division of labor among the components of the reading system and identifying the forces that constrain the solution the reading system settles on.

Differences among languages and writing systems provide excellent opportunities for investigating how the reading system is shaped by environmental regularities, although we would note that cross-language comparisons would benefit from a more detailed and sophisticated characterization of the relevant regularities than is currently available. (This is especially the case when one considers the interplay of phonological and morphological regularities, which are generally investigated independently of one another.) An emphasis on statistical regularities would also benefit more applied research focusing on the causes and treatment of dyslexia. For example, reading disabled and nonimpaired children likely differ in the amount and variety of their reading experiences. If so, to what extent might differences in outcome be causally related to these differences in experience?

Environmental regularities can also be manipulated experimentally in "artificial lexicon" studies (e.g., Bailey, Manis, Pedersen, & Seidenberg, 2004; Sandak et al., 2004), which also provide a means for investigating the learning process that attunes the reader to the mappings among orthography, phonology, and semantics. It is noteworthy that learning has typically not been seriously addressed by theories of skilled word recognition, which stipulate complex mental structures and processes but generally fail to consider how these hypothesized entities come into being. From our perspective this is a mistaken approach in that it leaves such theories underconstrained and limits their utility as frameworks for addressing theoretically important questions, including, in particular, the nature of the developmental trajectory (or trajectories) associated with reading disability. This is especially problematic given intriguing new results concerning the neurobiological correlates of learning in dyslexic readers (e.g., Pugh et al., in press).

Our account stresses that behavior reflects both environmental regularities and the learning process that attunes readers to these regularities, but in the end, behavior is most directly the consequence of the cooperative interactions among the neural subsystems that subserve reading. Although the research directions highlighted in the preceding paragraphs would shed light on the division of labor among these subsystems, other lines of research should also be directed toward this goal. In part this would involve developing experiments that, like the Strain paradigm, are explicitly designed with this goal in mind. One possibility would be to explore the interactions of phonological and morphological variables, which presumably differ in the degree to which they reflect the operation of the orth–phon and orth–sem pathways. Another important advance, especially in light of the growing importance of neuroimaging, would be the development of analytic techniques that are intended to characterize the interactions among regions rather than the activation of particular regions. Mencl, Frost, and Pugh (this volume) discuss some of the possibilities now on the horizon.

ACKNOWLEDGMENTS

This research was supported by National Institute for Child Health and Development grant HD-01994. We would like to thank Ken Pugh, Einar Mencl, Stephen Frost, Len Katz, Nicole Landi, Rebecca Sandak, Laurie Feldman, and other members of the Haskins community for their contributions to the ideas presented here.

NOTES

1. The term *dual-route model* is ambiguous because it also refers to models in which there are two procedures for mapping from spelling to phonology (e.g., Coltheart, Curtis, Atkins, & Haller, 1993; Marshall & Newcombe, 1973). These models have focused on normal and disordered reading aloud and said little about access of meaning. See Coltheart (2000) and Harm and Seidenberg (2004) for discussion.
2. Although there are models where the units in a network (at either the single-unit or collective level) are meant to correspond to specific neural circuits, in general this is not the case. For example, the structure of the triangle model is not based on any particular assumptions about the organization of the cortical regions underlying reading. (However, questions about the relationship between the organization of the model and the organization of the cortical reading system are not uninteresting and are likely to drive future research.)
3. This statement is true independent of the fact that some writing systems encode phonological information more directly than others (see discussion of orthographic depth). Even arbitrary symbols such as & and / are associated with both pronunciations and meanings.
4. There are other connectionist models of word reading that have employed so-called localist networks (e.g., Grainger & Jacob, 1996; McClelland & Rumelhart, 1981). This research, much of which focuses on orthographic phenomena, is not reviewed here because it incorporates very different assumptions about knowledge representation and processing.
5. See Plaut and Kello (1999) for a connectionist model of a multilevel speech perception/production system that learns to represent phonological structure based on acoustic and articulatory constraints.

REFERENCES

Bailey, C. E., Manis, F. R., Pedersen, W. C., & Seidenberg, M. S. (2004). Variation among developmental dyslexics: Evidence from a printed-word-learning task. *Journal of Experimental Child Psychology, 87*, 125–154.

Baron, J., & Strawson, C. (1976). Use of orthographic and word specific knowledge in reading words aloud. *Journal of Experimental Psychology: Human Perception and Performance, 2*, 386–393.

Bertelson, P., & de Gelder, B. (1989). Learning about reading from illiterates. In A. M. Galaburda (Ed.), *From reading to neurons* (pp. 1–23). Cambridge, MA: MIT Press.

Bick, A., Goelman, G., & Frost, R. (2008). Neural correlates of morphological processes in Hebrew. *Journal of Cognitive Neuroscience, 20*, 406–420.

Bishop, D. V. M., North, T., & Donlan, C. (1996). Nonword repetition as a behavioural marker for inherited language impairment: Evidence from a twin study. *Journal of Child Psychology and Psychiatry, 37*, 391–403.

Booth, J. R., Burman, D. D., Van Santen, F. W., Harasaki, Y., Gitelman, D. R., Parrish, T. B., & Mesulam, M. M. (2001). The development of specialized brain systems in reading and oral language. *Child Neuropsychology, 7*, 119–141.

Bozic, M., Marslen-Wilson, W. D., Stamatakis, E. A., Davis, M. H., & Tyler, L. K. (2007). Differentiating morphology, form, and meaning: Neural correlates of morphological complexity. *Journal of Cognitive Neuroscience, 19*, 1464–1475.

Carr, T. H., & Pollatsek, A. (1985). Recognizing printed words: A look at current models. In D. Besner, T. G. Waller, & G. E. MacKinnon (Eds.), *Reading research: Advances in theory and practice* (Vol. 5, pp. 1–82). Orlando, FL: Academic Press.

Castles, A., & Coltheart, M. (1993). Varieties of developmental dyslexia. *Cognition, 47*, 149–180.

Chee, M. W. L., O'Craven, K. M., Bergida, R., Rosen, B. R., & Savoy, R. L. (1999). Auditory and visual word processing studied with fMRI. *Human Brain Mapping, 7*, 15–28.

Cohen, L., & Dehaene, S. (2004). Specialization within the ventral stream: The case for the visual word form area. *NeuroImage, 22*, 466–476.

Coltheart, M. (1978). Lexical access in simple reading tasks. In G. Underwood (Ed.), *Strategies of information processing* (pp. 151–216). London: Academic Press.

Coltheart, M. (2000). Dual routes from print to speech and dual routes from print to meaning: Some theoretical issues. In A. Kennedy, R. Radach, J. Pynte, & D. Heller (Eds.), *Reading as a perceptual process*. Oxford, UK: Elsevier.

Coltheart, M., Curtis, B., Atkins, P., & Haller, M. (1993). Models of reading aloud: Dual-route and parallel-distributed-processing approaches. *Psychological Review, 100*(4), 589–608.

Coltheart, M., Rastle, K., Perry, C., Langdon, R., & Ziegler, J. (2001). DRC: A dual route cascaded model of visual word recognition and reading aloud. *Psychological Review, 108*, 204–256.

Cornelissen, P., Tarkiainen, A., Helenius, P., & Salmelin, R. (2003). Cortical effects of shifting letter position in letter strings of varying length. *Journal of Cognitive Neuroscience, 15*, 731–746.

Dehaene, S., Cohen, L., Sigman, M., & Vinckier, F. (2005). The neural code for written words: A proposal. *Trends in Cognitive Sciences, 9*, 335–341.

Dehaene, S., Le Clec'H, G., Poline, J. B., Bihan, D. L., & Cohen, L. (2002). The visual word form area: A prelexical representation of visual words in the left fusiform gyrus. *NeuroReport, 13*, 321–325.

Devlin, J. T., Jamison, H. L., Gonnerman, L. M., & Matthews, P. M. (2006). The role of the posterior fusiform gyrus in reading. *Journal of Cognitive Neuroscience, 18,* 911–922.

Devlin, J. T., Matthews, P. M., & Rushworth, M. F. S. (2003). Semantic processing in the left inferior prefrontal cortex: A combined functional magnetic resonance imaging and transcranial magnetic stimulation study. *Journal of Cognitive Neuroscience, 15,* 71–84.

Elman, J. L., Bates, E. A., Johnson, M., Karmiloff-Smith, A., Parisi, D., & Plunkett, K. (1996). *Rethinking innateness: A connectionist perspective on development.* Cambridge, MA: MIT Press.

Fiebach, C. J., Friederici, A. D., Muller, K., & von Cramon, D. Y. (2002). fMRI evidence for dual routes to the mental lexicon in visual word recognition. *Journal of Cognitive Neuroscience, 14,* 11–23.

Fiez, J. A., Balota, D. A., Raichle, M. E., & Petersen, S. E. (1999). Effects of lexicality, frequency, and spelling-to-sound consistency on the functional anatomy of reading. *Neuron, 24,* 205–218.

Fletcher, J. M., Shaywitz, S. E., Shankweiler, D. P., Katz, L., Liberman, I. Y., & Stuebing, K. K. (1994). Cognitive profiles of reading disability: Comparisons of discrepancy and low achievement definitions. *Journal of Educational Psychology, 86,* 6–23.

Frost, R. (1995). Phonological computation and missing vowels: Mapping lexical involvement in reading. *Journal of Experimental Psychology: Learning, Memory, and Cognition, 21,* 398–408.

Frost, R. (1998). Toward a strong phonological theory of visual word recognition: True issues and false trails. *Psychological Bulletin, 123,* 71–99.

Frost, S. J., Mencl, W. E., Sandak, R., Moore, D. L., Rueckl, J., Katz, L., et al. (2005). An fMRI study of the trade-off between semantics and phonology in reading aloud. *NeuroReport, 16,* 621–624.

Grainger, J., & Jacobs, A. M. (1996). Orthographic processing in visual word recognition: A multiple read-out model. *Psychological Review, 103,* 518–565.

Harm, M., McCandliss, B. D., & Seidenberg, M. S. (2003). Modeling the successes and failures of interventions for disabled readers. *Scientific Studies of Reading, 7,* 155–182 .

Harm, M. W., & Seidenberg, M. S. (1999). Phonology, reading acquisition, and dyslexia: Insights from connectionist models. *Psychological Review, 106,* 491–528.

Harm, M. W., & Seidenberg, M. S. (2004). Computing the meanings of words in reading: Cooperative division of labor between visual and phonological processes. *Psychological Review, 111,* 662–720.

Hebb, D. O. (1949). *The organization of behavior.* New York: Wiley.

Henderson, L. (1985). Towards a Psychology of morphemes. In A. W. Ellis (Ed.), *Progress in the psychology of language* (Vol. 1, pp. 15–72). London: Erlbaum.

Herbster, A., Mintun, M., Nebes, R., & Becker, J. (1997). Regional cerebral blood flow during word and pseudoword reading. *Human Brain Mapping, 5,* 84–92.

Hickok, G., & Poeppel, D. (2004). Dorsal and ventral streams: A framework for understanding aspects of the functional anatomy of language. *Cognition, 92,* 67–99.

Indefrey, P., & Levelt, W. J. M. (2004). The spatial and temporal properties of word production components. *Cognition, 92,* 101–144.

Joanisse, M. F., Manis, F. R., Keating, P., & Seidenberg, M. S. (2000). Language deficits in dyslexic children: Speech perception, phonology, and morphology. *Journal of Experimental Child Psychology, 77,* 30–60.

Jobard, G., Crivello, F., & Tzourio-Mazoyer, N. (2003). Evaluation of the dual route theory of reading: A meta-analysis of 35 neuroimaging studies. *NeuroImage, 20,* 693–712.

Jorm, A. F., & Share, D. L. (1983). Phonological recoding and reading acquisition. *Applied Psycholinguistics, 4,* 103–147.

Katz, L., Lee, C. H., Frost, S. J., Mencl, W. E., Rueckl, J., Sandak, R., et al. (2005). Effects of printed word repetition in lexical decision and naming on behavior and brain activation. *Neuropsychologia, 43,* 2068–2083.

Kello, C. T., & Plaut, D. C. (2003). Strategic control over rate of processing in word reading: A computational investigation. *Journal of Memory and Language, 48,* 207–232.

Kronbichler, M., Hutzler, F., Wimmer, H., Mair, A., Staffen, W., & Ladurner, G. (2004). The visual word form area and the frequency with which words are encountered: Evidence from a parametric fMRI study. *NeuroImage, 21,* 946–953.

Kuo, W. J., Yeh, T. C., Lee, C. Y., Wu, Y. T., Chou, C. C., Ho, L. T., et al. (2003). Frequency effects of Chinese character processing in the brain: An event-related fMRI study. *NeuroImage, 18,* 720–730.

Kuo, W. J., Yeh, T. C., Lee, J. R., Chen, L. F., Lee, P. L., Chen, S. S., et al. (2004). Orthographic and phonological processing of Chinese characters: An fMRI study. *NeuroImage, 21,* 1721–1731.

Liberman, I. Y., & Shankweiler, D. (1985). Phonology and the problems of learning to read and write. *Remedial and Special Education, 6,* 8–17.

Manis, F., Seidenberg, M., Doi, L., McBride-Chang, C., & Peterson, A. (1996). On the basis of two subtypes of developmental dyslexia. *Cognition, 58,* 157–195.

Marshall, J. C., & Newcombe, F. (1973). Patterns of paralexia: A psycholinguistic approach. *Journal of Psycholinguistic Research, 2,* 175–199.

McCandliss, B. D., Cohen, L., & Dehaene, S. (2003). The visual word form area: Expertise for reading in the fusiform gyrus. *Trends in Cognitive Sciences, 7,* 293–299.

McClelland, J. L., & Rumelhart, D. E. (1981). An interactive activation model of context effects in letter perception: I. An account of basic findings. *Psychological Review, 88,* 375–407.

McDermott, K. B., Petersen, S. E., Watson, J. M., & Ojemann, J. G. (2003). A procedure for identifying regions preferentially activated by attention to semantic and phonological relations using functional magnetic resonance imaging. *Neuropsychologia, 41,* 293–303.

Mechelli, A., Crinion, J. T., Long, S., Friston, K. J., Lambon-Ralph, M. A., Patterson, K., et al. (2005). Dissociating reading processes on the basis of neuronal interactions. *Journal of Cognitive Neuroscience, 17,* 1753–1765.

Mencl, W. E., Frost, S. J., Sandak, R., Lee, J. R., Jenner, A. R., Mason, S., et al. (2005). Effects of orthographic and phonological priming in printed word identification: An fMRI study. Manuscript submitted for publication.

Paap, K. R., & Noel, R. W. (1991). Dual route models of print to sound: Still a good horse race. *Psychological Research, 53,* 13–24.

Paulesu, E., Démonet, J.-F., Fazio, F., McCrory, E., Chanoine, V., Brunswick, N., et al. (2001). Dyslexia: Cultural diversity and biological unity. *Science, 291,* 2165–2167.

Paulesu, E., McCrory, E., Fazio, F., Menoncello, L., Brunswick, N., Cappa, S., et al. (2000). A cultural effect on brain function. *Nature Neuroscience, 3,* 91–96.

Perfetti, C. A. (1985). *Reading ability.* New York: Oxford University Press.

Plaut, D. (1995). Double dissociation without modularity: Evidence from connectionist neuropsychology. *Journal of Clinical and Experimental Neuropsychology, 17,* 291–321.

Plaut, D. C., & Gonnerman, L. M. (2000). Are non-semantic morphological effects incompatible with a distributed connectionist approach to lexical processing? *Language and Cognitive Processes, 15,* 445–485.

Plaut, D. C., & Kello, C. T. (1999). The emergence of phonology from the interplay of speech comprehension and production: A distributed connectionist approach. In B. MacWhinney (Ed.), *The emergence of language* (pp. 381–415). Mahwah, NJ: Lawrence Erlbaum Associates.

Plaut, D. C., McClelland, J. L., Seidenberg, M., & Patterson, K. E. (1996). Understanding normal and impaired word reading: Computational principles in quasi-regular domains. *Psychological Review, 103,* 56–115.

Plaut, D. C., & Shallice, T. (1993). Deep dyslexia: A case study of connectionist neuropsychology. *Cognitive Neuropsychology, 10,* 377–500.

Poldrack, R. A., & Gabrieli, J. D. E. (2001). Characterizing the neural mechanisms of skill learning and repetition priming: Evidence from mirror reading. *Brain, 124,* 67–82.

Price, C. J., Moore, C. J., Humphreys, G. W., & Wise, R. J. S. (1997). Segregating semantic from phonological processes during reading. *Journal of Cognitive Neuroscience, 9,* 727–733.

Pugh, K. R., Frost, S. J., Sandak, R., Rueckl, J. G., Constable, R. T., Della Porta, G., et al. (in press). An fMRI study of the effects of stimulus difficulty on printed word identification: A comparison of non-impaired and reading disabled adolescent cohorts. *Journal of Cognitive Neuroscience*

Pugh, K. R., Mencl, W. E., Jenner, A. J., Katz, L., Frost, S. J., Lee, J. R., et al. (2000). Functional neuroimaging studies of reading and reading disability (developmental dyslexia). *Mental Retardation and Developmental Disabilities Review, 6,* 207–213.

Pugh, K. R., Shaywitz, B. A., Shaywitz, S. A., Constable, R. T., Skudlarski, P., Fulbright, R. K., et al. (1996). Cerebral organization of component processes in reading. *Brain, 119,* 1221–1238.

Roskies, A. L., Fiez, J. A., Balota, D. A., Raichle, M. E., & Petersen, S. E. (2001). Task-dependent modulation of regions in the left inferior frontal cortex during semantic processing. *Journal of Cognitive Neuroscience, 13,* 829–843.

Rossell, S. L., Price, C. J., & Nobre, C. (2003). The anatomy and time course of semantic priming investigated by fMRI and ERPs. *Neuropsychologia, 41,* 550–564.

Rueckl, J. G. (2002). A connectionist perspective on repetition priming. In J. S. Bowers & C. Marsolek, (Eds.), *Rethinking Implicit Memory* (pp. 67–104). Oxford University Press.

Rueckl, J. G., Mikolinski, M., Raveh, M, Miner, C., & Mars, F. (1997). Morphological priming, fragment completion, and connectionist networks. *Journal of Memory and Language, 36,* 382–405.

Rueckl, J. G., & Raveh, M. (1999). The influence of morphological regularities on the dynamics of a connectionist network. *Brain and Language, 68,* 110–117.

Rumelhart, D. E., Hinton, G., & Williams, R. (1986). Learning internal representations by error propagation. In D. E. Rumelhart, J. McClelland, & the PDP Research Group (Eds.), *Parallel distributed processing: Explorations in the microstructure of cognition. Vol. 1: Foundation* (pp. 318–362). Cambridge, MA: MIT Press.

Rumsey, J. M., Horwitz, B., Donohue, B. C., Nace, K., Maisog, J. M., & Andreason, P. (1997). Phonological and orthographic components of word recognition: A PET-rCBF study. *Brain, 120,* 739–759.

Salmelin, R., Service, E., Kiesilä, P., Uutela, K., & Salonen, O. (1996). Impaired visual word processing in dyslexia revealed with magnetoencephalography. *Annals of Neurology, 40,* 157–162.

Sandak, R., Mencl, W. E., Frost, S. J., Rueckl, J. G., Katz, L., Moore, D., et al. (2004). The neurobiology of adaptive learning in reading: A contrast of different training conditions. *Cognitive, Affective, & Behavioral Neuroscience, 4,* 67–88.

Scott, S. K., & Johnsrude, I. S. (2003). The neuroanatomical and functional organization of speech perception. *Trends in Neuroscience, 26,* 100–107.

Seidenberg, M., & Gonnerman, L. (2000). Explaining derivational morphology as the convergence of codes. *Trends in Cognitive Sciences, 4,* 353–361.

Seidenberg, M. S. (1995). Visual word recognition: An overview. In P. Eimas & J. L. Miller (Eds.), *Handbook of perception and cognition: Language* (pp. 137–179). New York: Academic Press.

Seidenberg, M. S. (2005). Connectionist models of word reading. *Current Directions in Psychological Science, 14*(5), 238–242.

Seidenberg, M. S., & McClelland, J. L. (1989). A distributed, developmental model of visual word recognition. *Psychological Review, 96,* 523–568.

Shaywitz, B., Shaywitz, S., Blachman, B., Pugh, K. R., Fulbright, R., Skudlarski, P., et al. (2004). Development of left occipitotemporal systems for skilled reading following a phonologically based intervention in children. *Biological Psychiatry, 55,* 926–933.

Shaywitz, B. A., Shaywitz, S. E., Pugh, K. R., Mencl, W. E., Fulbright, R. K., Constable, R. T., et al. (2002). Disruption of posterior brain systems for reading in children with developmental dyslexia. *Biological Psychology, 52,* 101–110.

Shaywitz, S. E., Shaywitz, B. A., Pugh, K. R., Fulbright, R. K., Constable, R. T., Mencl, W. E., Shankweiler, D. P., Liberman, A. M., Skudlarski, P., Fletcher, J. M., Katz, L., Marchione, K. E., Lacadie, C., Gatenby, C., & Gore, J. C. (1998). Functional disruption in the organization of the brain for reading in dyslexia. *Proceedings of the National Academy of Sciences, 95,* 2636–2641.

Smith, F. (1978). *Understanding reading.* New York: Holt, Rinehart, & Winston.

Snowling, M. J. (1991). Developmental reading disorders. *Journal of Child Psychology and Psychiatry, 32,* 49–77.

Stanovich, K. E., & Siegel, L. S. (1994). Phenotypic performance profile of children with reading disabilities: A regression-based test of the phonological-core variable-difference model. *Journal of Educational Psychology, 86,* 24–53.

Strain, E., Patterson, K., & Seidenberg, M. S. (1995). Semantic effects in single word naming. *Journal of Experimental Psychology: Learning, Memory, and Cognition, 21,* 1140–1154.

Tan, L. H., Spinks, J. A., Gao, J. H., Liu, H. L., Perfetti, C. A., Xiong, J., et al. (2000). Brain activation in the processing of Chinese characters and words: A functional MRI study. *Human Brain Mapping, 10,* 16–27.

Turkeltaub, P. E., Gareau, L., Flowers, D. L., Zeffiro, T. A., & Eden, G. F. (2003). Development of neural mechanisms for reading. *Nature Neuroscience, 6,* 767–773.

Ungerleider, L. G., Doyon, J., & Karni, A. (2002). Imaging brain plasticity during motor skill learning. *Neurobiology of Learning and Memory, 78,* 553–564.

Van Orden, G. C., Pennington, B. F., & Stone, G. O. (1990). Word identification in reading and the promise of subsymbolic psycholinguistics. *Psychological Review, 97*(4), 488–522.

Vinckier, F., Dehaene, S., Jobert, A., Dubus, J. P., Sigmna, M., & Cohen, L. (2007). Hierarchical coding of letter strings in the ventral stream: Dissecting the inner organization of the visual word-form system. *Neuron, 55,* 143–156.

Visser, T., & Besner, D. (2001). On the dominance of whole-word knowledge in reading aloud. *Psychonomic Bulletin and Review, 8,* 560–567.

Wang, Y., Sereno, J. A., Jongman, A., & Hirsch, J. (2003). fMRI evidence for cortical modification during learning of Mandarin lexical tone. *Journal of Cognitive Neuroscience, 15,* 1019–1027.

Waters, G. S., Seidenberg, M. S., & Bruck, M. (1984). Children's and adults' use of spelling-sound information in three reading tasks. *Memory and Cognition, 12*, 293–305.

Yang, J., Zevin, J. D., Shu, H., McCandliss, B. D., & Li, P. (2006). A triangle model of Chinese reading. Proceedings of the Twenty-Eighth Annual Conference of the Cognitive Science Society. Mahwah, NJ: Lawrence Erlbaum.

Ziegler, J. C., & Goswami, U. (2005). Reading acquisition, developmental dyslexia, and skilled reading across languages: A psycholinguistic grain size theory. *Psychological Bulletin, 131*, 3–29.

Ziegler, J. C., Pech-Georgel, C., George, F., Alario, F. X., & Lorenzi, C. (2005). Deficits in speech perception predict language learning impairment. *Proceedings of the National Academy of Sciences, 102*, 14110–14115.

Ziegler, J. C., Perry, C., Jacobs, A. M., & Braun, M. (2001). Identical words are read differently in different languages. *Psychological Science, 12*, 379–384.

7 The Devil Is in the Details

Decoding the Genetics of Reading

Elena L. Grigorenko and Adam J. Naples

The last decade of research on the biological bases of reading has generated an exciting quilt of findings integrating what we currently know about the biological machinery behind the skill of reading. This machinery is impressive in many aspects, but mostly in its robustness. Given its complexity, it is quite amazing how relatively rarely it breaks down. In fact, there are relatively few cases in the literature of individuals who are absolutely unable to read. And most, if not all, of these cases present some other fundamental developmental problems, such as severe mental retardation. If taught, the overwhelming majority of people can learn to read, at least to some degree. Yet people exhibit significant variation in their number of errors when reading aloud, in their speed of reading (both aloud and silently), and in their degree of comprehension of the written material.

Everybody who contributed to this book is on the quest to understand how this biological machinery of reading is built in the course of development, how it constructs and installs various safety, efficiency, and flexibility mechanisms to achieve the highest possible levels of performance, and where its vulnerable spots are. Understanding these three aspects of the machinery (i.e., its formation, sustainment, and vulnerability) is crucial for understanding both typical and atypical reading.

In this chapter, capitalizing on contributions by many contributors to the symposium (see especially chapters in this volume by Olson, Byrne, & Samuelsson, and Rosen, Wang, Fiondella, & LoTurco), we offer some comments on the growing literature concerning genetic mechanisms underlying typical and atypical reading.

Our comments are organized around the following themes. First, we comment on the general landscape of the emerging findings in the field of specific reading disability (SRD). Specifically, we will discuss issues of replication and nonreplication in the context of the emerging landscape of genetic findings in the field of reading. Second, we consider what is known about the function of genes labeled as candidate genes for SRD. Finally, we offer our expectations on where the field of genetics of SRD appears to be going. In all of these commentaries, we view and understand SRD as a disorder of genetic origin with a basis in the brain (Saviour & Ramachandra, 2006).

REPLICATION OR NONREPLICATION?

During the last 5 years or so, since the draft completion of the Human Genome Project (www.ornl.gov/sci/techresources/Human_Genome/home.shtml) and the International HapMap Project (www.hapmap.org/)—the two projects that form the foundation of today's genetic sciences—the debate on issues concerning the replication and nonreplication of the reported connections between specific phenotypes and genes or alleles has become central to the field of the genetics of disorders and normal traits. There are many examples of "exciting" findings in genetics that were initially published in high-profile scientific journals and then knocked off their pedestals under the pressure of nonreplication. Thus, the question of sustaining the pressure of postreport inquiry is no less serious than Hamlet's "To be or not to be?"

In a general sense, replication means that a particular reported finding is validated by a subsequent independent investigation, thus strengthening the credibility of the first finding. On the contrary, a refutation or nonreplication means that a particular finding is not validated, thus weakening the credibility of that finding. Thus, the transition from the phrase "based on this finding, it is suggested that ..." to "based on the literature, it is accepted that ...," where the specific ending of this statement reflects the balance of replications and refutations, is made in accordance with the credibility curve of the first finding. In other words, a replication adds to and a nonreplication subtracts from such a credibility curve for any firsthand finding. However, whereas there is a clear understanding and broad support for the process of validation and accreditation of a firsthand finding, there is much uncertainty regarding the features of a finding that is worthy of attempts at replication, methodological details of an adequate replication study, and defining specifics of an outcome (i.e., distinctions between a replication and a refutation). Although these issues are debated in the literature (see, for example, NCI-NHGRI Working Group on Replication in Association Studies et al., 2007; Sullivan, 2007), here we briefly illustrate some of the points of contention and concern to the landscape of research on reading.

In providing such illustrations, we want to remind the reader of the distinction between *operational* and *constructive* replications (Lykken, 1968). Providing this distinction, Lykken wrote about the need for the field of psychology to produce constructive attempts at replication that challenge and extend original findings, not merely operationally reproduce them. Applying this distinction to the current debate on replication, Sullivan (2007), on the contrary, appears to call for operational (in his terms, "precise") replications, carried out at the best possible level of strict and rigorous criteria for comparisons (from as closely matched samples as possible to the same statistical strategies and techniques used in the original analyses).

Using Lykken's idea of constructive replications, through multiple studies that incrementally expanded the results of the previous studies, the field has arrived at a number of broad general conclusions. These conclusions are present in numerous reviews of the genetic studies of SRD published in the last 2 to 3 years (Bates, 2006; Caylak, 2007; Fawcett & Nicolson, 2007; Fisher & Francks,

2006; Kovas & Plomin, 2006; McGrath, Smith, & Pennington, 2006; Olson, 2006; Paracchini, Scerri, & Monaco, 2007; Saviour & Ramachandra, 2006; Sawyer, 2006; Schumacher, Hoffman, Schmäl, Schulte-Körne, & Nöthen, 2007; Shastry, 2007; Smith, 2007; Williams & O'Donovan, 2006) and can be summarized as follows. First, it is now accepted that the origin of SRD is genetic; thus, there is a quest for specific genes. Second, it is believed that SRD is caused not by a single gene, but by many genes, most likely by "conspiracies" of genes. Currently nine candidate regions of the human genome DYX1-DYX9—15q21 (DYX1), 6p21-p22 (DYX2), 2p12-p16 (DYX3), 6q11-q12 (DYX4), 3p12-q13 (DYX5), 18p11 (DYX6), 11p15 (DYX7), 1p34-p35 (DYX8), and Xq26-q27 (DYX9)—each of which is assumed to harbor at least one and possibly more candidate genes, are considered. Yet, new studies in new samples contribute new candidate regions and this tendency is expected to continue. Third, it is anticipated that, when considered individually, each of these genes contributes only small effects. A combined effect of many genes, whether linear or nonlinear (e.g., involving interactions between genes) is expected. Fourth, given that heritability estimates for SRD itself and its componential processes, although substantial, are far from being 1, it is assumed that environment plays an important role in mediating the effect of genetic risk factors. Fifth, genetic linkage and association have been shown not only with SRD as a categorical diagnosis, but also with SRD's many cognitive components (e.g., phonemic awareness, single-word identification), which are distributed quantitatively in disordered samples and in the general population. Sixth, there are six candidate genes currently being evaluated as causal genes for SRD: *DYX1C1, KIAA0319, DCDC2, ROBO1, MRPL2,* and *C2orf3.* Thus, in terms of Lykken's constructive replications, the field of genetics of SRD has advanced marvelously since the seminal 1983 paper by Smith and colleagues, which introduced the first candidate region for SRD, DYX1 (15q21), to the field. All in all, these 25 years of research present a very impressive picture of discovery.

Nonetheless, the perception of advances in the field gets attenuated when we consider Sullivan's (2007) concept of "strict" replication. First, using the current guidelines for qualification of a study as an attempt at replication, very few studies in the field of genetics of SRD would even qualify. In fact, not a single DYX1-DYX9 region has consistently been established as a susceptibility region; there is at least one nonsupportive result for each of the regions, and there is often more than one. Second, there is no single phenotype, either categorical or quantitative, that has been linked or associated consistently across multiple samples, genetic regions, or genes. Phenotypically, the presentation of SRD is complex, and when considered together (e.g., by means of Fisher product), the patterns of results for different phenotypes can negate one another (see the meta-analyses for DYC1-DYX8 for a constellation of different phenotypes in Grigorenko, 2005). Third, and most strikingly, of the six candidate genes at the scene, not a single gene meets Sullivan's criteria of producing replicable results. (Admittedly, these criteria were developed for case-control study and comparable criteria for family-based association studies might not be so stringent.)

To illustrate this last point, let us consider the stories of two of the six candidate genes, *KIAA0319*[1] and *DCDC2*.[2] Both genes are located in the same susceptibility region, DYX2 (6p21-p22). We selected these two genes because for each of them the literature refers to "discovery" studies, Francks et al. (2004) for *KIAA0319* and Meng et al. (2005) for *DCDC*; and "replication" studies, Cope et al. (2005) for *KIAA0319* and Schumacher et al. (2006) for *DCDC2*. The other candidate genes are referred to in the literature as awaiting replication (e.g., Paracchini et al., 2007; Schumacher et al., 2007), although some interesting if not fully convincing observations suggesting a possible involvement of at least *DYX1C1* with SRD (Brkanac et al., 2007; Marino et al., 2007; Wigg et al., 2004) have been made. Returning to *KIAA0319* and *DCDC2*, how strong is the attempt at replication, provided strict (precise) criteria? Sullivan's precise replication assumes, in the initial and replication studies, (a) the presence of association with identical genetic markers, (b) identical statistical tests, and (c) effects going in the same direction.

For *DCDC2*, the discovery sample was from the Colorado Learning Disabilities Research Center (CLDRC) sample (see Olson et al., this volume); the replication for this study was carried out with a German sample. The association was reported for only partially overlapping Single Nucleotide Polymorphisms (SNPs), rs793862, rs807724, and rs1087266 for the original (Meng et al., 2005), and rs793862 and rs807701 for the replication (Schumacher et al., 2006) studies, respectively; neither study carried out any type of correction for multiple comparisons. In addition, the associations were also reported for different phenotypes. The original study used 12 quantitative phenotypes, two of which, the discriminant score and the homonym choice phenotypes, were labeled as demonstrating "the peak of transmission disequilibrium." The replication study used the "disease status" (SRD in this sample was defined as "spelling disorder") phenotype and four quantitative phenotypes, which were conceptually close but not identical to those used in the discovery sample. None of the quantitative phenotypes showed evidence of association in the replication sample. The presence of genetic association was established by means of the QTDT software in the discovery and the TDT software in the replication sample. Finally, neither of the studies showed the direction of the established effects; neither article presented the corresponding analyses.

For *KIAA0319*, both the discovery and the replication studies included multiple samples: the CLDRC sample and the Oxford, United Kingdom, sample for the former, and the Cardiff, United Kingdom, sample for the latter. Similar, although not completely overlapping, panels of SNPs were used, but there were multiple SNPs (consistently, rs4504469, rs2179515, and rs2038137), which indicated the presence of association in multiple samples within the original study (Francks et al., 2004) and the replication study (Cope et al., 2005) and across the studies. The analyses were carried out with different statistical software (QTDT and Merlin for the discovery, and ENPHASED and custom-made regression routines for the replication sample). The phenotypes used were different, with the discovery study using the quantitative phenotypes and the replication study the categorical phenotypes. The direction of the effects was not discussed in either presentation.

The reports did not offer any evidence for systematic adjustments for multiple comparisons. The patterns of the association did not feature any specific SNP or haplotype; similarly, no specific phenotype was implicated. To at least partially homogenize this discrepant pattern of results, the U.K. discovery and the replication samples (i.e., the Oxford and Cardiff samples) were merged in a collaborative effort (Harold et al., 2006), and the resulting sample was reanalyzed with all old markers and a number of new markers for *KIAA0319* and *DCDC2*. Six quantitative phenotypes were used in the Oxford sample and one categorical phenotype was used in the Cardiff sample. The *p*-values were adjusted with Bonferroni corrections and combined via Fisher's probability test. These analyses revealed evidence of association between SRD (as captured by either the quantitative, in the Oxford sample, or qualitative, in the Cardiff sample, phenotypes) and five SNPs (rs4504469, rs2179515, rs761100, rs2038137, rs1555090) in both samples, whether analyzed separately or jointly.

It is important to comment on three additional details before making a summative statement. Specifically, the ascertainment schemes used in these studies are different. The CLDRC and the Cardiff samples were recruited from the general population through school systems. The German and Oxford samples are clinical samples, ascertained through families who approached clinical centers for assessment. Although the ascertainment criteria are not featured by Sullivan's (2007) discussion of precise replications, many studies in genetic epidemiology assert the importance of taking the ascertainment scheme into account in interpreting results of genetic studies. Another interesting detail is that, at some moment, both the *KIAA0319* and the *DCDC2* discovery groups were working with a substantially overlapping sample (the CLDRC sample), in which each of the groups saw "their" and not the "other group's" association. Moreover, each group attempted a replication of the other group's findings in separate samples and these attempts were unsuccessful. Finally, currently there is at least one more study that found no evidence for the association of SRD with either *KIAA0319* or *DCDC2* (Brkanac et al., 2007).

Thus, from the point of view of precise replications, the field looks substantially less inspiring than from the point of view of constructive replications. The worry is that the level of precision in establishing parameters for replication studies appears to be crucial for minimizing an astonishingly high rate of false positives, expected from attempts at replication based on simulation studies, up to 96% (Sullivan, 2007). It is also very worrisome that, empirically, only a fifth to a quarter of initially reported positive associations between genetic markers and complex diseases or traits tend to be replicated (Ioannidis, Trikalinos, Ntzani, & Contopoulos-Ioannidis, 2003). Since, as per current perceptions of the rate of false positives in genetic association studies based on empirical and simulated data, we anticipate that at least 75% (or more) of the originally reported findings will not be replicated, we need to be quite conservative in appraising the reported genetic associations. It appears that none of the candidate genes can be excluded from the candidate-gene list (e.g., Paracchini et al., 2007), but, at this point, none of them receive unequivocal or unified support from the field.

There is a distinct possibility that this current situation is recognizable as a winner's curse or Pyrrhic victory; whether in the economic markets, business, auctions, theaters of war or politics, literature, and sport, the costs of the "victory" cannot be justified, because the value of such a victory was falsely overstated. Sullivan's (2007) concern about overwhelming the field of genetics of complex behaviors with unreplicable false positives is a serious one because of its scientific, financial, and public implications. The excitement associated with the introduction of the first candidate gene for SRD (Taipale et al., 2003) has been replaced by cautious attitudes pertaining to replicability of the reported original findings. Now, even the first presentation of a candidate gene or genes in a prestigious journal routinely contains an original sample and a replication sample (Anthoni et al., 2007); subsequently more independent investigations from the field are expected to form an opinion on the new candidates.

WHAT DO SRD CANDIDATE GENES DO?

Although the field is divided behind the support for specific candidate genes (or lack thereof), the notion of candidate genes for SRD generates much excitement. One of the reasons for this excitement is a convergence of evidence regarding early work on structural peculiarities of postmortem brains of individuals with SRD (Galaburda, Sherman, Rosen, Aboitiz, & Geschwind, 1985), research on animal models of dyslexia (Galaburda, LoTurco, Ramus, Fitch, & Rosen, 2006), and functional profiles of the SRD candidate genes (Paracchini et al., 2007; Schumacher et al., 2007). The history and reasoning behind and evidence in support of this excitement are described by Rosen et al. (this volume). Here we briefly present a number of specific details that are of interest in the context of this discussion.

As of today, the field entertains six candidate genes for SRD. Four of these genes are discussed extensively in this volume (Olson et al. and Rosen et al.) and elsewhere (e.g., Galaburda et al., 2006; Paracchini et al., 2007; Schumacher et al., 2007; Smith, 2007). Two other "new" genes were introduced to the literature only recently and not enough time has passed yet for other laboratories to report on replicability of these findings. Here we briefly review major characteristics of these six gene candidates for SRD. In doing so, we present information on the structural and functional (known or inferred, based on recognizable DNA sequences present in a gene that are known to be coding for particular aspects/ components of proteins) characteristics of these genes.

DYX1C1 is located in 15q21.3; three isoforms[3] exist for this gene. Depending on which isoform is considered, the gene spans ~78–90 Kb and includes 9–10 exons. Its default isoform (isoform a) is characterized by 10 (9 coding) exons spread through 77,927 base pairs of DNA. This isoform encodes a protein (primary accession number Q8WXU2) that includes 420 amino acids and has 4 recognizable domains, 1 CS and 3 TPR (three tetratricopeptide repeat) domains[4] (http://ca.expasy.org/cgi-bin/niceprot.pl?Q8WXU2), with the TPR domain being generally involved in protein–protein interactions. This protein is expressed in a number of tissues (lung, kidney, and testes), including the brain, where it localizes to a fraction of cortical neurons and white matter glial cells.

ROBO1 is located in 3p12.3 and belongs to the immunoglobulin superfamily; there are two different isoforms of this gene. The isoforms cover ~422–992 Kb and include 29–30 exons. The isoform *a* has 30 exons spanning 992,672 base pairs and coding for a protein (Q9Y6N7, http://ca.expasy.org/cgi-bin/niceprot. pl?Q9Y6N7), including 1,651 amino acids and containing 3 fibronectin type-III and 5 Ig-like C2-type (immunoglobulin-like) domains. This protein is expressed widely (with the exception of the kidney) and is localized in cellular membranes. The name for this gene is "roundabout 1" and it is structurally similar to the roundabout gene (a member of the immunoglobin gene superfamily) in drosophila. In fruit flies, this gene encodes a protein that has two functions, exon guidance and cell adhesion receptor; the protein is involved in determining whether and at which axons to cross the central nervous system midline (a characteristic of all bilateral symmetric nervous systems). In humans, *ROBO1* acts as a receptor for chemorepellent proteins SLIT1 and SLIT2, whose function is assumed to be that of molecular guidance cue in cellular migration (including axonal migration across the ventral midline; Rajagopalan, Nicolas, Vivancos, Berger, & Dickson, 2000; Ward, McCann, DeWulf, Wu, & Rao, 2003).

KIAA0319 is situated at 6p22.2. The gene spans 102,052 base pairs and contains 21 (20 coding) exons. The protein encoded by this gene (Q5VV43) is localized to membranes, contains 1,072 amino acids, and is characterized by three recognizable (1 MANSC and 2 PKD) domains (http://ca.expasy.org/cgi-bin/ niceprot.pl?Q5VV43). The protein produced by this gene is expressed in brain and cerebellum tissue.

Just like *KIAA0319*, *DCDC2* is also located in 6p22.2; it is separated from *KIAA0319* only by ~170 Kb. It is present in two isoforms, covering ~33–211 Kb and including 3–10 exons. The isoform 1 spans 211,538 base pairs, contains 11 (10 coding) exons, and encodes 476 amino acids. The protein contains 2 doublecortin domains (therefore, the gene name, *DCDC2*, is an abbreviation of its full name, doublecortin domain-containing protein 2). This domain has been shown to bind certain types of globular proteins, tubulins, which make microtubules, structural components within cells participating in numerous cellular processes (one of the subtypes of tibulins, class III beta-globulin, is found exclusively in neurons). *DCDC2* shares features with the *DCX* gene (Sossey-Alaoui et al., 1998), coding for a cytoplasmic protein that regulates the organization of microtubules during neuronal migration (Gleeson, Lin, Flanagan, & Walsh, 1999). The expression of the protein (Q9UHG0) is ubiquitous (http://ca.expasy.org/cgi-bin/niceprot.pl?Q9UHG0).

MRPL19 is located in 2p12. This gene spans ~15–24 Kb and includes 6 coding exons, encoding a protein consisting of 292 amino acids. The protein (P49406) is localized in mitochondrion and recognized as a member of the ribosomal protein L19P family (http://ca.expasy.org/cgi-bin/niceprot.pl?P49406). Members of this family assist in protein synthesis within the mitochondrion.

The last current candidate, *C2orf3*, is also situated at 2p12, ~31 Kb from *MRPL19*. It spans ~49 Kb and includes 17 exons coding for a 781-aminoacid protein

(P16383), which is localized in nuclei. It is recognized as a member of the GCF (GC-rich sequence DNA-binding factor) gene family. Functionally, GCF proteins bind the GC-rich sequences present in the epidermal growth factor receptor, beta-actin, and calcium-dependent protease promoters, and represses transcription. It is widely expressed in all tissues (http://ca.expasy.org/cgi-bin/niceprot.pl?P16383).

Thus, for the six current candidate genes, there is prior evidence for involvement in axon growth and neuronal migration for only one of them, *ROBO1*. As for concurrent evidence, three candidate genes (*DYX1C1, KIAA0319, DCDC2*) have been subjected to interrogations in the developing rat cerebral neocortex (Meng et al., 2005; Threlkeld et al., 2007; Wang et al., 2006), using the technique known as in utero RNA interference (RNAi; Bai et al., 2003). This technique permits inhibition of the activity of a selected gene only in those neurons getting ready to move toward their ultimate positions in the hierarchical configuration of the cortex. Specifically, this technique relies on implantation into a cell of an RNA molecule that is capable of instigating the degradation of the complementary cellular mRNA ultimately resulting in the elimination of an activity of the targeted gene. Introduction of RNAi resulted in local loss of function for all three genes tested. The specifics of the outcomes, however, were somewhat different for the three interrogated genes.

RNAi against *Dyx1c1* (a rodent ortholog of the human *DYX1C1*) disrupts neuronal migration in the developing embryonic neocortex by resulting in pockets on unmigrated and faultily migrated neurons (Rosen et al., 2007; Threlkeld et al., 2007; Wang et al., 2006). The deficiencies in the migration patterns were observed through shortened migration distances 4 days after the transfection and abnormal placement, and were associated with specific phenotypical features (Threlkeld et al., 2007). It was hypothesized that the TRP domain of the gene plays a crucial role in the migration process.

The local loss of function for *Dcdc2* (a rodent ortholog of the human *DCDC2*) led to abnormal migration, evident through a reduced (by ~40%) average distance and percentage of migrated neurons as compared with that normally observed 4 days after the introduction of RNAi (Meng et al., 2005).

The RNAi of rat *Kiaa0319* (a rodent ortholog of the human *KIAA0319*) resulted in reduced migration distances and detectable changes in the morphology of migrating neurons 4 days after the introduction of RNAi (Paracchini et al., 2006). These changes in morphology generated a hypothesis that *KIAA0319* might be required to adhere migrating neurons to radial glial fibers. Given that the *KIAA0319* gene possesses polycystic kidney disease (PKD) domains, implicated in functions of cell adhesion, it is possible that some variants of the gene result in the changed forms of the protein, which can weaken the degree of adhesion between the neurons and the radial glia (Paracchini et al., 2006).

The difference in the outcomes of the RNAi studies with three of the six candidate genes for SRD resulted in the generation of a "role differentiation" hypothesis for the three genes (for details, see Rosen et al., this volume). Specifically, it has been hypothesized that *Kiaa0319* might be involved in the process of cell adhesion; *Dcdc2* might be involved in neuronal migration and processes of extension, and cell polarity determination; and *Dyx1c1* might participate in the transition to the multipolar stage of neuronal migration (LoTurco & Bai, 2006).

It is this intriguing set of findings and evidence for functional similarities among four of the six candidate genes that generates excitement in the field. Of these four candidate genes (the last two genes being offered to the field in the spring of 2007), one has been long implicated in neuronal migration, and three others have all sustained the pressure of RNAi experiments and encode for proteins with known domains that could well be involved with neuronal migration. Indeed, it is an intriguing and stimulating state of affairs, and amid the hype of attempting to comprehend these results, researchers readily close their eyes to the fact that genetic associations with either *ROBO1* or *DYX1C1* have not really been replicated in independent samples.

In addition, a number of other observations are relevant here. First, all RNAi experiments, so far, have been conducted in the same laboratory. It seems important that the impact of the local loss of function for the four candidate genes of interest be investigated in different laboratories. Second, the published experiments do not reveal information on the number of animals on which the impact of transfection was investigated. It seems important to replicate these experiments on a respectfully large number of animals, providing an account of the range of individual responses to the transfection. Third, it is important to place these findings in a larger context of developmental neuroscience. Neuronal migration is a fundamental process in the establishment of the neocortex. Migration involves multiple stages and agents such as cell adhesion, actin cytoskeleton, microtubules and their regulation, dynein and other molecular motors, centrosome, tyrosine phosphatases, and tyrosine kinases. Each of these processes and agents are controlled by numerous genes, which collectively amount to hundreds of genes (assuming that these processes are restricted to neuronal cells only). In this context, the fact that four of the six candidate genes appear to be somehow related to neuronal migration (that is, of course, if their association with SRD is confirmed) is no longer that astonishing. In addition, there are families of genes whose role in neuronal migration has been convincingly established (e.g., both ligands and receptors from the groups of the semaphorin genes and the fibroblast growth factor [FGF] genes, and many others). It is noteworthy that one of the semaphoring (SEMA) genes, *SEMA4F*, which maps to 2p13.1 (DYX3 susceptibility region for DD), has been evaluated as a candidate gene for SRD, and this evaluation did not produce affirmative results (Francks et al., 2002). In summary, although the information accumulated so far on the six candidate genes for SRD is promising and productive of hypotheses, at this stage, the genes themselves and their functions in SRD are still only that, hypotheses.

A SET OF CAUTIOUS EXPECTATIONS FOR THE FUTURE

So far, we have focused primarily on the candidate genes for SRD. We mentioned, in passing, the nine genomic regions of interest (DYX1–DYX9) for SRD and commented on the anticipation that more regions will be identified with the addition of new samples and the enhancement of technology. As we implied earlier, we also believe that some regions and genes that are currently on the table in the quest for "genes for reading" might end up not being reading specific at all. Here we expand these remarks and illustrate it with a number of recent studies. We summarize these studies, noting specific aspects that from our point of view are instrumental in terms of interpreting the current picture of genetic research in the field of SRD.

Years and years of research conducted on numerous families resulted in the field's firm belief that genes matter for typical and atypical reading acquisition (see Olson et al., this volume). In addition, this research resulted in a number of observations that are relevant to this discussion. Specifically, it is accepted that SRD presents through a complex componential phenotype, with the components demonstrating differential heritabilities (Grigorenko, 2004) whose magnitudes appear to fluctuate with age (Friend, DeFries, Wadsworth, & Olson, 2007). In addition, based on a number of twin and family studies, it is believed that reading-related componential processes are characterized by general (or shared; e.g., Harlaar, Dale, & Plomin, 2007) and specific (or unique; e.g., Zumberge, Baker, & Manis, 2006) variance. For example, one recent family study investigated a variety of reading-related indicators with a sample of 287 families with SRD and reported that the correlation between the component phenotypes of SRD varied from –0.1 to 0.7 and the familiality estimates ranged from 0.25 to 0.63 (Schulte-Körne et al., 2006). Similarly, twin studies indicate the contributions of common and specific genes when reading and reading-related measures are considered in multivariate analyses (see Olson et al., this volume).

When these observations are taken a step further, specific analytic procedures are used to decompose these shared and unique contributions of genes, so that an anticipated number of genes can be estimated for reading-related traits. A number of such traits have been investigated in the context of so-called segregation analyses (i.e., the patterns of transmission of strengths and weaknesses, or similarities and dissimilarities on particular traits among family members). The results indicated that it is likely that each reading-related trait is controlled by a number of genes, and these genes are only partially overlapping for different traits (Wijsman et al., 2000). Estimates indicate that there are might be three to six genes contributing to each of the reading-related processes, with only 50% of these genes contributing to more than one process (Naples, Chang, Katz, & Grigorenko, in press). Moreover, it is estimated that the contributions of genes are characterized by rather small effect sizes (Meaburn, Harlaar, Craig, Schalkwyk, & Plomin, 2008; Naples et al., in press).

Based on these findings, it is not surprising that nearly every new genome-wide scan for SRD returns new candidate regions (in addition to the nine mentioned above, DYX1–DYX9; e.g., Meaburn et al., 2008). That tendency is likely to continue with more and more powerful and well-characterized samples of individuals with SRD becoming available for analyses. Also of interest is that many, or all in some cases (Meaburn et al., 2008), of the previously identified regions are not confirmed as susceptibility regions for SRD in these new samples. Thus, the hunt is ongoing not only for specific genes that contribute to SRD, but also for specific regions that might harbor such genes.

In this discussion, it is important to mention a different class of studies in which genes and their allelic polymorphisms implicated as being associated with specific disorders are investigated in samples of typically developing individuals (e.g., Bates et al., 2007; Luciano et al., 2006). For example, the role of a set of unstable tetranucleotide repeats known to be associated with specific neurogenerative disorders (e.g., Huntington's chorea) has been investigated as a predictive source of variance for a variety of cognition-related indicators in an unselected sample of adolescent twins (Luciano et al., 2007). In selecting their cognitive indicators, the investigators focused on those indicators demonstrated to be affected in the repeat-dependent disorders, for example, visual reaction time (RT) and IQ (digit symbol processing, arithmetic, spatial ability, object assembly, general knowledge, and vocabulary). The researchers reported weak but present and, therefore, interesting consistent positive association of the repeat in the *SCA1* gene with the arithmetic subtest of an IQ test ($P = 0.04$).

Similarly, traits that are distributed normally in the general population (e.g., IQ or reading-related processes) are studied in well-characterized samples of individuals ascertained for a trait-unrelated disease (e.g., substance abuse; Dick et al., 2006). Of interest is that such studies of individuals who were not ascertained for specific deficits call to the field's attention some of the same candidate regions implicated for SRD (e.g., Posthuma & de Geus, 2006).

Another interesting line of inquiries is into disorders that present as highly comorbid with SRD, such as attention deficit/hyperactivity disorder (ADHD), a variety of speech and language conditions (e.g., speech and sound disorders, SSD; specific language impairment, SLI; stuttering), and other learning disabilities (e.g., specific math disability). Both behavior genetic and molecular literature contains evidence for the existence of overlapping genetic mechanisms for these disorders (e.g., SRD and ADHD: Caylak, 2007; Luca et al., 2007; Willcutt, Pennington, Olson, & DeFries, 2007; SRD, SSD and SLI: DeThorne et al., 2007; Lewis et al., 2007; Stein et al., 2004, 2006; White, 2007), and much more work is needed to sort out disorder-general and disorder-specific contributions of various SRD-related candidate regions and candidate genes. Of particular interest are overlapping procedural deficits between linguistic disorders, both pairwise (e.g., deficits that are shared between two conditions; Boets, Ghesquière, van Wieringen, & Wouters, 2007) and listwise (e.g., deficits that seem to be common to all developmental language disorders; Grigorenko, 2007).

Finally, there are certain regions in the genome that seem to be connected to a number of developmental disorders, some of which are comorbid and some of which are not. Specifically, the genetic linkage has been established for the long arm of chromosome 15 and SRD (DYX1), but also for autism, schizophrenia, major depressive disorder, juvenile epilepsy, Prader-Willi/Angelman syndrome, and spinocerebellar ataxia (for details, see Chagnon, 2005). Although these conditions were linked to somewhat different regions of the long arm, these differences need to be explored further and mapped more precisely to argue that these are differential linkages. It is possible that such popular chromosomal regions as 15q might be characterized by genome disregulation of a type that predisposes a developing organism for a number of possible disordered outcomes early in development, and the specific form of such an outcome is determined by some other genes or by environmental influences.

Thus, the future holds a number of serious tasks for the field of genetics of SRD. First, "real" candidate regions and candidate genes must be sorted out. Second, population risk factors, and trait-specific and general genetic risk factors for SRD must be identified. Third, there is the enormous task of translating statistical signals into animal models and understanding the biological machinery underlying these statistical signals. Finally, we must understand whether these mechanisms are limited to disordered reading or are important for the process of reading acquisition more generally, or whether in fact these genetic risk mechanisms are generic to many or some developmental disorders.

In summary, all these literatures are important in interpreting the current landscape of genetic research in the field of SRD. The biological machine of reading is only one of many sets of machinery engaged by the factory of human development. Understanding the mechanisms of "neighboring" machinery of language, attention, and learning in general is probably as important for understanding the "reading machinery" as inquiries into its own parts and mechanics. Although there is much excitement in the field regarding its current state, there is a tremendous amount to sort out. A string of recent publications indicating failures to replicate previously reported genetic associations for a number of complex human conditions and discussing the importance of replication has had a sobering impact on the field of neuropsychiatric genetics in general. Let's hope that all of the SRD-related findings withstand the durability and tests of replicability.

ACKNOWLEDGMENTS

Preparation of this chapter was supported in part by the following research grants from the National Institutes of Health: R01 DC007665 and P01 HD052120. Grantees undertaking such projects are encouraged to express their professional judgment freely. Therefore, this chapter does not necessarily reflect the position or policies of the National Institutes of Health, and no official endorsement should be inferred. We are thankful to Robyn Rissman for her editorial assistance.

NOTES

1. The abbreviation KIAA is used for all genes identified structurally through its cDNAs determined in the Kazusa cDNA sequencing project and identified as a Human Unidentified Gene-Encoded (HUGE) protein. The number after the abbreviation KIAA indicates the sequence number under which a particular gene was described.
2. Doublecortin domain containing 2.

3. That is, slightly different, but carrying the same function and versions of the coded protein.
4. A region of the protein that is defined structurally and functionally.

REFERENCES

Anthoni, H., Zucchelli, M., Matsson, H., Müller-Myhsok, B., Fransson, I., Schumacher, J., et al. (2007). A locus on 2p12 containing the co-regulated MRPL19 and C2ORF3 genes is associated to dyslexia. *Human Molecular Genetics, 16*, 667–677.

Bai, J., Ramos, R. L., Ackman, J. B., Thomas, A. M., Lee, R. V., & LoTurco, J. J. (2003). RNAi reveals doublecortin is required for radial migration in rat neocortex. *Nature Neuroscience, 6*, 1277–1283.

Bates, T. C. (2006). Genes for reading and spelling. *London Review of Education, 4*, 31–47.

Bates, T. C., Luciano, M., Castles, A., Coltheart, M., Wright, M. J., & Martin, N. G. (2007). Replication of reported linkages for dyslexia and spelling and suggestive evidence for novel regions on chromosomes 4 and 17. *European Journal of Human Genetics, 15*, 194–203.

Boets, B., Ghesquière, P., van Wieringen, A., & Wouters, J. (2007). Speech perception in preschoolers at family risk for dyslexia: Relations with low-level auditory processing and phonological ability. *Brain and Language, 101*, 19–30.

Brkanac, Z., Chapman, N. H., Matsushita, M. M., Chun, L., Nielsen, K., Cochrane, E., et al. (2007). Evaluation of candidate genes for DYX1 and DYX2 in families with dyslexia. *American Journal of Medical Genetics, Part B: Neuropsychiatric Genetics, 144*, 556–560.

Caylak, E. (2007). A review of association and linkage studies for genetical analyses of learning disorders. *American Journal of Medical Genetics, Part B: Neuropsychiatric Genetics, 144B*(7), 923–943.

Chagnon, Y. C. (2005). Shared chromosomal susceptibility regions between autism and other mental disorders. *International Review of Neurobiology, 71*, 419–443.

Cope, N., Harold, D., Hill, G., Moskvina, V., Holmans, P., Owen, M. J., et al. (2005). Strong evidence that KIAA0319 on chromosome 6p is a susceptibility gene for developmental dyslexia. *American Journal of Human Genetics, 76*, 581–591.

DeThorne, L. S., Hart, L. A., Petrill, S. A., Deater-Deckard, K., Thompson, L. A., Schatschneider, C., et al. (2007). Children's history of speech-language difficulties: Genetic influences and associations with reading-related measures. *Journal of Speech, Language, and Hearing Research, 49*, 1280–1293.

Dick, D. M., Aliev, F., Bierut, L., Goate, A., Rice, J., Hinrichs, A., et al. (2006). Linkage analyses of IQ in the Collaborative Study on the Genetics of Alcoholism (COGA) sample. *Behavior Genetics, 36*, 77–86.

Fawcett, A. J., & Nicolson, R. I. (2007). Dyslexia, learning, and pedagogical neuroscience. *Developmental Medicine & Child Neurology, 49*, 306–311.

Fisher, S. E., & Francks, C. (2006). Genes, cognition and dyslexia: Learning to read the genome. *Trends in Cognitive Sciences, 10*, 250–257.

Francks, C., Fisher, S. E., Olson, R. K., Pennington, B. F., Smith, S. D., DeFries, J. C., et al. (2002). Fine mapping of the chromosome 2p12-16 dyslexia susceptibility locus: Quantitative association analysis and positional candidate genes SEMA4F and OTX1. *Psychiatric Genetics, 12*, 35–41.

Francks, C., Paracchini, S., Smith, S. D., Richardson, A. J., Scerri, T. S., Cardon, L. R., et al. (2004). A 77-kilobase region on chromosome 6p22.2 is associated with dyslexia in families from the United Kingdom and from the United States. *American Journal of Human Genetics, 75*, 1046–1058.

Friend, A., DeFries, J. C., Wadsworth, S. J., & Olson, R. K. (2007). Genetic and environmental influences on word recognition and spelling deficits as a function of age. *Behavior Genetics, 37*, 477–486.

Galaburda, A. M., LoTurco, J. J., Ramus, F., Fitch, R. H., & Rosen, G. D. (2006). From genes to behavior in developmental dyslexia. *Nature Neuroscience, 9*, 1213–1217.

Galaburda, A. M., Sherman, G. F., Rosen, G. D., Aboitiz, F., & Geschwind, N. (1985). Developmental dyslexia: Four consecutive patients with cortical anomalies. *Annals of Neurology, 18*, 222–233.

Gleeson, J. G., Lin, P. T., Flanagan, L. A., & Walsh, C. A. (1999). Doublecortin is a microtubule-associated protein and is expressed widely by migrating neurons. *Neuron, 23*, 257–271.

Grigorenko, E. L. (2004). Genetic bases of developmental dyslexia: A capsule review of heritability estimates. *Enfance, 3*, 273–287.

Grigorenko, E. L. (2005). A conservative meta-analysis of linkage and linkage-association studies of developmental dyslexia. *Scientific Studies of Reading, 9*, 285–316.

Grigorenko, E. L. (2007). Understanding the etiology of complex traits; symbiotic relationships between psychology and genetics. *Mind, Brain, and Education, 1*(4), 193–199.

Harlaar, N., Dale, P. S., & Plomin, R. (2007). From learning to read to reading to learn: Substantial and stable genetic influence. *Child Development, 78*, 116–131.

Harold, D., Paracchini, S., Scerri, T., Dennis, M., Cope, N., Hill, G., et al. (2006). Further evidence that the KIAA0319 gene confers susceptibility to developmental dyslexia. *Molecular Psychiatry, 11*, 1085–1091.

Ioannidis, J. P., Trikalinos, T. A., Ntzani, E. E., & Contopoulos-Ioannidis, D. G. (2003). Genetic associations in large versus small studies: An empirical assessment. *Lancet, 361*, 567–571.

Kovas, Y., & Plomin, R. (2006). Generalist genes: Implications for the cognitive sciences. *Trends in Cognitive Sciences, 10*, 198–203.

Lewis, B. A., Freebairn, L. A., Hansen, A. J., Miscimarra, L., Iyengar, S. K., & Taylor, H. G. (2007). Speech and language skills of parents of children with speech sound disorders. *American Journal of Speech-Language Pathology, 16*, 108–118.

LoTurco, J. J., & Bai, J. (2006). The multipolar stage and disruptions in neuronal migration. *Trends in Neuroscience, 29*, 407–413.

Luca, P., Laurin, N., Misener, V. L., Wigg, K. G., Anderson, B., Cate-Carter, T., et al. (2007). Association of the dopamine receptor D1 gene, DRD1, with inattention symptoms in families selected for reading problems. *Molecular Psychiatry, 12*, 776–785.

Luciano, M., Hine, E., Wright, M. J., Duffy, D. L., MacMillan, J., & Martin, N. G. (2007). Effects of SCA1, MJD, and DPRLA triplet repeat polymorphisms on cognitive phenotypes in a normal population of adolescent twins. *American Journal of Medical Genetics, Part B: Neuropsychiatric Genetics, 144B*, 95–100.

Luciano, M., Wright, M. J., Duffy, D. L., Wainwright, M. A., Zhu, G., Evans, D. M., et al. (2006). Genome-wide scan of IQ finds significant linkage to a Quantitative Trait Locus on 2q. *Behavior Genetics, 31*, 45–55.

Lykken, D. (1968). Statistical significance in psychological research. *Psychological Bulletin, 70*, 151–159.

Marino, C., Citterio, A., Giorda, R., Facoetti, A., Menozzi, G., Vanzin, L., et al. (2007). Association of short-term memory with a variant within DYX1C1 in developmental dyslexia. *Genes, Brain, & Behavior, 6*, 640–646.

McGrath, L., Smith, S. D., & Pennington, B. F. (2006). Breakthroughs in the search for dyslexia candidate genes. *TRENDS in Molecular Medicine, 12*, 333–341.

Meaburn, E. L., Harlaar, N., Craig, I. W., Schalkwyk, L. C., & Plomin, R. (2008). Quantitative trait locus association scan of early reading disability and ability using pooled DNA and 100K SNP microarrays in a sample of 5760 children. *Molecular Psychiatry, 13*, 729–740.

Meng, H., Smith, S. D., Hager, K., Held, M., Liu, J., Olson, R. K., et al. (2005). DCDC2 is associated with reading disability and modulates neuronal development in the brain *Proceedings of the National Academy of Sciences of the United States of America, 102*, 17053–17058.

Naples, A. J., Chang, J. T., Katz, L., & Grigorenko, E. L. (2009). Same or different? Insights into the etiology of phonological awareness and rapid naming. Manuscript submitted for publication.

NCI-NHGRI Working Group on Replication in Association Studies, Chanock, S. J., Manolio, T., Boehnke, M., Boerwinkle, E., Hunter, D. J., et al. (2007). Replicating genotype-phenotype associations. *Nature, 447*, 655–660.

Olson, R. K. (2006). Genes, environment, and dyslexia. The 2005 Nonnan Geschwind Memorial Lecture. *Annals of Dyslexia, 56*, 205–238.

Paracchini, S., Scerri, T. S., & Monaco, A. P. (2007). The genetic lexicon of dyslexia. *The Annual Review of Genomics and Human Genetics, 8*, 57–79.

Paracchini, S., Thomas, A., Castro, S., Lai, C., Paramasivam, M., Wang, Y., et al. (2006). The chromosome 6p22 haplotype associated with dyslexia reduces the expression of KIAA0319, a novel gene involved in neuronal migration. *Human Molecular Genetics, 15*, 1659–1666.

Posthuma, D., & de Geus, E. J. C. (2006). Progress in the molecular-genetic study of intelligence. *Current Directions in Psychological Science, 15*, 151–155.

Rajagopalan, S., Nicolas, E., Vivancos, V., Berger, J., & Dickson, B. J. (2000). Crossing the midline: Roles and regulation of Robo receptors. *Neuron, 23*, 767–777.

Rosen, G. D., Bai, J., Wang, Y., Fiondella, C. G., Threlkeld, S. W., LoTurco, J. J., et al. (2007). Disruption of neuronal migration by RNAi of Dyx1c1 results in neocortical and hippocampal malformations. *Cerebral Cortex, 17*(11), 2562–2572.

Saviour, P., & Ramachandra, N. B. (2006). Biological basis of dyslexia: A maturing perspective. *Current Science, 90*, 168–175.

Sawyer, D. J. (2006). Dyslexia. A generation of inquiry. *Topics in Language Disorders, 26*, 95–109.

Schulte-Körne, G., Ziegler, A., Deimel, W., Schumacher, J., Plume, E., Bachmann, C., et al. (2006). Interrelationship and familiality of dyslexia related quantitative measures. *Annals of Human Genetics, 71*, 160–175.

Schumacher, J., Anthoni, H., Dahdouh, F., König, I. R., Hillmer, H. M., Kluck, N., et al. (2006). Strong genetic evidence of *DCDC2* as a susceptibility gene for dyslexia. *American Journal of Human Genetics, 78*, 52–62.

Schumacher, J., Hoffman, P., Schmäl, C., Schulte-Körne, G., & Nöthen, M. M. (2007). Genetics of dyslexia: The evolving landscape. *Journal of Medical Genetics, 44*, 289–297.

Shastry, B. S. (2007). Developmental dyslexia: An update. *Journal of Human Genetics, 52*, 104–109.

Smith, S. D. (2007). Genes, language development, and language disorders. *Mental Retardation and Developmental Disabilities, 13*, 95–105.

Sossey-Alaoui, K., Hartung, A. J., Guerrini, R., Manchester, D. K., Posar, A., Puche-Mira, A., et al. (1998). Human doublecortin (DCX) and the homologous gene in mouse encode a putative Ca2+-dependent signaling protein which is mutated in human X-linked neuronal migration defects. *Human Molecular Genetics, 7,* 1327–1332.

Stein, C. M., Millard, C., Kluge, A., Miscimarra, L. E., Cartier, K. C., Freebairn, L. A., et al. (2006). Speech sound disorder influenced by a locus in 15q14 region. *Behavior Genetics, 36,* 858–868.

Stein, C. M., Schick, J. H., Taylor, G. H., Shriberg, L. D., Millard, C., Kundtz-Kluge, A., et al. (2004). Pleiotropic effects of a chromosome 3 locus on speech-sound disorder and reading. *American Journal of Human Genetics, 74,* 283–297.

Sullivan, P. F. (2007). Spurious genetic associations. *Biological Psychiatry, 61,* 1121–1126.

Taipale, M., Kaminen, N., Nopola-Hemmi, J., Haltia, T., Myllyluoma, B., Lyytinen, H., et al. (2003). A candidate gene for developmental dyslexia encodes a nuclear tetratricopeptide repeat domain protein dynamically regulated in brain. *Proceedings of the National Academy of Sciences of the United States of America, 100,* 11553–11558.

Threlkeld, S. W., McClure, M. M., Bai, J., Wang, Y., LoTurco, J. J., Rosen, G. D., et al. (2007). Developmental disruptions and behavioral impairments in rats following in utero RNAi of Dyx1c1. *Brain Research Bulletin, 71,* 508–514.

Wang, Y., Paramasivam, M., Thomas, A., Bai, J., Kaminen-Ahola, N., Kere, J., et al. (2006). Dyx1c1 functions in neuronal migration in developing neocortex. *Neuroscience, 143,* 515–522.

Ward, M., McCann, C., DeWulf, M., Wu, J. Y., & Rao, Y. (2003). Distinguishing between directional guidance and motility regulation in neuronal migration. *Journal of Neuroscience, 23,* 5170–5177.

White, S. M. (2007). Talking genes. *Advances in Speech-Language Pathology, 8,* 2–6.

Wigg, K. G., Couto, J. M., Feng, Y., Anderson, T., Cate-Carter, D., Macciardi, F., et al. (2004). Support for EKN1 as the susceptibility locus for dyslexia on 15q21. *Molecular Psychiatry, 9,* 1111–1121.

Wijsman, E. M., Peterson, D., Leutenegger, A. L., Thomson, J. B., Goddard, K. A. B., Hsu, L., et al. (2000). Segregation analysis of phenotypic components of learning disabilities: I. Nonword memory and digit span. *American Journal of Human Genetics, 67,* 631–646.

Willcutt, E. G., Pennington, B. F., Olson, R. K., & DeFries, J. C. (2007). Understanding comorbidity: A twin study of reading disability and attention deficit/hyperactivity disorder. *American Journal of Medical Genetics, Part B: Neuropsychiatric Genetics, 144B*(6), 709–714.

Williams, J., & O'Donovan, M. C. (2006). The genetics of developmental dyslexia. *European Journal of Human Genetics, 14,* 681–689.

Zumberge, A., Baker, L. A., & Manis, F. R. (2006). Focus on words: A twin study of reading and inattention. *Behavior Genetics, 37,* 284–293.

Section III

Neurobiological, Genetic, and Cognitive Aspects

8 Understanding the Nature of the Phonological Deficit

Franck Ramus and Gayaneh Szenkovits

Phonologists and psycholinguists have described in great detail the structure of phonological representations, the rules (or computations) operating on them, and the various levels of representation and processing that must be involved in speech perception and production. That area has been reviewed before in relation to dyslexia (Ramus, 2001). Here we only recall the overall cognitive architecture that we assume (Figure 8.1) and will explain phonological and psycholinguistic concepts where they are necessary to understand our experiments.

More than 30 years of research on dyslexia have taught us that there are three main dimensions to the phonological deficit (Wagner & Torgesen, 1987):

- Poor phonological awareness (as exemplified in phoneme deletion tasks)
- Poor verbal short-term memory (as exemplified in digit span or nonword repetition tasks)
- Slow lexical retrieval (as exemplified in rapid automatic naming tasks)

The poor performance of people with dyslexia in most (if not all) verbal tasks can be explained by one or several of these dimensions. A pertinent question therefore is why this "dyslexic triad" and why the three dimensions are affected together more often than to be expected by chance. The answer seems to be that the three dimensions have something in common: They all implicate phonological representations, each in its own way. The first dimension concerns conscious access, attention to, and manipulation of those representations and their subunits. Within Figure 8.1, this can be viewed as a central executive processor (not represented) accessing the contents of sublexical phonological representations. The second dimension refers to their storage for a short period of time, either briefly copied in phonological buffers (typically, holding the first words of a sentence for the very short time necessary to process the end), or actively recycling them between input and output sublexical representations (also known as the phonological loop, typically recruited in span tasks). Finally, the third member of the triad involves the retrieval of lexical phonological representations from long-term memory.

Therefore, it should come as no surprise that the most commonly accepted hypothesis regarding the nature of the phonological deficit in dyslexia is that

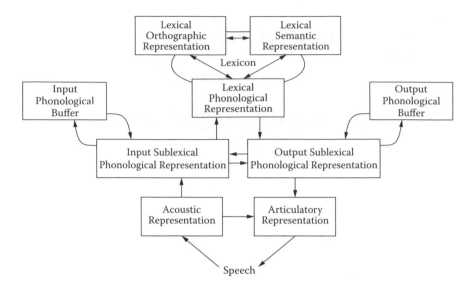

FIGURE 8.1   An information-processing model of speech perception and production, and lexical access.

phonological representations are degraded, that is, they are fuzzier, or noisier, or underspecified, or have a lower resolution or a larger grain size than they should, or are not sufficiently categorical and preserve too many acoustic or allophonic details (e.g., Adlard & Hazan, 1998; Elbro, 1998; Manis et al., 1997; Mody, Studdert-Kennedy, & Brady, 1997; Serniclaes, Van Heghe, Mousty, Carré, & Sprenger-Charolles, 2004; Snowling, 2000). Nevertheless, there is also much more to phonology than these three dimensions, and therefore the hypothesis of a deficit in phonological representations makes a host of additional predictions, concerning notably the early stages of phonological acquisition in the first few years of life and their consequences on on-line speech perception and production (Ramus, 2001).

EXPLORING THE PHONOLOGICAL DEFICIT

In the course of our investigations, we have tested French university students with dyslexia. Self-reports of persons with dyslexia have been supplemented by data from a diagnostic battery, ensuring they met predefined inclusion criteria in terms of nonverbal IQ, reading disability, and presence of a significant phonological deficit (in the sense of the classic triad). Control students were also recruited and underwent the same tests, ensuring that they did not present any reading disability and that they were matched to the students with dyslexia in age and nonverbal IQ (Szenkovits & Ramus, 2005).

This population of university students was thought to be appropriate for testing with psycholinguistic tasks, which tend to be long, boring, and demanding. This does not excuse us from testing a more representative sample of children with age-appropriate tasks, but this was considered a second step after having delineated the most promising hypotheses to warrant confirmation in children.

IN SEARCH OF A LOCUS

In the first series of experiments, we attempted to assess the most relevant levels of representations depicted in Figure 8.1 (Szenkovits & Ramus, 2005). Indeed, the general hypothesis of a phonological deficit does not by itself specify which of the different levels of phonological representation is presumed to be deficient.

To disentangle the various levels, we adopted the following strategy: We contrasted sublexical and lexical levels of representations by comparing tasks involving words and nonwords; and we contrasted input and output pathways by comparing repetition tasks (involving both) with auditory discrimination tasks (involving only input representations). To ensure that discrimination tasks were not performed by covert use of output representations (i.e., the phonological loop), we had an additional condition where the discrimination task was performed with concurrent articulatory suppression (uttering "bababa ..." for the whole duration of each trial, therefore keeping output representations busy). The material to be discriminated or repeated consisted of sequences of monosyllabic nonwords of increasing length (i.e., nonword matching span). Verbal short-term memory load was an important aspect of all the experiments. In the discrimination task, two sequences were heard and compared, which were either identical or differed by one phonetic feature in one of the nonwords.

We found significant group differences in all conditions, suggesting that the phonological deficit appears no matter what levels are involved: sublexical as well as lexical, input as well as output, whether or not articulatory suppression was applied. Furthermore, participants with dyslexia were relatively more impaired in discrimination than in repetition tasks, highlighting more specifically their deficit in input representations. On the other hand, articulatory suppression slightly decreased overall performance, but did not impact differently on the two groups of participants. Thus, we feel compelled to take a closer look at the input pathway.

REPRESENTATION VERSUS WORKING MEMORY PROCESSES

Why do people with dyslexia fail to correctly discriminate and repeat verbal material as soon as short-term memory load is significant? The previous series of experiments leaves open two broad classes of explanation that are not mutually exclusive. One is that phonological representations are degraded, so some phonetic features get lost in the process and are therefore missing when they must be compared or repeated. An alternative interpretation is that phonological representations are themselves intact, that is, all phonetic features are correctly encoded, but short-term memory processes are limited, and the poor performance of participants with dyslexia reflects a capacity limitation.

We have attempted to test these contrasting hypotheses using the phonological similarity effect: the more phonologically similar the words or nonwords in the sequence, the more difficult it is to recall the sequence (Baddeley, 1984). This effect shows that verbal short-term memory is limited not only by general capacity constraints but also by possible phonological confusion between the items to be remembered. If the phonological representations of people with dyslexia are degraded, they should have even more confusion between items and therefore show an increased phonological similarity effect. On the other hand, if their phonological representations are intact, they should show just as much phonological similarity effect as controls, not more. Yet another conceivable prediction would be that they show less similarity effect than controls, although this is predicted only in the case of known words for which conceptual or visual representations are available (McNeil & Johnston, 2004; Shankweiler, Liberman, Mark, & Fowler, 1979).

We therefore carried out a new series of experiments requiring participants to discriminate sequences of nonwords in two conditions (Szenkovits, Dupoux, & Ramus, 2009). In the minimal condition, sequences were made of repetitions of two to seven nonwords that differed by just one phonetic feature ([taz]-[taʒ]). The two sequences were either identical or differed by just one of the nonwords being changed into the other (i.e., they differed by one phonetic feature). In the maximal condition the two nonwords differed maximally ([taz]–[gum]), so that different sequences differed by three phonemes and quite a few phonetic features. Furthermore, to ensure that sequences were encoded at the phonological (rather than acoustic) level of representation, nonwords were uttered by two different voices, which alternated constantly within a sequence and in opposite orders between sequences. As a result, even phonologically identical sequences were different at the acoustic level.

The main results were that we found a phonological similarity effect (poorer performance in the minimal than in the maximal condition) and that participants with dyslexia performed more poorly. However, as phonological similarity decreased, the performance of the dyslexic group increased by the same magnitude as for controls. This pattern of results held under various replication variants, with concurrent articulatory suppression, with sequence repetition rather than discrimination, and whether minimal and maximal conditions were intermixed or administered in separate blocks.

Our results extend previous studies that also found no differential phonological similarity effect, during verbal recall or words or letter names (Hall, Wilson, Humphreys, Tinzmann, & Bowyer, 1983; Johnston, Rugg, & Scott, 1987; Swanson & Ramalgia, 1992), as well as during paired associate learning (Messbauer & de Jong, 2006). Overall, these results fail to confirm the predictions of the "degraded phonological representations" hypothesis. They are more compatible with the alternative hypothesis that the deficit might lie in the short-term memory processes operating on phonological representations (i.e., in Figure 8.1, the input and/or output phonological buffers, or the phonological loop between input and output sublexical representations).

UNIVERSAL OR HYPERNATIVE PHONOLOGY?

A great deal of phonology is specific to each particular language. This is best illustrated by the unique phonetic repertoire of each language, but is also true at other levels of the phonological hierarchy. It is generally agreed that the child acquires adequate language-specific phonological representations very early, by the end of the first year of life by some accounts and at any rate before the end of the third year. Given that the phonological deficit is presumed to be congenital, it should manifest itself early in an altered pattern of phonological acquisition. The few longitudinal studies starting at birth that have directly tested that prediction (although very succinctly) have generally supported it (Guttorm, Leppänen, Richardson, & Lyytinen, 2001; Leppänen et al., 2002; Molfese, 2000; Richardson, Leppänen, Leiwo, & Lyytinen, 2003; van Alphen et al., 2004).

Beyond the first year of life, altered phonological acquisition predicts an "atypical" structure of phonological representations. Indeed, hypotheses emphasizing poor categorical perception and/or preserved allophonic perception rest on the idea that phonological categories were not properly acquired. These hypotheses more specifically assume that phonology was incompletely acquired, so that the phonology of the child (or adult) with dyslexia is closer to the initial, universal stage of phonology: categories are less sharply defined, less specific to any particular language, and representations still incorporate some acoustic or allophonic details that should have been eliminated through phonological acquisition (e.g., Mody et al., 1997; Serniclaes et al., 2004).

One possible further prediction of this class of hypotheses is that, as a consequence, individuals with dyslexia might retain the ability to perceive and perhaps produce foreign speech sounds. This is because people's difficulties with foreign speech sounds are a direct outcome of their phonological acquisition, which rigidifies their phonology with the categories and processes of the native language, which are often in conflict with the categories and processes of a different, later-acquired language. If the phonology of a person is less rigidified by their native language, it might retain some plasticity for a second one. As an example, French and English both have two categories for voicing, but with a different boundary. Korean has three categories. If, for example, an English speaker with dyslexia has less well-defined English voicing categories, s/he might be less impaired in the perception of French voicing contrasts around a different boundary. They might be even less impaired in the perception of Korean voicing contrasts, if s/he has retained in his/her phonological representation the allophonic details that are the basis for the Korean contrast (as hypothesized by Serniclaes et al., 2004).

To tease apart the two hypotheses, we conducted a series of experiments testing the perception and production of foreign speech contrasts by people with dyslexia (Soroli, Szenkovits, & Ramus, 2009). To assess the role of short-term memory load, we conducted discrimination and repetition tasks using either single CVCV (consonant–vowel–consonant–vowel) nonwords, or sequences of two or three CVCV nonwords. We tested one segmental and one suprasegmental phonological contrasts. The segmental contrast was the voicing of stop consonants in Korean, which, as mentioned earlier, presents three categories (plain, tense, aspirated), instead of two in French (the native language of all participants). The suprasegmental contrast was lexical stress, a prosodic contrast present in many languages like Spanish or Italian, but not in French. In that condition, stress could fall either on the first or the second syllable of the nonword, and different pairs differed only by the location of the stress, phonemes being kept identical. In the repetition tasks, participants' production was recorded and coded off-line by a native speaker of Korean for segmental contrasts and a native speaker of Greek (a language with lexical stress) for stress contrasts.

Overall, the results showed that when discriminating or repeating single nonwords, participants with dyslexia showed the same performance as controls. However, group differences appeared when discriminating or repeating sequences of two or three nonwords, particularly so for the stress contrast. These results suggest that the native phonological representations of people with dyslexia are equally (un)able to represent foreign speech contrasts. Group differences appear only when short-term memory load increases. These results therefore do not support the hypothesis of a universal (initial stage) phonology. Again, they are more compatible with the hypothesis that the phonological representations of participants with dyslexia are intact and that short-term memory processes operating on them are impaired.

From the point of view of second-language acquisition, our results suggest that the difficulties of people with dyslexia in this domain may not result from the particular format of their phonological representations, but rather from their impaired verbal short-term memory and phonological awareness, and perhaps phonological learning, as these capacities must be heavily recruited during second-language acquisition (Service, 1992).

PHONOLOGICAL GRAMMAR

Another area of phonology that is potentially of interest with respect to dyslexia is what can be termed *phonological grammar*. This refers to a whole host of rule-like processes that apply (typically probabilistically) in speech production when phonological lexical items are retrieved from the lexicon and assembled (at the sublexical level) to make phrases (Chomsky & Halle, 1968). These phenomena are mainly described in speech production but similar phenomena occur in speech perception, either as a compensation for productive processes or simply as an adaptation to native phonological structure. Most of these phonological processes are language specific and therefore must be learned in the course of language acquisition. Do children with dyslexia acquire them as well as controls?

Based on a series of experiments by Darcy et al. (Darcy, Peperkamp, & Dupoux, 2007; Darcy, Ramus, Christophe, Kinzler, & Dupoux, in press), we tested one particular phonological process that occurs in French: voicing assimilation. In French, the voicing feature may spread backward from obstruents or fricatives to the preceding consonant; for instance, "cape grise" [kapgriz] → [kabgriz] (gray cloak). This assimilation process is both context specific (it does not occur before nasals: "cape noire" is always [kapnwar]; black cloak) and language specific (it does not occur in English, which instead shows assimilation of place of articulation: "brown bag" [brownbag] → [browmbag]).

In the production experiment, participants saw a sentence written on the computer screen, rehearsed it as much as needed, then were recorded as they pronounced it rapidly. Sentences were read without difficulty by participants with dyslexia, the rehearsal ensuring that each sentence could be produced accurately and rapidly (to maximize the likelihood of producing assimilations) without being hindered by reading fluency. Sentences contained either a legal context for voicing assimilation (according to French phonology) or an illegal context for voicing assimilation (to assess context specificity). Other sentences contained similar conditions for English place assimilation (to assess language specificity). The words that could be assimilated were excised from the recordings of all participants and played, one at a time, to a new set of native French listeners, together with the written version of both the assimilated and unassimilated forms. These participants judged whether the target word was assimilated or not (i.e., in the earlier example, whether they heard [kap] or [kab]). This yielded the probability of producing an assimilation for each target word, in each condition, by each subject. Results showed that French people with dyslexia, just like controls, produce voicing assimilations around 40% of the time in legal contexts, but not in illegal contexts, and do not produce place assimilations. Furthermore, voicing assimilations occur more frequently than devoicing assimilations (Snoeren, Halle, & Segui, 2006), to the same degree in the participants with dyslexia and controls.

In the perception experiment, similar sentences were played preceded by a target word (e.g., "cape"), the task being to detect if the target word was included and correctly pronounced in the sentence. The sentences again came in three conditions. They either contained (a) the target word in assimilated form in a legal context ("La petite fille jette sa cab grise"; this should go unnoticed if participants compensate perceptually for voicing assimilation) or (b) the target word in assimilated form in an illegal context ("la petite fille jette sa cab noire"; this should be noticed because no assimilation is expected in this context), or (c) did not contain the target word. Three additional conditions tested the possibility of compensation for place assimilation. Results showed that French participants with dyslexia compensate perceptually for voicing assimilations to the same extent as controls (see also Blomert, Mitterer, & Paffen, 2004), but only in legal contexts (like controls), and do not compensate for place assimilation (like controls). Furthermore, an asymmetry in perceptual compensation was observed in perception as in production, to the same extent in people with dyslexia as in controls.

In another experiment, we investigated assimilations induced by phonotactic constraints. The background is that each language has its own phonotactic constraints, forbidding certain consonant clusters in certain contexts. In French, as in English, clusters like [dl] or [tl] can never occur at the beginning of a word. The consequence is that when French or English listeners hear a nonword such as [dla] or [tla], they most often assimilate it to the closest legal cluster ([gla] or [kla], respectively), that is, they fail to hear the illegal cluster and report hearing the legal one (Hallé, Segui, Frauenfelder, & Meunier, 1998). This is also evident in discrimination tasks, where they, for instance, respond "same" to the "different" pair [dla]–[gla]. In such a discrimination task we found that listeners with dyslexia fall victim to this perceptual illusion just as much as controls, hearing [gla] instead of [dla]. Thus, their speech perception is constrained by the phonotactics of their native language as much as it is for controls.

In conclusion, the aspects of phonological grammar that we have investigated seem perfectly normal in people with dyslexia (Szenkovits, Darma, Darcy, & Ramus, 2009). Our results are consistent with the hypothesis that phonological representations are intact, that grammatical processes that operate on them are intact too, and that the deficit lies somewhere else.

UNCONSCIOUS SPEECH PROCESSING AND LEXICAL ACCESS

A recurrent problem in psycholinguistics is that tasks typically require explicit instructions, attention to stimuli, and introspection, which may blur the interpretation of the effects observed, particularly so when the population tested has problems with phonological awareness. One solution to this problem is to observe indirect effects of experimental manipulations of which the subject is unaware. In the case of visual presentation of linguistic stimuli, subliminal priming has provided a particularly elegant solution. The participant performs a task (typically lexical decision) on a target word, which is preceded by a prime word. When presentation duration is sufficiently reduced, and when the prime is preceded and followed by visual masks, it is not consciously perceived but may still be processed. One may therefore assess the effects of the prime on the recognition of the target, unbeknown to the subject. More recently, a similar technique has been used to render auditory primes subliminal (Kouider & Dupoux, 2005). Kouider and Dupoux (2005) have used a combination of time compression, amplitude attenuation, and masking with backward speech to achieve subliminal processing of the prime and have shown that subliminal repetition priming occurs, as evidenced by a decrease in reaction time compared to when the prime is unrelated to the target. Moreover, this priming is strictly lexical and it operates on an abstract lexical phonological representation, because subliminal priming occurs only for words and resists large acoustic differences between prime and target (i.e., there is as much priming when prime and target are spoken by speakers of different sexes; Kouider & Dupoux, 2005).

The availability of this new method gave us the opportunity to consider new questions to ask about the phonological deficit in dyslexia, namely: How efficient are unconscious lexical access processes in people with dyslexia? What is the nature of their lexical phonological representations? The degraded phonological representations hypothesis predicts reduced subliminal repetition priming, due to the fact that phonological details might be lost and therefore distort the identity relationship between prime and target. A more specific hypothesis, according to which their phonological representations would be less abstract and closer to acoustic representations, would predict decreased priming specifically across different speakers.

The findings from our study of control participants fully replicated those of Kouider and Dupoux (2005), and our results on dyslexia fully replicated those of controls (Ramus, Gaillard, Szenkovits, de Gardelle, & Kouider, 2009). In short, participants with dyslexia show as much subliminal repetition priming as controls, it is restricted to words like in controls, and it is of equal magnitude across and within speakers. These results do not support the predictions of the degraded phonological representations hypothesis, neither do they support the hypothesis that persons with dyslexia rely on acoustic rather than abstract phonological representations for their lexicon. Rather, they are compatible with the idea that their phonological representations and processes for lexical access are intact. Follow-up experiments manipulating the phonological relationship between prime and target will be needed to fully bolster the latter hypothesis.

A NEW HYPOTHESIS

The experiments that we have described were designed to test various hypotheses regarding the status of the phonological system in dyslexia. Overall, their findings converge toward one single conclusion: The phonological representations of people with dyslexia are normal. Of course, this conclusion cannot be considered as proven. Many aspects of the phonological representations of people with dyslexia still remain to be tested. Nevertheless, let us consider for the sake of discussion that our conclusion holds. What, then, might be the nature of the phonological deficit? If phonological representations are normal, if phonological grammar is acquired normally, then what's wrong with phonology?

The first important remark to make is that our results do not challenge in any way the very existence of a phonological deficit. Indeed, our own data attest that our participants with dyslexia have a phonological deficit, as measured in the traditional sense, using, for instance, spoonerisms, nonword repetition, and rapid naming tasks. So it is not time to abandon the phonological deficit hypothesis, merely to rethink its precise formulation.

A comparison of phonological tasks in which participants with dyslexia show normal as opposed to poor performance provides important clues. First, task requirements, and in particular short-term memory load, seem paramount. This is obvious in span tasks where difficulties appear as sequence length increases. It is also the case in most phonological awareness tasks, which require the subject to hold segmented phonological units in short-term memory and to have conscious access to those representations. In fact, the most difficult phonological awareness tasks for people with dyslexia turn out to be those that load most heavily on short-term memory (e.g., spoonerisms). One type of task that challenges people with dyslexia without recruiting verbal short-term memory is rapid naming. Given that they do not always have problems with single picture naming, it seems that in this case the crucial task constraint is speed (Marshall, Tang, Rosen, Ramus, & van der Lely, 2009; McCrory, 2001; Szenkovits, Ramus, & Dupoux, 2009; but see Snowling, van Wagtendonk, & Stafford, 1988; Swan & Goswami, 1997b).

In an attempt to provide a unifying explanation for those task constraints that seem to pose specific problems in dyslexia, we tentatively propose the concept of *phonological access*. By this, we mean all processes by which (lexical or sublexical) phonological representations are accessed for the purpose of external computations. Verbal short-term memory requires access to phonological representations for the purpose of copying them into buffers, then access to phonological buffers for retrieval (see Figure 8.1), access to input representations to copy them into output representations, and access to output representations tapping to recycle them into input representations (i.e., the phonological loop; Baddeley, 1984; Jacquemot & Scott, 2006). Phonological awareness tasks additionally involve *conscious access* to phonological representations, which may place special demands on access mechanisms. And rapid naming tasks require multiple fast accesses to lexical phonological representations. Therefore, it seems to us that people with dyslexia tend to fail at tasks that are particularly demanding in terms of phonological access. A relatively similar proposal was made by Shankweiler and Crain (1986) as the *processing limitation hypothesis*. There are also some commonalities with Hulme and Snowling's (1992) notion of an *output deficit*.

We acknowledge that, at the present stage, our notion of phonological access needs developing and that our analysis of which tasks are demanding in terms of access is rather ad hoc. Ultimately, computational models of the phonological system would be the best way to provide an operational definition of access and to make unambiguous predictions concerning the consequences of a phonological access deficit on the performance of various tasks.

DISCUSSION

The most striking aspect of the series of experiments we have reported here is our consistent failure to demonstrate a deficit in the phonological representations of people with dyslexia. Could obvious reasons explain our failure? Could it be that our unrepresentative, well-compensated participants with dyslexia were not dyslexic enough or did not present a phonological deficit at all? It should be recalled that all our participants were included on the basis of both a history of reading disability, and poor performance on reading and standard phonological tasks. In fact their performance on standard phonological tasks (spoonerisms, digit span, rapid naming) did not overlap at all with that of age- and IQ-matched participants. Therefore there is good evidence that our participants with dyslexia did present a phonological deficit. But this deficit surfaces in some tasks and not in others, and the whole point of our hypothesis is to explain why.

Another potential limitation of our findings is that, in working with adults, we cannot rule out the possibility that people with dyslexia may have deficient phonological representations as children, but these representations have recovered when we test them in adulthood (e.g., Goswami, 2003). However, this type of hypothesis does not easily explain why performance on tasks tapping fine aspects of the phonological representation would recover, while performance on the same tasks with additional short-term memory load, or conscious awareness, or time constraints would not. Clearly, the developmental critique is plausible to the extent that it is able to adequately explain what recovers and what doesn't. Nevertheless this type of critique must be taken seriously, and the only way to do so will be to replicate our main findings on children. In fact, some of our studies on 8- to 12-year-old children have found that dyslexic children seem to have little deficit with their phonology beyond the classic phonological skills. In particular, we found no problems with nonword discrimination and repetition when short-term memory load was minimized (Marshall, Tang, et al., 2009), with normal perception and production of prosody (Marshall, Harcourt-Brown, Ramus, & van der Lely, in press), and with normal compensation for assimilations, as reported here in adults (Marshall, Harcourt-Brown, Ramus, & van der Lely, in press).

More supportive evidence may come from a reinterpretation of earlier studies. For instance, we have always known that most children with dyslexia can repeat one- and two-syllable nonwords without much problem, and that difficulties appear only with three-, four-, and five-syllable nonwords. Such data do suggest that phonological representations are normal, and only memory load makes a difference. As another example, in a landmark study, Swan and Goswami (1997a) tested phonological awareness in children with dyslexia while controlling for their ability to correctly retrieve the phonological form of the target words. Although their findings are widely interpreted as supporting a form of the degraded phonological representations hypothesis, they have in fact shown that the phoneme awareness deficits of children with dyslexia cannot be entirely attributed to poor phonological representation of the target words.

Of course, it is expected that *some* dyslexic children have a real phonological deficit, in the sense of degraded phonological representations, if only because some dyslexic children have an auditory deficit, which inevitably impairs their correct acquisition of phonological categories. The interesting observation is that not all dyslexic individuals have auditory deficits and not all of them have the ensuing categorical perception deficit (e.g., Adlard & Hazan, 1998; Mody et al., 1997; Ramus et al., 2003; Rosen & Manganari, 2001; White et al., 2006). This suggests that degraded phonological representations, like basic auditory perception deficits, affect only a minority of people with dyslexia and may not be part of the core phonological deficit in dyslexia. Obviously, our focus on a high-achieving, adult population biases our recruitment against people with auditory deficits and degraded phonological representations. Nevertheless, these individuals did have difficulties acquiring literacy and still show the standard hallmarks of the phonological deficit (as assessed by phonological awareness, short-term memory, and rapid naming). The challenge is therefore to understand what the underlying nature of their phonological deficit is, if not a degradation of their phonological representations, and why this impairs reading acquisition so much. If we manage to do so, the explanation may well generalize to dyslexic people who have additional deficits.

Does our phonological access hypothesis imply a more general executive dysfunction in dyslexia? Certainly access to representations for the purpose of working memory or awareness is part of what could be termed executive function. Nevertheless, we are not proposing a general executive dysfunction in dyslexia in the same sense as executive dysfunction in autism or in frontal patients. This must be a very specific type of executive dysfunction, specific both in terms of executive processes and in terms of modality (e.g., Jeffries & Everatt, 2004). Executive function is a domain-general concept, but in practice it is plausible that the neural substrate of executive processes has central (frontal) components (which are not affected in dyslexia) and is partly distributed in each sensory modality and functional module (Carpenter, Just, & Reichle, 2000). Then it is possible to envision that, say, a left perisylvian dysfunction might disrupt executive processes only as applied to verbal (or auditory) material.

The matter of sensory deficits in dyslexia is also of interest here. Indeed, after years of investigations of auditory and visual deficits in dyslexia, some researchers have come to conclusions that are intriguingly similar to ours. Ahissar and colleagues have found that the difficulties of people with dyslexia never seem to be specific to a particular kind of stimulus, be it auditory or visual; rather they appear or disappear depending on task requirements, being particularly prominent when the stimuli must be stored in short-term memory (Amitay, Ben-Yehudah, Banai, & Ahissar, 2002; Banai & Ahissar, 2006; Ben-Yehudah, Sackett, Malchi-Ginzberg, & Ahissar, 2001). In their interpretation, the deficit lies in the ability to "form a perceptual anchor" (Ahissar, Lubin, Putter-Katz, & Banai, 2006). Similarly, working on visual processing, Sperling and colleagues concluded that the deficit in dyslexia does not lie specifically with stimuli tapping the magnocellular system, but rather lies in the ability to perform the task when the stimuli are noisy: in their own words, a deficit in "perceptual noise exclusion" (Sperling, Lu, Manis, & Seidenberg, 2005, 2006). This is not without recalling the finding that children's difficulties with speech perception are exacerbated by presentation in noise (Brady, Shankweiler, & Mann, 1983; Cornelissen, Hansen, Bradley, & Stein, 1996; but see Snowling, Goulandris, Bowlby, & Howell, 1986) or under conditions where the stimuli are extremely minimal (Serniclaes et al., 2004). Rephrased within our framework, the interpretation of these results is that the auditory and visual representations of people with dyslexia are intact, but that they have difficulties *accessing* them under certain conditions involving storage in short-term memory, speeded or repeated retrievals, extraction from noise, and other task difficulty factors. Does this imply that individuals with dyslexia in fact suffer from a *general deficit* in the capacity to access sensory representations? The critique of sensory theories of dyslexia retains its force (Ramus, 2003); simply, for those who, on top of their phonological deficit, do show auditory and/or visual deficits, these may be construed in terms of access to representations, like the phonological deficit. Therefore, individuals with dyslexia may have cognitive deficits of a single type but expressed in several domains, with most of them having a deficit in the phonological domain (hence the link with reading disability) and some having the same kind of deficit more generally in the auditory and/or visual domains (and possibly elsewhere). The range of deficits within a particular individual would presumably depend on the spatial extent of their cortical dysfunctions, for example, ectopias or related neuronal migration abnormalities (Galaburda, LoTurco, Ramus, Fitch, & Rosen, 2006; Ramus, 2004).

To summarize, a series of experiments conducted in our lab suggests that the phonological representations of people with dyslexia are basically intact, and the phonological deficit surfaces only as a function of certain task requirements, notably short-term memory, conscious awareness, and time constraints. In an attempt to reformulate those task requirements more economically, we propose that they have a deficit in access to phonological representations. The same type of deficient access to representations may turn out to adequately characterize the additional sensory and cognitive deficits of the subset of individuals who have them.

PERSPECTIVES

The present chapter underlines the fact that more than 30 years after the phonological deficit began to be theorized and experimentally investigated (Liberman, 1973) we still don't know what it is. If anything, the results reviewed here only suggest what it is not. This implies that there still is much more work to be done on this subject. A great deal of research has focused on reading acquisition and disability, which is of course very important, but we should always remember that reading disability is merely a symptom of dyslexia, albeit the most socially important one. Deep under this symptom lies a deficit in the mental processing of speech sounds. To really understand the nature of this deficit, we will have to learn and draw much more from research on language (phonological) acquisition and psycholinguistics. The present review has only skimmed the surface of the questions that can be asked and of the experimental methods that can be used to probe them. We hope that in the coming years a renewed interest in this area of research will eventually be able to tell us what the phonological deficit really is.

ACKNOWLEDGMENTS

This chapter is a modified version of Ramus and Szenkovits (2008). This work was supported by grants from the Fyssen Foundation and Ville de Paris.

REFERENCES

Adlard, A., & Hazan, V. (1998). Speech perception in children with specific reading difficulties (dyslexia). *Quarterly Journal of Experimental Psychology, 51A*(1), 153–177.

Ahissar, M., Lubin, Y., Putter-Katz, H., & Banai, K. (2006). Dyslexia and the failure to form a perceptual anchor. *Nature Neuroscience, 9*(12), 1558–1564.

Amitay, S., Ben-Yehudah, G., Banai, K., & Ahissar, M. (2002). Disabled readers suffer from visual and auditory impairments but not from a specific magnocellular deficit. *Brain, 125*(10), 2272–2285.

Baddeley, A. D. (1984). Exploring the articulatory loop. *Quarterly Journal of Experimental Psychology, 36*, 233–252.

Banai, K., & Ahissar, M. (2006). Auditory processing deficits in dyslexia: Task or stimulus related? *Cerebral Cortex, 16*(12), 1718–1728.

Ben-Yehudah, G., Sackett, E., Malchi-Ginzberg, L., & Ahissar, M. (2001). Impaired temporal contrast sensitivity in dyslexics is specific to retain-and-compare paradigms. *Brain, 124*(Pt 7), 1381–1395.

Blomert, L., Mitterer, H., & Paffen, C. (2004). In search of the auditory, phonetic and/or phonological problems in dyslexia: Context effects in speech perception. *Journal of Speech, Language and Hearing Research, 47*(5), 1030–1047.

Brady, S., Shankweiler, D., & Mann, V. (1983). Speech perception and memory coding in relation to reading ability. *Journal of Experimental Child Psychology, 35*(2), 345–367.

Carpenter, P. A., Just, M. A., & Reichle, E. D. (2000). Working memory and executive function: Evidence from neuroimaging. *Current Opinion in Neurobiology, 10*(2), 195–199.

Chomsky, N., & Halle, M. (1968). *The sound pattern of English.* New York: Harper and Row.

Cornelissen, P. L., Hansen, P. C., Bradley, L., & Stein, J. F. (1996). Analysis of perceptual confusions between nine sets of consonant-vowel sounds in normal and dyslexic adults. *Cognition, 59*(3), 275–306.

Darcy, I., Peperkamp, S., & Dupoux, E. (2007). Perceptual learning and plasticity in a second language: Building a new system for phonological processes. In J. Cole & J. I. Hualde (Eds.), *Labphon 9: Change in phonology.* Berlin: Mouton de Gruyter.

Darcy, I., Ramus, F., Christophe, A., Kinzler, K. D., & Dupoux, E. (in press). Phonological knowledge in compensation for native and non-native assimilation. In F. Kügler, C. Féry, & R. van de Vijver (Eds.), *Variation and gradience in phonetics and phonology.* Berlin: Mouton de Gruyter.

Elbro, C. (1998). When reading is "readn" or somthn. Distinctness of phonological representations of lexical items in normal and disabled readers. *Scandinavian Journal of Psychology, 39*(3), 149–153.

Galaburda, A. M., LoTurco, J., Ramus, F., Fitch, R. H., & Rosen, G. D. (2006). From genes to behavior in developmental dyslexia. *Nature Neuroscience, 9*(10), 1213–1217.

Goswami, U. (2003). Why theories about developmental dyslexia require developmental designs. *Trends in Cognitive Sciences, 7*(12), 534–540.

Guttorm, T. K., Leppänen, P. H. T., Richardson, U., & Lyytinen, H. (2001). Event-related potentials and consonant differentation in newborns with familial risk for dyslexia. *Journal of Learning Disabilities, 34*(6), 534–544.

Hall, J. W., Wilson, K. P., Humphreys, M. S., Tinzmann, M. B., & Bowyer, P. M. (1983). Phonemic-similarity effects in good vs. poor readers. *Memory & Cognition, 11*(5), 520–527.

Hallé, P. A., Segui, J., Frauenfelder, U., & Meunier, C. (1998). Processing of illegal consonant clusters: A case of perceptual assimilation? *Journal of Experimental Psychology: Human Perception & Performance, 24*(2), 592–608.

Hulme, C., & Snowling, M. (1992). Deficits in output phonology: An explanation of reading failure? *Cognitive Neuropsychology, 9*(1), 47–72.

Jacquemot, C., & Scott, S. K. (2006). What is the relationship between phonological short-term memory and speech processing? *Trends in Cognitive Sciences, 10*(11), 480–486.

Jeffries, S., & Everatt, J. (2004). Working memory: Its role in dyslexia and other specific learning difficulties. *Dyslexia, 10*(3), 196–214.

Johnston, R. S., Rugg, M., & Scott, T. (1987). Phonological similarity effects, memory span and developmental reading disorders: The nature of the relationship. *British Journal of Psychology, 78*, 205–211.

Kouider, S., & Dupoux, E. (2005). Subliminal speech priming. *Psychological Science, 16*(8), 617–625.

Leppänen, P. H., Richardson, U., Pihko, E., Eklund, K. M., Guttorm, T. K., Aro, M., et al. (2002). Brain responses to changes in speech sound durations differ between infants with and without familial risk for dyslexia. *Developmental Neuropsychology, 22*(1), 407–422.

Liberman, I. Y. (1973). Segmentation of the spoken word and reading acquisition. *Bulletin of the Orton Society, 23*, 65–77.

Manis, F. R., McBride-Chang, C., Seidenberg, M. S., Keating, P., Doi, L. M., Munson, B., et al. (1997). Are speech perception deficits associated with developmental dyslexia? *Journal of Experimental Child Psychology, 66*(2), 211-235.

Marshall, C. R., Harcourt-Brown, S., Ramus, F., & van der Lely, H. K. J. (2009). *Phonological knowledge in compensation for place assimilation in children with SLI and/or dyslexia.* Manuscript in preparation.

Marshall, C. R., Harcourt-Brown, S., Ramus, F., & van der Lely, H. K. J. (in press submitted). The link between prosody and language skills in children with SLI and/or dyslexia. *International Journal of Language and Communication Disorders.*

Marshall, C. R., Tang, S., Rosen, S., Ramus, F., & van der Lely, H. K. J. (2009). *The relationship between phonological, syntactic and morphosyntactic deficits in SLI and dyslexia.* Manuscript submitted for publication.

McCrory, E. (2001). *A neurocognitive investigation of phonological processing in dyslexia.* Unpublished doctoral dissertation, University College London.

McNeil, A. M., & Johnston, R. S. (2004). Word length, phonemic, and visual similarity effects in poor and normal readers. *Memory & Cognition, 32*(5), 687–695.

Messbauer, V. C. S., & de Jong, P. F. (2006). Effects of visual and phonological distinctness on visual–verbal paired associate learning in Dutch dyslexic and normal readers. *Reading and Writing, 19*(4), 393–426.

Mody, M., Studdert-Kennedy, M., & Brady, S. (1997). Speech perception deficits in poor readers: Auditory processing or phonological coding? *Journal of Experimental Child Psychology, 64*(2), 199–231.

Molfese, D. L. (2000). Predicting dyslexia at 8 years of age using neonatal brain responses. *Brain and Language, 72*(3), 238–245.

Ramus, F. (2001). Outstanding questions about phonological processing in dyslexia. *Dyslexia, 7*, 197–216.

Ramus, F. (2003). Developmental dyslexia: Specific phonological deficit or general sensorimotor dysfunction? *Current Opinion in Neurobiology, 13*(2), 212–218.

Ramus, F. (2004). Neurobiology of dyslexia: A reinterpretation of the data. *Trends in Neuroscience, 27*(12), 720–726.

Ramus, F., Gaillard, E., Szenkovits, G., de Gardelle, V., & Kouider, S. (2009). *Exploring dyslexics' phonological deficit VI: Unconscious lexical access.* Manuscript in preparation

Ramus, F., Rosen, S., Dakin, S. C., Day, B. L., Castellote, J. M., White, S., et al. (2003). Theories of developmental dyslexia: Insights from a multiple case study of dyslexic adults. *Brain, 126*(4), 841–865.

Ramus, F., & Szenkovits, G. (2008). What phonological deficit? *Quarterly Journal of Experimental Psychology, 61*(1), 129–141.

Richardson, U., Leppänen, P. H. T., Leiwo, M., & Lyytinen, H. (2003). Speech perception of infants with high familial risk for dyslexia differs at the age of six months. *Developmental Neuropsychology, 23*(3), 385–397.

Rosen, S., & Manganari, E. (2001). Is there a relationship between speech and nonspeech auditory processing in children with dyslexia? *Journal of Speech, Language, and Hearing Research, 44*(4), 720–736.

Serniclaes, W., Van Heghe, S., Mousty, P., Carré, R., & Sprenger-Charolles, L. (2004). Allophonic mode of speech perception in dyslexia. *Journal of Experimental Child Psychology, 87,* 336–361.

Service, E. (1992). Phonology, working memory, and foreign-language learning. *Quarterly Journal of Experimental Psychology, 45A*(1), 21–50.

Shankweiler, D., & Crain, S. (1986). Language mechanisms and reading disorder: A modular approach. *Cognition, 24*(1-2), 139–168.

Shankweiler, D., Liberman, I. Y., Mark, L. S., & Fowler, C. A. (1979). The speech code and learning to read. *Journal of Experimental Psychology: Human Learning and Memory, 5,* 531–545.

Snoeren, N. D., Halle, P. A., & Segui, J. (2006). A voice for the voiceless: Production and perception of assimilated stops in French. *Journal of Phonetics, 34*(2), 241–268.

Snowling, M. J. (2000). *Dyslexia* (2nd ed.). Oxford: Blackwell.

Snowling, M. J., Goulandris, N., Bowlby, M., & Howell, P. (1986). Segmentation and speech perception in relation to reading skill: A developmental analysis. *Journal of Experimental Child Psychology, 41*(3), 489–507.

Snowling, M. J., van Wagtendonk, B., & Stafford, C. (1988). Object-naming deficits in developmental dyslexia. *Journal of Research in Reading, 11*(2), 67–85.

Soroli, E., Szenkovits, G., & Ramus, F. (2009). *Exploring dyslexics' phonological deficit V: Universal or hyper-native phonology?* Manuscript in preparation.

Sperling, A. J., Lu, Z. L., Manis, F. R., & Seidenberg, M. S. (2005). Deficits in perceptual noise exclusion in developmental dyslexia. *Nature Neuroscience, 8*(7), 862–863.

Sperling, A. J., Lu, Z. L., Manis, F. R., & Seidenberg, M. S. (2006). Motion-perception deficits and reading impairment: It's the noise, not the motion. *Psychological Science, 17*(12), 1047–1053.

Swan, D., & Goswami, U. (1997a). Phonological awareness deficits in developmental dyslexia and the phonological representations hypothesis. *Journal of Experimental Child Psychology, 66*(1), 18–41.

Swan, D., & Goswami, U. (1997b). Picture naming deficits in developmental dyslexia: The phonological representations hypothesis. *Brain and Language, 56*(3), 334–353.

Swanson, H. L., & Ramalgia, J. M. (1992). The relationship between phonological codes on memory and spelling tasks for students with and without learning disabilities. *Journal of Learning Disabilities, 25*(6), 396–407.

Szenkovits, G., Darma, Q., Darcy, I., & Ramus, F. (2009). *Exploring dyslexics' phonological deficit II: Phonological grammar.* Manuscript submitted for publication.

Szenkovits, G., Dupoux, E., & Ramus, F. (2009). *Exploring dyslexics' phonological deficit III: Impaired representations or short-term memory processes?* Manuscript in preparation.

Szenkovits, G., & Ramus, F. (2005). Exploring dyslexics' phonological deficit I: Lexical vs. sub-lexical and input vs. output processes. *Dyslexia, 11*(4), 253–268.

Szenkovits, G., Ramus, F., & Dupoux, E. (2009). Exploring dyslexics' phonological deficit IV: The output pathway. Manuscript in preparation.

van Alphen, P., de Bree, E., Gerrits, E., de Jong, J., Wilsenach, C., & Wijnen, F. (2004). Early language development in children with a genetic risk of dyslexia. *Dyslexia, 10*(4), 265–288.

Wagner, R. K., & Torgesen, J. K. (1987). The nature of phonological processing and its causal role in the acquisition of reading skills. *Psychological Bulletin, 101,* 192–212.

White, S., Milne, E., Rosen, S., Hansen, P. C., Swettenham, J., Frith, U., et al. (2006). The role of sensorimotor impairments in dyslexia: A multiple case study of dyslexic children. *Developmental Science, 9*(3), 237–255.

9 Visual Word Recognition

Insights From MEG and Implications for Developmental Dyslexia

Piers L. Cornelissen

INTRODUCTION

The ability to fluently, and seemingly effortlessly, read words is one of a few unique human attributes, but one which has assumed inordinate significance because of the role that this activity has come to have in modern society. A disadvantage in reading ability not only has profound personal impact for the individuals concerned, but in terms of economic and social problems also has a wider negative influence on society at large. According to current government figures in the United Kingdom, some 22% of 11-year-olds do not reach the minimum standard required in English national curriculum tests. Despite its importance, the scientific understanding of the neural basis of reading, and more particularly the visual aspect of visual word recognition, is relatively poorly understood. Thus far, a coherent overarching model that spans the various conceptual levels from behavior through functional description to neuroanatomy has proven extraordinarily challenging to elucidate. A fuller understanding of the computational processing and neurophysiological basis of how the reading system functions would therefore represent significant progress.

As with most complex behaviors, visual word recognition is thought to result from the dynamic interplay between the elements of a distributed cortical and subcortical network. To fully understand how visual word recognition is achieved and how it may fail in developmental dyslexia, we need to identify not only the necessary and sufficient complement of nodes that comprise this network—its functional anatomy—but we also need to understand how information flows through this network with time and how the structure of the network itself may adapt in both the short and long term. In this chapter we take a historical approach to reviewing recent magnetoencephalography (MEG) research, which elucidates these temporal dynamics, focusing particularly on events with the first 300 ms of a visually presented word, and which we believe should set crucial constraints on models of visual word recognition and reading.

EQUIVALENT CURRENT DIPOLE (ECD) MODELING

In our first attempts to explore the temporal sequence of cortical activation for visually presented words, my colleagues and I used equivalent current dipole (ECD) modeling of MEG data. This technique is based on source modeling of evoked averaged data, and can therefore only reveal current sources in the brain that show a high degree of phase synchrony across trials. Unlike minimum current estimation (MCE; Uutela, Hämäläinen, & Somersalo, 1999) and minimum norm estimation (MNE; Hämäläinen & Ilmoniemi, 1984), whose solutions give a spatially distributed estimation of current spread, multidipole ECD models render a set of tightly focused point sources of each subject for each experimental condition. At the individual level, this can give the impression that activity is well localized in the brain with ECDs. Although this may be true for auditory and somaesthetic cortices, where very clear dipolar field patterns are readily seen, this is rarely the situation for tasks that involve a widely distributed cortical network, such as reading and visual word recognition. As a result, we tend to see considerable variability in terms of anatomical localization across different subjects. Therefore, we suggest that the best way to interpret the data from multidipole models is in terms of robust but rather simplified views of brain activation, in which the temporal sequence and response characteristics of a set of relatively coarsely defined regions of interest (ROIs) can be described.

In a series of four studies of word reading and visual word recognition (Cornelissen, Tarkiainen, Helenius, & Salmelin, 2003; Helenius, Tarkiainen, Cornelissen, Hansen, & Salmelin, 1999; Tarkiainen, Cornelissen, & Salmelin, 2002; Tarkiainen, Helenius, Hansen, Cornelissen, & Salmelin, 1999), we applied

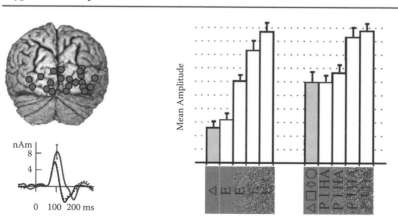

Type II 150ms post-stimulus

FIGURE 9.1A Type I ECDs and mean amplitude of response to one- and four-element symbol and letter strings.

Type II 150ms post-stimulus

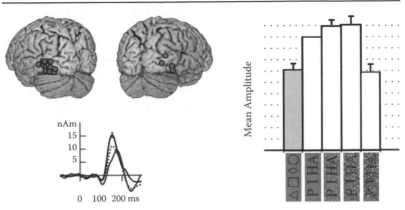

FIGURE 9.1B Type II ECDs and mean amplitude of response to one- and four-element symbol and letter strings.

the following logic to stimulus design. As Figure 9.1A shows, we presented dark gray stimuli, such as letter strings, symbol strings, objects, and faces, on a light gray background. We then systematically varied the visibility of such stimuli by adding increasing amounts of pixel noise. This manipulation has two useful properties that allow us to look for dissociations in the patterns of evoked response. First, as noise increases, stimulus visibility reduces. This means that cortical areas, which are sensitive to higher order stimulus properties, should show increasingly weaker responses as a function of increasing stimulus noise. Second, as pixel noise increases so does the number of contrasting edges in the image. Therefore, any neurons that are primarily tuned to low-level image properties, such as contrast borders, should show an increase in the amplitude of their responses as a function of stimulus noise. By using these manipulations, we identified two main response patterns, and these are illustrated in Figure 9.1A and Figure 9.1B.

The first of these, which we called Type I, took place around 100 ms after stimulus onset. It originated in the midline-occipital region the vicinity of V1/V2/V3 and was distributed along the ventral visual stream. This response was systematically and monotonically modulated by noise but was insensitive to the stimulus content, suggesting involvement in low-level analysis of visual features. The second pattern, which we call Type II, took place around 150 ms after stimulus onset and was concentrated in the inferior occipitotemporal region with left-hemisphere dominance. This activation was greater for letter strings than for symbol strings. The response to noise masking was nonlinear: Response amplitude increased moderately with increasing pixel noise, and then as stimulus visibility became severely impaired at even higher noise levels, response amplitude reduced back toward the baseline. We argue that this very different pattern of responses is likely to reflect an object-level processing stage that acts as a gateway to higher processing areas. In addition, we also identified a third pattern of response (Type III). This also occurred in the time window around 150 ms after stimulus onset, but originated mainly in the right occipital area. Like Type II responses, it was modulated by string length, but showed no preference for letters as compared with symbols.

These data suggest an important role for the inferior occipitotemporal cortex in reading within 200 ms after stimulus onset and are consistent with findings from intracranial recordings (Nobre, Allison, & McCarthy, 1994) and earlier MEG results (Salmelin, Service, Kiesilä, Uutela, & Salonen, 1996). Nobre et al. (1994) demonstrated letter-string specific responses bilaterally in posterior fusiform gyrus about 200 ms after stimulus onset. MEG recordings by Salmelin et al. (1996) showed strong transient responses to words and nonwords in the bilateral inferior occipitotemporal cortex in fluent readers at 150–200 ms. However, in dyslexic subjects, the left- but not right-hemisphere response was missing, suggesting a special role for the left inferior occipitotemporal cortex in fluent reading within the first 200 ms after seeing a letter string (Helenius et al., 1999).

The fact that the Type II occipitotemporal response at ~150 ms is stronger for letter strings than symbol strings in a silent reading task suggests a degree of orthographic selectivity. This raises the question whether it may also be sensitive to the lexical status of the letter string. However, other data suggests that the Type II response is prelexical. The strength of this response as well as its latency is very similar for words, nonwords, and consonant strings (Cornelissen et al., 2003; Salmelin et al., 1996). Moreover, in these studies the effect of lexicality (i.e., words > nonwords, or words > consonant strings) only starts to appear at about 200 to 300 ms after stimulus onset (see Figure 9.2) in the perisylvian cortex including the left superior temporal and inferior parietal areas (Cornelissen et al., 2003; Helenius, Salmelin, Service, & Connolly, 1998; Marinkovic et al., 2003) and at the base of the left anterior temporal lobe (Nobre et al., 1994).

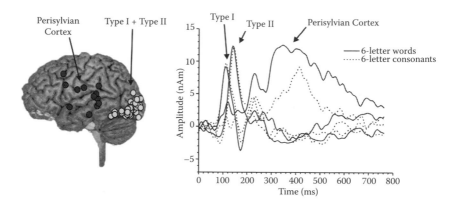

FIGURE 9.2 Type I and II ECDs together with ECDs showing significantly stronger responses to six-letter Finnish words than six-letter consonant strings. Plot showing gran average waveforms for each of the three ECD types, separately for words and consonant strings.

SOURCE RECONSTRUCTION WITH SYNTHETIC
APERTURE MAGNETOMETRY (SAM)

Synthetic aperture magnetometry (SAM) is an adaptive beamforming technique for the analysis of electroencephalography (EEG) and MEG data (Robinson & Vrba, 1999; Van Veen, van Drongelen, Yuchtman, & Suzuki, 1997; Vrba & Robinson, 2001). It is a second-order technique for solving the inverse problem and uses a linear weighting of the sensor channels to focus the array on a given target location or set of locations—in this case a regular array of virtual electrodes (or voxels) in the brain placed 5 mm apart from one another. The result is a reconstruction of the time series for every voxel or virtual electrode in the brain. Thereafter, for a nominated frequency range, it is possible to compare the power in the Fourier domain between a passive or baseline time window and a sequence of active time windows of interest, as well as to compute time-frequency plots for particular virtual electrodes of interest. As a result, it is possible to image changes in spectral power for both event-related synchronization (ERS; i.e., where power in the active window > passive window) and event-related desynchronization (ERD; i.e., where power in the active window < passive window).

The main advantages of source reconstruction techniques like SAM are twofold. First, unlike ECDs, it is possible to localize sources in the brain with SAM based on both evoked and induced activity, be they ERSs or ERDs. Epochs of evoked activity are those that are tightly phase-locked to the stimulus across successive trials, whereas induced activity is not (see Hillebrand & Barnes, 2005). In the amplitude domain, simple averaging across trials is sufficient to reveal an evoked signal component that will also be reflected in the frequency domain. In comparison, simple averaging in the amplitude domain will not reveal sources of induced activity because of phase jitter from one trial to the next, but such sources will still be revealed in the frequency domain. The second advantage is that using the appropriate anatomical information from an individual enables individual SAM statistical maps to be transformed to a standard MNI space and used to make group statistical inferences. The main limitation of adaptive beamformer techniques is dealing with sources that are perfectly temporally correlated. However, perfect neural synchrony between two sources in the brain over the entire course of an experiment is exceedingly unlikely, and it has been shown that two sources can be resolved even at relatively large temporal correlation levels (Sekihara, Nagarajan, Poeppel, & Marantz, 2002; Van Veen et al., 1997).

LEXICAL DECISION

We recently used SAM analysis of MEG data from a visual lexical decision task to map the spatiotemporal evolution of cortical events during visual word recognition (Pammer et al., 2004). As Figure 9.3 shows, during the first ~150 ms following the central presentation of five-letter words, we saw ERS in primary visual areas in the lingual gyrus, cuneus (BA17).

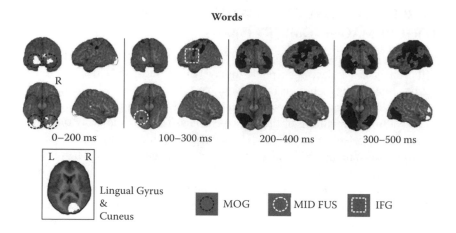

FIGURE 9.3 Group SAM maps of responses in the beta frequency band (10–20 Hz) to 5-letter words. MOG = Middle Occipital Gyrus; MID FUS = Mid Fusiform Gyrus (VWFA); IFG = Inferior Frontal Gyrus. ERS and ERD thresholded at p<0.05 are shown in white and black respectively.

In the same time frame, we also saw bilateral ERS in the inferior and middle occipital gyri (BA 18/19) with the responses being stronger in the left hemisphere (LH) than the right hemisphere (RH). These findings are entirely consistent with other MEG studies of visual word recognition and reading using equivalent current dipole modeling (Cornelissen et al., 2003; Salmelin, Schnitzler, Schmitz, & Freund, 2000; Tarkiainen et al., 1999), minimum norm current estimation (Dhond, Buckner, Dale, Marinkovic, & Halgren, 2001), and dynamic imaging of coherent sources (DICS; Kujala et al., 2007). After ~150 ms, we saw ERD in the left and right fusiform gyri (LH > RH), which expanded systematically in both the posterior–anterior and medial–lateral directions over the course of the next 500 ms. In the LH, that part of the mid-fusiform region, which has recently been dubbed the visual word form area (VWFA), was activated around ~200 ms poststimulus; this is in good agreement with the timing of word-specific responses from other neurophysiological recordings (Cohen et al., 2000; Nobre et al., 1994).

COMPARING SAM WITH ECDS AND fMRI

On the basis of anatomical location and timing, there appears to be good correspondence between the ERS in lingual gyrus and cuneus identified with SAM and the Type I sources defined with equivalent current dipole modeling. Similarly, the ERS in the left and right middle occipital gyrus (MOG) defined by SAM would appear to correspond reasonably with the Type II ECD response. Despite the fact that both sets of results are based on MEG data recorded during visual word recognition tasks, the SAM maps in Figure 9.3 show a much finer anatomical parcellation of functional activation than is the case with ECDs. For example, the SAM maps show activations in the MOG, which are distinctly separate from those in the fusiform gyri, whereas the published ECD results have never convincingly separated two such components. One explanation for this difference could be that the activation in MOG is largely phase-locked, whereas that in the fusiform is not. If so, ECD algorithms would likely fail to "see" the fusiform activation. Alternatively, it may be the case that fixed location, fixed orientation dipoles (as were used in Tarkiainen et al., 1999) are not sensitive enough to separate two sources that are both close to each other and active within a similar timeframe. Fortunately, the application of a third analysis technique to these kinds of MEG data, minimum norm estimation (see Marincovic et al., 2003), does help us to resolve this apparent discrepancy because it also suggests that there is a systematic spread of activation along the ventral stream, from V1 toward the lateral occipital complex and the fusiform gyrus, during visual word recognition.

The comparison between functional magnetic resonance imaging (fMRI) and SAM data shows another striking difference between the results from different imaging modalities. As Figure 9.4 shows, based on the meta-analysis of fMRI studies of reading by Vigneau, Jobard, Mazoyer, and Tzourio-Mazoyer (2005), the appropriate fMRI contrasts for visually presented words tend to reveal a spatially restricted response in the mid-fusiform gyrus (average Talairach coordinates: $x = -43$, $y = -54$, $z = 12$), even though this can extend as far as ~4 cm anteroposteriorly (see for example, Vinckier et al., 2007). Among many others, Cohen et al. (2000) showed that this so-called VWFA responds more strongly to alphabetic letter strings than to checkerboard stimuli, more strongly to words than to consonant strings, and demonstrates invariance with respect to retinal position. In addition, VWFA shows font-type invariance (Dehaene, Le Clec, Poline, Le Bihan, & Cohen, 2002). At issue here is not the validity of the interpretation as far as the role of this neuronal population is concerned. Instead, it is the very different impressions of what might be going on, depending on whether information about timing (in the millisecond range) is available. On the one hand, the fMRI

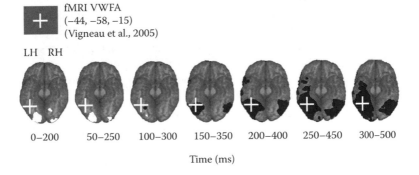

fMRI VWFA
(−44, −58, −15)
(Vigneau et al., 2005)

LH RH

0–200   50–250   100–300   150–350   200–400   250–450   300–500

Time (ms)

FIGURE 9.4 Group SAM maps of responses in the beta frequency band to centrally presented words. Left and right MOG activations appear as white ERS. Left and right fusiform gyus activations appear as black ERD.

data tend to produce a single, static blob of activation in the left mid-fusiform or VWFA because information is integrated over a long (~500 ms) window. This gives the strong impression that a relatively fixed population of neurons is doing something that contributes en masse to letter-string processing—whatever that is. On the other hand, it is very tempting to interpret the SAM and minimum norm estimates as evidence of a progressive sweep of corticocortical activation along the fusiform gyrus that evolves with time. This more dynamic pattern is consistent with recent computational and conceptual models of visual word recognition (see, for example, Whitney, 2001; Dehaene, Cohen, Sigman, & Vinckier, 2005), which suggests the idea of a time-dependent sequence along the fusiform in which progressively complex attributes of letter strings are extracted: from simple lines and edges in a retinotopic spatial framework, through to font and case invariant letters, letter clusters, and ultimately whole words. For example, the LCD model proposed by Dehaene et al. (2005) suggests a succession of larger and larger receptive fields, from V1, though V2, V4, and V8 to OTS, which extract letter fragments, then case-specific letter shapes, then abstract letter identities, then letter clusters, and so on. Therefore, in skilled readers in whom the visual word recognition network has been trained over hundreds of thousands of hours on central presentations of words, we ought to expect stimulus driven, bottom-up responses, which reflect this tuning (see, e.g., Nazir, Ben-Boutayab, Decoppet, Deutsch, & Frost, 2004; Polk & Farah, 1998).

RETINOTOPICITY AND HEMIFIELD PRESENTATIONS

In languages where the orthography is read from left to right, we tend to fixate on letters situated somewhere between the beginning and the middle of a word. According to recent research (Lavidor, Ellis, Shillcock, & Bland, 2001; Lavidor & Walsh, 2004; Monaghan, Shillcock, & McDonald, 2004), this means that the letters falling to the left of fixation project initially *only* to the visual cortex in the right cerebral hemisphere, while letters to the right of fixation project initially *only* to the visual cortex in the left cerebral hemisphere. There appears to be *no* overlap between the two. Consistent with this split fovea model, Cohen et al. (2000) recorded fMRI activations during the presentation of words, consonant strings, and checkerboards to the left and right halves of the visual field. As expected, they found position-invariant activation in the VWFA, especially for words. However, this activation was distinct from more posterior hemifield-dependent middle occipital gyrus (BA 19) responses. These were stronger for contralateral than for ipsilateral stimulation, irrespective of whether the participants viewed words, consonant strings, or checkerboards. Therefore, these data are consistent with retinotopic coding at this location in the reading network. Ultimately, however, to confirm retinotopicity, it would be necessary to view these posterior activations in individual participants where not only have the boundaries between visual areas been carefully demarcated by retinotopic mapping (see, for example, Dougherty et al., 2003), but also the word stimuli have been systematically shifted across the visual field relative to a fixation point.

Figure 9.5 shows results from our own MEG data in which five-letter words were presented to the left and right upper and lower quadrants of the visual field. In these analyses, the data are averaged across the upper and lower quadrants to compare the left- and right-hemisphere responses with each other. They show that within the first 250 ms after stimulus presentation, the response to words in the region of the middle occipital gyrus is largely contralateral, suggesting

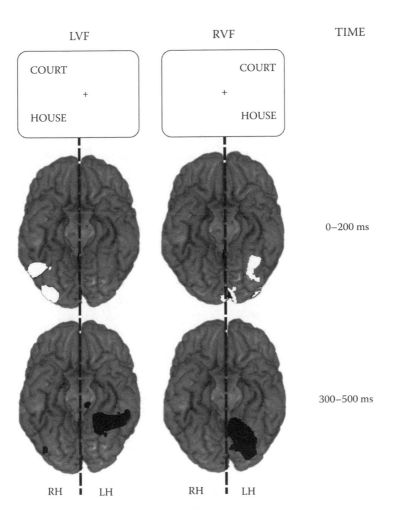

FIGURE 9.5 Group SAM maps of responses in the beta frequency band to 5-letter words presented to either the left or the right visual field. ERS and ERD thresholded at p<0.05 are shown in white and black respectively.

processing within a retinotopic spatial framework. However, by around 300 ms, the responses have become lateralized to the left fusiform. Thus, the left and right halves of words appear initially to be processed independently in retinotopic cortical representations in the right and left occipital cortex, respectively. Some 50–100 ms later, processing appears to localize and to lateralize to the left hemisphere's (nonretinotopic) mid-fusiform cortex.

EARLY BROCA'S ACTIVATION

Surprisingly, Pammer et al. (2004) found an ERD in the left pars opercularis of the inferior frontal gyrus (IFG) and the precentral gyrus (BA44/6) which started early, at around ~100–200 ms poststimulus. This early IFG activity followed immediately after the bilateral ERS in the middle occipital gyrus and overlapped in time with the onset of activation in the LH mid-fusiform. Together, these findings suggest that the interplay between the vision and language domains starts early during visual word recognition.

The early involvement of Broca's area in visual word recognition may at first seem puzzling, but in fact a number of other studies have also found indications of this. For example, in their analysis of evoked responses in a reading task, measured with MEG, Salmelin et al. (2000) reported an early left frontoparietal activation (between 100–200 ms poststimulus) in 5/10 stutterers and 5/10 controls. Kober et al. (2001) used MEG to identify responses in Broca's and Wernicke's areas in patients who carried out a silent reading task. Although Kober et al.'s (2001) report focuses attention on the response in Broca's area at 720 ms poststimulus, nevertheless an earlier peak is clear in their data at around 170 ms poststimulus. Finally, Lachaux et al. (2008) measured cortical activity from surface electrodes implanted in epilepsy patients. Subjects were presented two interleaved stories in a rapid serial visual presentation (RSVP) format. Words from the story to be attended to appeared in one color, while words from the story to be ignored appeared in a different color. Time-frequency analysis based on data averaged in relation to word onset showed clear, early beta frequency band activity for both storylines.

The required connectivity between extrastriate visual areas and posterior superior IFG could be supplied via the arcuate fasciculus. Recent diffusion tensor imaging (DTI) and histological studies of the arcuate fasciculus in human brains (Bürgel et al., 2006; Makris et al., 2005) support Dejerine's (1895/1980) original proposals and suggest direct connections between Brodmann's areas 18 and 19 and the lateral frontal association areas. Moreover, DiVirgilio and Clarke (1997) used the Nauta technique to demonstrate anterograde axonal degeneration in a postmortem brain that had suffered a right inferior temporal infarction. These authors found crossed monosynaptic connections between extrastriate visual cortex and Wernicke's and Broca's areas. In the current study we found a difference in latency between the MOG (i.e., BA 18/19) and IFG of 10–15 ms. Therefore, assuming no additional synaptic delays, this latency difference is consistent with the conduction velocity of a myelinated fiber of about 1μ diameter over an 8–10 cm distance (Patton, 1982). In summary, there is good reason to suppose that early activation in the IFG to visually presented words is both plausible as an empirical phenomenon and supportable by the known anatomical connectivity. Consistent with this, a Granger causality analysis reported in a recent MEG study of continuous reading (Kujala et al., 2007) also suggests that there are direct functional connections between occipitotemporal cortex and left hemisphere frontal areas during reading (see Figure 9.6).

The role of the IFG in visual word recognition is well established from a number of neuroimaging studies (Bookheimer, 2002). The cortical regions in and around Broca's area in the IFG appear to be associated with fine-grained, speech-gestural, phonological recoding; direct stimulation/recording studies have shown very fast connections between this region in the IFG and motor neurons in the motor strip that drive the speech articulators (Greenlee et al., 2004). This system has been found to function in silent reading and naming (Fiez & Petersen, 1998; Pugh et al., 1996, 1997) and is thought to be more strongly engaged by low-frequency words and pseudowords than by high-frequency words (Fiebach, Friederici, Muller, & von Cramon, 2002; Fiez & Petersen, 1998; Pugh et al., 1996, 1997). Moreover, functional connectivity between the left dorsal IFG and occipitotemporal cortex for words, pseudowords, and letter strings, but not false fonts, has been demonstrated (Bokde, Tagamets, Friedman, & Horwitz, 2001; Mechelli et al., 2005). Hemodynamic functional imaging has therefore delimited quite precisely the anatomical extent of left posterior IFG activation during visual word recognition and elucidated a likely role for it in phonological encoding.

However, while the functional connectivity data imply direct interplay between the vision and language domains, they cannot inform us about the time course of these effects nor how they evolve over time. In contrast, neurophysiological studies using event-related potentials (ERPs) or event-related fields (ERFs) can pinpoint events in time with millisecond precision, but they often face the converse

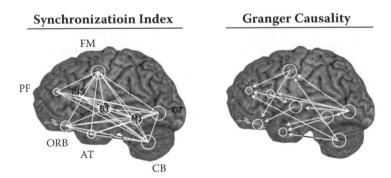

FIGURE 9.6   Phase synchronization and Granger causality estimates between left hemisphere cortical network nodes during continuous reading. OT, inferior occipitotemporal cortex; MT, medial temporal cortex; ST, superior temporal cortex; AT, anterior part of the inferior temporal cortex; FM, face motor cortex; INS, insula; CB, cerebellum; PF, prefrontal cortex; ORB, orbital cortex.

problem that they lack anatomical precision. Nevertheless, a number of such studies have been carried out which indicate that interactions between visual and linguistic factors during visual word recognition do begin early. For example, Assadollahi and Pulvermüller (2003) showed an interaction between word length and frequency in MEG, with short words exhibiting a frequency effect around 150 ms but long words at around 240 ms. Effects of lexicality (i.e., a differential response between words and pseudowords) have been reported as early as 110 ms (Sereno, Rayner, & Posner, 1998), though more commonly around 200 ms (Cornelissen et al., 2003; Martin-Loeches, Hinojosa, Gomez-Jarabo, & Rubia, 1999). Lexico-semantic variables have been found to influence brain responses as early as 160 ms after visual word onset (Pulvermüller, Assadollahi, & Elbert, 2001; Pulvermüller, Lutzenberger, & Birbaumer, 1995), as has semantic coherence, which is a "measure that quantifies the degree to which words sharing a root morpheme, (e.g., gold, golden, goldsmith) are related to each other in meaning" (Hauk, Davis, Ford, Pulvermüller, & Marslen-Wilson, 2006, p. 1386). Intriguingly, Figures 5 and 7 in Hauk et al. (2006) suggest early left frontal involvement particularly for semantic coherence, but unfortunately it is not possible to be more anatomically precise from their data.

VIRTUAL ELECTRODE ANALYSIS OF RESPONSES IN BROCA'S AREA, VWFA, AND MOG

Recently, my colleagues and I sought further evidence for early activation of the IFG—specifically in the pars opercularis and precentral gyrus—in response to visually presented words. Based on our previous work and the studies reviewed earlier, we hypothesized that IFG activation should first be detected in a time window between the start of bilateral activation of the middle occipital gyri (MOG, BA 18/19) and the start of activation of the LH mid-fusiform (BA 37). Therefore, we used SAM analysis to identify six ROIs: one in each of the left and right MOG, the VWFA in left mid-fusiform and its right hemisphere homologue, and the left posterior IFG and its right hemisphere homologue. We tested the specificity of any early IFG activation by comparing responses to centrally presented words, consonant strings, and faces. In addition, we wanted to ensure that the cognitive and attentional demands of the experimental task were held constant across different stimulus types by asking subjects to fixate on a central cross continuously, and to simply monitor and respond to any color change of the cross. For each site and for each subject, we then calculated the time course of the MEG signal to compare the relative timings and amplitudes of responses to words, faces, and consonants.

AMPLITUDE DOMAIN ANALYSIS: ERFS IN BROCA'S AREA, VWFA, AND MOG

To examine the relative timings of evoked activity in these six ROIs, and also to compare responses to words, faces, and consonant strings, we carried out further analyses in the domain, restricted to the time window 0–300 ms poststimulus. Significant differences between conditions in the resultant difference waveforms were computed using a nonparametric randomization technique, the record orthogonality test by permutations (ROT-p; Achim, 1995; Achim, Alain, Richer, & Saint-Hilaire, 1988).

Figure 9.7a and 9.7b show the normalized ERFs for centrally presented words in the left IFG ROI, compared with its RH homologue, as well as word responses in the VWFA ROI compared to its RH homologue. Consistent with our hypothesis, the left IFG showed a significantly stronger early response at ~125 ms to words than its RH homologue. As would be expected on the basis of hemodynamic neuroimaging studies, we also found a significantly stronger response to words in the VWFA at ~150 ms than its RH homologue.

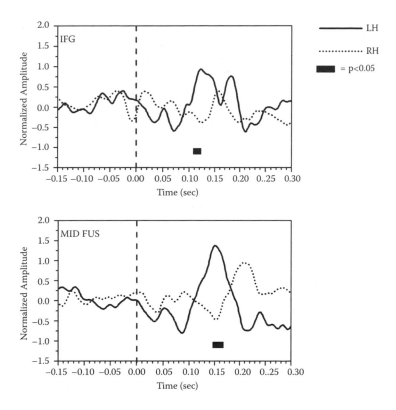

FIGURE 9.7   (a) the normalised ERFs for centrally presented words in the left IFG (solid), compared with its right hemisphere homologue (dotted). (b) word responses in the VWFA (solid) compared to its right hemisphere homologue (dotted). Black bars illustrate significant differences between each pair of time series (P <0.05) as computed with ROT-p.

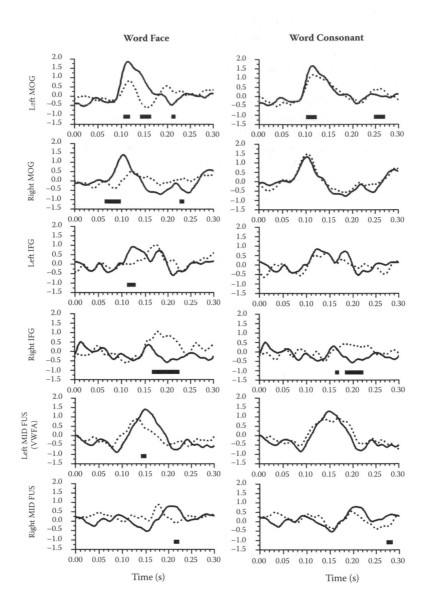

FIGURE 9.8   (a) the normalised ERFs for centrally presented words (dotted) and faces (dotted). (b) words (solid) and consonants (dotted) in all six virtual electrodes. Black bars illustrate significant differences between each pair of time series (P <0.05) as computed with ROT-p.

Figure 9.8 shows pairwise comparisons between words and faces (Figure 9.8a), and words and consonant-strings (Figure 9.8b) for all six ROIs. ROT-p analyses showed significantly stronger responses to words than to faces in left and right MOG, left IFG, and VWFA, between ~80 and 150 ms poststimulus. We also found a significantly stronger response to faces than to words in right IFG between ~150 and 200 ms. Moreover, Figure 9.8a shows that the peak response to words in the left IFG ROI occurred ~10–15 ms later than the commensurate peaks in left and right MOG but ~20 ms earlier than that in VWFA. Formal statistical comparisons showed the former difference, but not the latter, to be significant at $p < 0.05$.

FREQUENCY DOMAIN ANALYSIS: SPECTROGRAMS IN BROCA'S AREA AND VWFA

Since the domain analysis failed to show a significant difference between the evoked responses to words and consonants in the left IFG and left mid-fusiform, my colleagues and I also carried out the complementary analysis for these ROIs in the frequency domain. To examine the time course of any changes in oscillatory activity within each ROI, time-frequency plots (or spectrograms) were calculated using a Morlet wavelet transform. Time-frequency plots contain information about both the evoked and the induced components of the neuronal response (Hillebrand & Barnes, 2005; Hillebrand et al., 2005). Figure 9.9 illustrates the results. Each plot represents the grand average of the differences between each participant's word and consonant spectrograms.

Figure 9.9 shows the left IFG responses to words were stronger than those to consonants in both the alpha and beta frequency bands first around ~130 ms poststimulus and also later at ~400 ms poststimulus. In the left mid-fusiform

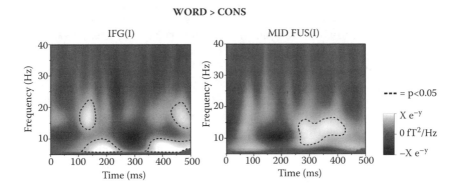

FIGURE 9.9   The difference between time-frequency plots for words and consonant strings for the left IFG and left mid-fusiform ROIs. The black dotted lines represent regions in the time-frequency plots within which the difference between conditions reached significance at $p < 0.05$, according to a general linear mixed model. To interpret the power scales, the values of x and y for IFG(l) are 5 and 19, respectively. The values of x and y for MID-FUS(l) are 3.5 and 18, respectively.

(VWFA), Figure 9.9 shows a stronger response to words than consonants at ~300 ms poststimulus. The dotted black lines in Figure 9.9 represent regions in the time-frequency plots where mixed modeling showed significantly more power for words than consonants at $p < 0.05$, controlling for any effects of spatial time-frequency covariation.

RESPONSE SPECIFICITY: MOG AND VWFA

The domain analyses showed stronger responses to words than faces in left and right MOG, where retinotopicity is maintained. Our experimental task arguably minimized differences in attentional demands and cognitive loading between stimulus classes because participants only had to monitor and respond to color changes in the fixation cross. Therefore, this leaves two main reasons in principle for stronger responses to words than faces. Consistent with the electrophysiological findings reviewed earlier (e.g., Cornelissen et al., 2003; Hauk et al., 2006; Pulvermüller et al., 1995, 2001; Sereno et al., 1998; Tarkiainen et al., 1999), one possibility is that these differences may genuinely reflect word specific effects related to early interactions between the vision and language domains. However, there is a second possibility. The MOG ROIs were located in retinotopic extrastriate visual cortex (see, e.g., Brewer, Liu, Wade, & Wandell, 2005; Dougherty et al., 2003). Therefore, since the horizontal extent of the words on the retina exceeded that of the faces, it is quite possible that the stronger response to words merely reflected activity in more peripheral receptive fields. The word/consonant string comparisons allow us to disambiguate these possibilities for MOG, because, unlike faces, word and consonant strings were the same size. For left MOG, Figure 9.8 shows that evoked word responses were stronger than consonant-string responses around 100 ms poststimulus. This differential response for stimuli with the same retinal subtens is therefore more consistent with word-specific than low-level visual effects (where we would have expected no differences between words and consonant strings). However, for right MOG, the picture is less clear because responses to consonant strings were no different from those to words.

At the VWFA site, we found an evoked response to words that peaked around 150 ms poststimulus and was stronger at this time point for words than faces, but was not distinguishable from the commensurate evoked response to consonant strings. However, the frequency-domain analyses for words demonstrated both ERD and ERS in the alpha and beta frequency bands respectively from ~120 ms poststimulus onward. Critically, the direct comparison between words and consonants revealed a significantly stronger response to words in the beta band between ~250 and 450 ms poststimulus. These results are consistent with hemodynamic neuroimaging studies, which suggest word-specific responses in the left mid-fusiform (e.g., Ben-Sachar, Dougherty, Deutsch, & Wandell, 2006; Cohen et al., 2000; Dehaene et al., 2002).

Put together, the results for left MOG and left mid-fusiform are consistent with recent models for letter strings encoding along the occipitotemporal complex, which assume that there is a hierarchy of information processing on a continuum from simple features through to increasingly elaborate and abstracted objects as discussed earlier.

RESPONSE SPECIFICITY: IFG

Left IFG gave a stronger evoked response at ~125 ms to words than right IFG. Moreover, the evoked response in left IFG at this time was stronger to words than to faces. In the frequency domain, we found a significantly stronger response to words than consonants in both the alpha and beta bands at around ~125 ms post-stimulus as well as later at ~400 ms poststimulus.

The simplest way to interpret this pattern of results is to assume that the same stereotypical response to any equivalent length string of letter-like objects would always be produced, irrespective of task demands, that is, whether explicit naming is required or whether stimuli are viewed passively as in the current experiment. If so, this might suggest that for a skilled reader who has had many thousands of hours of experience with print, the very presence of word-like stimuli in the visual field can trigger a response in IFG, and its role is to prime the rest of the language system to prepare for upcoming cross-modal interactions between the vision and language systems—a stimulus-driven anticipatory response. It is also possible that such an effect, if true, may have been further enhanced by the blocked design of the current study. This proposal is similar to recent claims by Bar et al. (2006), who showed that low spatial frequencies can facilitate visual object recognition by initiating top-down processes projected from the orbitofrontal to visual cortex; object recognition elicited differential activity that developed in the left orbitofrontal cortex 50 ms earlier than it did in recognition-related areas in the temporal cortex.

An alternative possibility is that early IFG activation in response to visually presented words reflects grapheme-to-phoneme conversion processes, perhaps along the sublexical route for reading (Coltheart, Curtis, Atkins, & Haller, 1993; Harm & Seidenberg, 2004). This interpretation is in line with other imaging studies that have implicated this frontal area in phonological processing during visual word recognition (Burton, LoCasto, Krebs-Noble, & Gullapalli, 2005; Joubert et al., 2004), and with priming studies showing early activation of phonological representations (Carreiras, Ferrand, Grainger, & Perea, 2005; Lee, Rayner, & Pollatsek, 1999; Lukatela, Carello, Savic, Urosevic, & Turvey, 1998; Lukatela & Turvey, 1994). Moreover, this possibility is in alignment with research on verbal short-term memory. Effects of word length and phonological similarity indicate that visually presented items, such as letters or numerals, are recoded into phonological form prior to storage in short-term memory (Baddeley, 1986; Conrad & Hull, 1964). Articulatory suppression removes the phonological similarity effect, indicating the importance of articulatory processes for such recoding (Baddeley, 1986). Indeed, one fMRI study specifically showed activation of the IFG, inferior parietal cortex, and posterior temporal cortex in response to working memory for letters versus abstract symbols (Henson, Burgess, & Frith, 2000). Imaging studies have also indicated that the inferior parietal cortex encodes the phonological information itself, providing the so-called phonological store (Baddeley, 1986), while the IFG also controls the rehearsal process via reactivation of information within the phonological store (Awh et al., 1996; Henson et al., 2000; Paulesu, Frith, & Frackowiak, 1993). Thus, it appears that visual information is recoded into an articulatory-phonological form in the IFG, which activates an auditory-phonological representation in the inferior parietal cortex, which in turn activates lexical forms in the temporal cortex (Henson et al., 2000).

IMPLICATIONS FOR DEVELOPMENTAL DYSLEXIA

The overriding impression from the MEG studies of visual word recognition reviewed here is that the functional connections between the nodes of the reading network seem to ignite multiple and/or parallel routes very quickly after words are presented. This runs counter to the idea of an orderly sequence from visual processing of letter strings, to grapheme–phoneme mapping, to semantic mapping to spoken output. Moreover the MEG data from the reading and visual word recognition studies of dyslexic individuals, reported by Salmelin et al. (1996) and Helenius et al. (1999) are very compelling. They suggest that the first detectable differences between the reading networks in dyslexic and nondyslexic readers emerge very early and are located essentially in extrastriate visual cortex. While the designs of these studies do not allow us to identify the causes of these differences, there is a range of possible explanations consistent with the data that lie between two extreme positions. At one extreme, these differences could in principle derive from a low-level deficit in visual processing of letter strings. This represents a strictly bottom-up account of the problem, placing the primary impairment squarely in the visual domain. At the opposite extreme, we can imagine either top-down or feedback-feedforward influences at work over the months and years that children learn to read. For example, it is possible that either a failure of network integration or a primary deficit higher up in the network—such as a tatty phonological representation—could result in differences in the way that the reading network crystallizes out over time. In this view, there is nothing particularly special about the lack of a left hemisphere occipitotemporal node in the dyslexic brain. It is merely one of a cluster of differences between the normal and dyslexic reading network, and is notable only for being the first to emerge in the temporal sequence of events in the cortex during visual word recognition.

Intriguingly, the data from Rosen, Wang, Fiondella, and LoTurco (this volume) suggest that developmental dyslexia is indeed associated with genetically determined differences in anatomical network integrity. If true, this may well impact on: (a) the spatiotemporal precision of information flow between the nodes of a distributed network, such as that for reading, and (b) the precision with which information may be transformed at the synapses contained within the nodes of the distributed network. If the integrity of thalamocortical and corticocortical loops is compromised, we might also predict that MEG could identify differences of at-rest measures of oscillatory activity in the brains of dyslexics. Moreover, while there is still debate about the prevalence and the impact of low-level visual processing differences in developmental dyslexia, the elegant findings from Ramus and Szenkovits (this volume) suggest that there may not be an isolable deficit with phonological representations in developmental dyslexia. In our own work measuring perceptual confusions between spoken consonant–vowel syllables in noise (Cornelissen, Hansen, Bradley, & Stein, 1996), we also struggled to find any convincing evidence for systematic differences between the input phonological representations of nondyslexic and dyslexic adult readers.

Given these challenges to the phonological deficit theory of dyslexia, let us go out on a limb here and suppose that dyslexics do *not* have visual processing deficits and do *not* suffer distorted phonological representations. How then could we explain impaired visual word recognition? Before we go further, I want to acknowledge that a long history of experimental research in psychology has taught us to be extremely cautious about developing arguments and theories based on personal experience and anecdote. Nevertheless, particularly in the clinical world, it is frequently the anecdotal story—the patient with the odd symptoms who doesn't seem to fit a recognized pattern—that leads to new insights. So, with these caveats in mind, I offer the following observation as an inspiration for how we might conceive of impaired reading without visual/phonological representational deficits.

At Chirk Castle in Wrexham, North Wales, United Kingdom, there is displayed on one wall of the museum a written proclamation dating from the time of Charles I. The manuscript is written in a flowing, highly decorative calligraphy in unfamiliar Old English that is peppered with unfamiliar spellings. What surprised me on a visit there was the complete inability of a highly literate English-speaking colleague of mine to read this manuscript. Though normally completely fluent in reading, this manuscript completely stumped him. There was no doubt he could slowly make out individual letters and work out individual sounds. But with this manuscript, what he could not do was to string the letters and sounds together quickly enough into working memory to obtain any sense of fluency. It was as if the extra burden the unfamiliar script imposed on his decoding skills pushed him to a tipping point and precipitated a catastrophic collapse. As a result, any possibility of his extracting meaning and context from the text completely evaporated.

What, if anything, can we draw from this anecdote? The first point to make, especially given the claims for impaired working memory in dyslexia, is the importance of integrating enough information into a large enough memory buffer quick enough to obtain fluency in reading. The second point to this story is that the noise introduced into my colleague's reading system was at a minimum caused by the slow extraction of orthographic features. But it is not hard to see how the bottleneck(s) could be placed a little further into the system, so that there is no longer a problem with feature extraction per se nor a lack of fidelity of representation, but slowed transmission and integration of information within and between network nodes. Arguably, and now I really want to go out on a limb here, reading is also one of the very few cognitive tasks where deficits in network integrity might be *expected* to cause the greatest devastation.

From a purely visual perspective, printed words represent a very unusual visual stimulus and are quite unlike images from the natural world (Cornelissen & Hansen, 1998). Specifically, all the information available in a line of text is compressed into three discrete spatial scales, to a first approximation: coarse, intermediate, and fine. Roughly speaking, these scales correspond to: the average size of a word, the average size of a letter, and the average thickness of the lines that make up each letter. There is no other useful information at intermediate spatial scales. This contrasts dramatically with natural images, which contain a smooth continuum of information across all spatial scales (Tolhurst, Tadmor, & Chao, 1992). Over and above their visual peculiarities, printed words are also unusual in the sense that the cognitive targets of familiar words are pre-existing semantic concepts that can only be reached via a complex set of learned transforms involving the vision and language systems. When we read for meaning, the sensory inputs for visual word recognition are not the direct sensory correlates of the semantic targets themselves, as is the case with seen objects, heard sounds, or felt objects. Instead, the situation with reading is much more indirect; printed words are visual symbolic representations of the speech/sound codes for the *verbal labels* for the semantic targets. This suggests to me, at least, that reading may make an anomalously high demand on an individual's capacity to integrate information across different domains, so that network integrity becomes absolutely key to success in reading. Commensurately, failure of network integrity may in and of itself be sufficient to explain reading failure.

REFERENCES

Achim, A. (1995). Signal detection in averaged evoked potentials: Monte Carlo comparison of the sensitivity of different methods. *Electroencephalography and Clinical Neurophysiology, 96*, 574–584.

Achim, A., Alain, C., Richer, F., & Saint-Hilaire, J. M. (1988). A test of model adequacy applied to the dimensionality of multi-channel average auditory evoked potentials. In D. Samson-Dollfus (Ed.), *Statistics and topography in quantitative EEG* (pp. 161–171). Amsterdam: Elsevier.

Assadollahi, R., & Pulvermüller, F. (2003). Early influences of word length and frequency: A group study using MEG. *NeuroReport, 14*, 1183–1187.

Awh, E., Jonides, J., Smith, E. E., Schumacher, E. H., Koeppe, R. A., & Katz, S. (1996). Dissociation of storage and rehearsal in verbal working memory: Evidence from positron emission tomography. *Psychological Science, 7*, 25–31.

Baddeley, A. D. (1986). *Working memory*. Oxford, UK: Oxford University Press.

Bar, M., Kassam, K. S., Ghuman, A. S., Boshyan, J., Schmid, A. M., Dale, A. M., et al. (2006). Top-down facilitation of visual recognition. *Proceedings of the National Academy of Sciences USA, 103*, 449–454

Ben-Sachar, M., Dougherty, R. F., Deutsch, G. K., & Wandell, B. A. (2006). Differential sensitivity to words and shapes in ventral occipito-temporal cortex. *Cerebral Cortex, 17*(7), 1604–1611.

Bokde, A. L., Tagamets, M. A., Friedman, R. B., & Horwitz, B. (2001). Functional interactions of the inferior frontal cortex during the processing of words and word-like stimuli. *Neuron, 30*, 609–617.

Bookheimer, S. (2002). Functional MRI of language: New approaches to understanding the cortical organization of semantic processing. *Annual Review of Neuroscience, 25*, 151–188.

Brewer, A. A., Liu, J. J., Wade, A. R., & Wandell, B. A. (2005). Visual field maps and stimulus selectivity in human ventral occipital cortex. *Nature Neuroscience, 8*, 1102–1109.

Bürgel, U., Amunts, K., Hoemke, L., Mohlberg, H., Gilsbach, J. M., & Zilles, K. (2006). White matter fibre tracts of the human brain: Three-dimensional mapping at microscopic resolution, topography and intersubject variability. *NeuroImage, 29*, 1092–1105.

Burton, M. W., LoCasto, P. C., Krebs-Noble, D., & Gullapalli, R. P. (2005). A systematic investigation of the functional neuroanatomy of auditory and visual phonological processing. *NeuroImage, 26*, 647–661.

Carreiras, M., Ferrand, L., Grainger, J., & Perea, M. (2005). Sequential effects of phonological priming in visual word recognition. *Psychological Science, 16*(8), 585–589.

Cohen, L., Dehaene, S., Naccache, L., Lehericy, S., Dehaene-Lambertz, G., Henaff, M. A., et al. (2000). The visual word form area: Spatial and temporal characterization of an initial stage of reading in normal subjects and posterior split-brain patients. *Brain, 123*(Pt 2), 291–307.

Coltheart, M., Curtis, B., Atkins, P., & Haller, M. (1993). Models of reading aloud: Dual-route and parallel-distributed-processing approaches. *Psychological Review, 100*, 589–608.

Conrad, R., & Hull, A. J. (1964). Information, acoustic confusion and memory span. *British Journal of Psychology, 55*, 429–432.

Cornelissen, P. L., & Hansen, P. C. (1998). Motion detection, letter position encoding and single word reading. *Annals of Dyslexia, 48*, 155–188.

Cornelissen, P. L., Hansen, P. C., Bradley, L., & Stein, J. F. (1996). Analysis of perceptual confusions between 9 sets of consonant-vowel sounds in normal and dyslexic adults. *Cognition, 59*, 275–306.

Cornelissen, P. L., Tarkiainen, A., Helenius, P., & Salmelin, R. (2003). Cortical effects of shifting letter-position in letter-strings of varying length. *Journal of Cognitive Neuroscience, 15*(5), 731–748.

Dehaene, S., Cohen, L., Sigman, M., & Vinckier, F. (2005). The neural code for written words: A proposal. *Trends in Cognitive Sciences, 9*, 335–341.

Dehaene, S., Le Clec, H., G., Poline, J. B., Le Bihan, D., & Cohen, L. (2002). The visual word form area: A prelexical representation of visual words in the fusiform gyrus. *NeuroReport, 13*, 321–325.

Dejerine, J. (1980). *Anatomie des Centres Nerveux*. Paris: Masson. (Original work published 1895)

Dhond, R. P., Buckner, R. L., Dale, A. M., Marinkovic, K., & Halgren, E. (2001). Spatiotemporal maps of brain activity underlying word generation and their modification during repetition priming. *Journal of Neuroscience, 21*(10), 3564–3571.

DiVirgilio, G., & Clarke, S. (1997). Direct interhemispheric visual input to human speech areas. *Human Brain Mapping, 5*, 347–354.

Dougherty, R. F., Koch, V. M., Brewer, A. A., Fischer, B., Modersitzki, J., & Wandell, B. A. (2003). Visual field representations and locations of visual areas V1/2/3 in human visual cortex. *Journal of Vision, 3*, 586–598.

Fiebach, C. J., Friederici, A. D., Muller, K., & von Cramon, D. Y. (2002). fMRI evidence for dual routes to the mental lexicon in visual word recognition. *Journal of Cognitive Neuroscience, 14*, 11–23.

Fiez, J. A., & Petersen, S. E. (1998). Neuroimaging studies of word reading. *Proceedings of the National Academy of Sciences USA, 95*, 914–921.

Greenlee, J. D. W., Oya, H., Kawasaki, H., Volkov, I. O., Kaufman, O. P., Kovach, C., et al. (2004). A functional connection between inferior frontal gyrus and orofacial motor cortex in human. *Journal of Neurophysiology, 92*, 1153–1164.

Hämäläinen, M., & Ilmoniemi, R. (1984). Interpreting measured magnetic fields of the brain: Estimates of current distributions (Technical Report, TKK-F-A559). Helsinki, Finland: Helsinki University of Technology.

Harm, M. W., & Seidenberg, M. S. (2004). Computing the meanings of words in reading: Cooperative division of labor between visual and phonological processes. *Psychological Review, 111*, 662–720.

Hauk, O., Davis, M. H., Ford, M., Pulvermüller, F., & Marslen-Wilson, W. D. (2006). The time course of visual word recognition as revealed by linear regression analysis of ERP data. *NeuroImage, 30*, 1383–1400.

Helenius, P., Salmelin, R., Service, E., & Connolly, J. F. (1998). Distinct time courses of word and sentence comprehension in the left temporal cortex. *Brain, 121*, 1133–1142.

Helenius, P., Tarkiainen, A., Cornelissen, P. L., Hansen, P. C., & Salmelin, R. (1999). Dissociation of normal feature analysis and deficient processing of letter-strings in dyslexic adults. *Cerebral Cortex, 9*, 476–483.

Henson, R. N. A., Burgess, N., & Frith, C. D. (2000). Recoding, storage, rehearsal and grouping in verbal short-term memory: An fMRI study. *Neuropsychologia, 38*, 426–440.

Hillebrand, A., & Barnes, G. R. (2005). Beamformer analysis of MEG data. *International Review of Neurobiology, 68*, 149–171.

Hillebrand, A., Singh, K. D., Holliday, I. E., Furlong, P. L., & Barnes, G. R. (2005). A new approach to neuroimaging with magnetoencephalography. *Human Brain Mapping, 25*(2), 199–211.

Joubert, S., Beauregard, M., Walter, N., Bourgouin, P., Beaudoin, G., Leroux, J. M., et al. (2004). Neural correlates of lexical and sublexical processes in reading. *Brain and Language, 89*, 9–20.

Kober, H., Möller, M., Nimsky, C., Vieth, J., Fahlbusch, R., & Ganslandt, O. (2001). New approach to localize speech relevant brain areas and hemispheric sominance using spatially filtered magnetoencephalography. *Human Brain Mapping, 14*, 236–250.

Kujala, J., Pammer, K., Cornelissen, P. L., Roebroeck, P., Formisano, E., & Salmelin, R. (2007). Phase coupling in a cerebro-cerebellar network at 8-13Hz during reading. *Cerebral Cortex, 17*, 1476–1485.

Lachaux, J. P., Jung, J., Mainy, N., Dreher, J. C., Bertrand, O., Baciu, M., et al. (2008). Silence is golden: Transient neural deactivation in the prefrontal cortex during attentive reading. *Cerebral Cortex, 18*, 443–450.

Lavidor, M., Ellis, A. W., Shillcock, R., & Bland, T. (2001). Evaluating a split processing model of visual word recognition: Effect of word length. *Cognitive Brain Research, 12*, 265–272.

Lavidor, M., & Walsh, V. (2004). The nature of foveal representation. *Nature Reviews Neuroscience, 5*, 729–735.

Lee, H. W., Rayner, K., & Pollatsek, A. (1999). The time course of phonological, semantic, and orthographic coding in reading: Evidence from the fast-priming technique. *Psychonomic Bulletin & Review, 6*, 624–634.

Lukatela, G., Carello, C., Savic, M., Urosevic, Z., & Turvey, M. T. (1998). When nonwords activate semantics better than words. *Cognition, 68*, B31–B40.

Lukatela, G., & Turvey, M. T. (1994). Visual lexical access is initially phonological. 2. Evidence from phonological priming by homophones and pseudohomophones. *Journal of Experimental Psychology-General, 123*, 331–353.

Makris, N., Kennedy, D. N., McInerney, S., Sorensen, G. A., Wang, R., Caviness, V. S., et al. (2005). Segmentation of subcomponents within the superior longitudinal fascicle in humans: A quantitative, in vivo, DT-MRI study. *Cerebral Cortex, 15*, 854–869.

Marinkovic, K., Dhond, R. P., Dale, A. M., Glessner, M., Carr, V., & Halgren, E. (2003). Spatiotemporal dynamics of modality specific and supramodel word processing. *Neuron, 38*, 487–497.

Martin-Loeches, M., Hinojosa, J. A., Gomez-Jarabo, G., & Rubia, F. J. (1999). The recognition potential: An ERP index of lexical access. *Brain and Language, 70*, 364–384.

Mechelli, A., Crinion, J. T., Lons, S., Friston, K. J., Lambon Ralph, M. A., Patterson, K., et al. (2005). Dissociating reading processes on the basis of neuronal interactions. *Journal of Cognitive Neuroscience, 17*, 1753–1765.

Monaghan, P., Shillcock, R., & McDonald, S. (2004). Hemispheric asymmetries in the split-fovea model of semantic processing. *Brain and Language, 88*(3), 339–354.

Nazir, T. A., Ben-Boutayab, N., Decoppet, N., Deutsch, A., & Frost, R. (2004). Reading habits, perceptual learning, and recognition of printed words. *Brain and Language, 88*, 294–311.

Nobre, A. C., Allison, T., & McCarthy, G. (1994). Word recognition in the human inferior temporal-lobe. *Nature, 372*, 260–263.

Pammer, K., Hansen, P. C., Kringelbach, M. L., Holliday, I., Barnes, G., Hillebrand, A., et al. (2004). Visual word recognition: The first half-second. *NeuroImage, 22*, 1819–1825.

Patton, H. D. (1982). Special properties of nerve trunks and tracts. In T. Ruch & H. D. Patton (Eds.), *Physiology and biophysics* (Vol. 4, pp. 101–127). Philadelphia: WB Saunders.

Paulesu, E., Frith, C. D., & Frackowiak, R. S. J. (1993). The neural correlates of the verbal component of working memory. *Nature, 362*, 342–345.

Polk, T. A., & Farah, M. J. (1998). The neural development and organization of letter recognition: Evidence from functional neuroimaging, computational modeling, and behavioral studies. *Proceedings of the National Academy of Sciences USA, 95*(3), 847–852.

Pugh, K. R., Shaywitz, B. A., Shaywitz, S. E., Constable, R. T., Skudlarski, P., Fulbright, R. K., et al. (1996). Cerebral organization of component processes in reading. *Brain, 119*, 1221–1238.

Pugh, K. R., Shaywitz, B. A., Shaywitz, S. E., Shankweiler, D. P., Katz, L., Fletcher, J. M., et al. (1997). Predicting reading performance from neuroimaging profiles: The cerebral basis of phonological effects in printed word identification. *Journal of Experimental Psychology-Human Perception and Performance, 23*, 299–318.

Pulvermüller, F., Assadollahi, R., & Elbert, T. (2001). Neuromagnetic evidence for early semantic access in word recognition. *European Journal of Neuroscience, 13*, 201–205.

Pulvermüller, F., Lutzenberger, W., & Birbaumer, N. (1995). Electrocortical distinction of vocabulary types. *Electroencephalography and Clinical Neurophysiology, 94*, 357–370.

Robinson, S. E., & Vrba, J. (1999). Functional neuroimaging by synthetic aperture magnetometry (SAM). In T. Yoshimoto, M. Kotani, S. Kuriki, H. Karibe, & N. Nakasato (Eds.), *Recent advances in biomagnetism* (pp. 302–305). Sendai, Japan: Tohoku University Press.

Salmelin R., Schnitzler, A., Schmitz, F., & Freund, H.-J. (2000). Single word reading in developmental stutterers and fluent speakers. *Brain, 123*, 1184–1202.

Salmelin, R., Service, E., Kiesilä, P., Uutela, K., & Salonen, O. (1996). Impaired visual word processing in dyslexia revealed with magnetoencephalography. *Annals of Neurology*, *40*, 157–162.

Sekihara, K., Nagarajan, S. S., Poeppel, D., & Marantz, A. (2002). Performance of an MEG adaptive-beamformer technique in the presence of correlated neural activities: Effects on signal intensity and time-course estimates. *IEEE Transactions on Biomedical Engineering*, *49*, 1534–1546.

Sereno, S. C., Rayner, K., & Posner, M. I. (1998). Establishing a time-line of word recognition: Evidence from eye movements and event-related potentials. *NeuroReport, 9*, 2195–2200.

Tarkiainen A., Cornelissen P. L., & Salmelin, R. (2002). Dynamics of visual feature analysis and object-level processing in face vs. letter-string perception. *Brain*, *125*, 1125–1136.

Tarkiainen, A., Helenius, P., Hansen, P. C., Cornelissen, P. L., & Salmelin, R. (1999). Dynamics of letter-string perception in the human occipito-temporal cortex. *Brain*, *122*(11), 2119–2131.

Tolhurst, D. J., Tadmor, Y., & Chao, T. (1992). Amplitude spectra of natural images. *Ophthalmic and Physiological Optics*, *12*(2), 229–232.

Uutela, K., Hämäläinen, M., & Somersalo, E. (1999). Visualization of magnetoencephalographic data using minimum current estimates. *NeuroImage*, *10*, 173–180.

Van Veen, B. D., van Drongelen, W., Yuchtman, M., & Suzuki, A. (1997). Localization of brain electrical activity via linearly constrained minimum variance spatial filtering. *IEEE Transactions on Biomedical Engineering*, *44*, 867–880.

Vigneau, M., Jobard, G., Mazoyer, B., & Tzourio-Mazoyer, N. (2005). Word and non-word reading: What role for the visual word form area? *NeuroImage*, *27*, 694–705.

Vinckier, F., Dehaene, S., Jobert, A., Dubus, J. S., Sigman, M. and Cohen, L. (2007). Hierarchical coding of letter strings in the ventral stream: dissecting the inner organization of the visual word-form system. *Neuron*, *55*, 143–156.

Vrba, J., & Robinson, S. E. (2001). Signal processing in magnetoencephalography. *Methods*, *25*, 249–271.

Whitney, C. (2001). How the brain encodes the order of letters in a printed word: The SERIOL model and selective literature review. *Psychonomic Bulletin and Review*, *8*, 221–243.

10 Reading Comprehension
Cognition and Neuroimaging

Laurie E. Cutting, Sarah H. Eason,
Katherine M. Young, and Audrey L. Alberstadt

Successful reading comprehension has long been known to be a complex and multifaceted process. The existing body of knowledge about early reading acquisition identifies word-level processes as the primary contributor to reading comprehension; yet much remains to be understood about what other processes impact a child's reading ability. Cognitive models of reading comprehension, such as Kintsch's (1998) construction-integration model, offer significant insights into the complexity of reading comprehension. Still, to date, the application of cognitive models to reading development and disability has been limited. Generally, the developmental research has constructed a model of reading based on two broad elements—word-level processes and oral language—theorizing that both factors are essential for successful comprehension. However, the constructs of both word-level processes and oral language contain many unexplored subquestions and issues regarding processes critical for successful reading comprehension. For example, what evidence do we have that reading comprehension consists of multiple processes, and which processes appear to be critical? When do different processes become more/less important? How does the measure of reading comprehension that we use influence our findings? And, finally, what are the potential explanations/origins for difficulties with reading comprehension, and how might future research address these?

In this chapter, we review what appear to be guiding principles/questions with regard to research in this area. Within this framework, we examine (a) the evidence for multiple types of processes involved in reading comprehension and when each becomes important, (b) the issue of measurement, and (c) possible explanations for why children struggle with reading comprehension. Finally, we address the next steps that may help frame future reading comprehension research.

EVIDENCE FOR MULTIPLE PROCESSES INVOLVED IN READING COMPREHENSION

A significant body of literature has accumulated indicating that poor basic reading skills (poor word recognition/decoding) cause poor reading comprehension

(Adams, 1990; Lyon, 1995; Torgesen, 2000), especially in younger children, but questions remain regarding other potential processes that are important for reading comprehension. Research examining the simple view of reading, including longitudinal studies, has long provided support for a multiple-factor model of reading comprehension and has also helped establish an understanding of how these processes (i.e., word recognition and language, most commonly listening comprehension) differentially contribute to reading comprehension at various points in development. Furthermore, studies that have specifically examined individuals with good word recognition but poor reading comprehension also suggest specific processes important for reading comprehension. Some of these processes fit within the simple view framework, but others are beyond the scope of word-level and listening comprehension in the simple view. Moreover, contributions from neuroimaging also help to understand potential origins of difficulty with reading comprehension.

EVIDENCE FROM THE SIMPLE VIEW OF READING: WHAT AND WHEN

The simple view of reading (Hoover & Gough, 1990) proposes that reading comprehension is a combination of word recognition and listening comprehension. These two factors are found to closely approximate reading comprehension; research examining contributions of word recognition and listening comprehension indicate that they account for 62% to 80% of the variance in reading comprehension ability.

Despite the fact that word recognition and listening comprehension each uniquely contributes to reading comprehension, the relative contribution of each appears to change over time (Catts, Adlof, & Weismer, 2006; Catts, Hogan, Adlof, & Barth, 2003; Storch & Whitehurst, 2002). Catts et al. (2003) administered measures of word recognition, listening comprehension, and reading comprehension to students in second, fourth, and eighth grade and found that both word recognition and listening comprehension accounted for a significant amount of the variance in reading comprehension. The unique variance accounted for by each factor, however, differed when comparing the three grade levels. Word recognition accounted for a smaller amount of variance in fourth grade than in second grade, and decreased even further by eighth grade. Conversely, the contribution of listening comprehension steadily increased from second to eighth grade. This exemplifies the common finding that as children progress in school, word recognition becomes less influential, and other language skills become more essential in reading comprehension.

In a longitudinal study, Storch and Whitehurst (2002) assessed code-related skills (e.g., print concepts, phonological awareness) and oral language skills (e.g., expressive and receptive vocabulary, conceptual knowledge) related to reading in preschool and kindergarten, followed by examining reading accuracy and reading comprehension skills in first through fourth grade. In preschool, oral language and code-related skills were strongly linked; however, by first and second grade, there was no significant correlation between the two domains. With regard to reading ability, in early grades (first and second), reading was best represented by a composite measure, with high correlations between reading accuracy and reading comprehension. Using this model, the strongest predictor of reading ability in second grade was a child's code-related skills in kindergarten. However, by third and fourth grade, reading accuracy and reading comprehension became separate subdomains of reading ability. During this later phase, reading accuracy continued to be determined by decoding abilities, while reading comprehension, on the other hand, was influenced by oral language skills (including language measured in preschool) as well as reading accuracy.

The changing contributions of word-level and oral language skills to reading comprehension are additionally supported by the results of studies on specific reading comprehension deficits (Catts et al., 2006). Eighth graders who struggled with reading comprehension but not word recognition (described as "poor comprehenders") demonstrated deficits in oral language and normal phonological abilities, while "poor decoders" exhibited an opposite pattern; they struggled with phonological processing, but their performance on oral language measures was normal. Longitudinal data from the same eighth graders, collected since kindergarten showed that oral language deficits in earlier grades were predictive of poor reading comprehension in eighth grade. Yet reading comprehension performance in early grades was not necessarily associated with later reading comprehension. Catts et al. (2006) propose that this disassociation may be attributed to the changing nature of reading comprehension in school over time with increasing demands on listening comprehension. Therefore, a child's particular strengths and weaknesses in reading may lead to inconsistency in reading comprehension performance over time. Indeed, Catts et al. (2003) found that in second grade, students identified as poor readers were more commonly classified as dyslexic (word recognition deficit only), but by eighth grade, hyperlexia (listening comprehension deficit only) was more common among poor comprehenders.

Although the simple view of reading has been supported by a variety of studies, the findings from the aforementioned studies are particularly illustrative of the differential contributions of word recognition and language skills to comprehension at different stages of development; predictors of reading comprehension at one snapshot of time may be quite different from predictors in another snapshot. This is illustrated in the study by Storch and Whitehurst (2002), in which they found that code-related skills, but not language, best predicted reading at second grade; however, by fourth grade, preschool oral language was a significant predictor of reading comprehension. Thus, a seemingly nonsignificant predictor in the early grades may have simply been lying dormant until such a time where greater demands on oral language in reading comprehension emerged. This very phenomenon was found by Catts et al. (2006), whereby language did not really appear to have any significant impact on reading comprehension in the early grades, but was a strong predictor of reading comprehension difficulty (despite normal word-level skills) by eighth grade.

What accounts for the changing roles of word recognition and language skills over time? It is important to examine how the nature of reading in school changes from the primary grades (kindergarten through third) to later elementary school and into secondary school. Early curriculum emphasizes phonics and decoding monosyllabic words, whereas after fourth grade, there is greater focus on fluency and comprehension, with more polysyllabic words being introduced. Additionally, reading material shifts from narratives to expository texts, and most practice becomes silent, independent reading instead of oral reading in a group. Therefore, children who have mastered word recognition but have other, underlying deficits in areas of language important for reading more complex words and understanding text (e.g., vocabulary) may suddenly appear to struggle with reading. Indeed, research supports the concept of a second wave of reading disabilities emerging during and after fourth grade (Chall, 1983), with as many as 36% to 46% of the students meeting diagnosis for a reading disability qualifying as "late-emerging" (Badian, 1999; Leach, Scarborough, & Rescorla, 2003; Lipka, Lesaux, & Siegel, 2006; Shaywitz, Escobar, Shaywitz, Fletcher, & Makuch, 1992). Given the changing demands of reading in later grades, older children may be required to rely on a variety of skills, including oral language, working memory, and processing speed, to successfully complete reading-related tasks. If a child has a deficit in one or more of these areas, he/she could potentially struggle with reading comprehension, even if his/her word recognition and/or language skills are sufficient.

It is clear that findings from studies on the simple view suggest that listening comprehension is a key component for reading comprehension. There are, however, multiple processes that feed into listening comprehension itself, such as vocabulary and syntax, that have yet to be fully explored and dissected in terms of their unique contributions to reading comprehension. Furthermore, it is not clear what other factors outside of language may influence a child's reading comprehension; for example, studies that have added a speed factor to the simple view have found that it contributes an additional amount of significant variance, suggesting that efficiency also needs to be considered as a component (Joshi & Aaron, 2000). Research on children with specific reading comprehension deficits (S-RCD) is also supportive of the suggestion that areas outside of word-level and language need to be considered.

Good Word Recognition/Poor Reading Comprehension

Approximately 3% to 10% of school age children fall into the category of having an S-RCD (Aaron, Joshi, & Williams, 1999; Catts et al., 2003; Leach et al., 2003; Nation, 2001; Shankweiler et al., 1999; Torppa et al., 2007). Previous research on S-RCD has sought to identify factors that lead to poor reading comprehension in children who demonstrate normal word recognition. As mentioned earlier, speed appears to account for additional variance in the word recognition/listening comprehension model of reading (Joshi & Aaron, 2000). Therefore, an open question with regard to S-RCD is whether a child can not only *accurately* read a word, but also *quickly* or automatically recognize words in isolation and/or context. In addition to the concept of fluency, research has also examined and linked S-RCD to a variety of deficits in both language skills (vocabulary and syntax) and executive functioning tasks such as comprehension monitoring, making inferences, finding main ideas, self-monitoring, and verbal working memory.

Fluency and Reading Comprehension

It has been suggested that fluency, or being able to read words efficiently in isolation or context, is an essential component of comprehension. Words must be read both accurately and quickly to easily comprehend. As children get older and reading material places greater demands on higher level processes (i.e., working memory), it creates what has been described as a "bottleneck" (Shankweiler, 1999). If a child is capable of accurately but not automatically recognizing words, necessary processes for reading comprehension (i.e., working memory) may have to compete with decoding for the same resources (Shankweiler, 1999). However, many of the studies on S-RCD have examined only accuracy of recognizing words and not how fast or automatically they are able to read them. There is a need for researchers to measure efficiency of word recognition in isolation or context as well as to examine the other skills necessary for comprehension with which non-fluent word recognition may compete. In particular, the language and executive function skills relevant to advanced (post primary grades) reading comprehension need to be examined in connection to fluency.

Oral Language and Reading Comprehension

Language skills, combined with word recognition, have consistently proven to be an influence on reading comprehension. Particularly for older readers, oral language accounts for more variance than word recognition (e.g., Catts et al., 2003). The construct of oral language, however, includes a variety of skills such as vocabulary, syntax, and inferential language, and each skill may contribute individually to reading comprehension, as is supported by numerous studies. In a study by Catts, Fey, Zhang, and Tomblin (1999), over 70% of poor comprehenders in second grade had exhibited a language deficit in kindergarten. Although the largest group of children showed deficits in both oral language (syntax and vocabulary) and phonological processing, there were also children who only had problems in one of the two areas, indicating that both components account for unique variance in reading.

In investigating language deficits in children with S-RCD, Nation and Snowling (1998, 1999, 2000) have found correlations between reading comprehension deficits and both syntactic and semantic difficulties. In a study comparing children with S-RCD to controls, the S-RCD group had more difficulty with identifying synonyms (Nation & Snowling, 1998). Nation and Snowling (1999) also found that, when asked to determine whether an item was a word or nonword, poor comprehenders and good comprehenders performed similarly when an item was primed by a functionally associated word. However, with categorically associated words, good comprehenders consistently demonstrated priming, while poor comprehenders did not show priming for pairs with a weaker association. These findings suggest that poor comprehenders may have a less developed ability to recognize semantic relationships.

Syntactic awareness also appears to be problematic for children with S-RCD. Nation and Snowling (2000) asked children to reorganize scrambled sentences and found that children with comprehension deficits were not as successful at correcting the word order of sentences. It is important to note, however, that this task required that children retain the words presented to them, and difficulty forming sentences could be reflective of a working memory deficit as opposed to or as well as a syntax deficit.

Executive Function and Reading Comprehension

In addition to skills related to language, other cognitive factors have been hypothesized to relate to reading comprehension, particularly factors that fall under the category of executive function, including abilities such as response inhibition; response preparation; ability to plan, organize, and self-monitor/regulate; working memory; initiation; and efficiently sustained and sequenced behavior. In later grades, reading becomes the main method of obtaining information; the ability to retain information and relate it to prior knowledge while reading becomes crucial. Thus, children with deficits in the areas of executive functioning may perform poorly on reading comprehension tasks. Executive function has been linked to reading comprehension primarily through verbal and visual working memory; the ability to make inferences; and the ability to plan, organize, and monitor.

Many studies have identified a link between verbal working memory and reading comprehension (Carpenter & Just, 1988; Daneman & Carpenter, 1980; Just & Carpenter, 1992; Swanson, 1999; Swanson & Alexander, 1997; Swanson, Ashbaker, & Lee, 1996; Swanson & Berninger, 1995; Swanson & Trahan, 1996). In Baddeley's (1986) model, working memory is conceptualized as a central executive that is supported by both verbal and visuospatial slave systems. Poor readers demonstrate impairments in the verbal system, as supported by observed deficits in phonological short-term memory, which would interfere with the transfer of information into working memory and consequently, comprehension. However, studies of children with S-RCD show that poor comprehenders have verbal working memory deficits, despite no evidence of phonological short-term memory deficits (Nation, Adams, Bowyer-Crane, & Snowling, 1999; Oakhill & Yuill, 1996; Oakhill, Yuill, & Parkin, 1986).

In addition to working memory, the ability to make inferences also has the potential to be a contributing factor to reading comprehension, and is supported by research findings (e.g., Barnes & Dennis, 1996; Oakhill, 1993; Oakhill & Garnham, 1988; Oakhill & Yuill, 1996; Perfetti, Marron, & Foltz, 1996). Planning, organizing, and monitoring, which are essential to developing reading strategies (e.g., knowing when to re-read, how to find the main idea), also need to be considered in terms of their influence on reading comprehension (Swanson, 1999; Swanson & Trahan, 1996).

Although many studies have examined elements of fluency, language, and executive function as related to reading, few have examined all of these elements in one study. A recent study by Cutting et al. (in press) sought to address this issue by examining language skills, executive function, and fluency in adolescents in three groups. Based on both their word recognition and reading comprehension scores, adolescents ages 9 to 14 were assigned to one of three groups: controls, word recognition deficits (WRD), and S-RCD. Reading fluency as well as components of both oral language (receptive vocabulary, receptive and expressive grammar, and inferential language) and executive function (spatial planning, inhibition, organization, and working memory) were assessed. Both poor reader groups exhibited deficits in language skills; however, only the S-RCD students had difficulties with executive function tasks. Specifically, students in the control group scored significantly higher than both poor reader groups on measures of inferential language, ambiguous sentences, combining sentences, and vocabulary. The WRD and S-RCD groups differed, however, on a measure of grammatic comprehension; although the S-RCD students performed similarly to the control group, the WRD group's scores were significantly lower.

On a measure of spatial planning, rule learning, and inhibition of impulsive responding, the S-RCD group performed significantly lower than the control and WRD groups. This is indicative of a possible distinguishing factor between those who struggle with word recognition and those who have specific deficits in reading comprehension. Similarly, fluency also appears to differentiate between the groups. Although students with S-RCD recognized words in isolation as fluently as controls, there was a significant difference between the two groups when measuring contextual fluency.

CONTRIBUTIONS FROM NEUROIMAGING

Although behavioral studies provide an important understanding of which cognitive/neuropsychological processes are critical for reading comprehension, functional neuroimaging offers a window into the *neurobiological* underpinnings of comprehension. In particular, neuroimaging offers a way to potentially understand contributions of different component processes to reading comprehension, especially those beyond the word level. Functional neuroimaging studies of comprehension have by and large focused on sentence processing, and the majority has been limited to adult skilled readers. Sentence comprehension in adult skilled readers has been associated with patterns of activation that are similar to those involved with processing isolated words; however, the activation is more widespread, with more right hemisphere activation, including bilateral activation of the inferior frontal gyrus (Left > Right) and the posterior, superior, and middle temporal gyri (e.g., Caplan et al., 2001; Cooke et al., 2006; Cutting et al., 2006; Ferstl & von Cramon, 2001; Friederici, Ruschemeyer, Hahne, & Fiebach, 2003; Grossman et al., 2002; Jobard, Vigneau, Mazoyer, & Tzourio-Mazoyer, 2007; Keller, Carpenter, & Just, 2001; Meyer, Friederici, & von Cramon, 2000). Greater left frontal and partial lobe activation for sentences versus words has also been reported (Bottini, Corcoran, & Sterzi, 1994; Stowe, Paans, & Wijers, 1999). More recently, studies have begun to explore the neurobiological correlates of text (paragraph) comprehension; this approach may prove fruitful in terms of understanding abnormalities in not only sentence-level but also discourse-level processing in various reader types (Ferstl, Rinck, & von Cramon, 2005; Jobard et al., 2007; Karunanayaka et al., 2007; Schmithorst, Holland, & Plante, 2006; Virtue, Haberman, Clancy, Parrish, & Beeman, 2006; Wilson, Molnar-Szakacs, & Iacoboni, 2008; Xu, Kemeny, Park, Frattali, & Braun, 2005).

The functional neuroimaging literature on sentence comprehension in individuals with reading disabilities is limited; however, a few studies have demonstrated that individuals with word recognition/decoding difficulties show abnormal patterns of activation while comprehending sentences (e.g., Breznitz & Leikin, 2000, 2001; Helenius, Salmelin, Service, & Connolly, 1999; Kronbichler, Hutzler, & Staffen, 2006; Leikin, 2002; Meyler et al., 2007; Rumsey et al., 1994; Sabisch, Hahne, Glass, von Suchodoletz, & Friederici, 2006; Seki, Koeda, & Sugihara, 2001). It is important to note that the abnormalities found in sentence comprehension studies concerning individuals with WRD appear to be present in higher level language comprehension independent of the word recognition requirements, as differences have been found between WRD and control groups for both *auditorally* and *visually* presented sentences (e.g., Leikin, 2002; Rumsey et al., 1994; Sabisch et al., 2006). For example, in a PET study comparing adults with WRD to skilled readers, Rumsey et al. (1994) found that while the patterns of activation associated with auditorally presented sentences was generally the same between groups, activating temporal and inferior frontal gyrus sites (L > R), the WRD group showed some abnormalities. These included reversed asymmetry in the temporoparietal region (R > L) and increased right anterior frontal activation as compared to controls.

In a recent fMRI study, Meyler et al. (2007) found in adolescents that while comprehending visually presented sentences, decreased activation in the left middle temporal gyrus, right inferior partial lobule, and left postcentral gyrus was associated with lower reading ability. Studies of sentence comprehension in individuals with impaired reading skills in languages other than English have also reported differences between WRD and control groups (e.g., Breznitz & Leikin, 2000, 2001; Helenius et al., 1999; Karni, Morocz, & Bitan, 2005; Kronbichler et al., 2006; Sabisch et al., 2006; Seki et al., 2001). For example, Kronbichler et al. (2006) found that while reading simple sentences in German, the WRD group showed reduced activation in the left lateral temporal cluster (posterior temporal cortex into inferior occipitotemporal cortex) and increased activation in the left medial temporal cortex, as compared to controls. However, similar to other studies, globally the two groups showed similar patterns of activation (left temporal cortex, inferior frontal gyrus, and precentral regions). Thus, it is important to note that most studies of sentence comprehension in people with WRD show that although they are processing sentences somewhat differently than controls, the overall regions that the two groups are relying upon do not appear to be *radically* different from each other, which is different from what is found when WRD and control groups are processing isolated words. This suggests that the complexity of sentence comprehension requires multiple resources and therefore may give rise to more compensatory mechanisms.

Collaborative research projects between Kennedy Krieger Institute and Haskins Laboratories have yielded findings with regard to neurobiological circuitry associated more specifically with comprehension processes. In an effort to understand sentence comprehension from a component process, Cutting et al. (2006) examined patterns of activation associated with the word recognition requirements of sentence comprehension and the short-term memory requirements of sentence comprehension in skilled readers. Findings revealed that left inferior frontal, fusiform (including visual word form area), and occipital gyri were associated with word recognition, and right middle frontal and cingulate gyri as well as left precuneous were associated with short-term memory; comprehension itself was associated with extensive bilateral temporal lobe activation. More recently, Rimrodt et al. (2008) examined patterns of activation associated with sentence comprehension after controlling for word recognition in 15 typical and 14 impaired readers with WRD (ages 9–14 years old). Both groups showed activation in bilateral extrastriate and left inferior frontal gyrus; impaired readers showed greater activation than typical readers in areas associated with linguistic processing (left middle and superior temporal gyri) as well as attention and response selection (bilateral insula, right cingulate gyrus, right superior frontal gyrus, and right parietal lobe). Additional analyses revealed that differences in activation between the groups were mostly driven by the impaired readers' response to incongruous sentences. Across the range of reading ability, more efficient reading of isolated words and connected text (out-of-scanner measures) was positively correlated to left occipitotemporal activation; in contrast, performance on most reading and language measures was negatively correlated with activation in right hemisphere regions.

In summary, neuroimaging studies provide guidance for understanding brain regions/circuits important for comprehension. Although studies with impaired readers (particularly various subtypes of impaired readers) are limited at this time, these types of experiments may be particularly revealing in terms of providing insights into where breakdowns that are linked with word-level or comprehension may occur, and where overlapping areas may exist. In turn, these brain–behavior connections, along with cognitive models of comprehension applied to a neuropsychological framework can help provide a link to specific brain circuitry and/or areas that may be particularly problematic for some children as they try to comprehend text. This approach may help pinpoint specific subtypes of reading comprehension disorder. Future neuroimaging studies with impaired readers that use various stimuli that tax different types of comprehension may be especially fruitful in terms of understanding how readers process various types of text. Thus, neuroimaging studies can help provide the foundation for understanding more about the neurobiological basis of the multifaceted nature of reading comprehension. In particular, neuroimaging may help to provide some guidance as to which brain systems may be involved in which types of comprehension for which type of reader.

THE ISSUE OF MEASUREMENT

Measurement is often discussed as a central issue in reading comprehension, as there are many ways to measure reading comprehension. Assessment tools for reading comprehension vary in numerous ways, such as the format of the text (e.g., type, length, read out loud or silently) and how comprehension is assessed (e.g., cloze items, multiple-choice questions, open-ended questions). Such issues are extremely important for diagnoses and defining groups, as different measurements could potentially be targeting different skills relevant to comprehension. Indeed, word recognition and decoding have been found to account for more variance in comprehension scores from tests with cloze items than from tests with question and answer items (Bowey, 1986; Nation & Snowling, 1997; Spear-Swerling, 2004). Recently Francis, Fletcher, Catts, and Tomblin (2005) found that a cloze test was more strongly linked to decoding skills, whereas both silent and oral passage reading, followed by multiple choice questions, had a stronger relation to language skills.

To assess the variance among different measures of reading comprehension, Cutting and Scarborough (2006) compared students' performances on three assessment tools, each containing both expository and narrative passages. The Gates-MacGinitie Reading Test–Revised (G-M; MacGinitie, MacGinitie, Maria, & Dreyer, 2000) requires students to read 3 to 15 sentence passages silently, and then answer written multiple-choice questions while still having access to the passage. There is a 35-minute time limit. The Gray Oral Reading Test–Third Edition (GORT-3; Wiederholt & Bryant, 1992), on the other hand, contains six to seven sentence passages, which are read aloud as quickly as possible. Multiple-choice questions pertaining to each passage are read out loud by the examiner after the passage is removed from view. Finally, the Wechsler Individual Achievement Test (WIAT; Wechsler, 1992) consists of two to three sentence passages read silently, followed by two open-ended questions asked orally by the examiner while the student is still able to view the passage. Word recognition/decoding accounted for significantly more variance for the WIAT than for the G-M and GORT-3, whereas oral language was a stronger predictor for the G-M than for the WIAT or GORT-3. Furthermore, the three comprehension measures varied in the extent to which two components of oral language (vocabulary and sentence processing) accounted for unique variance. Although the G-M relied on both factors, only sentence processing was a predictor for the WIAT, and vocabulary was the sole language composite significantly correlated with the GORT-3. These findings are supportive of the suggestion that there is variance in the specific skills measured by different reading comprehension assessment tools. A recent study by Keenan, Betjemann, and Olson (2008), also examined the variance among tests of reading comprehension. Their findings were in keeping with the results of previous studies, with the actual contributions of word-level and language skills varying quite significantly among comprehension tests.

An awareness of this variance among reading comprehension measures is crucial when diagnosing deficits in reading comprehension. In the Cutting and

Scarborough study (2006), although over 43% of the participants were identified as having a reading comprehension deficit (RCD) by at least one of the tests, only 9.4% (21.6% of those identified by at least one test) were consistently classified as having an RCD by all three measures. Clearly the selection of measures to use when assessing a child can have a great impact on the results and interpretation of a child's performance. Similarly, in research, different measures of reading comprehension may yield different findings, and this should be considered especially when examining inconsistencies between studies.

POTENTIAL EXPLANATIONS/ORIGINS FOR DIFFICULTIES WITH READING COMPREHENSION

Although it is apparent that reading comprehension involves many different processes and that difficulty in reading comprehension can result from various weaknesses, it is not entirely clear where these difficulties may originate. There may be many different reasons for a resulting end difficulty in reading comprehension; however, two overarching hypotheses seem to be on the forefront for consideration: (a) difficulties with comprehension are a downstream result of poor decoding skills (subtle decoding and/or Matthew effects) or (b) difficulties arise from deficits in other processes, either separate from word-level processes or in addition to them. Additionally, with regard specifically to the observance of late-emerging reading disabilities—are they *really* late-emerging—do comprehension deficits simply appear, or are there some cognitive indications long before these comprehension deficits become noticeable?

With regard to the hypothesis that comprehension deficits are downstream of decoding problems, there are two possibilities. One possibility is that comprehension deficits could arise due to concurrent subtle deficits in word recognition/decoding, such as a lack of fluency. In this case, the bottleneck hypothesis would apply—such effort is going into decoding that few resources are left for comprehension, thus weaknesses in comprehension are seen. The reason for not seeing these deficits would be that our standardized measures might not place enough demands on word recognition. Another possibility is that comprehension could be impacted over many years, as is described by the classic Matthew effects hypothesis (Stanovich, 1986); that is, difficulties with word recognition/decoding lead to reading less year after year, which then would result in less growth in vocabulary and other processes important for reading comprehension.

The alternative hypothesis is that reading comprehension difficulties may be a result of true weaknesses in other processes that cannot be attributed to word-level difficulties. In other words, deficits in other areas (e.g., language and executive function) are *not* downstream from difficulties of word recognition/decoding, but rather are areas of weakness in and of themselves. In this scenario, it would be possible for an individual to show difficulties with reading comprehension either solely from these other processes (S-RCD) or in addition to word-level processes.

Despite the noteworthy numbers of late-emerging reading disability, this is an area that to date has not been examined in great depth by the field. Understanding late emergers is an important issue as children who are late emergers may have origins of reading difficulties that are distinct—and therefore possibly differentially remediated—in comparison to children who show early reading difficulty. Although it is possible that these cognitive deficits only develop at a later stage, a more plausible hypothesis is that the cognitive deficits that cause late-emerging reading disability are longstanding deficits, but for various reasons (e.g., demands of reading do not tax these processes heavily, the measures of reading are not sensitive enough) simply weren't observed until later. In this case, one would surmise that the cognitive deficits that impact the late emerger's reading were present long before the appearance of his/her reading difficulties, but reading did not place demands on these processes until later.

Knowing early on which cognitive/neuropsychological deficits will later give rise to reading comprehension deficits is critical. One could envision a child who had weaknesses in language and executive function since preschool, but because beginning reading did not place demands on either of these processes, it wasn't until fourth grade, when suddenly both language and executive function were heavily relied upon for reading comprehension, that the reading comprehension problems became apparent. If we know executive function plays a role in later reading comprehension difficulties, measuring executive function in preschool, long before this process becomes critical for reading comprehension, would be important for designing interventions to prevent late-emerging reading disabilities. Additionally, developing measures of reading comprehension for younger children that are more sensitive to these processes would be important.

NEXT STEPS THAT MAY HELP FRAME FUTURE READING COMPREHENSION RESEARCH

Although there are many different potential directions for future research, in reviewing the reading comprehension and other literature, several seem to stand out as areas to pursue. The measurement of reading comprehension is probably the most central area of need in reading comprehension research because it is critical for defining the dependent variable(s) in the field—both for our research studies and for measuring practical outcomes in schools and states. Several studies have established that commonly used standardized measures of reading comprehension yield significant differences from one another in terms of which cognitive processes are most important. One important question about these current measures is whether these differences actually reflect subtypes of reading comprehension difficulty. Therefore, at the very least, researchers need to include multiple measures of reading comprehension in their studies. However, significant additional work needs to be pursued in terms of actually developing assessments that reflect and measure the types of comprehension skills that children need to have for positive long-term reading and educational outcomes.

It is important to keep in mind the present state of affairs, which is that, clearly, from a practical day-to-day standpoint, the outcome that matters is performance on high-stakes reading comprehension measures (state assessments). Therefore, performance on state tests may be our best proxy right now for providing the ultimate outcome for the entity of reading comprehension (i.e., "positive reading and educational outcomes"). From this current public health and public policy standpoint, understanding how and why an individual succeeds or fails on these outcome measures is a critical next research step. Our suggestion would be to pursue understanding what combination of weaknesses and strengths in various processes, together with various text demands, allows for a reader to succeed or fail on high-stakes tests.

For example, take two children, one who scores Proficient on the state test and another who scores Basic. Each will probably have various cognitive strengths and weaknesses that impact how he/she comprehends; furthermore, these cognitive strengths and weaknesses will interact with the type of text demands. Understanding the interaction between cognitive profile and text type will result in a greater understanding of how the end result of a score of Basic or Proficient is achieved. It may be that the child who scores Proficient has poor language skills, but has strong executive function skills that allow for a compensatory effect on tests that are highly executively demanding. The converse could be true for the child who scores Basic. To explore this issue, a series of experimental texts could be given that were each manipulated to demand substantial reliance on various dimensions of text, thereby isolating that feature (e.g., a text that isolated vocabulary, another text that isolated reading strategies, another that isolated syntax). Each of these manipulations, in combination with establishing the child's cognitive/neuropsychological profile, would further reveal a child's strengths and weaknesses and in particular how a child's cognitive weaknesses resulted in struggling with comprehending text X but not Y—and how this comes together to ultimately deem him/her an Advanced, Proficient, or Basic reader on a state outcome test. This in turn would help pinpoint which types of comprehension are critical (i.e., text type X for the state test but not text type Y for the state test[1]). It also would pave the way for pursuing the development of more refined measures of reading comprehension and perhaps lead to conceptualizing reading comprehension as a multifaceted construct versus the more unitary one that is traditional for the present-day, practical-outcome, state-test assessments.

In addition to helping with refining the measurement of and cognitive processes important for reading comprehension, the aforementioned course of research would enable for more specific characterization of potentially different subtypes of reading comprehension deficits. The usage of neuroimaging methodologies in concert with behavioral experiments would be especially crucial for characterizing these subtypes. Although it is feasible that each type of reading comprehension difficulty presents with a unique neurobiological profile, it is more plausible that a more limited neurobiological set of abnormalities gives rise to multiple behavioral manifestations/profiles. Pinpointing these more universal neurobiological deficits would be crucial for being able to characterize as well as provide appropriate intervention for individuals with poor reading comprehension. It would be important that these neurobiological profiles not simply be defined by use of functional MRI, which may still reflect multiple outcomes from a more confined set of neurobiological abnormalities, but instead with methods of imaging that tap more basic structural and chemical properties of the brain. For example, diffusion tensor imaging, which provides a proxy for the degree of organization of white matter by measuring the preferential direction of diffusion of water molecules in white matter tracts, may reveal that individuals with X-, Y-, or Z-type comprehension difficulties all have one specific pathway/tract impacted (tract "A"); thus, while these behavioral manifestations may vary (X, Y, or Z), neurobiologically, the manifestation may be confined to one pathway ("A"). This type of understanding would be very helpful to illuminating origins of seemingly variable types of difficulties observed at the behavioral level. It also makes even more apparent the importance of merging cognitive models of comprehension with a neuropsychological framework, and then to actual neurobiological measures, as such an integration will allow for the brain–behavior connections needed for understanding origins of reading comprehension deficits (Schmalhofer & Perfetti, 2007).

   Another important area of research is that which can help disentangle the issue of whether long-standing cognitive deficits can manifest in late-emerging reading difficulties. Clearly longitudinal studies are the approach that is needed to address this issue. For example, if we know that executive function is associated with late-emerging reading disabilities, then we need to determine whether these deficits in executive function can be found as far back as preschool. Knowing if these risk factors are present at an early age will be essential for prevention of late-emerging reading disabilities. Longitudinal studies would also be helpful in terms of determining one possibility that we raised—that is, whether downstream deficits in word recognition (Matthew effects) are a central cause of difficulty for S-RCD; although, in general, studies have revealed mixed support for Matthew effects (e.g., Scarborough & Parker, 2003; Tunmer, Chapman, & Prochnow, 2004), Matthew effects could more definitively be revealed as an origin of difficulty (or not) specifically for S-RCD.

   In summary, we would propose that the following lines of research are especially important for the next steps in understanding reading comprehension: (a) measurement of reading comprehension; (b) refining the understanding of which cognitive/neuropsychological processes are important for reading comprehension; (c) defining subtypes of reading comprehension; (d) examining the learner–text interaction; and (e) understanding the origins of late-emerging reading disability. It will be critical when carrying out research in the aforementioned areas to do so within the context of connecting the rich line of research on cognitive theories of reading comprehension (e.g., Britton & Graesser, 1996; Cromley & Azevedo, 2007; Kintsch, 1998; Schmalhofer & Perfetti, 2007; Trabasso & Wiley, 2005; van den Broek, Rapp, & Kendeou, 2005) to a neuropsychological framework, and then in turn connect these to neurobiological findings (Schmalhofer & Perfetti, 2007). It should be noted that while we have conceptualized these five lines of research as seemingly separate, it of course would be almost impossible in investigating one area to not overlap to a great degree with another. However, we nonetheless feel that conceptualizing these lines of research this way may be fruitful for achieving the goals of *understanding what type of reader struggles with which type of text, the origins (both behavioral and neurobiological) of these comprehension difficulties, and, ultimately, how to best intervene and prevent reading comprehension difficulties.*

NOTE

1. We recognize, of course, that state outcome tests also vary *across* states.

REFERENCES

Aaron, P. G., Joshi, R. M., & Williams K. A. (1999). Not all reading disabilities are alike. *Journal of Learning Disabilities, 32,* 120–137.

Adams, M. J. (1990). *Beginning to read: Thinking and learning about print.* Cambridge, MA: MIT Press.

Baddeley, A. D. (1986). *Working memory.* Oxford, UK: Clarendon Press.

Badian, N. A. (1999). Reading disability defined as a discrepancy between listening and reading comprehension: A longitudinal study of stability, gender differences, and prevalence. *Journal of Learning Disabilities, 32,* 138–148.

Barnes, M. A., & Dennis, M. (1996). Reading comprehension deficits arise from diverse sources: Evidence from readers with and without developmental brain pathology. In C. Cornoldi & J. Oakhill (Eds.), *Reading comprehension difficulties: Processes and intervention* (pp. 251–278). Mahwah, NJ: Lawrence Erlbaum Associates.

Bottini, G., Corcoran, R., & Sterzi, R. (1994). The role of the right hemisphere in the figurative aspects of language: A positron emission tomography activation study. *Brain: A Journal of Neurology, 117,* 1241–1253.

Bowey, J. (1986). Syntactic awareness in relation to reading skill and ongoing reading comprehension monitoring. *Journal of Experimental Child Psychology, 41,* 282–299.

Breznitz, Z., & Leikin, M. (2000). Syntactic processing of Hebrew sentences in normal and dyslexic readers: Electrophysiological evidence. *Journal of Genetic Psychology, 161,* 359–380.

Breznitz, Z., & Leikin, M. (2001). Effects of accelerated reading rate on processing words' syntactic functions by normal and dyslexic readers: Event related potentials evidence. *Journal of Genetic Psychology, 162,* 276–296.

Britton, B. K., & Graesser, A. C. (1996). *Models of understanding text.* Hillsdale, NJ: Lawrence Erlbaum Associates.

Caplan, D., Vijayan, S., Kuperberg, G., West, C., Waters, G., Greve, D., et al. (2001). Vascular responses to syntactic processing: Event-related fMRI study of relative causes. *Human Brain Mapping, 15,* 26–38.

Carpenter, P. A., & Just, M. A. (1988). The role of working memory in language comprehension. In D. Klahr & K. Kotovasky (Eds.), *Complex information processing: The impact of Herbert A. Simon* (pp. 31–68). Hillsdale, NJ: Lawrence Erlbaum Associates.

Catts, H. W., Adlof, S. M., & Weismer, S. E. (2006). Language deficits in poor comprehenders: A case for the simple view of reading. *Journal of Speech, Language, and Hearing Research, 29,* 278–293.

Catts, H. W., Fey, M. E., Zhang, X., & Tomblin, J. B. (1999). Language basis of reading and reading disabilities: Evidence from a longitudinal investigation. *Scientific Studies of Reading, 3,* 331–361.

Catts, H. W., Hogan, T. P., Adlof, S. M., & Barth, A. E. (2003, June). *The simple view of reading: Changes over time.* Poster session presented at the annual conference of the Society for Scientific Study of Reading, Boulder, CO.

Chall, J. S. (1983). *Stages of reading development.* New York: McGraw-Hill.

Cooke, A., Grossman, M., DeVita, C., Gonzalez-Atavales, J., Moore, P., Chen, W., et al. (2006). Large-scale neural network for sentence processing. *Brain and Language, 96,* 14–36.

Cromley, J. G., & Azevedo, R. (2007). Testing and refining the direct and inferential mediation model of reading comprehension. *Journal of Educational Psychology, 99,* 311–325.

Cutting, L. E., Clements, A. M., Courtney, S., Rimrodt, S. R., Schafer, J. G. B., Wilkins, J., et al. (2006). Differential components of sentence comprehension: Beyond single word reading and memory. *NeuroImage, 29,* 429–438.

Cutting, L. E., Materek, A., Cole, C. A. S., Levine, T., & Mahone, E. M. (in press). Effects of language, fluency, and executive function on reading comprehension performance. *Annals of Dyslexia.*

Cutting, L. E., & Scarborough, H. S. (2006). Prediction of reading comprehension: Relative contributions of word recognition, language proficiency, and other cognitive skills can depend on how comprehension is measured. *Scientific Studies of Reading, 10,* 277–299.

Daneman, M., & Carpenter, P. (1980). Individual differences in working memory and reading. *Journal of Verbal Learning and Verbal Behavior, 19,* 450–466.

Ferstl, E. C., Rinck, M., & von Cramon, D. Y. (2005). Emotional and temporal aspects of situation model processing during text comprehension: An event-related fMRI study. *Journal of Cognitive Neuroscience, 17,* 724–739.

Ferstl, E. C., & von Cramon, D. Y. (2001). The role of coherence and cohesion in test comprehension: An event-related fMRI study. *Cognitive Brain Research, 11,* 325–340.

Francis, D. J., Fletcher, J. M., Catts, H. W., & Tomblin, J. B. (2005). Dimensions affecting the assessment of reading comprehension. In S. G. Paris & S. A. Stahl (Eds.), *Children's reading comprehension and assessment* (pp. 369–394). Mahwah, NJ: Lawrence Erlbaum Associates.

Friederici, A. D., Ruschemeyer, S. A., Hahne, A., & Fiebach, C. J. (2003). The role of left inferior frontal and superior temporal cortex in sentence comprehension: Localizing syntactic and semantic processes. *Cerebral Cortex, 13,* 170–177.

Grossman, M., Cooke, A., DeVita, C., Alsop, D., Detre, J., Chen, W., & Gee, J. (2002). Age-related changes in working memory during sentence comprehension: An fMRI study. *NeuroImage, 15,* 302–317.

Helenius, P., Salmelin, R., Service, E., & Connolly, J. F. (1999). Semantic cortical activation in dyslexic readers. *Journal of Cognitive Neuroscience, 11,* 535–550.

Hoover, W. A., & Gough, P. B. (1990). The simple view of reading. *Reading and Writing, 2,* 127–160.

Jobard, G., Vigneau, M., Mazoyer, B., & Tzourio-Mazoyer, N. (2007). Impact of modality and linguistic complexity during reading and listening tasks. *NeuroImage, 34,* 784–800.

Joshi, R., & Aaron, P. G. (2000). The component model of reading: Simple view of reading made a little more complex. *Reading Psychology, 21,* 85–97.

Just, M. A., & Carpenter, P. A. (1992). A capacity theory of comprehension: Individual differences in working memory. *Psychological Review, 99,* 122–149.

Karni, A., Morocz, I. A., & Bitan, T. (2005). An fMRI study of the differential effects of word presentation rates (reading acceleration) on dyslexic readers' brain activity patterns. *Journal of Neurolinguistics, 18,* 197–219.

Karunanayaka, P. R., Holland, S. K., Schmithorst, V. J., Solodkin, A., Chen, E. E., Szaflarski, J. P., et al. (2007). Age-related connectivity changes in fMRI data from children listening to stories. *NeuroImage, 34,* 349–360.

Keenan, J. M., Betjemann, R. S., & Olson, R. K. (2008). Reading comprehension tests vary in the skills they assess: Differential dependence on decoding and oral comprehension. *Scientific Studies of Reading, 12*(3), 281–300.

Keller, T. A., Carpenter, P. A., & Just, M. A. (2001). The neural bases of sentence comprehension: A fMRI examination of syntactic and lexical processing. *Cerebral Cortex, 11,* 223–237.

Kintsch, W. (1998). *Comprehension: A paradigm for cognition.* New York: Cambridge University Press.

Kronbichler, M., Hutzler, F., & Staffen, W. (2006). Evidence for a dysfunction of left posterior reading areas in German dyslexic readers. *Neuropsychologia, 44,* 1822–1832.

Leach, J. M., Scarborough, H. S., & Rescorla, L. (2003). Late-emerging reading disabilities. *Journal of Educational Psychology, 95,* 211–224.

Leikin, M. (2002). Processing syntactic functions of words in normal and dyslexic readers. *Journal of Psycholinguistic Research, 31,* 145–163.

Lipka, O., Lesaux, N. K., & Siegel, L. S. (2006). Retrospective analyses of the reading development of grade 4 students with reading disabilities: Risk status and profiles over 5 years. *Journal of Learning Disabilities, 39,* 364–378.

Lyon, G. R. (1995). Toward a definition of dyslexia. *Annals of Dyslexia, 45,* 3–27.

MacGinitie, W. H., MacGinitie, R. K., Maria, K., & Dreyer, L. G. (2000). *Gates-MacGinitieReading Tests* (4th ed.). Itasca, IL: Riverside.

Meyer, M., Friederici, A. D., & von Cramon, D. Y. (2000). Neurocognition of auditory sentence comprehension: Event related fMRI reveals sensitivity to syntactic violations and task demands. *Cognitive Brain Research, 9,* 19–33.

Meyler, A., Keller, T. A., Cherkassky, V. L., Lee, D., Hoeft, F., Whitfield-Gabrieli, S., et al. (2007). Brain activation during sentence comprehension among good and poor readers. *Cerebral Cortex, 17*(12), 2780–2787.

Nation, K. (2001). Reading and language in children: Exposing hidden deficits. *The Psychologist, 14,* 238–242.

Nation, K., Adams, J. W., Bowyer-Crane, C. A., & Snowling, M. J. (1999). Working memory deficits in poor comprehenders reflect underlying language impairments. *Journal of Experimental Child Psychology, 73,* 139-158.

Nation, K., & Snowling, M. J. (1997). Assessing reading difficulties: The validity and utility of current measures of reading skill. *British Journal of Educational Psychology, 67,* 359–370.

Nation, K., & Snowling, M. J. (1998). Semantic processing and the development of word-recognition skills: Evidence from children with reading comprehension difficulties. *Journal of Memory and Language, 39,* 85–101.

Nation, K., & Snowling, M. J. (1999). Developmental differences in sensitivity to semantic relations among good and poor comprehenders: Evidence from semantic priming. *Cognition, 70,* B1–B13.

Nation, K., & Snowling, M. J. (2000). Factors influencing syntactic awareness skills in normal readers and poor comprehenders. *Applied Psycholinguistics, 21,* 229–241.

Oakhill, J. (1993). Children's difficulties in reading comprehension. *Educational Psychology Review, 5,* 223–237.

Oakhill, J., & Garnham, A. (1988). *Becoming a skilled reader.* Oxford, UK: Basil Blackwell.

Oakhill, J., & Yuill, N. M. (1996). Higher order factors in comprehension disability: Processes and remediation. In C. Cornoldi & J. Oakhill (Eds.), *Reading comprehension difficulties: Processes and intervention* (pp. 69–92). Mahwah, NJ: Lawrence Erlbaum Associates.

Oakhill, J. V., Yuill, N. M., & Parkin, A. J. (1986). On the nature of the difference between skilled and less-skilled comprehenders. *Journal of Research in Reading, 9,* 80–91.

Perfetti, C. A., Marron, M. A., & Foltz, P. W. (1996). Sources of comprehension failure: Theoretical perspectives and case studies. In C. Cornoldi & J. Oakhill (Eds.), *Reading comprehension difficulties: Processes and intervention* (pp. 137–166). Mahwah, NJ: Lawrence Erlbaum Associates.

Rimrodt, S. L., Clements-Stephens, A. M., Pugh, K. R., Courtney, S., Blankner, J. G. B., Bisesi, J., et al. (2008). *Functional MRI of sentence comprehension in adolescents with reading disabilities: Neurobiology beyond the single word.* Manuscript submitted for publication.

Rumsey, J. M., Zametkin, A. J., Andreason, P., Hanahan, A. P., Hamburger, S. D., Aquino, T., et al. (1994). Normal activation of frontotemporal language cortex in dyslexia, as measured with oxygen 15 positron emission tomography. *Archives of Neurology, 51,* 27–38.

Sabisch, B., Hahne, A., Glass, E., von Suchodoletz, W., & Friederici, A. D. (2006). Auditory language comprehension in children with developmental dyslexia: Evidence from event-related brain potentials. *Journal of Cognitive Neuroscience, 18,* 1676–1695.

Scarborough, H. S., & Parker, J. D. (2003). Children's learning and teachers' expectations: Matthew effects in children with learning disabilities: Development of reading, IQ, and psychosocial problems from grade 2 to grade 8. *Annals of Dyslexia, 53,* 47–71.

Schmalhofer, F., & Perfetti, C. A. (2007). *Higher level language processes in the brain: Inference and comprehension processes.* Mahwah, NJ: Lawrence Erlbaum Associates.

Schmithorst, V. J., Holland, S. K., & Plante, E. (2006). Cognitive modules utilized for narrative comprehension in children: A functional magnetic resonance imaging study. *NeuroImage, 29,* 254–266.

Seki, A., Koeda, T., & Sugihara, S. (2001). A functional magnetic resonance imaging study during sentence reading in Japanese dyslexic children. *Brian & Development, 23,* 312–316.

Shankweiler, D. (1999). Words to meanings. *Scientific Studies of Reading, 3,* 113–127.

Shankweiler, D., Lundquist, E., Katz, L., Stuebing, K. K., Fletcher, J. M., Brady, S., et al. (1999). Comprehension and decoding: Patterns of association in children with reading difficulties. *Scientific Studies of Reading, 3,* 69–94.

Shaywitz, S. E., Escobar, M. D., Shaywitz, B. A., Fletcher, J. M., & Makuch, R. (1992). Evidence that dyslexia may represent the lower tail of a normal distribution of reading ability. *The New England Journal of Medicine, 326,* 145–150.

Spear-Swerling, L. (2004). Fourth graders' performance on a state-mandated assessment involving two different measures of reading comprehension. *Reading Psychology, 25,* 121–148.

Stanovich, K. E. (1986). Matthew effects in reading: Some consequences of individual differences in the acquisition of literacy. *Reading Research Quarterly, 21,* 360–406.

Storch, S. A., & Whitehurst, G. J. (2002). Oral language and code-related precursors to reading: Evidence from a longitudinal structural model. *Developmental Psychology, 38,* 934–947.

Stowe, L. A., Paans, A. M. J., & Wijers, A. A. (1999). Sentence comprehension and word repetition: A positron emission tomography investigation. *Psychophysiology, 36,* 786–801.

Swanson, H. L. (1999). Reading comprehension and working memory in learning-disabled readers: Is the phonological loop more important than the executive system? *Journal of Experimental Child Psychology, 72,* 1–31.

Swanson, H. L., & Alexander, J. E. (1997). Cognitive processes as predictors of word recognition and reading comprehension in learning-disabled and skilled readers: Revisiting the specificity hypothesis. *Journal of Educational Psychology, 89,* 128–158.

Swanson, H. L., Ashbaker, M., & Lee, C. (1996). Learning-disabled readers' working memory as a function of processing demands. *Journal of Experimental Child Psychology, 61,* 242–275.

Swanson, H. L., & Berninger, V. (1995). The role of working memory in skilled and less skilled readers' comprehension. *Intelligence, 21,* 83–108.

Swanson, H. L., & Trahan, M. (1996). Learning disabled and average readers' working memory and comprehension: Does metacognition play a role. *British Journal of Educational Psychology, 66,* 333–355.

Torgesen, J. K. (2000). Individual differences in response to early interventions in reading: The lingering problem of treatment resisters. *Learning Disabilities Research and Practice, 15,* 55–64.

Torppa, M., Tolvanen, A., Poikkeus, A. M., Eklund, K., Lerkkanen, M. K., Leskinen, E., et al. (2007). Reading development subtypes and their early characteristics. *Annals of Dyslexia, 57,* 3–32.

Trabasso, T., & Wiley, J. (2005). Goal plans of action and inferences during comprehension of narratives. *Discourse Processes, 39,* 129–164.

Tunmer, W. E., Chapman, J. W., & Prochnow, J. E. (2004). Why the reading achievement gap in New Zealand won't go away: Evidence from the PIRLS 2001 International Study of Reading Achievement. *New Zealand Journal of Educational Studies, 39,* 127–145.

van den Broek, P., Rapp, D. N., & Kendeou, P. (2005). Integrating memory-based and constructionist processes in accounts of reading comprehension. *Discourse Processes, 39,* 299–316.

Virtue, S., Haberman, J., Clancy, Z., Parrish, T., & Beeman, M. J. (2006). Neural activity of inferences during story comprehension. *Brain Research, 1084,* 104–114.

Wechsler, D. L. (1992). *Wechsler Individual Achievement Test.* San Antonio, TX: Psychological Corporation.

Wiederholt, L., & Bryant, B. (1992). *Examiner's manual: Gray Oral Reading Test-3.* Austin, TX: Pro-Ed.

Wilson, S. M., Molnar-Szakacs, I., & Iacoboni, M. (2008). Beyond superior temporal cortex: Intersubject correlations in narrative speech comprehension. *Cerebral Cortex, 18*(1), 230–242.

Xu, J., Kemeny, S., Park, G., Frattali, C., & Braun, A. (2005). Language in context: Emergent features of word, sentence, and narrative comprehension. *NeuroImage, 25,* 1002–1015.

11 Reconciling Strong Genetic and Strong Environmental Influences on Individual Differences and Deficits in Reading Ability

Richard Olson, Brian Byrne, and Stefan Samuelsson

INTRODUCTION

Reading is a uniquely human activity that is strongly dependent both on our shared genetic endowment that distinguishes us from other primates and on the environment, typically through universal and formal reading instruction in modern societies. Thus, strong genetic and strong environmental influences are both apparent when we think of reading as a species-specific and culturally dependent skill. It is less obvious how genes and the environment influence *individual differences* and *deficits* in reading ability within modern societies that support universal reading education.

Recent studies with identical and fraternal twins from Australia, England, Scandinavia, and the United States have provided evidence for strong genetic and relatively weak environmental influences on reading disability (RD) and on individual differences in reading across the normal range. These results may seem to suggest that the educational environment for reading is of little importance, but there is evidence from remedial training studies for RD (see Foorman & Al Otaiba, this volume), and from whole-school or district-wide reading reforms (see Siegel, this volume) that experimentally demonstrate strong environmental influences on reading development. One of the goals of this chapter is to work toward a reconciliation between the evidence for both strong environmental and strong genetic influences on deficits and individual differences in reading development.

This is important because as Sherman and Cowen (this volume) point out, children with RD, their parents, their teachers, and educational policymakers might draw the wrong conclusions regarding the etiology and remediation of RD unless we are clear about the implications of our genetic and neurological research. It is also important that we understand the implications of genetic research for individual differences across the normal range when considering broad public educational policies such as No Child Left Behind (NCLB; 107th Congress, 2002) that often seem to ignore the possibility of genetic and other biological influences on reading ability.

The present review of the behavior genetic evidence from studies of identical and fraternal twins is divided into two main sections. The first section includes a brief review of results from studies where school-age twins were selected for low performance in reading or related skills, and the average relative influences of genes and environment were estimated for low group membership. We will pay particular attention to studies conducted in the Colorado Learning Disabilities Research Center (CLDRC; DeFries et al., 1997; Olson, 2006). The second and main section of the chapter focuses on results from several ongoing longitudinal twin studies of early reading development in unselected population samples that allow us to estimate the average influence of genes and environment on individual differences across the normal range. We will focus primarily on results from our International Longitudinal Twin Study (ILTS) of early reading development from preschool through the second grade that includes twin cohorts from Australia, the United States, and Scandinavia.

The concluding section of the chapter attempts to reconcile the evidence for both strong environmental and strong genetic influences on RD and individual differences across the normal range. We acknowledge that our twin samples may not include the full environmental range, particularly the extremely negative educational environments that exist in some impoverished communities. We also note the impact from extraordinary environmental interventions for many children with RD and from school district reading reforms, and we discuss why this experimental evidence for strong environmental influences is not inconsistent with the evidence for strong genetic influences on RD and individual differences in reading development.

Before proceeding with the rest of the chapter, some explanation is needed for our reference to RD in place of dyslexia. The term dyslexia may be associated with specific diagnostic criteria including failure in spite of normal educational opportunity to learn to read and a discrepancy between reading ability and general cognitive ability (Lyon, Shaywitz, & Shaywitz, 2003). The twin samples in the behavior genetic studies reviewed in this chapter include individuals with a broad range of general cognitive abilities that may be more or less discrepant from their reading abilities, and the home and school environments related to reading development are variable. We will explore the relations between these variables and the genetic and environmental etiology of individual differences and group deficits in reading.

TWIN STUDIES OF READING DISABILITY

Reading disability has long been thought to be at least partly due to genes because it tends to run in families (for review, see Grigorenko & Naples, this volume; Pennington & Olson, 2005). However, families also share their environment, so other converging behavior genetic evidence is needed to estimate the relative influences of genes and environment on RD. Most of this evidence has come from the wonderful natural experiment afforded by identical and fraternal twins. Identical twins share all their genes because they derive from the same fertilized egg or zygote (i.e., they are monozygotic or MZ twins). In contrast, fraternal twins share half of their segregating genes on average because they develop from two different fertilized eggs (i.e., they are dizygotic or DZ twins). Both types of twin pairs share their family environment and nearly always attend the same schools. Therefore, if MZ twins are more likely to share RD than DZ twins, this would provide evidence for genetic influence on dyslexia (see Plomin, DeFries, McClearn, & McGuffin, 2001, for a discussion of behavior genetic methods and assumptions in twin studies).

Early twin studies that compared groups of MZ and DZ twins with at least one member of each pair categorically diagnosed as "dyslexic" generally found that MZ twins are more likely than DZ twins to share or be "concordant" for dyslexia, thus providing evidence for at least some average genetic influence across the group with dyslexia. However, the categorical diagnosis of dyslexia versus normal reading is problematic because reading ability is continuously and normally distributed (i.e., the bell curve) in the population (Rodgers, 1983), as are most behavioral traits that have many independent genetic and/or environmental influences (see Olson, 2006, for further discussion of this point). Therefore, DeFries and Fulker (1985, 1988) developed the more appropriate DeFries–Fulker (DF) method for estimating genetic and environmental influences on deviant group membership for normally distributed behavioral dimensions such as reading. MZ and DZ twins that fall below some specified level of reading ability are identified as "probands" or affected twins, and then the averages for the MZ and DZ cotwins' mean performance levels are compared across the normally distributed dimension of reading ability.

The details of the DF method are beyond the scope of this chapter, but three extreme hypothetical examples may serve to clarify how the DF method is able to estimate the relative influences on RD from genes, shared family environment, and nonshared environment. First, if genes are completely responsible for RD and there is no measurement error, all of the cotwins of MZ probands with RD would also have RD because MZ twins share the same genes. In contrast, DZ cotwins, who share half of their segregating genes on average, would be expected to have reading skills that fall halfway on average between the mean of the RD group and the unselected population mean. Second, if shared family environment was the only influence on dyslexia, the cotwins of both MZ and DZ probands would also have RD because both types of twins share their family environment. Third, if nonshared environment (i.e., nonshared disease, birth problems, accidents, etc.)

was the only influence on RD, both the MZ and DZ cotwin groups would exhibit average reading performance levels close to the unselected population mean. The actual results from applying the DF method to twin data on reading and related skills from the CLDRC have fallen between these extreme examples, indicating that genes, shared family environment, and nonshared environment influences all contribute significantly to RD group membership.

Recent DF analyses of CLDRC data have estimated that genes account for about 60%, shared environment about 30%, and nonshared environment about 10% of the average influences on RD group membership. The exact percentages vary somewhat across the different reading and related skills and IQ cutoff scores that are used to define deviant group membership (see Pennington & Olson, 2005, for review). Similar DF estimates for genetic and environmental influences on low reading performance near the end of first grade have recently been reported from a large population study of twins in England and Wales (Harlaar, Spinath, Dale, & Plomin, 2005).

It is important to note that the estimates for genetic and environmental influences on RD group membership do not necessarily apply to any individual within the RD group. These estimates only indicate the average influence of genes and environment across the group. Extensions of the DF model that test for differences in the genetic etiology of RD depending on other variables have shown that the average genetic influence on RD varies significantly depending on the twins' component reading process profiles (higher heritability for phonological vs. surface dyslexia; Castles, Datta, Gayán, & Olson, 1999), on their IQ (higher heritability with higher IQ; Wadsworth, Olson, Pennington, & DeFries, 2000), on their parents' years of education (higher heritability with higher education; Friend, DeFries, & Olson, 2007), and on their comorbidity of RD with attention deficit/hyperactivity disorder (higher heritability for RD comorbid with ADHD; Willcutt, Pennington, Olson, & DeFries, 2007). However, these are estimates of the average influence of the moderator variables on the level of genetic influence across the RD group, so it is still not possible to specify the level of genetic etiology for any individual within the group.

Molecular genetic studies conducted by investigators in the CLDRC and other laboratories have found preliminary evidence for the role of specific genes in reading and related disabilities that may be linked to differences in neuronal migration (cf. Deffenbacher et al., 2004; Meng et al., 2005; Rosen, Wang, Fiondella, & LoTurco, this volume). The identification of these and other genes yet to be discovered may someday allow us to better understand the genetic etiology of RD in specific individuals by analyzing their DNA. The evidence from behavior genetic studies may be helpful in guiding the search for genes influencing RD by identifying the most heritable phenotypes for molecular genetic and related neurological studies.

In addition to estimating genetic and environmental influences on a single variable, studies with identical and fraternal twins are also able to estimate these influences on the covariation between two different variables. In DF analyses of group deficits, this is done by selection of probands on one variable and comparing MZ and DZ cotwins' mean performance on a second variable. For example, investigators in the CLDRC have explored the bivariate heritability of RD and ADHD and found that the group-deficit covariation for these often comorbid disorders is largely due to genes that influence both RD and ADHD (Willcutt et al., 2007). Willcutt et al. (2007) conducted bivariate linkage analyses of subjects' DNA that identified a region on the short arm of chromosome 6 that contained a gene or genes influencing both RD and ADHD, and Gayán et al. (2005) found suggestive evidence in their DNA linkage study for the approximate locations of several additional pleiotropic genes for RD and ADHD.

Other bivariate DF analyses have shown that group deficits in the phonological decoding of printed nonwords share most of their genetic influence with deficits in phonological awareness (Gayán & Olson, 2001), and this finding may be consistent with the relation between reading skill and the synchronicity of activity between Broca's speech area and visual word processing areas in the brain (Cornelissen, this volume). Similar kinds of bivariate behavior genetic analyses have been used in studies of individual differences across the normal range that we discuss in the next section.

TWIN STUDIES OF INDIVIDUAL DIFFERENCES IN EARLY READING DEVELOPMENT

In this section we turn to the genetic and environmental etiology of individual differences in early reading development across the normal range in unselected population samples of MZ and DZ twins. As mentioned earlier, reading and related skills are normally distributed in the general population and this is true for twins as well, who are similar in their reading performance to nontwin samples. These normal distributions allow us to compare the average similarity for MZ and DZ twins in unselected samples by computing and comparing their correlations or variance–covariance matrices. For example, if individual differences in a normally distributed variable were entirely due to additive genetic influences, there would be a perfect correlation of 1 for the MZ twins because they have the same genes, and the correlation would be .5 for DZ twins because they share half of their segregating genes on average. If individual differences were entirely due to shared family environment, the correlations would be 1 for both MZ and DZ twins because both types of twins share their environments. If individual differences were entirely due to nonshared environment, the correlations would be 0 for both MZ and DZ twins because they would be no more similar on average than pairs of individuals who were chosen randomly from the population. Of course, as with the extreme examples cited in the previous section on DF analyses for RD, we do not observe such extreme results for individual differences in complex behavioral variables such as reading. Instead, we commonly see MZ correlations that are significantly less than 1, with the difference from a perfect MZ correlation indicating nonshared environmental influences, including measurement error. DZ twin correlations are commonly lower than those for MZ twins, indicating some degree of genetic influence. As a rule of thumb, the heritability or the proportion of the population variance accounted for by additive genetic influences can be estimated from twice the difference between the correlations for MZ and DZ twins. Shared environment influence is indicated if the DZ correlation is greater than half of the MZ correlation, and it can be approximately estimated by the difference between the MZ correlation and the heritability estimate (Plomin et al., 2001). For the studies reviewed in this section, estimates of genetic and environmental influences were computed from the MZ and DZ twins' variance–covariance matrices using the Mx program (Neale, Boker, Xie, & Maes, 2002).

Results From the International Longitudinal Twin Study

We begin this review with a discussion of results from our International Longitudinal Twin Study (ILTS) of individual differences in early reading development. The ILTS was initiated in the Sydney area of Australia in 1999 under the direction of Brian Byrne. Subsequently the same measures were employed with twins in Colorado beginning in 2000 under the direction of Richard Olson, and in Scandinavia beginning in 2002 under the direction of Stefan Samuelsson, with measures translated for twins in Norway and Sweden. We exclude twins with profound metal retardation or sensory deficits such as blindness or deafness, but otherwise we attempt to make our samples representative of same-sex twins in the population that are learning to read in their first language.

The ILTS begins its assessment in the last preschool year between age 4 and 5, prior to the kindergarten year. This pre-reading assessment allows us to evaluate the relations between various pre-reading skills and subsequent reading development before those skills, such as phoneme awareness, may be strongly influenced by learning to read. Follow-up assessments of reading and related skills are conducted at the end of kindergarten, first grade, and second grade.

The rich multivariate database of the ILTS has allowed us to address many important questions about the genetic and environmental etiology of early reading and related cognitive development. In this review we discuss the evidence related to three of these questions: (a) How does the balance of genetic and environmental influences on reading skills change across our longitudinal assessments of early reading development in the different countries? (b) How does the evidence for very strong genetic influences on reading ability at the end of first grade comport with evidence on environmental influences related to different teachers, schools, and parents' education? (c) What is the evidence that genes influence individual differences in reading development through their direct influence on individual differences in learning rates?

Developmental and Country Differences in the Etiology of Reading Ability

Here we ask if there are developmental differences in the genetic and environmental etiology of individual differences in reading ability, and if these developmental differences vary across countries in relation to different educational practices in preschool and the early grades. The results from recent latent-trait analyses by

Samuelsson and colleagues (Samuelsson et al., 2008; Samuelsson, Olson, et al. 2007) for preschool print knowledge and for the Test of Word Reading Efficiency (TOWRE) (Torgesen, Wagner, & Rashotte, 1999) at the end of kindergarten and first grade are presented in Table 11.1. Note that the heritability (a^2) and non-shared environment (e^2) estimates for preschool print knowledge (mostly letter name and sound knowledge) are consistently low and shared environment influence (c^2) is consistently high across all three samples. In contrast to the preschool print knowledge results, large sample differences in genetic and shared environmental influences emerged from assessments at the end of kindergarten for the TOWRE latent trait. Heritability was highest for the Australian sample, lowest for the Scandinavian sample, and the U.S. sample fell in between. By the end of first grade, the sample differences at the end of kindergarten had largely disappeared. Now all three samples exhibited strikingly high heritabilities for individual differences in the TOWRE latent trait.

Samuelsson and colleagues (Samuelsson et al., 2008; Samuelsson, Olson, et al., 2007) accounted for the striking sample differences in mean reading performance and heritability at the end of kindergarten by noting that formal reading instruction was not included in the Norwegian and Swedish kindergarten curriculum. This contrasts with a strong emphasis on beginning reading instruction in the

---

TABLE 11.1

MX Model Fitting Estimates (and Confidence Intervals) for Latent Traits of Preschool Print Knowledge, Kindergarten Word Reading Efficiency, and Grade 1 Word Reading Efficiency within Each Twin Sample

	Heritability (a^2)	Shared Environment (c^2)	Non-Shared Environment (e^2)
Preschool Print Knowledge			
Australian sample	.25 (.00, .59)	.62 (.30, .84)	.13 (.07, .22)
U.S. sample	.26 (.13, .41)	.65 (.51, .76)	.09 (.06, .14)
Scandinavian sample	.20 (.11, .60)	.74 (.51, .89)	.07 (.02, .14)
Kindergarten Word Reading Efficiency			
Australian sample	.84 (.61, .94)	.09 (.00, .31)	.08 (.05, .11)
U.S. sample	.68 (.54, .84)	.25 (.09, .39)	.07 (.05, .09)
Scandinavian sample	.33 (.11, .60)	.52 (.26, .71)	.15 (.10, .23)
First-Grade Word Reading Efficiency			
Australian sample	.80 (.52, .87)	.02 (.00, .28)	.18 (.13, .26)
U.S. sample	.83 (.65, .92)	.07 (.00, .24)	.11 (.08, .14)
Scandinavian sample	.79 (.46, .89)	.07 (.00, .38)	.14 (.09, .22)

Note: Estimates with 95% confidence intervals including .00 are not significantly greater than 0.

Australian full-day kindergarten classes, and a more intermediate and less consistent emphasis on reading in the half-day kindergarten classes in the U.S. sample from Colorado. Formal reading instruction in Norway and Sweden was initiated in first grade for the ILTS twin cohort, and individual differences in response to this first year of instruction were strongly influenced by genetic factors.

In 2006, Norway introduced formal reading instruction in the kindergarten year. Samuelsson was able to collect data on a small sample of Norwegian twins at the end of kindergarten who were trained under this new curriculum. Their reading scores were significantly higher than those in the Norwegian ILTS twin cohort that had the previous curriculum, and the heritability estimates for individual differences in reading were also higher under the new curriculum (Samuelsson, Byrne, Hulslander, & Olson, 2007). Of course the goal of the new Norwegian reading curriculum in kindergarten is not to increase genetic influence or just improve kindergarten reading. It is intended to raise literacy levels through the later school years. It remains to be seen if this goal can be met, but it should be noted that other countries such as Sweden and Germany that continue to defer formal reading instruction until the first grade do quite well in international literacy assessments in the later grades (OECD, n.d.).

In summary, the results of the Samuelsson and colleagues (Samuelsson et al., 2008; Samuelsson, Olson, et al., 2007) analyses make clear that following the first year of consistent formal reading instruction, whether that begins in kindergarten or first grade, estimates of genetic influences on individual differences in the TOWRE latent trait for word and nonword reading efficiency are strikingly high, accounting for an average of 81% of individual differences across the three samples. The estimates of shared family environment accounted for an average of only 5% across samples, and nonshared environment influences averaged 14%. Samuelsson et al. (2008) also reported similar results for individual differences in a single measure of spelling at the end of first grade, where genes accounted for 70%, shared environment 7%, and nonshared environment 22% including measurement error related to the use of a single spelling measure. Similarly high genetic (77%) and low shared environment (2%) estimates averaged across the Australian and U.S. samples have been reported by Byrne, Samuelsson, et al. (2007) for a measure of reading comprehension at the end of first grade.

Two other longitudinal twin studies of reading development are underway that also report strong genetic and relatively weaker shared environment influences on individual differences in reading near the end of first grade. Petrill et al. (2007) reported stronger genetic (58%) than shared environment (33%) estimates for a single untimed measure of word reading accuracy that was administered in their Western Reserve Reading Project. These estimates are less extreme than we found for our TOWRE latent trait in the ILTS. However, Petrill et al. (2007) also used the same measure of reading comprehension that we used in the ILTS, and their genetic (76%) and shared environment (11%) estimates were similar to our ILTS estimates of 77% and 2% (Byrne, Samuelsson, et al., 2007).

The second independent twin study of individual differences in reading near the end of first grade was reported by Harlaar et al. (2005) for a large sample of twins in the United Kingdom that were tested by the same TOWRE measure that we used in the ILTS, although it had to be administered by phone due the sample size, and the investigators added the standard scores for word and nonword reading to create a composite variable instead of modeling a latent trait for the TOWRE as we did. Nevertheless, their estimates of genetic (70%) and shared environment (15%) influences were not far from what we found for our TOWRE latent trait.

Many readers of our articles and people who hear our conference presentations say that they find our very high genetic and low shared environment estimates hard to believe. Some wonder why the strong shared family environment influences on preschool print knowledge would not transfer to individual differences in reading after the first year of formal reading instruction. Others wonder if the assumptions behind our analyses of twin data might be incorrect, including the assumption of additive genetic influences and equal shared environment for MZ and DZ twins. We are also concerned about the validity of these assumptions. It is possible that there are some nonadditive genetic influences at play, such as dominance or other complex interactions between genes, that might lead us to overestimate genetic influences and underestimate shared environment influences when we assume complete genetic additivity. Unfortunately, without direct molecular genetic evidence for nonadditive genetic influences related to reading, we can not confirm these influences unless the MZ correlations are significantly more than twice the DZ correlations, which they are not.

It is also possible that the equal shared environment assumption for MZ and DZ twins is incorrect. If there is greater shared environment for MZ than DZ twins, this might lead us to overestimate genetic influences and underestimate shared environment influences. There is evidence for gene–environment correlations wherein MZ twins are more likely to select similar environments such as the amount of print exposure (Harlaar, Dale, & Plomin, 2007). However, if this is due to direct genetic influences on their ease in learning to read that subsequently influence their level of interest in reading and amount of print exposure, it is not considered to be a violation of the basic equal shared environment assumption (Plomin et al., 2001). Of greater concern is the possibility that MZ twins reared together might collaborate in their reading practice more than DZ twins for other reasons outside of direct genetic influences on their learning rates for reading skills. Finally, some critics of our results are concerned that the environmental range within our twin samples is constrained below that of the general population. We will consider this possibility in the final section of the chapter.

Now we will turn to our second question regarding external evidence for environmental influences related to possible teacher effects, school effects, and the effects of parents' educational background. If these are strong effects, as many believe they are, that would seem to be inconsistent with our high estimates of genetic influence and low estimates of shared environment influence.

Teacher, School, and Parent Education Influences on Early Reading

Many believe that teachers are largely responsible for individual differences in students' success or failure in learning to read. For example, Jonathan Alter (2007)

recently opined that "anyone with an ounce of brains knows what must be done....
It's time to move from identifying failing schools to identifying failing teachers."
Of course, on average, teachers do have a great deal of influence on children's
early reading development. This is clear from the studies of schooling effects on
early reading development by Morrison and colleagues who compared the early
reading progress of near same-age children who attended or did not attend school
because of the age cut off (Morrison, Alberts, & Griffith, 1997). Children in the
study who did not attend school made only a small fraction of the growth in reading skills compared to the near same-age children who attended school. But our
question about teacher effects is the degree to which *differences* between teachers
influence individual differences in students' early reading development within the
same school grade.

Byrne, Olson, et al. (2007) compared the end-of-first-grade TOWRE, spelling,
and reading comprehension correlations for twins in the ILTS who shared the
same teacher and for twins who had different teachers in the first grade. If teachers
are a significant cause of students' individual differences in early reading development, the correlation should be significantly higher for twins who share the same
teacher versus twins who have different teachers. The correlations for TOWRE
are presented separately for MZ and DZ twins in Figure 11.1, bracketed by their
95% confidence intervals. It is obvious that there are significant differences in
correlations between MZ and DZ twins regardless of their having the same or
different teachers, and this is the basis for our estimates of genetic and environmental influences in our behavior genetic analyses. It is also obvious, because
the confidence intervals overlap, that there are no statistically significant differences for either MZ or DZ twin correlations depending on whether the twins in
each pair had the same or different teachers. Very similar results were obtained

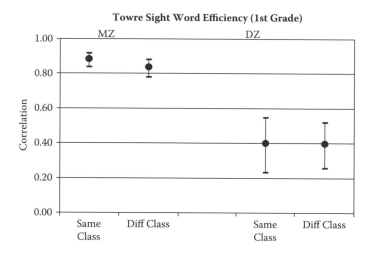

FIGURE 11.1 TOWRE composite score correlations for MZ and DZ twins who had the
same or different first-grade teachers.

for TOWRE nonword reading efficiency, and measures of spelling and reading comprehension.

This convergence of results for same versus different class correlations across the different reading and spelling measures in the ILTS is impressive, but the 95% confidence intervals leave open the possibility of modest differences in same- versus different-teacher correlations and the modest teacher effects that these differences would imply. Therefore it is fortunate that same versus different first-grade teacher twin correlations are also available for the TOWRE from a much larger twin sample in the United Kingdom that yielded much smaller confidence intervals (Nicole Harlaar, personal communication, September 10, 2006). The correlations and 95% confidence intervals were .86 (.84–.88) for 1,038 MZ twin pairs with the same teachers, .85 (.82–.87) for 578 MZ twin pairs with different teachers, .56 (.52–.60) for 939 DZ twin pairs with the same teachers, and .48 (.41–.54) for 528 DZ twin pairs with different teachers. None of the same- versus different-teacher correlation differences were statistically significant and the confidence intervals were quite small, indicating that any differential teacher effects on the TOWRE, if they exist at all, must be very small, on average, in this large and representative U.K. population sample. Kovas, Haworth, Dale, and Plomin (2007) have provided additional support for this conclusion by finding no significant differences in their estimates of genetic and shared environment influences on the TOWRE when comparing twins in the first grade who had the same or different teachers. Of course these group results from the ILTS and U.K. studies do not preclude the possibility of large but rare individual teacher effects in our samples.

The apparent absence of significant differential teacher effects provides no challenge to our high genetic and low shared environment estimates for the end of first-grade reading assessments in the ILTS, but many find the absence of significant differential teacher effects difficult to believe (Susan Brady, Louisa Moats, and Barbara Wise, personal communication, May 7, 2007). One response has been that maybe "bad" teachers migrate to "bad" schools and "good" teachers migrate to "good" schools. Since the twins' teachers are embedded in schools and the twins in each pair nearly always attend the same school, we could be missing teacher effects that are associated with schools.

To explore the possibility of teacher effects embedded within schools, Olson et al. (2006) examined the correlations between the average school score on the Colorado standardized reading assessment test administered in the third grade and the twins' reading scores on the ILTS measures administered at the end of second grade. The correlations were .13 with the TOWRE, .14 with reading comprehension, and .13 with spelling, all significantly greater than 0. These modest correlations open the possibility of modest teacher effects associated with differences in average school performance, but the mean school scores were also correlated with parents' years of education at .4, and parents' years of education were correlated with the twins ILTS second-grade reading scores at .29 for the TOWRE, .28 for reading comprehension, and .24 for spelling. Therefore, it is possible that differences related to parental education and not the twins' teachers are the real source of the school correlations with the twins' reading performance.

To provide a partial test of this hypothesis, we computed the partial correlations between the twins' ILTS test scores and mean reading score for their school after controlling for parents' years of education. The resulting partial correlations ranged from .01 to .02 and none approached significance. In contrast, the partial correlations between parents' years of education and their twins' ILTS reading scores after controlling for the twins' mean school score were only very slightly and nonsignificantly lower (.01 to .02 difference) than the first order correlations of .29, .28, and .24. Thus, the small but significant school correlations with the twins' ILTS reading scores are almost completely confounded with parents' years of education, but the stronger correlations between parents' years of education and their twins' ILTS reading scores are not mediated by the twins' school score. There may still be modest school/ teacher effects within the Colorado ILTS cohort that are linked to parents' years of education through economic constraints on their choice of residence and schools. There also could be genetic or other family environment constraints that mediate the parents' education and the twins' test correlations with mean school score.

In summary, there was no clear evidence that the results of our behavior genetic analyses are incorrect because we are missing environmental influences associated with teacher effects that are embedded within schools. Moreover, possible environmental influences from schools suggested by the modest correlations between the twins' average school score and their ILTS test performance could not be separated from genetic and/or environmental influences associated with parent education.

Our work on teacher and school effects is not completed. We will repeat the analyses with a larger ILTS sample and also include assessments of teacher effects on end-of-kindergarten and end-of-second-grade reading and spelling. We will also check to see if teacher effects might be more evident among children who are struggling in learning to read, a possibility suggested by Barbara Wise (personal communication, May 7, 2007). It has also been suggested that differential teacher effects might be eliminated for our twin pairs because they share their classroom experiences when they are at home. We agree that this might possibly dilute some differential teacher effects. However, if the twins' sharing of reading classroom experiences when they are at home had a strong influence on their similarity in reading ability, we would expect to see high correlations for *both* MZ and DZ twin pairs, and high estimates of shared environment influences, which we do not. At present, the results certainly do not support the contention of Alter (2007) that bad teachers are the main reason that children fail.

How Genes Influence Early Reading Development

Our third question pertains to the mechanisms of genetic influences on early reading development. Estimates of average genetic influence in the population that we presented in answer to the first question are certainly important, but they do not tell us how genes influence individual differences and deficits in early reading development. Of course the how question will have to be addressed at many different levels, including genetic influences on early brain development (Rosen et al., this volume). Here we address the how question at the behavioral level.

One way that genes might influence early reading development could be through genetic influences on children's motivation to practice reading. We do see wide variation in preschool children's early interest in books and in their subsequent level of reading practice across the early grades. It is also clear from many studies that there is a correlation between the amount of reading practice and performance on tests of reading ability. Another way genes might influence early reading abilities and practice is through their direct influence on learning rates for print knowledge and phonological awareness in preschool, and subsequently for learning new words through the early grades.

Byrne, Fielding-Barnsley, and Ashley (2000) assessed preschool children's learning rates for phoneme awareness in a well-controlled training study. The number of training sessions needed for children to reach a criterion level of phoneme awareness was the best predictor of their rate of reading growth through the early grades. Therefore we included several experimental measures of learning rate in the ILTS test battery. One of these is a measure of orthographic learning that we administer at the end of second grade (Byrne et al., 2008). The children's task was to read short passages containing novel words such as *laif* that can be spelled in two or more ways (e.g., *lafe*). Subsequently we asked the children to spell the new words and used their accuracy as an index of their orthographic learning rate. We also assessed their accuracy in decoding the novel words in the passages (they were told the correct pronunciation if it was incorrect) and their performance on a standardized spelling test. We found that the genes influencing children's orthographic learning in this experimental task were largely the same genes that influenced their decoding accuracy and their performance on the standardized spelling test.

We also asked if genetic influences on orthographic learning might simply reflect genetic influences on general cognitive ability. To address this question we calculated the genetic correlation between orthographic learning and an IQ measure that was given in preschool. The resulting genetic correlation was .5, indicating significant overlap, but also significant independent genetic influences on orthographic learning at the end of second grade. Gayán and Olson (2003) found a similar genetic correlation (.44) between IQ and a measure of orthographic knowledge administered in the same test session to a sample of older twins from 8 to 18 years of age. Thus, there seems to be at least some specificity for genetic influences on orthographic learning rates beyond genetic influences on general cognitive ability.

Could genetic influences on learning rates for reading and related skills be the cause of individual differences in preschool print interest, reading practice in the early grades, and related differences in reading ability? We can't entirely rule out some other genetic influences on reading practice, but it seems likely that children who find it relatively easy to learn to read with fluency will find reading more pleasant and will read more than children who have more difficulty in learning to read. This unfortunate gene–environment correlation would mean that children who may need more than a normal level of reading practice to reach or more closely approach the "grade level" reading goal of the NCLB legislation are likely to choose a less than normal level of reading practice. We will return to this problem and its implications for educational policy at the end of the chapter.

RECONCILING STRONG GENETIC AND STRONG ENVIRONMENTAL INFLUENCES

The behavior genetic studies with twins that we have reviewed in this chapter do not show strong shared environmental influences on individual differences or deficits in early reading development, so what is the evidence for strong environmental influences, and how can they be reconciled with the evidence for strong genetic influences? First, we need to consider the environmental range within our twin samples. Twin studies are sometimes criticized for downplaying the importance of the environment because they do not include the full environmental range that might yield lower estimates of genetic influence and higher estimates of environmental influence. We do constrain the ILTS sample to twins learning to read in their first language. Nevertheless, the reading skills of the ILTS twins in Colorado at the end of first grade are very similar to the standardizing sample for the TOWRE at the end of first grade, with a mean standard score close to 100 and a standard deviation close to 15. Moreover, 90% of families with twins that we were able to contact through Colorado state birth records agreed to participate in the study. The large Twins Early Development Study (TEDS) in the United Kingdom has also been very successful in recruiting a representative population sample of twins (Kovas et al., 2007).

However, these representative samples only yield *average* estimates of environmental influence that may conceal the importance of extremely bad or extremely beneficial environmental influences that are present for a small minority of the twins in the sample. There can be no doubt that extremely negative educational environments can have a very negative influence on early reading development (Kozol, 1985, 2005). If half of a twin sample was drawn from these very bad educational environments described by Kozol and half from the schools along the Colorado front range, we would likely see higher estimates of shared environment influence and lower estimates of genetic influence in the combined sample. The same point can be made from a comparison of the kindergarten reading levels of the Australian ILTS twins who received reading instruction and the Scandinavian twins who did not. When we combine these samples in a behavior genetic analysis without standardizing within the samples, the estimates of shared environment influence increase.

Another source of evidence for strong environmental influences on reading development comes from reports of school or district-wide reading reforms, including the very successful reform in the North Vancouver School District with many ESL (English as a second language) children described by Siegel (this volume), and in the Pueblo 60 district in Colorado that has many low SES (socioeconomic status) families (Sadoski & Wilson, 2006). The Pueblo 60 district steadily improved its level of reading performance in the early grades from 1998 to 2003 as it increasingly implemented more systematic and intensive reading instruction, reading practice, and special remedial programs for children making the least progress. Foorman and Al Otaiba (this volume) review the results of other promising school and district-wide reading reforms.

Further evidence for environmental influences from remedial interventions for RD has been reviewed by Torgesen (2002, 2004), and significant brain activity changes related to such interventions are being studied with modern imaging techniques (Frost et al., this volume). One of the intervention studies reviewed by Torgesen was directed by Barbara Wise, a coinvestigator in the CLDRC, who is using computer-based programs to promote and study response to instruction (RTI) for children with RD in the early grades and children at risk for RD in kindergarten. Precursors to these programs were used in 40-hour pull-out training studies in the Boulder, Colorado, schools for second- through fifth-grade children with RD that yielded strong average gains in standard scores for word recognition of 10 points, compared to gains of 3 points (effect size ~1) for children with RD who remained in their regular reading classrooms (Wise, Ring, & Olson, 1999, 2000).

With all the evidence for the positive effects of remedial interventions and for benefits from school and district-wide reading reform, can we ignore genetic influences on reading ability and disability when crafting public education laws such as NCLB? It would seem so when schools and teachers may be required to bring all children up to grade level in reading, and now in math and science as well, by 2014! But the real story from the district reform and intervention studies is that many children will still be left behind if grade-level performance in reading is the criterion for success. (It is not clear what is meant by "grade level" in the proposed legislation, but its traditional meaning in standardized tests is the average level of performance among children at a given school grade level.)

Many intensive intervention studies for RD have been successful in raising the average standard scores for children in the treatment groups compared to untreated control groups, but individual responses to these interventions are typically normally distributed. Some of the children with remediation for RD may reach or exceed grade level on standardized reading and spelling tests, but many do not, even though they may show functionally significant gains. Similarly, studies of school or district-wide reading reforms have left many children below grade level in spite of their average improvement in reading. Many of these so-called treatment resistors may have genetic or nongenetic biological constraints on their development that may make it impossible for them to reach grade-level performance, even if they were to far exceed the amount of effort and reading practice required by most children who perform at or above grade level. More generally, it is likely that the *differences* among children that remain after average gains in levels of reading have been achieved will in large part be genetically determined.

We understand the concern some may have that if we acknowledge genetic constraints on children's reading development, that might become an excuse for not providing sufficient remedial intervention for children with RD who could benefit. This is a realistic concern, and something we must guard against as best we can. But we think the opposite conclusion is warranted. That is, children whose responsiveness to available instruction is hampered by their genetic endowment need *increased* learning opportunities. This is where the high art of teaching is called upon to be at its most creative because of the likely decline in motivation that attends lower levels of early reading success.

Unfortunately, our population twin studies that point to strong *average* genetic influences on RD and individual differences in reading are not presently accompanied by molecular genetic evidence that can accurately specify genetic constraints on reading development at the individual level. That is a hope for the future. Children being studied by Barbara Wise for their response to intervention in the CLDRC help us approach this goal when we compare their response to intervention with their DNA.

For now, failure to acknowledge the possible genetic or other biological constraints on some children's treatment-resistant RD and setting unrealistic goals (i.e., "grade level") is grossly unfair to those children, their parents, their teachers, and their schools. We hope that the reauthorization of the NCLB law that is currently being considered in Congress as we write this chapter will retain the positive aspects of NCLB that help promote better education for all children in the United States, particularly those with RD, while also recognizing that some children with RD may not be able to reach grade level even with the best remedial programs, and that these children, their parents, their teachers, and their schools should be congratulated for their functionally important gains from effective remedial reading programs, even if they do fall short of grade level.

ACKNOWLEDGMENTS

The Colorado Learning Disabilities Research Center is supported by grant HD-27802 from the National Institute of Child Health and Human Development (NICHD). The International Longitudinal Twin Study is funded by the Australian Research Council (A79906201), the National Institute for Child Health and Human Development (HD27802 and HD38526), the Research Council of Norway (154715/330), the Swedish Research Council (345-2002-3701), and University of Stavanger, Norway.

REFERENCES

107th Congress. (2002). The no child left behind act of 2001. Washington, DC: United States Congress.

Alter, J. (2007, February 10). Stop pandering on education; It's time to move from identifying failing schools to identifying failing teachers. Sounds obvious, but it hasn't happened in American education. *Newsweek*, p. 55.

Byrne, B., Fielding-Barnsley, R., & Ashley, L. (2000). Effects of phoneme identity training after six years: Outcome level distinguished from rate of response. *Journal of Educational Psychology, 92,* 659–667.

Byrne, B., Olson, R. K., Hulslander, J., Samuelsson, S., Harlaar, N., & Coventry, W. (2007, July 13). *Exploring environmental influences on literacy development in a genetically-sensitive research design: The case of teacher effects.* Paper presented at the meeting of the Society for the Scientific Study of Reading, Prague.

Byrne, B., Olson, R. K., Hulslander, J., Samuelsson, S., Wadsworth, S., DeFries, J. C., et al. (2008). A behavior genetic analysis of orthographic learning, spelling, and decoding. *Journal of Research in Reading, 31,* 8–21.

Byrne, B., Samuelsson, S., Wadsworth, S., Hulslander, J., Corley, R., DeFries, J. C., et al. (2007). Longitudinal twin study of early literacy development: Preschool through Grade 1. *Reading and Writing: An Interdisciplinary Journal, 20,* 77–102

Castles, A., Datta, H., Gayán, J., & Olson, R. K. (1999). Varieties of developmental reading disorder: Genetic and environmental influences. *Journal of Experimental Child Psychology, 72,* 73–94.

Deffenbacher, K. E., Kenyon, J. B., Hoover, D. M., Olson, R. K., Pennington, B. F., DeFries, J. C., et al. (2004). Refinement of the 6p21.3 QTL influencing dyslexia: Linkage and association analysis. *Human Genetics, 115,* 128–138.

DeFries, J. C., Filipek, P. A., Fulker, D. W., Olson, R. K., Pennington, B. F., Smith, S. D., et al. (1997). Colorado Learning Disabilities Research Center. *Learning Disabilities, 8,* 7–19.

DeFries, J. C., & Fulker, D. W. (1985). Multiple regression analysis of twin data. *Behavior Genetics, 15,* 467–473.

DeFries, J. C., & Fulker, D. W. (1988). Multiple regression analysis of twin data: Etiology of deviant scores versus individual differences. *Acta Geneticae Medicae et Gemellologiae, 37,* 205–216.

Friend, A., DeFries, J. C., & Olson, R. K. (2008). Parental education moderates genetic influences on reading disability. *Psychological Science, 19,* 1124–1130.

Gayán, J., & Olson, R. K. (2001). Genetic and environmental influences on orthographic and phonological skills in children with reading disabilities. *Developmental Neuropsychology, 20*(2), 487–511.

Gayán, J., & Olson, R. K. (2003). Genetic and environmental influences on individual differences in printed word recognition. *Journal of Experimental Child Psychology, 84,* 97–123.

Gayán, J., Willcutt, E. G., Fisher, S. E., Francks, C., Cardon, L. R., Olson, R. K., et al. (2005). Bivariate linkage scan for reading disability and attention-deficit/hyperactivity disorder localizes pleiotropic loci. *Journal of Child Psychology and Psychiatry, 46,* 1045–1056.

Harlaar, N., Dale, P. S., & Plomin, R. (2007). *ART and reading: Genetic and shared environmental mediation of the association between reading experience and reading achievement in 10-year-old twins.* Manuscript submitted for publication.

Harlaar, N., Dale, P. S., & Plomin, R. (2007, July 13). *How are reading experience and reading achievement related over time?* Paper presented at the meeting of the Society for the Scientific Study of Reading, Prague.

Harlaar, N., Spinath, F. M., Dale, P. S., & Plomin, R. (2005). Genetic influences on early word recognition abilities and disabilities: A study of 7-year-old twins. *Journal of Child Psychology and Psychiatry, 46,* 373–384.

Kovas, Y., Haworth, C. M. A., Dale, P. S., & Plomin, R. (2007). The genetic and environmental origins of learning abilities and disabilities in the early school years. *Monographs of the Society for Research in Child Development, 72,* 1–144.

Kozol, J. (1985). *Illiterate America.* Garden City, NY: Anchor Press/Doubleday.

Kozol, J. (2005). *The shame of the nation: The restoration of apartheid schooling in America.* New York: Crown.

Lyon, G. R., Shaywitz, S. E., & Shaywitz, B. A. (2003). A definition of dyslexia. *Annals of Dyslexia, 53,* 1–14.

Meng, H., Smith, S. D., Hager, K., Held, M., Liu, J., Olson, R. K., et al. (2005). DCDC2 is associated with reading disability and modulates neuronal migration in the brain. *Proceedings of the National Academy of Sciences, 102*(47), 17053–17058.

Morrison, F. J., Alberts, D., & Griffith, E. M. (1997). Nature-nurture in the classroom: Entrance age, school readiness, and learning in children. *Developmental Psychology, 33,* 254–262.

Neale, M. C., Boker, S. M., Xie, G., & Maes, H. H. (2002). *Mx: Statistical modeling* (6th ed.). (Available from Department of Psychiatry, VCU Box 900126, Richmond, VA 23298.)

Olson, R. K. (2006). Genes, environment, and dyslexia: The 2005 Norman Geschwind Memorial Lecture. *Annals of Dyslexia, 56*(2), 205–238.

Olson, R. K., Lefly, D., Byrne, B., Samuelsson, S., Corley, R., Hulslander, J., et al. (2006, July 6). *School and genetic influences on early reading and related skills.* Paper presented at the meeting of the Society for the Scientific Study of Reading, Vancouver, British Columbia.

Organization for Economic Cooperation and Development (OECD) Program for International Student Assessment (PISA) (n.d.). Retrieved September 18, 2004, from www.pisa.oecd.org.

Pennington, B. F., & Olson, R. K. (2005). Genetics of dyslexia. In M. Snowling, C. Hulme, & M. Seidenberg (Eds.), *The science of reading: A handbook* (pp. 453–472). Oxford, UK: Blackwell.

Petrill, S. A., Deater-Deckard, K., Thompson, L. A., Schatschneider, C., DeThorne, L. S., & Vandenbergh, D. J. (2007). Longitudinal genetic analysis of early reading: The Western Reserve Reading Project. *Reading and Writing, 20,* 127–146.

Plomin, R., DeFries, J. C., McClearn, G. E., & McGuffin, P. (2001). *Behavioral genetics* (4th ed.). New York: Worth Publishers.

Rodgers, B. (1983). The identification and prevalence of specific reading retardation. *British Journal of Educational Psychology, 53,* 369–373.

Sadoski, M., & Wilson, V. L. (2006). Effects of a theoretically based large-scale reading intervention in a multicultural urban school district. *American Educational Research Journal, 43*(1), 137–154.

Samuelsson, S., Byrne, B., Hulslander, J., & Olson, R. K. (2007, July 13). *A new curriculum for reading and spelling: Changes in estimated genetic and environmental influences on early literacy development in Norway.* Paper presented at the meeting of the Society for the Scientific Study of Reading, Prague.

Samuelsson, S., Byrne, B., Wadsworth, S., Corley, R., DeFries, J. C., Willcutt, E. G., et al. (2008). Response to early literacy instruction in the United States, Australia, and Scandinavia: A behavior-genetic analysis. *Learning and Individual Differences, 18*(3), 289–295.

Samuelsson, S., Olson, R. K., Wadsworth, S., Corley, R., DeFries, J. C., Willcutt, E., et al. (2007). Genetic and environmental influences on pre-reading skills and early reading and spelling development: A comparison among United States, Australia, and Scandinavia. *Reading and Writing: An Interdisciplinary Journal, 20,* 51–75.

Torgesen, J. (2002). The prevention of reading difficulties. *Journal of School Psychology, 40*, 7–26.

Torgesen, J. (2004). Lessons learned from research on interventions for students who have difficulty learning to read. In P. McCardle & V. Chhabra (Eds.), *The voice of evidence in reading research* (pp. 355–382). Baltimore: Paul H. Brookes.

Torgesen, J., Wagner, R., & Rashotte, C. A. (1999). *A Test of Word Reading Efficiency (TOWRE)*. Austin, TX: PRO-ED.

Wadsworth, S. J., Olson, R. K., Pennington, B. F., & DeFries, J. C. (2000). Differential genetic etiology of reading disability as a function of IQ. *Journal of Learning Disabilities, 33*, 192–199.

Willcutt, E. G., Pennington, B. F., Olson, R. K., & DeFries, J. C. (2007). Understanding comorbidity: A twin study of reading disability and attention deficit/hyperactivity disorder. *American Journal of Medical Genetics (Neuropsychiatric Genetics), 8*, 709–714.

Wise, B. W., Ring, J., & Olson, R. K. (1999). Training phonological awareness with and without attention to articulation. *Journal of Experimental Child Psychology, 72*, 271–304.

Wise, B. W., Ring, J., & Olson, R. K. (2000). Individual differences in gains from computer-assisted remedial reading with more emphasis on phonological analysis or accurate reading in context. *Journal of Experimental Child Psychology, 77*, 197–235.

12 Reading in Hebrew Versus Reading in English

Is There a Qualitative Difference?

Ram Frost

To rapidly perceive, recognize, and process printed words, some well-defined organization of word units must exist in the mental lexicon. Models of visual word recognition are concerned with the principles of this organization. For example, the entry-opening model (Forster, 1999; Forster & Davis, 1984) assumes that lexical entries are organized into bins based on their orthographic form. Thus, words sharing similar letter sequences (or orthographic neighbors) would be located in the same bin. Upon presentation of a printed word, the orthographic properties of the input are used to calculate an approximate address (i.e., a bin number), and a frequency-ordered search within that bin is performed to locate the matching entry. Alternatively, attractor-based models of reading (e.g., Rueckl, 2002) assume that printed words are represented as points in a perceptual space that is defined in terms of orthographic properties. Words that are close together in this perceptual space will tend to overlap in their orthographic structure. The process of word recognition is then described in terms of a trajectory of the system through its state space, where the initial point of this trajectory is some random position in the state space and the final point is an attractor basin corresponding to the input word. Each word has a unique attractor, and the positions of the attractors in the state space are organized to reflect similarities in spelling.

The present chapter is concerned with the following question: Could there be *qualitative* differences in the principles of lexical organization and lexical processing in different alphabetic orthographies? Within this context, two contrasting theoretical approaches can be outlined. What I will label here as the *universal view* suggests that similar principles of lexical organization and processing apply to different languages. Obviously, languages with alphabetic orthographies may differ in their statistical properties (i.e., number of words, word length, distributional properties of sublinguistic units such as bigrams and trigrams, etc.). However, these differences are quantitative in nature, and, hence, the resulting processing differences will be quantitative as well. The universal view is best represented by current parallel-distributed processing models of word recognition that focus on statistical learning and the search for orthographic regularities in the printed input (e.g., Seidenberg, McDonald, & Safran, 2003). In contrast, what I label here as the *structural-ecological view* suggests that the principles of organization and processing of words in alphabetic orthographies are not determined exclusively by orthographic constraints but may be shaped by the language's morphological characteristics. According to the structural-ecological view, reading entails not only the unequivocal recognition of a letter string, but also an efficient on-line process of morphological and semantic analysis. Hence, reading processes in two languages that have very different morphological structures may differ qualitatively, even if they employ similar orthographic systems (e.g., Frost, Kugler, Deutsch, & Forster, 2005).

How would we know that cross-linguistic processing differences are qualitative rather than quantitative? Admittedly, this is a tough question. Since the distributional properties of words and sublinguistic orthographic and phonological units differ from language to language, some processing differences are necessarily expected. A convincing case for qualitative cross-linguistic differences would be established, therefore, only by finding points of discontinuity, where patterns of performance in one language are opposed to the patterns found in another language, and by demonstrating converging results from several research paradigms. Obviously, the most convincing case would be made by bilingual experiments in which very similar linguistic manipulations are used on identical subjects, producing different patterns of results. The aim of the present chapter is to argue for the ecological-structural view by examining two languages: Hebrew and English. Both have an alphabetic orthography, but they differ in their morphological structure. The following review and discussion will demonstrate that reading processes in these languages are qualitatively different. This will be done by assembling evidence from masked orthographic priming, masked morphological priming, the measurement of parafoveal preview benefits, and by monitoring the impact of letter transposition. Finally, converging evidence from reading disorders will be discussed as well. I will first begin with a brief description of the orthographic and morphological characteristics of the two languages.

HEBREW AND ENGLISH: ORTHOGRAPHIC STRUCTURE VERSUS MORPHOLOGICAL STRUCTURE

Hebrew and English are both considered deep alphabetic orthographies, where letters represent phonemes, but the mapping of graphemes-to-phonemes is not entirely transparent (Frost, Katz, & Bentin, 1987; Katz & Frost, 1992). Yet, whereas the English alphabet has 26 letters, the Hebrew alphabet consists of only 22 letters, which mostly represent consonants. Hebrew vowels can optionally be superimposed on the consonants as diacritical marks ("points"); in addition, some vowels may also be represented by letters, depending on the orthographic or phonological context. Since different vowels may be inserted into the same string of consonants to form different words or nonwords, Hebrew unpointed print cannot specify a unique phonological unit, and a printed consonant string is phonologically ambiguous, often representing more than one word. Thus, the depth of the Hebrew orthography is different by nature from that of English orthography. Whereas in English the opaque relations of spelling to sound are related to the *inconsistency* of letter clusters, in Hebrew, opaque spelling-to-sound connections arise simply from *missing* phonemic information, mainly vowel information. Extensive research has consistently revealed that in contrast to English, reading in Hebrew involves interplay of two computational processes that are defined by the size of the computed units. The first process is characterized by the conversion of units of single letters into consonantal information (Frost, 1994, 1995). This process provides an impoverished phonological representation that is often sufficient for lexical access (Frost, 1998). However, a detailed and complete phonological representation that is necessary for reading is produced by using morphological information. As will be explained later, this morphological information provides the cluster of all missing vowels as one morphemic unit: the *word pattern* (see Frost, 2006, for a discussion).

The main difference between Hebrew and English thus concerns their morphological structure. The morphological structure of Indo-European languages can be characterized by a linear and sequential concatenation of morphemic units to form multimorphemic words. Thus, both inflectional and derivational morphology are based on appending prefixes or suffixes to a base morpheme. As a general rule, the orthographic integrity of the base form remains intact, and, in fact, in most languages with concatenated morphology, the base forms function not only as morphemes in complex forms but also constitute free word-forms in their own right (such as *dark* in *darkness,* or *dream* in *dreamer).*

Hebrew, on the other hand, is a Semitic language. Hence, most words can be decomposed into two abstract morphemes: the root and the word pattern. Roots in most cases consist of three consonants whereas word patterns can be either a sequence of vowels or a sequence consisting of both vowels and consonants. However, the most salient feature of Semitic languages' morphology concerns the special manner in which these morphemic units are combined to form morphological complexity. Roots and word patterns are not appended to one another linearly, as in languages with concatenated morphology. Rather, the consonants of the root are intertwined with the phonemes (and, therefore, the corresponding letters) of the word pattern. Unlike base forms in English, roots and word patterns are abstract structures because only their joint combination results in specific phonemic word-forms with specific meanings. These meanings cannot necessarily be predicted by analyzing each of the two morphemes independently. For example, the Hebrew word TIZMORET ("orchestra") is a derivation of the root ZMR. This root is mounted onto the phonological pattern TI--O-ET (each dash indicates the position of a root consonant). The root ZMR alludes to anything related to the concept of singing, and the phonological pattern TI--O-ET is often (but not always) used to form feminine nouns. It is the merging of the root

with the word pattern that forms the word meaning "orchestra." Other phonological word patterns may combine with the same root to form different words with
different meanings that can be either closely or remotely related to the notion of
singing. Other roots may also be combined with the word pattern TI--O-ET to
form various feminine nouns. For example, the root LBŠ (conveying the action
of dressing) can be combined with TI--O-ET, to form the word TILBOŠET ("an
outfit"). Similarly, the word ZAMAR ("a singer") is formed by combining the
root ZMR with the phonologic pattern -A-A-, which carries the information that
the word is a noun that signifies a profession.

The two basic morphemic units in Hebrew (the root and the word pattern) differ in their linguistic characteristics. Whereas word patterns, at least in the nominal system, convey primarily vague grammatical information about word class
(there are more than a hundred such patterns), the root carries the core meaning
of the word. Given the important role of the root morpheme in forming word
structure and word meaning, word recognition studies explore the possibility that
the root plays a significant role in lexical organization. Indeed, numerous experiments that examined visual word recognition in Hebrew showed that root primes
facilitate both lexical decision and the naming of target words that are derived
from these roots. These findings suggested that in the course of word recognition, words are decomposed into their constituent morphemes and root units are
the target of lexical search (e.g., Frost, Deutsch, & Forster, 2000; Frost, Deutsch,
Gilboa, Tannenbaum, & Marslen-Wilson, 2000; Frost, Forster, & Deutsch, 1997).
In a recent study, Frost et al. (2005) have consequently argued that the lexical
architecture of Hebrew is primarily determined by morphological rather than by
orthographic characteristics. According to this view, lexical space in Hebrew is
organized so that all words derived from the same root are clustered together;
therefore, the initial stage of word recognition entails the extraction of the root
letters. This theoretical claim is in accordance with the structural-ecological
view, as it suggests that the principle of organization and processing of words
in alphabetic orthographies is primarily determined by the language's morphological characteristics. In Semitic languages, lexical neighborhoods are, thus,
defined by root units and not by simple orthographic structure. Hence, whereas
in English two words that share all of their letters but one are considered to be
neighbors (e.g., Coltheart, Davelaar, Jonasson, & Besner, 1977), in Hebrew such
words would be far apart in lexical space if they share a different root. The question at hand is whether the results obtained in visual word recognition in Hebrew
are qualitatively different from those obtained in English. The following sections
will review the empirical evidence for this claim.

THE EFFECT OF PRIME–TARGET ORTHOGRAPHIC OVERLAP

The most promising method for studying the properties of lexical space is to
use a priming paradigm with very short exposure duration (masked priming).
Considering, for example, attractor-based models, their basic account of facilitation is that for any prime–target pair, if the properties of the prime overlap with

those of the target, then they must be "near" each other. Hence, moving toward the rhyme location will also involve moving toward the target location. When the prime is replaced by the target, the starting point for the new trajectory will be closer to the final destination than if the prime had been unrelated to the target, and, consequently, target recognition latencies are shorter in the related condition than in the unrelated one. In interactive activation models, it is assumed that words that are located in adjacent regions of lexical space somehow interact, so that activation of the central correlates of one word has an effect on the central correlates of the other words. The very nature of the access architecture in parallel activation models guarantees that through *cross-activation* the input stimulus will activate (or suppress) a wide range of word units to varying degrees, depending on the amount of orthographic overlap. Finally, in search models such as the entry-opening model, priming reflects a transfer effect. The results of processing carried out on the prime are transferred across to the target. In other words, most of the processing operations involved in analyzing the prime can serve for the identification and recognition of the target, resulting in a gain of processing time. This transfer is made possible when the primes and targets have overlapping orthographic structures. The theoretical question is, therefore, by what principle are words positioned one next to the other or by what principles are they interconnected. The definition adopted by most researchers in visual word recognition is that two words are considered as neighbors if they have a similar orthographic structure; for example, if they are of the same length but differ by a single letter (e.g., *face* and *race*; Coltheart et al. 1977), or if they share the body (the vowel plus the following consonants of the first syllable; Ziegler & Perry, 1998).

The empirical support for the claim that words are lexically organized by a principle of letter-sequence similarity comes from masked priming experiments in which primes and targets have a similar orthographic structure (i.e., form priming). The magnitude of the priming effect and whether it is facilitatory or inhibitory depends on factors such as exposure duration, prime–target relative frequency, the lexical status of the prime, and neighborhood density. For example, in short exposure durations, the prime is not consciously perceived. If the primes and targets have overlapping orthographic structures, any processing carried out on the prime could be used to locate the target, shortening its recognition. In contrast, with longer exposure duration, the prime may be recognized, and since orthographically similar word forms may compete with one another as part of the recognition process, the prime may suppress the processing of the target. In line with this argument, Chateau and Jared (2000) indeed reported strong effects of orthographic facilitation with a prime exposure of 30 ms but strong inhibition with a prime exposure of 60 ms. Regarding frequency, in general, stronger facilitation or inhibition is expected when the frequency of the prime exceeds that of the target (e.g., Segui & Grainger, 1990). As to the lexical status of the prime, nonword primes that are orthographically similar to the targets produce stronger priming, since no prime–target competition is expected for nonword primes (e.g., Holyk & Pexman, 2004). Finally, form-priming facilitation also depends on neighborhood density: Strong facilitation is obtained for word targets having few orthographic neighbors and weak facilitation for words having many (e.g., Forster & Taft, 1994). This is because the prime predicts the target with greater efficiency when the orthographic neighborhood includes but a few candidates than when it includes many.

Masked form priming (positive or negative) is a robust effect in visual word recognition and has been repeatedly demonstrated in numerous studies across many Indo-European languages, such as English (e.g., Davis & Lupker, 2006), French (Ferrand & Grainger, 1992), Dutch (Van Heuven, Dijkstra, Grainger, & Schriefers, 2001), and Spanish (e.g., Perea & Rosa, 2000). In accordance with the aforementioned various experimental factors, most masked priming studies reported either significant facilitation or significant inhibition when primes and targets shared orthographic form.[1] Taken together, these studies are compatible with the suggestion that orthographic constraints determine the structure of lexical space in Indo-European languages.

What about Hebrew then? In a recent study, Frost et al. (2005) have shown a very different pattern of results in this language. In a set of eight experiments, they reported that no form-orthographic priming could be obtained in Hebrew or in Arabic, also a Semitic language. Thus, orthographically similar prime–target pairs differing by one letter only did not show any significant facilitation or inhibition in any experimental condition. Moreover, in sharp contrast to Indo-European languages, masked form priming seemed unaffected by the lexical status of the prime or by neighborhood density. Of special interest in the present context were two experiments involving bilingual subjects. In these two experiments, Hebrew–English (Experiment 3a) and English–Hebrew (Experiment 3b) bilinguals were presented with form-related primes and targets in Hebrew and in English. When tested in English, these bilingual speakers indeed demonstrated robust form priming. However, in both experiments, no such effect was obtained when these same subjects were tested with Hebrew material.

The interpretation of these findings was that the Hebrew lexical space is organized in a radically different manner from that of English and other Indo-European languages. In the latter case, the orthographic dimensions of the space specify words in terms of the constituent letters and their absolute and relative positions. In contrast, the Hebrew lexical space may be structured according to the morphological roots. This would mean that all words that contain the same root would be clustered together, and the perceptual distance between two words containing different roots would be uncorrelated with their overall orthographic similarity. This conclusion is further supported when considering masked morphological priming.

THE EFFECT OF PRIME–TARGET MORPHOLOGICAL OVERLAP

In contrast to the form-orthographic priming effects that were consistently found to be small and unreliable in Hebrew, robust masked morphological priming effects have been repeatedly reported in a series of studies. The main finding concerns the role of the root morpheme in visual word recognition. Root primes presented in isolation or contained in verbal or nominal derivations were found to facilitate both lexical decision and the naming of target words that were derived from these roots (e.g., Deutsch, Frost & Forster, 1998; Frost et al., 1997, 2005; Frost, Deutsch, & Foster, 2000; Frost, Deutsch, Gilboa et al., 2000). In other words, masked morphological priming is always obtained when the prime consists of the root letters or a derivation of that root, and the target consists of the root letters or a derivation of the root. Finally, the morphological priming effect seems unaffected by semantic transparency or lack thereof. These findings strongly suggest that Hebrew readers extract the root morpheme during word recognition and that these morphemic units govern lexical access.

The results from Indo-European languages are more difficult to assess. At first glance, masked morphological priming is also consistently found in Indo-European languages. Significant priming effects were reported in English (e.g., Rastle & Davis, 2003), in Dutch (e.g., Diependaele, Sandra, & Grainger, 2005), in French (e.g., Longtin, Segui, & Halle, 2003), and in Spanish (Badecker & Allen, 2002). The crucial question is, however, whether these effects are comparable to those obtained in Hebrew. One striking feature of masked morphological priming studies in Indo-European languages is an asymmetry in the position of primes and targets. It seems that robust morphological priming is obtained when the prime is a derivation and the target is a stem (*darkness–dark*), but less so when this order is reversed. A recent review of masked morphological priming effects (Brysbaert & Rastle, 2006) reveals that out of two dozen reported studies, more than 20 followed the derivation-stem procedure. Although a few studies (e.g., Feldman & Soltano, 1999) have reported significant morphological priming when the prime was the stem rather than the derivation (*dark–darkness*) or when both primes and targets were derivations (*darkly–darkness*), in general it is safe to say that such priming effects are not as robust. In Hebrew, on the other hand, the position of the prime and target is of no consequence. Identical effects are obtained whether the prime is a root or a derivation.

The second issue concerns the impact of semantic transparency on morphological priming. In Hebrew, semantic transparency does not modulate priming. Thus, two root derivations such as *targil–meragel* (both derived from the root *RGL*, which conveys the meaning of foot action, the former meaning "exercise," the latter meaning "spy") produce priming effects similar in magnitude to two derivations that are semantically related. The results from English are mixed. Although most studies suggested that masked morphological priming is not modulated by semantic transparency (e.g., Rastle, Davis, & New, 2004) some studies found an opposite trend (e.g., Diependaele et al., 2005; also see Rastle & Davis, in press, for a review). One striking feature of masked morphological priming in English is the facilitation obtained by prime–target pairs such as *brother–BROTH*, which are pseudoderived. It is this finding that is taken as evidence that masked morphological priming effects in English are independent of semantic transparency (e.g., Rastle et al., 2004), in sharp contrast to the Hebrew studies that examined true morphological derivations rather than pseudoderivations. However, it is possible that *brother–BROTH* priming simply reflects a morpho-orthographic automatic parsing procedure characteristic of languages based on the concatenation of highly frequent prefix or suffix bigrams such as *ER* (see Diependaele et al., 2005, and Rastle & Davis, in press, for a discussion).

Are masked morphological priming effects in Hebrew and English different? Since it is difficult to compare different studies in different languages, the most compelling evidence for cross-linguistic differences should come from experiments that employ identical experimental manipulations on bilingual subjects. Such a study was recently conducted in our laboratory. In this experiment Hebrew–English bilingual subjects were presented with an identical morphological priming manipulation in Hebrew and in English. The stimuli in the experiment were 48 prime–target pairs in Hebrew and 48 in English. All pairs were comprised of root or stem primes and derivation targets. For example, the prime *fail* was paired with the target *failure* in the related condition, and *failure* was primed by *lure* in the control condition, a word–prime contained in the target yet not the stem. The priming effect was, thus, determined by the facilitation caused by *fail* relative to that of *lure* for the target *failure*. The stimuli in Hebrew were constructed in the same way. In fact, many of the Hebrew prime–target pairs consisted of actual translations of the English stimuli. For instance, the prime root *KŠL* (meaning "to fail") was followed by the target *kišalon* ("a failure"). In the control condition, the letters of the prime *ŠLO* (meaning "his") were again contained in the target but were not the root morpheme. As in English, the priming effect was determined by the facilitation caused by *KŠL* relative to *ŠLO* for the target *kišalon*. The experiment consisted of two blocks: one with the English stimuli and one with the Hebrew stimuli. Thirty-six Hebrew–English balanced bilinguals participated in the study. The procedure and apparatus were identical to the masked priming experiments reported by Frost et al. (2005) with form priming.

The left side of Table 12.1 presents the morphological priming effects obtained in Hebrew and in English, and the right side of the table summarizes the combined orthographic priming effects reported in Experiments 3a and 3b by Frost

---

TABLE 12.1

The Double Dissociation: Masked Morphological and Masked Orthographic Priming Effects in Hebrew and in English

Condition	Morphological Priming			Orthographic Priming		
	Related	Unrelated	Priming Effect	Related	Unrelated	Priming Effect
Hebrew	540	557	17**	570	578	8 (*ns*)
English	563	573	10 (*ns*)	605	635	30**

Note: Results reported by Frost et al. (2005) and Frost (2006). Subjects are balanced bilinguals.
**$p < .01$.

et al. (2005), both with bilingual subjects. The pattern of results seems straight-forward, demonstrating a double dissociation. Whereas in Hebrew orthographic priming effects were small and unreliable, in English they were significant and robust. In contrast, morphological priming effects in Hebrew were significant and robust, whereas in English they were small and unreliable.

Taken together, these results suggest again that word organization in lexical space of Semitic languages and Indo-European languages is defined by differ-ent principles. In Hebrew, words are organized by root morphemes. Therefore, root priming produces significant facilitation, whereas orthographic priming does not. Conversely, words in English are aligned in lexical space by orthographic similarity. As a result, form priming is robust and masked morphological priming appears to be more fragile.

PROCESSING MORPHOLOGICAL INFORMATION IN THE PARAFOVEA

The evidence reported so far for early morphological decomposition is based on prim-ing under masked presentations. The masked-priming paradigm is particularly useful for exploring early processes of word recognition because the brief presentation of the prime combined with forward and backward masking prevents the full conscious identification of the prime. Consequently, the priming effect obtained in this proce-dure is not influenced by the participants' appreciation of the prime–target morpho-logical or orthographic relation, as is the case with some long-term priming effects.

Recently, converging evidence for morphological decomposition was obtained in Hebrew by measuring preview benefit effects induced by presenting morpho-logical information in the parafovea. This procedure measures how the informa-tion extracted from a word before the eyes land on it affects the identification of that word. This information is considered parafoveal because it is typically about 5 to 10 characters from fixation and, thus, is near, but not in, the foveal region. A large body of research on eye movements in reading (see Rayner, 1998, for a review) has revealed that although the perceptual span from which readers extract information is small, it is not restricted to the fixated word, and readers can extract information from the next word or two as well. The common finding (in languages written from left to right) is that reading is significantly slowed if the parafoveal information about the word to the right of the fixated word is withheld. A detailed assessment of the benefit from a parafoveal preview can be provided using the boundary technique (Rayner, 1975). This technique involves rapidly changing a single word during the saccade in which the eyes move to fixate the word. The display change is triggered when the eyes cross an invisible boundary just prior to the target word. When preview benefit is assessed during sentence reading, the fixation time on the target word is the primary dependent measure. Thus, participants are not required to perform any external task aside from naturally reading the text.

An important feature of the boundary technique is that readers are virtually unaware of the display change and are also unable to identify the stimulus in the parafovea. Nevertheless, the parafoveal information is apparently integrated with the subsequent activation of the foveal word, as parafoveal information was found to facilitate the identification of the foveal target word (Rayner, McConkie, & Zola, 1980). Using the boundary technique, it has been shown that both orthographic (Inhoff, 1989; Rayner, Well, Pollatsek, & Bertera, 1982) and phonological information (Henderson, Dixon, Peterson, Twilley, & Ferreira, 1995; Pollatsek, Lesch, Morris, & Rayner, 1992) are extracted from the parafovea. The explanation for parafoveal benefit resembles the one for masked priming effects: Information extracted from the parafovea leads to partial activation of the lexicon, and this activation is integrated with the later activation caused by the processing of the foveal word (Rayner, 1998; see Forster & Davis, 1984, for masked priming).

Interestingly, only a few studies have manipulated morphological factors in the parafovea while measuring preview effects in English (Inhoff, 1989; Kambe, 2004; Lima, 1987; Rayner, Juhasz, White, & Liversedge, 2007). These studies used previews that shared a morpheme with the target word. The overall pattern of results obtained from studies in English is consistent: No greater benefit from morphologically related previews was found relative to control previews that shared as many letters with the target (in the same positions) as the morphemic previews. These findings do not converge with morphological priming effects found in English under masked presentation, as previously described.

What about Hebrew? Using a manipulation similar to the English studies, Deutsch, Frost, Pollatsek, and Rayner (2000) examined parafoveal preview benefit effects in Hebrew, focusing on morphological relatedness between previews and targets. The results showed that lexical decisions for root derivation targets were facilitated when the root letters were presented in the parafovea, relative to a control condition in which three other letters were presented parafoveally. Figure 12.1 illustrates an example of the preview manipulation in Hebrew. The parafoveal stimulus is the root ברש BRŠ ("to brush"). While the eye crosses the invisible boundary, the parafoveal stimulus is replaced by the target word מברשת MBRŠT ("a brush").

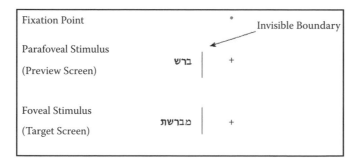

FIGURE 12.1 The parafoveal preview benefit paradigm. Example of the stimuli employed by Deutsch et al. (2000).

TABLE 12.2
Parafoveal Preview Benefit Effects with Morphologically Related Preview

	Morphological Preview	Orthographic Control
Deutsch et al. (2000), Lexical decision latencies	566 15 ms**	581
Deutsch et al. (2003), First fixation in milliseconds	226 12 ms**	238
Deutsch et al. (2003), Gaze duration in milliseconds	267 12 ms**	279

Note: Results reported by Deutsch et al. (2000) monitoring lexical decisions, and by Deutsch et al.
        (2003) monitoring first fixation and gaze duration during sentence reading.
**$p < .01$.

In a subsequent study, Deutsch, Frost, Peleg, Pollatsek, and Rayner (2003) examined sentence processing rather than single word identification. The measure employed in this study was *gaze duration*, the sum of the durations of all fixations made on a target word from the first time the reader's eyes land on the word until the eyes move to preceding or following parts of the sentence. Deutsch and her colleagues demonstrated that a preview of a word derived from the same root morpheme as the foveal target word shortened processing of the target word, compared to a preview that was as orthographically similar to the target as the morphemic preview.

Taken together, these studies stand in sharp contrast to results obtained in English. The results suggest that morphological information is extracted from the parafovea in the initial phases of word recognition in Hebrew. The target of this search is the root (although some facilitation was recently demonstrated for verbal word patterns as well; Deutsch, Frost, Pollatsek, & Rayner, 2005). In other words, whereas English readers seem to simply register the orthographic structure of words in the parafovea, Hebrew readers seem to engage in extensive morphological processing, including searching for the root information. The findings using parafoveal presentation, therefore, provide additional support for the structural-ecological view.

THE IMPACT OF LETTER TRANSPOSITION

In recent years, several studies have consistently reported robust form-orthographic priming effects when primes and targets shared the identity of individual letters but in a different order (e.g., *gadren* priming *garden*; Perea & Lupker, 2003; Schoonbaert & Grainger, 2004; for a discussion, Grainger & Van Heuven, 2003). Masked priming with transposed letters was reported in several Indo-European languages including English (e.g., Lupker & Perea, 2003), French (Schoonbaert & Grainger, 2004), and Spanish (Perea & Lupker, 2004). The finding that robust form-orthographic priming can be obtained even with changes in letter order has revolutionized the modeling of visual word recognition. It presented immense difficulties for slot-based coding computational models, which encode letter position in absolute terms (e.g., the interactive activation [IA] model by McClelland & Rumelhart, 1981, or the dual-route cascaded [DRC] model by Coltheart, Rastle, Perry, Langdon, & Ziegler, 2001). Consequently, a new generation of computational models that focus on context-sensitive coding of relative letter position has emerged (e.g., Grainger & Van Heuven, 2003; Grainger & Whitney, 2004; Whitney, 2001; see Schoonbaert & Grainger, 2004, for a discussion). For example, to account for the letter transposition effect, Grainger and Whitney have offered a new approach to letter position coding that is based on "open bigram" units (Grainger & Whitney, 2004; Whitney, 2001). Open bigrams do not contain precise information about which letter is adjacent to which (i.e., contiguity), meaning the word *FORM*, for example, would be represented by activation of the bigram units *FO, FR, OR, OM*, and *RM*. A transposition prime, such as *from*, would then share all but one of these units, namely *FR, FO, RM,* and *OM*.

Perhaps the most dramatic demonstration of how reading is resilient to letter transposition in Indo-European languages is a paragraph that has been circulating via the Internet, especially in the reading research community. The paragraph alluded to some fictitious research conducted at Cambridge University effectively demonstrating a puzzling phenomenon: the text could be read without much difficulty despite the fact that almost every word included letter-transpositions: "Aoccdrnig to rscheearch at Cmabrigde Uinervtisy, it deosn't mttaer in waht oredr the ltteers in a wrod are, the olny iprmoetnt tihng is taht the frist and lsat ltteer be at the rghit pclae ...." The phenomenon has been labeled the "Cambridge University effect," and since its first appearance in 2003, it has become somewhat of an urban legend. The English text has since been translated into French, Spanish, Italian, Dutch, German, Danish, Finnish, Icelandic, Portuguese, Swedish, Russian, Hungarian, Irish, Polish, and Albanian. A recent study monitoring eye movements showed that although some transpositions pose some difficulty, others are pretty easy to read (Rayner, White, Johnson, & Liversedge, 2006).

How would letter transpositions affect reading in Hebrew? The structural-ecological view has clear predictions: If lexical access in Hebrew is indeed based on a preliminary search of a triliteral root entry, then the sensitivity of Hebrew readers to letter transposition may be significantly increased relative to readers of Indo-European languages. The a priori support for such a hypothesis is based on simple combinatorial arguments. The Hebrew language has a listing of about 3,000 triconsonantal roots (Ornan, 2003), which are represented by the 22 letters of the alphabet. The immediate combinatorial implication is that many roots have to share the same set of three consonants (or letters) but in a different order. For example, the letter order of the root Š.L.X ("to send") can be altered to produce the root X.L.Š ("to dominate"), X.Š.L ("to toughen"), and L.X.Š ("to whisper"). In fact, one can hardly find a triconsonantal root that does not share its set of three letters with other roots. If lexical access in Hebrew requires the identification of a specific root, then letter order is critical, and the processing system should not be able to tolerate transpositions involving root letters. This is because all derivations of X.Š.L, for example, need to be differentiated from those of Š.L.X, L.X.Š, and X.Š.L. If this hypothesis is correct, the Cambridge University effect will not work in a Semitic language such as Hebrew. The effect could then be taken to reflect the specific characteristics of Indo-European languages, rather than a general property of the visual processing of words in alphabetic orthographies.

Velan and Frost (2007) investigated this intriguing possibility by examining reading performance of Hebrew–English bilinguals, using rapid serial visual presentation (RSVP; see Potter, 1984). In this study, 28 Hebrew–English balanced bilinguals were presented with 20 sentences in English and 20 in Hebrew, 10 of which had transposed-letter words and 10 of which were intact. The sentences were presented on the screen word by word, and each word appeared for 200 ms. Following the final word, subjects had to vocally produce the entire sentence. The aim of the experiment was to measure the relative level of performance in Hebrew and in English on sentences that involved the transposition of letters and to compare these with the presentation of the intact sentences. Velan and Frost also examined whether the subjects were at all aware of the transposition manipulation in each language, given the rapid presentation of words on the screen.

The results of Velan and Frost (2007) are presented in Figure 12.2. The figure demonstrates a marked difference in the effect of letter transposition in the two languages. For English materials, the report of words was virtually unaltered when sentences included words with transposed letters. Moreover, Velan and Frost found that subjects were virtually unaware of the transposition manipulation. For about one-third of their subjects, detection of transpositions in English materials was at chance level. Measuring the sensitivity of subjects to the transposition manipulation, d', detecting transpositions for English material was found to be relatively low, about 0.86. This finding seems to converge with recent results reporting strong masked-priming effects with transposed letters. The striking feature of Figure 12.2, however, is the contrast with Hebrew. The correct report of Hebrew words dropped

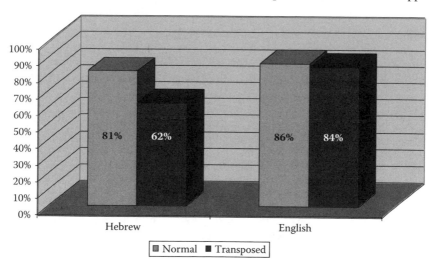

FIGURE 12.2   Effects of letter transposition in Hebrew and in English using rapid serial visual presentation. Data from Velan and Frost (2007).

dramatically in sentences containing transpositions, from 81% correct to 62% correct. Also, for the Hebrew material, detection of transposition was immediate, and d' values were exceedingly high, about 2.51. Since the participants in the present study were bilingual subjects in a within-subject design, the difference between the Hebrew and the English blocks can only be attributed to a linguistic factor and not to experimental procedures or to individual differences between the speakers of the two languages. Moreover, as performance in English and in Hebrew was very similar with normal sentences, the poor performance with transposed stimuli cannot be attributed to content complexity; rather, this reflects a genuine difference in sensitivity to transposition in the two languages.

What then is the source of the dramatic cross-linguistic differences in the impact of letter transposition on reading? Similar to the previous experimental manipulations, the effects of letter transposition probably reflect the principles of how lexical space is defined and organized and do not emerge from the peripheral registering of letters in alphabetic orthographies. If lexical access in a language such as Hebrew indeed requires the correct identification of a specific root morpheme and many roots share the same set of letters, the primary task of the lexical system is to determine the exact identity and order of letters constituting the root morpheme. Root-letter transpositions will, therefore, prevent the processing system from extracting the correct root identity necessary for the lexical search. This would produce genuine differences in sensitivity to letter transpositions in Hebrew, when compared with English. Thus, whereas readers of English seem to display some "blindness" to transpositions in RSVP, readers of Hebrew seem to display extreme difficulties in reading transposed text. Thus, the dramatic difference in the impact of letter transposition in English and in Hebrew provides additional support for the structural-ecological view.

EVIDENCE FROM READING DISORDERS

The final argument in support of the structural-ecological view concerns converging evidence from reading disorders in Hebrew. The question is whether the morphological constraint on lexical structure in Hebrew can be demonstrated in some specific forms of dyslexia that are characteristic to Hebrew readers only. Bearing in mind the impact of letter transposition, the possible relevant disorders to consider are those related to the visual processing of printed words, especially those related to the encoding of letter position. According to Ellis and Young (1988), three distinct functions are relevant to peripheral disorders related to visual analysis of print: letter identification, letter-to-word binding, and encoding of letter position. The first two concern letter agnosia (e.g., Marshall & Newcombe, 1973) and letter migration problems (e.g., Shallice & Warrington, 1977), which are characteristic of any alphabetic orthography. The third dysfunction, however, may have immediate relevance to reading Hebrew. The question is whether it is possible to demonstrate a *selective* impairment related only to the positions of letters, and, if so, whether readers of Hebrew would be more affected by it than readers of English.

The answer to both questions seems to be positive. Friedmann and Gvion (2001, 2005) have reported two cases of Hebrew-speaking acquired dyslexic patients with left parieto-occipital damage (BS, 75 years old, with ischemic infarct; and PY, 70 years old, with a lesion following tumor removal), who both had intact letter identification and intact binding of letters to words but a deficit in the positioning of letters within a word. The deficit was hence labeled *letter position dyslexia* (LPD). Interestingly, as Friedmann and her colleagues suggested, pure cases of LPD were never reported in Indo-European languages. Recently, Friedmann and Rahamim (in press) reported 11 cases of developmental LPD, again, a selective deficit of letter position within words, without letter identity errors or word migration errors and without phonemic awareness deficit or output deficit. All of these cases involve Hebrew speakers. Why then is LPD more prevalent in Hebrew? Considering, the characteristics of LPD, the answer seems straightforward. First, errors in LPD occur almost exclusively in the middle letters so that initial and final letters remain in their original position. Second, the LPD patients reported by Friedmann and her colleagues tended to naturally search for a lexical candidate and to produce words. Consequently, errors occurred mainly in "migratable" words, when transpositions produce another lexical candidate— another word. What is then the main difference between Hebrew and English? First, because in Hebrew most vowels are not represented in print, on average, words are shorter than in English and each word has many orthographic neighbors. Second, because of the combinatorial aspect of root letters, letter transpositions would in all probability result in an existing word. Thus, in English, patients who suffer from a dysfunction related to letter position encoding perform quite well, like normal readers would perform when reading a text with jumbled letters. Most texts would appear to them as the text implicated in the Cambridge University effect. As we found with normal subjects, reading of transposed letters in English does not significantly hinder performance. In contrast, in Hebrew, letter transpositions have dramatic impact on reading. Patients who suffer from LPD would then show a marked deficit. Since migratable words are the rule in Hebrew, LPD is instantly detected. Patients do not simply "recover" from transposition and "fix" the correct letter order; rather, they produce another word derived from a root that has the same letter cluster but with a different sequence. In English, migratable words such as *clam–calm* are the exception, not the rule. Thus, it is more difficult to diagnose LPD in English, and the dysfunction related to letter order is often covert.

SUMMARY AND CONCLUSIONS

The present discussion raises a fundamental question in visual word recognition: Could there be a qualitative difference in the principles of lexical organization and visual word recognition processes in different alphabetic orthographies? The empirical evidence reviewed here covers a variety of experimental paradigms that were employed in English, an Indo-European language, and in Hebrew, a Semitic language. First, when masked orthographic and masked morphological priming effects are compared, a double dissociation emerges, and Hebrew and English seem to present opposite results: unconstrained morphological priming and weak orthographic priming effects in Hebrew versus constrained morphological priming and robust orthographic priming in English. Second, converging evidence is provided by comparing parafoveal preview benefits in these two languages. Strong morphological preview effects are consistently obtained in Hebrew, yet these are not found in English. Third, a marked difference in the effects of letter transposition is found in these two languages. Whereas reading in English seems almost unaffected by jumbled letters, reading in Hebrew is seriously hindered. Finally, reading disorders, such as letter-position dyslexia, are prevalent in Hebrew but not in English.

Taken together, these findings seem to reveal a qualitative difference between Hebrew and English, suggesting that their respective lexical spaces are defined according to different principles: In English, lexical space is defined according to linear alphabetic constraints, whereas in Hebrew it is defined according to root morphemes. How to implement these cross-linguistic differences in current models of visual word recognition necessarily depends on the type of model chosen. For example, in attractor-based models (Rueckl, 2002), the position of attractors in lexical space would be determined by all of the letters in Indo-European languages, but only by the root letters in Hebrew. In practical terms, this would mean that for English, words are aligned in lexical space taking their full sequence of letters into account, whereas for Hebrew, all words derived from a given root would presumably be clustered together. An active search model, such as the entry-opening model (Forster, 1999; Forster & Davis, 1984), would need to propose that in English, allocation of words into bins is based on orthographic neighborhoods, whereas in Hebrew, the grouping of entries into bins would be based on the root letters only. Hence, all words that contain the same root letters would be located in the same bin. But note that whatever type of model is chosen, it seems evident that the processing of print would necessarily reflect the structural differences between Hebrew and English. Findings from beginner and skilled readers indeed show interplay between a computational process that involves letter-by-letter units, along with a parallel computational process that involves the search for morphemic units (see Frost, 2006, for a discussion). Subsequently, the comparison of English and Hebrew demonstrates that linguistic considerations should be the main source of constraints on any theory of lexical organization. This is the essence of the structural-ecological view.

NOTE

1. I am indebted to Marc Brysbaert who provided an extensive and illuminating review of masked form-priming effects in an unpublished manuscript.

REFERENCES

Badecker, W., & Allen, M. (2002). Morphological parsing and the perception of lexical identity: A masked priming study of stem homographs. *Journal of Memory and Language, 47*, 125–144.

Brysbaert, M., & Rastle, K. (2009). *Are form priming and morphological priming different for Hebrew than for Indo-European languages? Not if you look at the evidence*. Unpublished manuscript.

Chateau, D., & Jared, D. (2000). Exposure to print and word recognition processes. *Memory & Cognition, 28*, 143–153.

Coltheart, M., Davelaar, E., Jonasson, J. T., & Besner, D. (1977). Access to the mental lexicon. In S. Dornic (Ed.), *Attention and performance VI* (pp. 535–555). London: Academic Press.

Coltheart, M., Rastle, K., Perry, C., Langdon, R., & Zeigler, J. (2001). A dual route cascaded model of visual word recognition and reading aloud. *Psychological Review, 108*, 204–256.

Davis, C. J., & Lupker, S. J. (2006). Masked inhibitory priming in English: Evidence for lexical inhibition. *Journal of Experimental Psychology: Human Perception and Performance, 32*, 668–687.

Deutsch, A., Frost, R., & Forster, K. I. (1998). Verbs and nouns are organized and accessed differently in the mental lexicon: Evidence from Hebrew. *Journal of Experimental Psychology: Learning, Memory, and Cognition, 24*, 1238–1255.

Deutsch, A., Frost, R., Peleg, S., Pollatsek, A., & Rayner, K. (2003). Early morphological effects in reading: Evidence from parafoveal preview benefit in Hebrew. *Psychonomic Bulletin & Review, 10*, 415–422.

Deutsch A, Frost, R., Pollatsek A., & Rayner, K. (2000). Early morphological effects in word recognition in Hebrew: Evidence from parafoveal preview benefit. *Language and Cognitive Processes, 15*, 487–506.

Deutsch, A., Frost, R., Pollatsek, A., & Rayner, K. (2005). Morphological parafoveal preview benefit effects in reading: Evidence from Hebrew. *Language and Cognitive Processes, 20*, 341–371.

Diependaele, K., Sandra, D., & Grainger, J. (2005). Masked cross-modal morphological priming: Unravelling morpho-orthographic and morpho-semantic influences in early word recognition. *Language and Cognitive Processes, 20*, 75–114.

Ellis, A. W., & Young, A. W. (1988). *Human cognitive neuropsychology*. Hove, UK: Lawrence Erlbaum Associates.

Feldman, L. B., & Soltano, E. G. (1999). Morphological priming: The role of prime duration, semantic transparency, and affix position. *Brain and Language, 68*, 33–39.

Ferrand, L., & Grainger, J. (1992). Phonology and orthography in visual word recognition: Evidence from masked nonword priming. *Quarterly Journal of Experimental Psychology, 45A*, 353–372.

Forster, K. I. (1999). The microgenesis of priming effect in lexical access. *Brain and Language, 68*, 5–15.

Forster, K. I., & Davis, C. (1984). Repetition priming and frequency attenuation in lexical access. *Journal of Experimental Psychology: Learning, Memory, and Cognition, 10*, 680–698.

Forster, K. I., & Taft, M. (1994). Bodies, antibodies, and neighborhood-density effects in masked form priming. *Journal of Experimental Psychology: Learning, Memory, and Cognition, 20*, 844–863.

Friedmann, N., & Gvion, A. (2001). Letter position dyslexia. *Cognitive Neuropsychology, 18*(8), 673–696.

Friedmann, N., & Gvion, A. (2005). Letter form as a constraint for errors in neglect dyslexia and letter position dyslexia. *Behavioral Neurology, 16*(2-3), 145–158.

Friedmann, N., & Rahamim, E. (2007). Developmental letter position dyslexia. *Journal of Neuropsychology, 1*, 201-236.

Frost, R. (1994). Prelexical and postlexical strategies in reading: Evidence from a deep and a shallow orthography. *Journal of Experimental Psychology: Learning, Memory, and Cognition, 20,* 116–129.

Frost, R. (1995). Phonological computation and missing vowels: Mapping lexical involvement in reading. *Journal of Experimental Psychology: Learning, Memory, and Cognition, 21,* 398–408.

Frost, R. (1998). Towards a strong phonological theory of visual word recognition: True issues and false trails. *Psychological Bulletin, 123,* 71–99.

Frost, R. (2006). Becoming literate in Hebrew: The grain-size hypothesis and Semitic orthographic systems. *Developmental Science, 9*(5), 439–444.

Frost, R., Deutsch, A., & Forster, K. I. (2000). Decomposing complex words in a nonlinear morphology. *Journal of Experimental Psychology: Learning, Memory, and Cognition, 26,* 751–765.

Frost, R., Deutsch, A, Gilboa, O., Tannenbaum M., & Marslen-Wilson, W. D. (2000). Morphological priming: Dissociation of phonological, semantic, and morphological factors. *Memory & Cognition, 28,* 1277–1288.

Frost, R., Forster, K. I., & Deutsch, A. (1997). What can we learn from the morphology of Hebrew: A masked priming investigation of morphological representation. *Journal of Experimental Psychology: Learning Memory, and Cognition, 23,* 829–856.

Frost, R., Katz, L., & Bentin, S. (1987). Strategies for visual word recognition and orthographical depth: A multilingual comparison. *Journal of Experimental Psychology: Human Perception and Performance, 13*(1), 104–115.

Frost, R., Kugler, T., Deutsch, A., & Forster, K. I. (2005). Orthographic structure versus morphological structure: Principles of lexical organisation in a given language. *Journal of Experimental Psychology: Learning, Memory, and Cognition, 31,* 1293–1326.

Grainger, J., & Van Heuven, W. J. B (2003). Modeling letter position coding in printed word perception. In P. Bonin (Ed.), *The mental lexicon* (pp. 1–23). New York: Nova Science.

Grainger, J., & Whitney, C. (2004). Does the huamn mnid raed words as a whole? *Trends in Cognitive Sciences, 8,* 58–59.

Henderson, J. M., Dixon, P., Peterson, A., Twilley, L. C., & Ferreira, F. (1995). Evidence for the use of phonological representation during transaccadic word recognition. *Journal of Experimental Psychology: Human Perception and Performance, 21,* 82–97.

Holyk, G. G., & Pexman, P. M. (2004). The elusive nature of early phonological priming effects: Are there individual differences? *Brain and Language, 90,* 353–367.

Inhoff, A. W. (1989). Parafoveal processing of words and saccade computation during eye fixations in reading. *Journal of Experimental Psychology: Human Perception and Performance, 15,* 544–555.

Kambe, G. (2004). Parafoveal processing of prefixed words during eye fixations in reading: Evidence against morphological influences on parafoveal preprocessing. *Perception & Psychophysics, 66*(2), 279–292.

Katz, L., & Frost, R. (1992). Reading in different orthographies: The orthographic depth hypothesis. In R. Frost & L. Katz (Eds.), *Orthography, phonology, morphology, and meaning* (pp. 67–84). Holland: Elsevier.

Lima, S. D. (1987). Morphological analysis in sentence reading. *Journal of Memory and Language, 26,* 84–99.

Longtin, C. M., Segui, J., & Halle, P. A. (2003). Morphological priming without morphological relationship. *Language and Cognitive Processes, 18,* 313–334.

Lupker, S., & Perea, M. (2003). Transposed-letter confusability effects in masked form priming. In S. Kinoshita & S. J. Lupker (Eds.), *Masked priming: State of the art* (pp. 97–120). Hove, UK: Psychology Press.

Marshall, J. C., & Newcombe, F. (1973). Patterns of paralexia: Psycholinguistic approach. *Journal of Psycholinguistic Research, 2*(3), 175–199.

McClelland, J. L., & Rumelhart, D. E. (1981). An interactive activation model of context effects in letter perception: Part 1. An account of basic findings. *Psychological Review, 88*, 375–407.

Ornan, U. (2003). *The final word: Mechanism for Hebrew word deneration* [in Hebrew]. Haifa, Israel: Haifa University Press.

Perea, M., & Lupker, S. J. (2003). Does *judge* activate *court*? Transposed-letter similarity effects in masked associative priming. *Memory & Cognition, 31*(6), 829–841.

Perea, M., & Lupker, S. J. (2004). Can CANISO activate CASINO? Transposed-letter similarity effects with nonadjacent letter positions. *Journal of Memory and Language, 51*, 231–246.

Perea, M., & Rosa, E. (2000). Repetition and form priming interact with neighbourhood density at a brief stimulus onset asynchrony. *Psychonomic Bulletin & Review, 7*, 668–677.

Pollatsek, A., Lesch, M., Morris, R. K., & Rayner, K. (1992). Phonological codes are used in integrating information across saccades in word identification and reading. *Journal of Experimental Psychology: Human Perception and Performance, 18*, 148–162.

Potter, M. C. (1984). Rapid serial visual presentation (RSVP): A method for studying language processing. In D. E. Kieras & M. A. Just (Eds.), *New methods in reading comprehension research* (pp. 91–118). Hillsdale, NJ: Erlbaum.

Rastle, K., & Davis, M. H. (2003). Reading morphologically-complex words: Some thoughts from masked priming. In S. Kinoshita & S. J. Lupker (Eds.), *Masked priming: The state of the art* (pp. 279–305). Hove, UK: Psychology Press.

Rastle, K., & Davis, M. H. (in press). Morphological decomposition based on the analysis of orthography. *Language and Cognitive Processes.*

Rastle, K., Davis, M. H., & New, B. (2004). The broth in my brother's brothel: Morpho-orthographic segmentation in visual word recognition. *Psychonomic Bulletin & Review, 11*, 1090–1098.

Rayner, K. (1975). The perceptual span and peripheral cues in reading. *Cognitive Psychology, 7*, 65–81.

Rayner, K. (1998). Eye movements in reading and information processing: 20 years of research. *Psychological Bulletin, 124*, 372–422.

Rayner, K., Juhasz, B. J., White, S. J., & Liversedge, S. P. (2007, June). *Does morphological processing in the parafovea influence eye movements in reading?* Paper presented at the 5th workshop on morphological processing, Marseille, France.

Rayner, K., McConkie, G. W., & Zola, D. (1980). Integrating information across eye movements. *Cognitive Psychology, 12*, 206–226.

Rayner, K., Well, A. D., Pollatsek, A., & Bertera, J. H. (1982). The availability of useful information to the right of fixation in reading. *Perception & Psychophysics, 31*, 537–550.

Rayner, K., White, S. J., Johnson, R. L., & Liversedge, S. P. (2006). Raeding wrods with jubmled lettrs: There's a cost. *Psychological Science, 17*, 192–193.

Rueckl, J. (2002). The dynamics of visual word recognition. *Ecological Psychology, 14*, 5–19.

Schoonbaert, S., & Grainger, J. (2004). Letter position coding in printed word perception effects of repeated and transposed letters. *Language and Cognitive Processes, 19*, 333–367.

Segui, J., & Grainger, J. (1990). Priming word recognition with orthographic neighbors: Effects of relative prime target frequency. *Journal of Experimental Psychology: Human Perception and Performance, 16*, 65–76.

Seidenberg, M. S., MacDonald, M. C., & Saffran, J. R. (2003). Are there limits to statistical learning? *Science, 300*, 51–52.

Shallice, T., & Warrington, E. K. (1977). The possible role of selective attention in acquired dyslexia. *Neuropsychologia, 15*(1), 31–41.

Van Heuven, W. J. B., Dijkstra, T., Grainger, J., & Schriefers, H. (2001). Shared neighborhood effects in masked orthographic priming. *Psychonomic Bulletin & Review, 8*, 96–101.

Velan, H., & Frost, R. (2007). Cambridge University vs. Hebrew University: The impact of letter transposition on reading English and Hebrew. *Psychonomic Bulletin & Review, 14*, 913–918.

Whitney, C. (2001). How the brain encodes the order of letters in a printed word: The SERIOL model and selective literature review. *Psychonomic Bulletin & Review, 8*, 221–243.

Ziegler, J. C., & Perry, C. (1998). No more problems in Coltheart's neighborhood: Resolving neighborhood conflicts in the lexical decision task. *Cognition, 68*, 53–62.

Section IV

Intervention

13 Reading Remediation
State of the Art

Barbara Foorman and Stephanie Al Otaiba

The state of the art in reading remediation is prevention and early intervention. The word-recognition skills of students with identified reading disabilities can be normalized with effective interventions. However, normalizing the fluency and comprehension skills of these students has proven extremely difficult. Because of the difficulty of remediating older students and the relative success of early intervention efforts, policy in the United States has shifted to encourage prevention. Under the Individuals with Disabilities Educational Improvement Act of 2004, districts are allowed to use up to 15% of special education funds for prevention and early intervention. This shift in federal law allows districts to use funds to provide intervention to struggling readers *before* they fail to meet grade-level achievement standards. In addition, the new law provides an alternative to the previous requirement that a student's low achievement be unexpected (i.e., discrepant) relative to their intelligence in order to qualify them for special education services. The alternative approach, called response to intervention (RTI), means that a local education agency "may use a process that determines if the child responds to scientific, research-based intervention as a part of the evaluation procedures" (Pub. L. No. 108-446 § 614 [b][6][A]; § 614 [b] [2 & 3]).

In this chapter we will review the evidence for effective reading interventions. First, we will look at landmark studies that focus on classroom prevention, early intervention, or remedial intervention. Second, we will describe other intervention studies, including ones involving community volunteers, to distill characteristics necessary and sufficient for positive student response. Finally, we will reflect on the promise of implementing an RTI model in schools.

LANDMARK INTERVENTION STUDIES

We will describe the landmark studies of (a) Foorman and colleagues, (b) Vellutino and colleagues, and (c) Torgesen and colleagues that examined effective classroom instruction and the duration and intensity of treatment protocols needed to remediate students with reading disabilities. First, however, we need to acknowledge the prior work on effective schools during the 1980s and comprehensive school reform during the 1990s that described the systemic characteristics of successful schools.

A reform model that made the reduction of the number of students in special education a central goal was Success for All (SFA; Slavin & Madden, 2001).

Building on the finding of the early 1980s that increasing time on task was crucial to increasing achievement (Stallings, 1980), school reform models such as SFA and direct instruction (Carnine, Silbert, & Kameenui, 1997), extended time for classroom reading instruction, and added additional small group or tutorial practice for struggling readers. These layers of instruction were seen as instrumental to the effectiveness of these models (Borman, Hewes, Overman, & Brown, 2003). Several publications have described characteristics of "beat the odds" schools—schools that score highly on state accountability tests in spite of high minority enrollment and high free and reduced lunch participation—and extended time for reading instruction is central (Denton, Foorman, & Mathes, 2003; Taylor, Pearson, Clark, & Walpole, 2000). Other important characteristics of these schools are strong instructional leadership, positive climate, strong accountability, ongoing professional development based on demonstrably effective reading strategies, continuous monitoring of student learning, and involved parents and decision-making teams.

FOORMAN AND COLLEAGUES

More than 36% of fourth graders and 27% of eighth graders performed below basic on the reading portion of the National Assessment of Educational Progress (NAEP; National Center for Education Statistics, 2005). Percentages for minority students are even higher (e.g., 58% of Blacks and 54% of Hispanics at fourth grade performed below basic). The national percentage for students with reading disabilities from epidemiological studies is approximately 17.5% (Shaywitz, Fletcher, & Shaywitz, 1995). With such a high proportion of students reading below grade level and, therefore, candidates for reading remediation, the obvious policy question is this: How can public schools afford to tutor so many students? Obviously, the cheapest solution is prevention. Improve classroom reading instruction, reduce the numbers needing remediation.

The 1998 study by Foorman, Francis, Fletcher, Schatschneider, and Mehta addressed this crucial policy question of whether classroom reading instruction could reduce the numbers of students at risk for reading failure. They hypothesized that explicitness of instruction in the alphabetic principle would predict growth in word reading and reading comprehension in 285 first and second graders in 66 classrooms in eight Title I schools. Teachers in these schools used one of three experimental approaches to classroom reading instruction, with at least two approaches in any one school: direct instruction in sequenced, letter–sound correspondences practiced in decodable text (direct code; Open Court Reading, 1995); less explicit instruction in sound–spelling patterns embedded in trade books (embedded phonics; Hiebert, Colt, Catto, & Gury, 1992); and implicit, incidental instruction of the alphabetic principle while reading trade books (implicit code; e.g., Weaver, 1994). All three approaches included instruction in reading comprehension and the language arts. What differed was that the direct and embedded approaches emphasized decontextualized phonics instruction, with the former providing more explicit instruction and practice in phonics. Teachers in all three experimental approaches received professional development and ongoing support, and fidelity of implementation was high. All three approaches were contrasted with standard instruction in the school district, which was implicit.

Growth curve analyses, with students nested within teachers, were conducted on literacy data collected four times across the school year. Students in the direct code group improved at a faster rate in word reading, spelling, and phonological awareness, compared to students in the implicit group. The means for students in the embedded phonics group were between those of the other two groups. In addition, the relationship between phonological awareness and word reading was stronger for students in the direct code group compared to those in the implicit code group, suggesting that effects of explicit instruction in the alphabetic principle on word reading emanated from its effects on phonological awareness. At the end of the year, 35% of these Title I students remained below the 30th percentile in word recognition. These students represented the bottom-achieving 18% of students in the eight participating schools. By multiplying 35% times 18%, the figure of 5% to 6% is obtained to represent the percent of students in the overall population that would remain poor readers based on widespread implementation of this classroom intervention.

The fact that a child characteristic such as initial phonological awareness interacts with instruction in determining effectiveness is reminiscent of aptitude-treatment interactions evident throughout the history of educational research. The idea that child-by-instruction interactions can be used to differentiate instruction for individual students is, however, a new concept, fueled in part by new statistical techniques for modeling multilevel relationships between students, teachers, and schools. For example, research by Foorman and colleagues (2006) and Connor and colleagues (Connor, Morrison, & Katch, 2004; Connor, Morrison, & Slominski, 2006) found that effective teachers allocated time to instructional activities differentially, depending on students' initial skills. By providing teachers with software that inputs students' initial skills and outputs recommended time allocations, differentiating instruction can become a more scientific process (e.g., Connor, Morrison, Fishman, Schatschneider, & Underwood, 2007).

VELLUTINO AND COLLEAGUES

In the Vellutino et al. (1996) study, 118 children from middle- and upper-class homes whose pseudoword and word reading scores were in the bottom 15th percentile received one-on-one tutoring 30 minutes daily for 15 weeks in the spring of first grade. Those children whose scores were below the 40th percentile at the end of first grade received an additional 8 to 10 weeks of tutoring in second grade. Thus, the amount of tutoring ranged from 35–65 hours. The intervention was adapted to individual student's needs and consisted of phonemic awareness, decoding, sight word practice, comprehension strategies, and text reading and writing. After one semester, 67% of the students were reading on grade level. A reading failure rate for those reading below the 26th percentile was 1.5% of the population if only severely impaired readers were included and 3% of the population if moderately impaired readers were included as well.

In a follow-up evaluation through fourth grade, Vellutino et al. (2003) compared the skill development of normal readers to poor readers who varied in how difficult they were to remediate. What differentiated the most difficult to remediate poor readers was their poor performance on phonological measures. They did not differ on semantic, syntactic, or visual measures, although all poor readers tended to perform below the normal readers on these measures as well as on most phonological measures.

TORGESEN AND COLLEAGUES

The work of Torgesen and colleagues is relevant to the question of whether earlier and longer intervention can further reduce the percentage of difficult to remediate students (Torgesen et al., 1999). They compared the effects of three intensive one-on-one interventions on decoding and comprehension skills of beginning readers that varied in socioeconomic status and ethnicity (53% minority). Students were identified in kindergarten based on low scores in letter names and phonological awareness. The 180 students in the participating sample were randomly assigned to four conditions: (a) *phonological awareness training plus synthetic phonics* (PASP), which consisted of explicit instruction in phonological awareness using articulatory cues plus extensive practice in decontextualized phonetic decoding; (b) *embedded phonics* (EP), which also consisted of instruction in explicit phonics but placed more emphasis on practice in reading and writing connected text and on acquisition of sight words; (c) *regular classroom support* (RCS), which consisted of tutorial assistance for the reading instruction provided in the regular classroom; and (d) a no-treatment control group. Students in each instructional condition received one-on-one tutoring for 20 minutes daily, 4 days a week, for 2½ years, beginning in the second half of kindergarten. Half the sessions were led by well-trained teachers, half by less well-trained paraprofessionals. Over the duration of the tutorials, students received an average of 47 hours from teachers and 41 hours from paraprofessionals.

Torgesen et al. (1999) found that at the end of the year, the PASP group significantly outperformed the other groups on phonemic decoding. On word reading, the PASP group significantly outperformed the control group and the RCS group. On spelling, the PASP group outperformed the control group. There were no differences between groups in reading comprehension. At the end of grade 2, students in the PASP program had significantly stronger word reading skills (i.e., in the middle of the average range) than students who received no intervention. However, 24% of the PASP students were still below the 26th percentile, which is a 2.4% failure rate in the population from which these students were selected.

The work of Torgesen and his colleagues is also highly relevant to the issue of intensity, duration, and supportiveness of reading remediation. Torgesen and his colleagues (2001) studied the effectiveness of interventions for older children (between the ages of 8 and 10) with identified reading disabilities. They randomly assigned 60 students with severe reading disabilities—in the bottom 2% in word decoding skills—to either the Auditory Discrimination in Depth program (ADD; Lindamood & Lindamood, 1984) or EP, which consisted of direct instruction in phonemic awareness and alphabetic coding practiced in writing and reading of text. Note that this EP condition is more similar to the direct code rather than the embedded code instruction of Foorman et al. (1998). The difference between the ADD and EP treatments was that EP provided more practice in writing and reading of text, whereas ADD provided more practice with phonemic awareness (down to the articulatory level) and phonological recoding.

The 60 students in Torgesen et al.'s (2001) study received 67.5 hours of one-on-one instruction in two, 50-minute sessions per day for 8 weeks. The intervention teachers had at least 1 year's experience teaching ADD or EP in clinic settings. Both interventions produced large effect sizes on reading achievement (4.4 and 3.9, respectively) that were stable 2 years later. Although students achieved mean scores in the normal range on reading accuracy and comprehension, their average reading rates continued to be severely impaired. Nonetheless, 40% of children returned to regular education, well above the 5% typical of special education programs.

REMEDIAL INTERVENTIONS

In addition to the Torgesen et al. (2001) study, there are several other researchers who have obtained impressive results with remedial interventions (e.g., Berninger et al., 2003; Blachman et al., 2004; Olson & Wise, 2006). One of the longest standing research programs is Lovett and colleagues' intervention with severely impaired upper elementary and middle school readers using a modification of the direct instruction program Reading Mastery (Englemann & Bruner, 1995), called Phonological Analysis and Blending/Direct Instruction (PHAB/DI), and a program that teaches word identification strategy training (WIST). Lovett et al. (2000) conducted a study that compared five conditions: (a) 35 hours of instruction in PHAB/DI followed by 35 hours of WIST, (b) 35 hours in WIST followed by 35 hours of PHAB/DI, (c) 70 hours of PHAB/DI, (d) 70 hours of WIST, and (e) 70 hours of a control condition that combined 35 hours of study skills and 35 hours of math instruction. They found that the combination was better than either method alone or the control condition on measures of nonword reading, letter–sound knowledge, and word recognition. Subsequently, PHAB/DI and WIST were combined into a PHAST (phonological and strategy training) Track Reading Program and contrasted with the old PHAB/DI combined either with study skills training or with Wolf's RAVE-O program (Wolf, Miller, & Donnelly, 2002). RAVE-O stands for Retrieval, Automaticity, Vocabulary elaboration, and Enrichment with language-Orthography. Results showed that the combined approaches worked better than PHAB/DI alone (i.e., gains of about 0.5 standard deviations) and that all three approaches worked better than a math control group. For about 50% of the students, the combined approaches led to word recognition skills in the average range.

These remedial reading studies, in conjunction with the landmark intervention studies, show us what is possible *outside* the typical public school delivery system for students identified with reading disabilities. We know that poor outcomes are apparent for special education students both in resource room settings (Foorman, Francis, Fletcher, Winikates, & Mehta, 1997; Moody, Vaughn, Hughes, & Fischer, 2000; Vaughn, Moody, & Schumm, 1998) and in inclusionary settings (Klingner, Vaughn, Schumm, Hughes, & Elbaum, 1997; Zigmond, 1996). Given the difficulty of normalizing older, impaired readers once they have fallen behind, researchers have turned to *early* reading interventions with children in kindergarten, first grade, and second grade.

EFFECTIVE EARLY INTERVENTIONS

Many early reading intervention studies have been conducted in the past two decades. They vary with respect to who delivers the intervention (teachers, peers, paraprofessionals, or community volunteers), as well as the explicitness, intensity, and duration of the intervention.

MATHES AND COLLEAGUES

A theoretically important question for early intervention research is how systematic alphabetic code instruction needs to be to be effective (Rayner, Foorman, Perfetti, Pesetsky, & Seidenberg, 2001). Mathes and colleagues (2005) addressed this question by contrasting enhanced classroom reading instruction with two kinds of interventions that varied in how prescriptive they were. The first, Proactive, focused on systematic phonics instruction using a scope and sequence and decodable text. The second intervention, Responsive, also taught phonics explicitly but without a scope and sequence or decodable text. Instead, the teacher responded to the student's needs as they were observed during the lesson. Both interventions consisted of work on decoding, fluency, and comprehension but time allocation emphasized phonemic decoding accuracy in Proactive, and supported reading and writing in Responsive. Enhanced classroom instruction meant that teachers were given feedback on at-risk students' progress in oral reading fluency and received professional development regarding linking assessment data to instruction.

Students in the Mathes et al. (2005) study were 100 normally developing kindergarteners and 292 kindergarteners designated as at risk (i.e., below the 20th percentile) based on a state-mandated early reading assessment in six non-Title I schools. In grade 1, the at-risk students were randomly assigned to enhanced classroom intervention or to Proactive or Responsive interventions. Six intervention teachers, who worked for the school district but were recruited and trained by the researchers, provided intervention, and there were 30 classroom teachers. Both interventions were delivered 40 minutes daily, 5 days a week for 30 weeks, in small groups (1:3) as a supplement to classroom reading instruction. Results showed that all three groups scored in the average range at the end of the year on reading and spelling measures. The two intervention groups did not differ from each other, on average, and outperformed the enhanced classroom group on outcomes of phonological awareness, word reading, and oral reading fluency. Based on an effectiveness criterion of scoring above the 30th percentile in word recognition skills, 16% of the enhanced classroom group did not achieve the criterion, which translates to 3% of the schools' first-grade population of students. Less than 10% of the intervention students fell below that criterion: 1% of the Proactive students (i.e., 0.2% of the schools' population) and 7% of the Responsive students (i.e., 1.5% of the schools' population).

PEER-ASSISTED LEARNING STRATEGIES (PALS)

Converging findings have established that classwide peer tutoring interventions can reduce the number of children at risk for reading difficulties by increasing students' reading practice time, their opportunities to respond, and their engagement in literate discourse (Greenwood, Carta & Hall, 1988). Peer tutoring has also improved verbal skills (Shaver & Nuhn, 1971) and self-concept (Scruggs & Osguthorpe 1986). One of the most researched peer-mediated programs is Peer-Assisted Learning Strategies or PALS (Simmons, Fuchs, Fuchs, Mathes, & Hodge, 1995). An impressive research program of empirical studies has demonstrated that participating in PALS three to four times per week for 16–20 weeks has improved reading achievement for students in kindergarten through sixth grade (Fuchs, Fuchs, Mathes, & Simmons, 1997; Fuchs et al., 2001; Mathes, Howard, Allen, & Fuchs, 1998; Simmons et al., 1995). Furthermore, PALS is an effective strategy for helping teachers adapt instruction for students with different levels of achievement (i.e., high, average, low, learning disabled; Fuchs et al., 1997, 2001; Mathes et al., 1998). Researchers have estimated that if PALS were available in first-grade classrooms, all but about 5% to 6% of students could be brought to achieve word-level reading scores above the 30th percentile (Denton & Mathes, 2003), a finding similar to the classroom intervention of Foorman et al. (1998).

To understand more about how teachers use PALS to supplement reading instruction to reduce the incidence of reading problems in their classrooms, we examine three related studies conducted in kindergarten and first grade (Al Otaiba & Fuchs, 2006; Fuchs et al., 2001; McMaster, Fuchs, Fuchs, & Compton, 2005). During PALS, teachers provide scripted reading lessons, and pairs of higher and lower performing readers practice these lessons. Fuchs and colleagues conducted a large randomized field trial involving 33 kindergarten teachers in eight culturally diverse urban schools, in which about 15% of students received special education services and 6% of students were ESL (English as a second language) learners (Fuchs et al., 2001). For 20 weeks, teachers were assigned to a control group or to provide one of two treatments: (a) phonological and print awareness activities selected from Ladders to Literacy (or Ladders; O'Connor, Notari-Syverson, & Vadasy, 1998), totaling 15 hours; or (b) a combination of Ladders activities and Kindergarten Peer-Assisted Learning Strategies (K-PALS; Fuchs et al., 2001), totaling 35 hours. K-PALS activities included phonological awareness, letter–sound and decoding, and sight word training three times a week for 20 minutes. On average, students receiving this combined approach outperformed controls on phonological awareness, reading, and spelling measures.

The following year, all first-grade teachers in the same eight schools were randomly assigned to first-grade PALS or control conditions. The first-grade PALS instructional routine is highly similar to K-PALS, in that teachers led three 20-minute sessions a week for 20 weeks that provided children a teacher-directed lesson followed by peer-mediated practice in phonological awareness, decoding, and sight word training, but added partner reading in connected text. PALS students outperformed controls across most measures of reading achievement, with large effects favoring children identified as low achieving at the start of the study. However, at the end of first grade, 2% of students had word attack skills below the 30th percentile on a standardized reading measure and 4% had similarly low word-identification scores. In a subsequent follow-up study, Al Otaiba and Fuchs (2006) reported that these children scored 1.5 standard deviations (*SD*) lower than responsive students on measures of vocabulary, rapid naming, and problem behavior and 1.0 *SD* lower on a measure of verbal memory. An implication is that peer tutoring may not be intensive enough to prevent reading problems for children with very low vocabulary, phonological processing deficits, or serious attention and behavior issues. When children's school records were examined at the end of third grade, all but one of these nonresponsive students were receiving special education services in reading (Al Otaiba & Fuchs, 2006).

Another first-grade PALS study was conducted by McMaster et al. (2005) to examine what might improve outcomes for children who did not benefit from 7 weeks of PALS (defined as .50 *SD* below average on level of performance and rate of growth). These children were randomly assigned to an additional 13 weeks of (a) typical PALS; (b) modified PALS, in which children progressed more slowly in the program; or (c) tutoring by an adult for about 35 minutes, 3 days per week. No statistically significant differences favored any of the treatments, although effect sizes favored tutoring by the adults. At the end of first grade, about 2% of PALS, modified PALS, or adult-tutored students performed below the 30th percentile on either word identification or word attack.

READING RECOVERY

Reading Recovery (RR) is currently used in 20% of U.S. schools (Gomez-Bellenge, 2002) and is implemented by specially trained teachers who create individualized lessons for their students. In the most recent study of RR (Schwartz, 2005), eligible students of RR teachers who volunteered to submit student data for the project were randomly assigned to an immediate-treatment or waiting-for-treatment control group. Roughly 51% of children received free or reduced lunch; 40% were White, 40% African American, 12% Hispanic, and 2% Asian (which Schwartz reported was consistent with the national RR database). After 20 weeks of daily 30-minute sessions, treatment students outperformed controls on a range of alphabetic, print, and reading measures, but not on phonemic awareness measures. Because children began the study in the lowest 20th percentile relative to their classmates, and 27% of treatment students were referred for additional support, Schwartz estimated that in most schools, roughly 5% of RR graduates could not read on grade level. These estimates may not be reliable because (a) no standardized testing was used to provide scores that may be compared to national norms or percentiles, (b) RR teachers did all the testing, and (c) reading on grade level was defined as reading a leveled text. However, the proportion is comparable to data from the RR national database reporting that 79% of successfully discontinued children were on grade level.

This finding is corroborated in the limited research base regarding the longer term effects of RR. One study in Australia followed successful graduates for a year (Center, Wheldall, Freeman, Outhred, & McNaught, 1995) and reported that 35% had below-average reading levels; similarly, in Texas, 30% of RR graduates did not pass the fourth-grade criterion-referenced portion of the Texas Assessment of Academic Skills (Askew, Fountas, Lyons, Pinnell, & Schmitt, 1998). However, it is important to note that estimates of success are likely inflated because substantial numbers of children do not complete the program if they are referred for special education or are frequently absent (Shanahan & Barr, 1995). Indeed a recent meta-analysis of one-to-one tutoring reported that effect sizes for RR were strong for successfully discontinued students, but were small or nonexistent for the discontinued students (Elbaum, Vaughn, Hughes, & Moody, 2000).

INTERVENTIONS DELIVERED BY COMMUNITY VOLUNTEERS

It is difficult for most schools to garner the necessary resources to conduct and sustain the intensive interventions just described. This is because of the cost of hiring personnel qualified to deliver intensive interventions with fidelity. Even in studies of classwide peer tutoring programs like PALS that were conducted by classroom teachers and their young students, research staff provided support. This resource issue is particularly acute in schools attended by children living in poverty, who are likely to begin school less prepared to read than children from middle-class families. Consequently, there has been increasing interest in lower cost tutoring models that utilize community members, college students, and other volunteers (Juel, 1994, 1996; Morrow & Woo, 2001). America Reads, AmeriCorps, and other grassroots reading initiatives are attempting to put more volunteers into schools to work with high-risk students. Although these initiatives are well intended, it is important to examine the evidence about their efficacy and to distill characteristics of interventions and interventionists that are necessary and sufficient for positive student response.

PRIOR TUTORING RESEARCH

Prior meta-analytic reviews of the broader tutoring literature (Cohen, Kulik, & Kulik, 1982; Elbaum et al., 2000) have demonstrated that tutoring improves reading outcomes for many students (mean effect size [ES] = .40). Elbaum et al. (2000)

reported that only a handful of studies used community volunteers as tutors; their mean weighted effect size was 0.59, but the range was from −0.25 to .98. Higher effect sizes were generally reported for programs that described tutors' training.

In a narrative review of the extant volunteer tutoring literature, Wasik (1998a) described findings from 11 studies that specifically examined the efficacy of using volunteers as literacy tutors. Tutors included college students, parents, and retirees. Wasik (1998b) reported that tutoring was generally effective, but noted that at that time only 3 of the 11 studies had equivalent treatment and no-treatment comparison groups. Wasik concluded that more rigorous evaluations were needed, but she made a series of recommendations that she found were associated with successful tutoring programs:

- Specialists to supervise tutors and to provide ongoing training and feedback
- Structured tutoring sessions that incorporate important reading components
- Access to high-quality materials and engaging texts
- Consistent/intensive tutoring for struggling readers that is coordinated with classroom instruction
- Ongoing assessment of student progress

CURRENT TUTORING RESEARCH

To learn whether Wasik's recommendations are supported by more recent studies involving more rigorous examinations of the effects of community literacy tutors, we searched the literature. An exhaustive review is beyond the scope of this chapter, so we highlight findings from three programs shown to be effective through randomized field trials.

Sound Partners

Perhaps the most thoroughly researched volunteer tutoring program is Sound Partners. For over a decade, Vadasy and colleagues have conducted several experimental and quasi-experimental studies of Sound Partners (Jenkins, Vadasy, Firebaugh, & Profilet, 2000; Vadasy, Jenkins, Antil, Wayne & O'Connor, 1997; Vadasy, Jenkins, & Pool, 2000). Sound Partners is a code-oriented supplemental tutoring program (100 lessons) provided to struggling beginning readers in first and second grade for about 30 minutes, 4 days per week. Scripted lessons follow a structured routine, including learning letter–sound correspondences, decoding words with familiar sounds or from common word families, practicing sight words, and demonstrating fluency on decodable text.

Research staff trained tutors and then provided weekly supervisory visits that included ongoing coaching and modeling. Staff also conducted fidelity of implementation checks and assessed students' progress at pre- and posttest. Across several studies, effect sizes in phonological awareness, spelling, word reading, and fluency consistently favored treatment students (ranging from small to large).

It was noteworthy, however, that once the responsibility for training and supervision was transferred to the schools, there were no differences between treatment and untutored controls, and that when staff reassumed their technical assistance, effect sizes again favored treatment students (Jenkins et al., 2000). Furthermore, even when their project staff supervised tutors, Vadasy et al. (2000) reported an important interaction between effectiveness and quality of tutoring; large effect sizes (mean of .83) favored students whose tutors had a higher fidelity of implementation scores.

Tutor-Assisted Intensive Learning Strategies (TAILS)

A randomized field trial investigated the effectiveness of a tutoring intervention provided by community tutors to kindergarten students at risk for reading difficulties (Al Otaiba, Schatschneider, & Silverman, 2005). All 243 kindergarteners in four high-poverty schools (12 classrooms) were screened; children were selected who had the lowest pretreatment letter naming (<2 letter names correct per minute) or letter–sound awareness (<3 letter–sounds). Nearly all of the students were African American and a very high proportion (over 80%) received free and reduced lunch. Of primary interest was to compare the effects of two versus four one-on-one tutoring sessions per week. The 73 participating students were randomly assigned within the classroom to tutoring 4 days a week, tutoring 2 days a week, or to a control condition that provided small-group storybook reading 2 days a week.

Similar to the instructional routine of lessons in the Sound Partners program, during each TAILS lesson, students received 10–15 minutes of scripted explicit instruction in phonological awareness and phonics. TAILS lessons borrowed some components from PALS (Fuchs et al., 2001), but also provided practice with movable tiles and letters with Elkonin sound boxes and introduced fluency practice in game-like formats that increased in difficulty from letter–sounds to connected text. TAILS lessons were designed to be a consistent supplement to children's explicit classroom core-reading program. During the 10–15 minute book-reading component of TAILS, adults read to children using dialogic reading strategies with engaging stories to develop vocabulary and comprehension (Beck, McKeown, & Kucan, 2002; Lonigan, Anthony, Bloomfield, Dyer, & Samwel, 1999); children also read simple decodable texts. TAILS tutors received relatively longer training (over 13 hours) than Sound Partners, but supervision was similar (weekly visits and modeling or coaching by research staff). Fidelity of TAILS implementation was consistently above 85%.

Staff administered standardized reading pre-, mid-, and posttreatment tests and weekly curriculum-based measures that were used to track student progress. Analyses revealed that students in the 4-day condition outperformed students in either the 2-day or control condition on three reading measures. Effect sizes favoring students in the 4-day versus control condition were .79, .90, and .83, on word identification, passage comprehension, and basic reading skills, respectively.

Start Making a Reader Today (SMART)

Baker, Gersten, and Keating (2000) evaluated the effectiveness of a 2-year, large-scale volunteer tutoring program. SMART differs from Sound Partners and TAILS in that it is not a scripted program but rather a governor's initiative operating in Oregon that served more than 7,100 students per year (grades K–2). Teachers nominate students for the program, which provides two 30-minute sessions per week during which tutors read with and listen to children read and ask them questions. The SMART initiative provided minimal training (1–2 hours) for tutors that incorporated mostly logistical issues rather than instructional techniques. Tutors were also provided a handbook with guidance about supporting children's reading comprehension and encouraging their interest in reading. Although Baker et al. (2000) conducted informal observations in two schools to understand the nature of tutoring, which they described as generally supportive, they also reported that "it is unclear just exactly what the sessions consisted of" (p. 510).

Baker et al. (2000) used a randomized treatment and control within classroom design. Their final sample of students who received 2 full years of tutoring included 43 SMART students and 41 controls. Results indicated that SMART students showed significantly greater improvement than controls on word identification (ES = .44) and reading fluency (ES = .48 at end of first grade and .53 at end of second grade); but there were no differences between groups on comprehension. Students showed the greatest growth in first grade.

SUMMARY OF CHARACTERISTICS NECESSARY AND SUFFICIENT FOR POSITIVE STUDENT RESPONSE

How important is having a specialist who supervises tutors and provides ongoing training and feedback? Additional research is warranted that manipulates the amount of support tutors need to achieve favorable outcomes because no causal conclusions can be drawn from the existing studies. It seems logical to agree with Wasik (1998a) that most successful programs include supervision, ongoing training, and feedback, especially given Vadasy and colleague's findings (e.g., Jenkins et al., 2000) that (a) higher fidelity of implementation was associated with greater reading growth, and (b) when training and supervision provided by the research team was withdrawn, schools were unable to sustain the efficacy of their program. However, contradictory findings from Baker et al.'s (2000) evaluation of SMART suggest tutors can be successful in improving students' fluency and word identification by administering an unstructured program with only minimal training.

How critical are structured tutoring sessions that incorporate all the important reading components? Sound Partners and TAILS sessions include both code-focused (phonological awareness, phonics, and fluency) and meaning-focused (vocabulary and comprehension) aspects of reading; although Sound Partners does not include vocabulary instruction. The SMART initiative focused more narrowly on book reading fluency and comprehension. Effect sizes were lower for SMART than the other two programs and no differences were found between SMART and control students on comprehension. Additional research is warranted that contrasts structured and less structured approaches. One study directly compared these approaches (Al Otaiba et al., 2005) and found similar outcomes for children receiving either approach for 2 days a week. By contrast, large effect sizes favored students receiving structured tutoring 4 days per week over students in the book reading condition.

Access to high quality materials and engaging texts. None of the studies manipulated the type of texts provided for tutees, and Baker et al. (2000) did not specify the type of books used in the SMART program. Vadasy and colleagues (1997; 2000) used mostly decodable texts for Sound Partners. Children reportedly enjoyed these books, which is likely because they could read them successfully and independently. The TAILS program incorporated the same decodable texts, but also required tutors to read aloud to children from storybooks and expository text. Critics might argue that a wider selection of books, such as the leveled text used by RR teachers, or more storybooks or informative texts would better support comprehension strategy development.

Consistent/intensive tutoring for struggling readers that is coordinated with classroom instruction. Only Al Otaiba et al. (2005) had the necessary resources to observe typical classroom instruction to ensure it was consistent in instructional approach with tutoring. Both followed similar direct instruction formats. It seems logical that students would benefit more from a consistent approach, but additional research is warranted.

Ongoing assessment of student progress. Sound Partners, SMART, and TAILS have been evaluated using pre- and posttest designs; additionally, TAILS incorporated more frequent progress monitoring. However, tutors were not expected to modify instruction based on student data.

Additional research is needed to learn the most appropriate role volunteers could play in successfully reducing the incidence of reading difficulties. Should their impact be considered similar to peer-tutoring approaches? If so, it might be reasonable to consider that their optimal contribution should be as a support and supplement to well-implemented general classroom reading instruction. Another contribution could be to support literacy centers in the classroom to allow teachers to provide more intensive instruction to the most struggling readers. Or, could volunteers deliver a standard treatment protocol such as the one used by paraprofessionals in the Torgesen et al. (1999) study? Findings from TAILS and Sound Partners suggest that scripting and training may support consistent fidelity of treatment. Or, with adequate supervision by a reading coach or specialist, could volunteers ever be expected to deliver a more individualized intervention based on student progress similar to RR or the Responsive approach used by Mathes et al. (2005)?

CONCLUSION

Several decades of research on effective reading interventions shows us that it is possible to substantially reduce the 36% of fourth graders reading below grade level on NAEP or the 17.5% of students with reading disabilities. Better classroom instruction can reduce the numbers of low-achieving students to around 5%. Supplemental small-group or one-on-one tutoring can reduce the numbers even further to 1%–3%. Such reductions in numbers of struggling and impaired readers requires well-trained teachers implementing with fidelity a comprehensive literacy curriculum that emphasizes explicit instruction in the alphabetic principle with ample opportunity to practice and receive corrective feedback. Such reductions in numbers also require the integration of general and special education into a layered or tiered system of service delivery.

The Reading First component of NCLB and the RTI approach to identifying students with learning disabilities encouraged in IDEA 2004 can work together to effect this multilayered service delivery system. By utilizing special education and Title I funds to provide classroom prevention and early intervention in kindergarten and first grade, struggling readers can be identified and helped before their achievement falls below grade level. Lessons learned from Reading First can be helpful to successful implementation of RTI (e.g., Foorman, Kalinowski, & Sexton, 2007). For example, staff development in the selection and use of scientifically based materials and assessments mean that teachers and principals are equipped to implement assessment-driven, differentiated instruction. Mentoring provided by coaches or well-trained paraprofessionals can ensure that teachers receive help with classroom management and with creating meaningful center-based activities that will engage students while the teacher works with reading groups. Specialists can collaborate with classroom teachers to reduce teacher–student ratios so that small-group instruction on targeted skills is possible for sufficient duration and intensity to normalize reading achievement. The principal's leadership is crucial to guaranteeing a minimum of 90 minutes a day of uninterrupted reading/language arts instruction, with flexible scheduling to allow supplemental small-group instruction that addresses the needs of individual students not responding adequately to classroom instruction. Schools as well as entire districts (e.g., Fielding, Kerr, & Rosier, 2007) have implemented a successful RTI model based on these principles. We are fortunate that national policy has been informed by a substantial research base to make the delivery of effective reading interventions within reach of the majority of elementary schools. It's now up to the educators at each school to realize this significant opportunity.

ACKNOWLEDGMENTS

This work was supported by grant R305W020001, "Scaling Up Assessment-Driven Intervention Using the Internet and Handheld Computers," from the Institute of Education Sciences in the U.S. Department of Education, and by a Multidisciplinary Learning Disabilities Center Grant P50HD052120 from the National Institute of Child Health and Human Development.

REFERENCES

Al Otaiba, S., & Fuchs, D. (2006). Who are the young children for whom best practices in reading are ineffective? An experimental and longitudinal study. *Journal of Learning Disabilities*, *39*(5), 414–431.

Al Otaiba, S., Schatschneider, C., & Silverman, E. (2005). Tutor-assisted learning strategies in kindergarten: How much is enough? *Exceptionality*, *13*(4), 195–208.

Askew, B. J., Fountas, I. C., Lyons, C. A., Pinnell, G. S., & Schmitt, M. C. (1998). *Reading Recover review: Understandings, outcomes and implications.* Columbus, OH: Reading Recovery Council of North America.

Baker, S., Gersten, R., & Keating, T. (2000). When less may be more: A 2-year longitudinal evaluation of a volunteer tutoring program requiring minimal training. *Reading Research Quarterly, 35*(4), 494–519.

Beck, I. L., McKeown, M. G., & Kucan, L. (2002). *Bringing words to Life: Robust vocabulary instruction.* New York: Guilford Press.

Berninger, V. W., Nagy, W. E., Carlisle, J., Thompson, J., Hoffer, D., Abbott, S., et al. (2003). Effective treatment for children with dyslexia in grades 4-6: Behavioral and brain evidence. In B. R. Foorman (Ed.), *Preventing and remediating reading difficulties: Bringing science to scale* (pp. 381–418). Baltimore: York Press.

Blachman, B. A., Schatschneider, C., Fletcher, J. M., Francis, D. J., Clonan, S., Shaywitz, B., et al. (2004). Effects of intensive reading remediation for second and third graders. *Journal of Educational Psychology*, *96*, 444–461.

Borman, G. D., Hewes, G. M., Overman, L. T., & Brown, S. (2003). Comprehensive school reform and achievement: A meta-analysis. *Review of Educational Research, 73*(2), 125-130.

Carnine, D. W., Silbert, J., & Kameenui, E. J. (1997). *Direct instruction reading* (3rd ed.). Upper Saddle River, NJ: Merrill/Prentice Hall.

Center, Y., Wheldall, K., Freeman, L., Outhred, L., & McNaught, M. (1995). An experimental evaluation of Reading Recovery. *Reading Research Quarterly, 30*, 240–263.

Cohen, P., Kulik, J. A., & Kulik, C. C. (1982). Educational outcomes of tutoring: A meta-analysis of findings. *American Educational Research Journal, 19*, 237–248.

Connor, C. M., Morrison, F. J., Fishman, B. J., Schatschneider, C., & Underwood, P. (2007, January). Algorithm-guided individualized reading instruction. *Science, 315*, 464–465.

Connor, C. M., Morrison, F. J., & Katch, L. E. (2004). Beyond the reading wars: Exploring the effect of child-instruction interactions on growth in early reading. *Scientific Studies of Reading, 8*(4), 305–336.

Connor, C. M., Morrison, F. J., Slominski, L. (2006). Preschool instruction and children's emergent literacy growth. *Journal of Educational Psychology*, *98*(4), 665–689.

Denton, C., Foorman, B., & Mathes, P. (2003). Schools that "Beat the Odds": Implications for reading instruction. *Remedial and Special Education*, *24*, 258–261.

Denton, C. A., & Mathes, P. G. (2003). Intervention for struggling readers: Possibilities and challenges. In B. R. Foorman (Ed.). *Preventing and remediating reading difficulties: Bringing science to scale* (pp. 229–252). Baltimore: York.

Elbaum, B., Vaughn, S., Hughes, M. T., & Moody, S. W. (2000). How effective are one-on-one tutoring programs in reading for elementary students at risk for reading failure? A meta-analysis of the intervention research. *Journal of Educational Psychology*, *92*(4), 605–619.

Englemann, S., & Bruner, E. (1995). *Reading Mastery I*. Chicago: SRA/McGraw-Hill.

Fielding, L., Kerr, N., & Rosier, P. (2007). *Annual growth for all students, catch-up growth for those who are behind*. Kennewick, WA: The New Foundation Press.

Foorman, B. R., Francis, D. J., Fletcher, J. M., Schatschneider, C., & Mehta, P. (1998). The role of instruction in learning to read: Preventing reading failure in at-risk children. *Journal of Educational Psychology, 90*, 37–55.

Foorman, B. R., Francis, D. J., Fletcher, J. M., Winikates, D., & Mehta, P. (1997). Early interventions for children with reading problems. *Scientific Studies of Reading, 1*, 255–276.

Foorman, B. R., Kalinowski, S. J., & Sexton, W. L. (2007). Standards-based educational reform is one important step toward reducing the achievement gap. In A. Gamoran (Ed.), *Standards-based reform and the poverty gap: Lessons from "No Child Left Behind"* (pp. 17–42). Washington, DC: Brookings Institution.

Foorman, B. R., Schatschneider, C., Eakin, M. N., Fletcher, J. M., Moats, L. C., & Francis, D. J. (2006). The impact of instructional practices in grades 1 and 2 on reading and spelling achievement in high poverty schools. *Contemporary Educational Psychology, 31*, 1–29.

Fuchs, D., Fuchs, L. S., Mathes, P. G., & Simmons, D. C. (1997). Peer-assisted learning strategies: Making classrooms more responsive to academic diversity. *American Educational Research Journal, 34*, 174–206.

Fuchs, D., Fuchs, L. S., Thompson, A., Svenson, E., Al Otaiba, S., Yang, N., et al. (2001). Peer-Assisted Learning Strategies in reading: Extensions to kindergarten/first grade and high school. *Remedial and Special Education, 22*, 15–21.

Gomez-Bellenge, F. X. (2002). *Reading Recovery and Decubriendo la Lectura National Report 2000–2001*. Columbus: The Ohio State University, National Data Evaluation Center.

Greenwood, C. R., Carta, J. J., & Hall, R. V. (1988). The use of peer-tutoring strategies in classroom management and educational instruction. *School Psychology Review, 17*(2), 258–275.

Hiebert, E., Colt, J., Catto, S., & Gury, E. (1992). Reading and writing of first-grade students in a restructured chapter 1 program. *American Educational Research Journal, 29*, 545–572.

Individuals with Disabilities Education Improvement Act of 2004 (IDEA), Pub. L. No. 108-446, 118 Stat 614 (2004).

Jenkins, J. R., Vadasy, P. F., Firebaugh, M., & Profilet, C. (2000). Tutoring first-grade struggling readers in phonological reading skills. *Learning Disabilities Research & Practice, 15*, 75–84.

Juel, C. (1994). At risk university students tutoring at-risk elementary school children: What factors make it effective? In E. H. Hiebert & B. M. Taylor (Eds.), *Getting reading right from the start: Effect early interventions* (pp. 39–62). Boston: Allyn & Bacon.

Juel, C. (1996). What makes literacy tutoring effective? *Reading Research Quarterly, 31*, 268–289.

Klingner, J. K., Vaughn, S. R., Schumm, J. S., Hughes, M., & Elbaum, B. (1997). Outcomes for students with and without learning disabilities in inclusive classrooms. *Learning Disabilities Research & Practice, 13*, 153–161.

Lindamood, C. H., & Lindamood, P. C. (1984). *Auditory discrimination in depth*. Austin, TX: PRO-ED.

Lonigan, C. J., Anthony, J. L., Bloomfield, B. G., Dyer, S. M., & Samwel, C. S. (1999). Effects of two shared-reading interventions on emergent literacy skills of at-risk pre-schoolers. *Journal of Early Intervention, 22*, 306–322.

Lovett, M. W., Lacerenza, L., Borden, S. L., Frijters, J. C., Steinbach, K. A., & DePalma, M. (2000). Components of effective remediation for developmental reading disabilities: Combining phonological and strategy-based instruction to improve outcomes. *Journal of Educational Psychology, 92*, 263–283.

Mathes, P. G., Denton, C. A., Fletcher, J. M., Anthony, J. L., Francis, D. J., & Schatschneider, C. (2005). The effects of theoretically different instruction and student characteristics on the skills of struggling readers. *Reading Research Quarterly, 40*(2), 148–183.

Mathes, P. G., Howard, J. K., Allen, S. H., & Fuchs, D. (1998). Peer-assisted learning strategies for first grade readers: Responding to the needs of diverse learners. *Reading Research Quarterly, 33*, 62–94.

McMaster, K. L., Fuchs, D., Fuchs, L. S., & Compton, D. L. (2005). Responding to nonresponders: An experimental field trial of identification and intervention methods. *Exceptional Children, 71*, 445–463.

Moody, S. W., Vaughn, S. R., Hughes, M. T., & Fischer, M. (2000). Reading instruction in the resource room: Set up for failure. *Exceptional Children, 16*, 305–316.

Morrow, L. M., & Woo, D. G. (2001). *Tutoring programs for struggling readers: The America Reads Challenge.* New York: Guilford Press.

National Center for Education Statistics. (2005). *The nation's report card: Reading 2005.* Washington, DC: Author.

O'Connor, R. E., Notari-Syverson, A., & Vadasy, P. (1998). Ladders to literacy: The effects of teacher-led phonological activities for kindergarten children with and without disabilities. *Exceptional Children, 63*, 117–130.

Olson, R. K., & Wise, B. (2006). Computer-based remediation for reading and related phonological disabilities. In M. McKenna, L. Labbo, R. Kieffer, & D. Reinking (Eds.), *Handbook of literacy and technology* (Vol. 2, pp. 57–74). Mahwah, NJ: Erlbaum.

Open Court Reading. (1995). *Collections for young scholars.* Chicago and Peru, IL: SRA/McGraw-Hill.

Rayner, K., Foorman, B., Perfetti, C. A., Pesetsky, D., & Seidenberg, M. S. (2001). How psychological science informs the teaching of reading. *Psychological Science in the Public Interest, 2*, 31–74.

Schwartz, R. M. (2005). Literacy learning of at-risk first-grade students in the Reading Recovery early intervention. *Journal of Educational Psychology, 97*(2), 257–267.

Scruggs, T., & Osguthorpe, R. T. (1986). Tutoring interventions within special educational settings: A comparison of cross-age and peer tutoring. *Psychology in Schools, 23*(2), 187–193.

Shanahan, T., & Barr, R. (1995). Reading recovery: An independent evaluation of the effects of an early instructional intervention for at-risk learners. *Reading Research Quarterly, 30*, 958–996.

Shaver, J., & Nuhn, D. (1971). The effectiveness of tutoring under-achievers in reading and writing. *Journal of Educational Research, 65*, 107–112.

Shaywitz, B. A., Fletcher, J. M., & Shaywitz, S. E. (1995). Defining and classifying learning disabilities and attention-deficit/hyperactivity disorder. *Journal of Child Neurology, 10*(Suppl. 1), S50–S57.

Simmons, D. C., Fuchs, L. S., Fuchs, D., Mathes, P. G., & Hodge, J. (1995). Effects of explicit teaching and peer-mediated instruction on the reading achievement of learning disabled and low performing students. *Elementary School Journal, 95*, 387–408.

Slavin, R. E., & Madden, N. A. (2001). *One million children: Success for All.* Thousand Oaks, CA: Corwin.

Stallings, J. A. (1980). Allocated academic reading time revisited, or beyond time on task. *Educational Researcher, 9,* 11–16.

Taylor, B. M., Pearson, P. D., Clark, K., & Walpole, S. (2000). Effective schools and accomplished teachers: Lessons about primary-grade reading instruction in low-income schools. *The Elementary School Journal, 101,* 121–165.

Torgesen, J. K., Alexander, A. W., Wagner, R. K., Rashotte, C. A., Voelier, K. K. S., & Conway, T. (2001). Intensive remedial instruction for children with severe reading disabilities: Immediate and long-term outcomes from two instructional approaches. *Journal of Learning Disabilities, 34*(1), 33–58.

Torgesen, J. K., Wagner, R. K., Rashotte, C. A., Rose, E., Lindamood, P., Conway, T., et al. (1999). Preventing reading failure in young children with phonological processing disabilities: Group and individual responses to instruction. *Journal of Educational Psychology, 91*(4), 579–593.

Vadasy, P. F., Jenkins, J. R., Antil, L. R., Wayne, S. K., & O'Connor, R. E. (1997). The effectiveness of one-to-one tutoring by community tutors for at-risk beginning readers. *Learning Disability Quarterly, 20,* 126–139.

Vadasy, P. F., Jenkins, J. R., & Pool, K. (2000). Effects of tutoring in phonological and early reading skills on students at risk for reading disabilities. *Journal of Learning Disabilities, 33,* 579–590.

Vaughn, S. R., Moody, S. W., & Schuman, J. S. (1998). Broken promises: Reading instruction in the resources room. *Exceptional Children, 64*(2), 211–225.

Vellutino, F. R., Scanlon, D. M., & Jaccard, J. (2003). Toward distinguishing between cognitive and experiential deficits as primary sources of difficulty in learning to read: A two year follow-up study of difficult to remediate and readily remediated poor readers. In B. R. Foorman (Ed.), *Preventing and remediating reading difficulties: Bringing science to scale* (pp. 73–120). Baltimore: York Press.

Vellutino, F. R., Scanlon, D. M., Sipay, E. R., Small, S. G., Pratt, A., Chen, R., et al. (1996). Cognitive profiles of difficult to remediate and readily remediated poor readers: Early intervention as a vehicle for distinguishing between cognitive and experiential deficits as basic causes of specific reading disability. *Journal of Educational Psychology, 88*(4), 601–638.

Wasik, B. A. (1998a). Volunteer tutoring programs in reading: A review. *Reading Research Quarterly, 33*(3), 266–292.

Wasik, B. A. (1998b). Using volunteers as reading tutors: Guidelines for successful practices. *The Reading Teacher, 51*(7), 562–570.

Weaver, C. (1994). *Understanding whole language: From principles to practice.* Portsmouth, NH: Heinemann.

Wolf, M., Miller, L., & Donnelly, K. (2002). Retrieval, Automaticity, Vocabulary Elaboration, Orthography (RAVE-O): A comprehensive, fluency-based reading intervention program. *Journal of Learning Disabilities, 33,* 375–386.

Zigmond, N. (1996). Organization and management of general education classrooms. In D. L. Speece & B. K. Keough (Eds.), *Research on classroom ecologies* (pp. 163–190). Mahwah, NJ: Lawrence Erlbaum Associates.

14 Remediation of Reading Difficulties in English-Language Learning Students

Linda S. Siegel

INTRODUCTION

Research has shown that for a number of children (i.e., 15%–20%), basic reading skills do not develop or improve with time (e.g., Fletcher & Foorman, 1994; Francis, Shaywitz, Stuebing, Shaywitz, & Fletcher, 1996). Children who fall behind in kindergarten and grade 1 fall further behind over time in reading and related areas (e.g., Lyon, 1995; Stanovich, 1986).

Clearly, it is important to identify early the children at risk for dyslexia and to provide an appropriate intervention. The accurate identification of children with reading difficulties, at as early a time as possible, is a central concern for society (e.g., Snow, Burns & Griffin, 1998). Due to the relationship between reading disability and negative life outcomes, it is critical that identification practices are accurate.

Reading failure has a negative impact on achievement in all academic areas as well as extracurricular activities and peer relations (e.g., Stanovich, 1986). With time, the disabled reader becomes unable to read age-appropriate material, and, as a result, reads less, is less likely to enjoy reading as compared to successful readers (Blachman, 1996), and lags in vocabulary development and acquisition of knowledge (Stanovich, 1986). A high prevalence of reading disabilities has been identified among adolescent homeless youth and adolescents who have committed suicide (Barwick & Siegel, 1996; McBride & Siegel, 1997). In addition to academic problems such as grade retention (e.g., McLeskey & Grizzle, 1992) and dropping out (e.g., Lichtenstein & Zantol-Wiener, 1988; National Center for Education Statistics, 1999), adolescents with learning disabilities are at increased risk of developing social problems (e.g., Sabornie, 1994; Wiener & Schneider, 2002) and emotional difficulties such as depression (e.g., Gregg, Hoy, King, Moreland, & Jagota, 1992). As well, this is a population at risk for problems with self-concept (e.g., Boetsch, Green, & Pennington, 1996; Chapman, 1988), juvenile delinquency, and substance use and abuse (Beitchman, Wilson, Douglas, Young, & Adlaf, 2001).

It is very important to identify children at risk for dyslexia early in their schooling when intervention is easier and less expensive. The model described in this chapter represents a shift away from the traditional model in which children who have experienced reading failure are evaluated and then receive intervention. This "wait until they fail" model usually means that struggling readers do not receive help until the later grades when issues of self-esteem become more pronounced. The study that I describe is a type of response-to-instruction (RTI) model. In this model, children are given a brief assessment to identify the children at risk for reading difficulties. Then all children are given appropriate phonological awareness reading instruction in the classroom. The teacher is trained to pay close attention to the children who have been identified as being at risk. Sometimes the teacher works with the at-risk children in small groups. Sometimes the at-risk children receive resource help from a special teacher. The present study was guided by three questions: (a) Could we develop a simple, effective system to detect children at risk for reading problems? (b) Would it be possible to provide a suitable intervention to overcome these early reading difficulties? (c) Would the system work as well with children, called English-language learners (ELL), whose first language is not English but who are being educated in English.

METHOD

PARTICIPANTS

The participants were 792 children in grade 6 from 30 schools in one school district in Canada. Of this sample, 658 had English as their first language and 124 had English as a second or additional language. All the children in this study were part of a longitudinal study that began in their kindergarten year.

ELL students were defined as students whose first spoken language at home to their parents, siblings, and grandparents was not English. Most of the students with ELL were immigrants to Canada, although some were born in Canada but did not speak English until they began to attend school. ELL students in the district studied receive the same classroom instruction as their native English-speaking (L1) peers. The sample represented students from a wide range of socioeconomic backgrounds.

DESIGN AND TASKS

Kindergarten Measures
In kindergarten, children were administered a battery of tests and tasks to assess early literacy, phonological processing, spelling, grammatical sensitivity, lexical access, and memory.

Early Literacy

WRAT3 (Wilkinson, 1993). The WRAT3 Reading subtest (blue form) was used. Each child was asked to name capital letters and to read some simple words.

Letter identification. Each child was presented with 26 written lowercase letters, in a random order, and was asked to name the letter. This task has a maximum score of 26 and a Cronbach's alpha of .94.

Spelling. In the spelling task, the children were asked to print their names and five words: mom, no, I, dad, cat. This task had a Cronbach's alpha of .76.

Phonological Processing

GFW sound mimicry. This subtest from Goldman, Fristoe, and Woodcock (1974) was used to assess the child's skill at recognizing and reproducing sounds presented orally. In this task, each child was asked to repeat pseudowords of increasing difficulty that had been read by the examiner. Pseudowords ranged in difficulty from vowel–consonant syllables (e.g., ab, id) to polysyllabic pseudowords (e.g., depnoniel, bafmotbem). This task had a Cronbach's alpha of .89.

Rhyme detection task. This task is from the Phonological Abilities Test (Muter, Hulme, & Snowling, 1997). In this task, the child was shown four pictures. A picture of the target word appeared above three pictures. Each child was asked which of the three words rhymed with the target word. For example: "What rhymes with boat? Foot, bike, or coat?" There were three demonstration items and 10 test items. If the child failed the demonstration item and the first five items, the administration was discontinued. This task had a Cronbach's alpha of .83.

Syllable identification and phoneme identification. These tasks are from the Phonological Abilities Test (Muter et al., 1997). In these tasks, each child was required to complete words. In the syllable identification part, the examiner presented a picture (i.e., table) to the children. The examiner said the first part of the word (i.e., "ta") and asked the child to complete the word (i.e., "ble"). In the phoneme identification task, the examiner presented a picture (e.g., fish) and said the first part of the word (i.e., "fi") and asked the child to complete the word (i.e., "sh"). The task consisted of eight syllable identification items, eight phoneme identification items, and two demonstration items for each section. If the child failed the demonstration items and the first four test items, the task was discontinued. This task had a Cronbach's alpha of .91.

Phoneme deletion task. This task is from the Phonological Abilities Test (Muter et al., 1997). In this task, the examiner presented the child with a picture of a word and the child was asked to delete a phoneme (initial or final) from the word. The task consisted of eight initial phoneme deletion items, eight final phoneme deletion items, and four demonstration items for each section. If the child failed the demonstration items and the first four test items, the task was discontinued. Examples of initial phoneme deletion included: "Seat without /s/ says …"; "Cake without /c/ says …" Examples of the final phoneme deletion included: "Sad without the /d/ says …"; "Cup without the /p/ says …" This task had a Cronbach's alpha of .92.

Lexical Access

Rapid automatized naming (RAN). This task was used to assess phonological recoding in lexical access, or word retrieval (Denckla & Rudel, 1976). In this task, each child was asked to name 40 items on a page consisting of line drawings of five different items (i.e., tree, chair, bird, pear, car) repeated in random order eight times. A practice trial of the five items was presented before the presentation of the 40 items to ensure the child knew the target words. The score was the time taken (in seconds) to name the 40 items.

Syntactic Awareness

Oral cloze. The oral cloze task was used to assess syntactic awareness (Siegel & Ryan, 1989; Willows & Ryan, 1981). Each child was required to listen to the examiner read 12 sentences, each with a missing word and then, for each sentence, provide a word that created a semantically and syntactically well-formed sentence. The class of the missing word varied as nouns, adjectives, prepositions, and verbs. An example of a sentence is: "The moon shines bright in the _____." This task had a Cronbach's alpha of .84.

Memory for Sentences

Memory for sentences. The Stanford Binet Memory for Sentences Test (Thorndike, Hagen, & Sattler, 1986) was used. Each child was asked to repeat sentences ranging from simple two-word sentences to complex sentences. The task was discontinued when a child failed at least three out of four items at two consecutive levels. Examples of sentences included: "Tall girl"; "The airplane's engines sputtered, then stopped, forcing an emergency landing." This task had a Cronbach's alpha of .86.

Grade 6 Measures

Reading

WRAT3 Reading subtest, blue form (Wilkinson, 1993). Children were asked to read as many words as possible from a list containing words of increasing difficulty (e.g., in, cat, stretch, triumph). The task administration was discontinued when 10 consecutive words were read incorrectly. This task had a Cronbach's alpha of .92.

Woodcock Reading Mastery Test–Revised: Word Identification, Form G (Woodcock, 1987). This subtest consists of a list of words of increasing difficulty (e.g., is, find, mathematician) and children were asked to read as many words as possible from the list. The task administration was discontinued when all items in a given level were failed and had a Cronbach's alpha of .97–.99.

Woodcock Reading Mastery Test–Revised: Word Attack, Form G (Woodcock, 1987). This subtest is made up of a list of pseudowords of increasing difficulty (e.g., dee, ap, straced) to measure decoding skills. Children were required to decode as many pseudowords as possible from the list. The task administration was discontinued when all items in a given level were failed. This task had a Cronbach's alpha of .97–.99.

Word Reading Fluency

One-minute word reading. Children were presented with a list of real words of increasing difficulty (e.g., as, because) and asked to read as many words as possible within a one-minute time period. This task had a Cronbach's alpha of .85.

One-minute pseudoword reading task. Children were presented with a list of pseudowords (e.g., yee, dreek) and asked to read as many words as possible within a one-minute time period. Form H of the Word Attack test was used as a word list to obtain a fluency measure; the number of words read correctly determined the score for this task. Standardized norms are not available when the list is used as a timed task and it had a Cronbach's alpha of .91.

Memory

Working memory for words. In the working memory for words task (Siegel & Ryan, 1989) children were presented with sets of sentences where the final word was missing (e.g., "Snow is white, grass is _____."); each sentence was read aloud by the examiner. Children were asked to provide the missing word of each sentence and then repeat all the missing words from each set of sentences for a total of three trials within each set of sentences. The number of sentences in each set increased beginning with two sentences in the first set and then increasing by an additional sentence up to a possible five sentences. To minimize word-finding problems, the sentences were chosen so that the word was virtually predetermined, which was reflected in the responses, because the children did not experience any difficulty in supplying the missing words. The task administration was discontinued when a child failed all the items in a given level. This task had a Cronbach's alpha of .53.

Working memory for numbers. In the working memory for numbers task (Siegel & Ryan, 1989), children were asked to count yellow dots within a field of blue and yellow dots arranged in a randomly determined irregular pattern on a 5 × 8 inch index card. For each set, the child was asked to recall the number of yellow dots on each card and the order in which they were presented with three trials within each set of cards. The number of cards in each set increased, beginning with two cards and increasing by an additional card up to a possible five cards. The task administration was discontinued when the child failed all the items of a given set. This task had a Cronbach's alpha of .69.

Phonological Processing

Rosner's Auditory Analysis Test. Rosner's Auditory Analysis Test (Rosner & Simon, 1971) includes both syllable and phoneme deletion. Children were asked to say a word and then to say the word again without one of its sounds (e.g., the directions were "Say smell" and then "Now say smell without the /m/ sound."). Overall, children were asked to delete syllables, single phonemes from both the initial and final positions in each word, and single phonemes from blends. Two practice items and 40 test items were administered; the 40 items were arranged in increasing order of difficulty. The administration of the test items was discontinued after five consecutive errors. This task had a Cronbach's alpha of .90.

Syntactic Awareness

Oral cloze. In the oral cloze task (Siegel & Ryan, 1989; Willows & Ryan, 1981), 20 sentences were read to each child and the children were asked to provide the missing word in each sentence (e.g., "Jane _____ her sister ran up the hill"; "The brown dog is small, the gray dog is smaller, but the white one is the _____."). The 20 items in the syntactic awareness task can be classified into six categories based on the target word that was missing in each sentence: past tense (regular and irregular forms), comparative and superlative items, conjunctions, prepositions, pronouns, and past participles.

Stanford Diagnostic Reading Test: Reading comprehension (SDRT; Karlsen & Gardner, 1994). Examiners administered this test in groups in each of the grade 6 classrooms. Each child was required to read the short passages within a booklet and provided responses to multiple-choice questions within a prescribed time limit.

Lexical Access

Rapid automatized naming (RAN). To assess efficiency in lexical retrieval, the children were requested to name individual numbers (1–9) presented in a random order in a 5×5 array. Each child's performance was timed in seconds.

Spelling

Woodcock–Johnson Spelling of Symbols. The children were administered the Spelling of Symbols subtest of Woodcock–Johnson (WJ). The task is made up of orally presented nonwords. Each child was asked to spell words that were read aloud. Sample words include: jesh and imbaf. Any acceptable phonetic equivalent was scored as correct (e.g., imbaf, imbaff). This task had a Cronbach's alpha of .70.

Wide Range Achievement Test–3, Spelling (blue form; Wilkinson, 1993): This subtest was administered in groups to assess real-word spelling. The children were presented orally with words of increasing difficulty and were required to generate the correct spelling.

PROCEDURE

Trained graduate students conducted individual assessments in the schools. Each child was assessed individually in a quiet room. In grade 6, the spelling, arithmetic, and reading comprehension tasks were administered in a group setting in the classrooms.

DISTRICT READING PROGRAM

In the North Vancouver school district, all children received phonological awareness instruction in kindergarten. The phonological awareness program Firm Foundations was a classroom-based program for both L1 and ELL students. The students that were identified as being at risk for reading problems received additional phonological awareness training provided by the classroom and resource teachers in small groups and on an individual basis. This phonological awareness training was based on the prototype of the program Launch into Reading Success (Bennett & Ottley, 2000). In addition, the Firm Foundations program consisted of early literacy skills development, letter–sound relationships, and language development. For instance, small groups and individuals are provided with different activities in a play format such as rhymes, sound–symbol, early writing activity (keeping journals), and letter-identification activities (baking letter-shaped cookies). Overall, the intervention was provided three to four times a week for 20 minutes. The intervention occurred in the context of developing a language and literacy rich environment with story reading and retelling, journals, and reading children's books of different levels.

In grade 2 and later, the district implemented the Reading 44 program (North Vancouver School District, 1999), a classroom program that was written by the teachers of North Vancouver. The program included the "Daily Dozen" or 12 reading strategies, and instructional activities and graphic organizers for classroom use to encourage students to learn these strategies.

RESULTS

In kindergarten, we defined a child as being at risk if they had a standard score ≤85 on the WRAT Reading subtest or a score of 0 on the phoneme-identification task or a score of <12 on the letter-identification task. The latter two scores represented scores approximately one standard deviation below the mean or lower. Of the English L1 group, 44% of the children were at risk and 54% of the ELL group were at risk for reading difficulties. Although this procedure may appear to be identifying too many children at risk, we thought it was important that we identify all the children with potential difficulties. As there was no stigma attached to this identification because it was merely for the benefit of the teacher and not for a special education designation, we thought it was an appropriate procedure.

In grade 6, children were defined as dyslexic if they had a standard score ≤85 on the WRAT Reading or the WJ Word Identification or the WJ Word Attack. The percentage of English L1 who had a reading disability was 1.9% and the percentage of ELL children was 2.3%. It should be noted that this is a very liberal criterion and had we used a stricter one, fewer children would have been identified.

Table 14.1 shows the scores of the dyslexics and normal readers on the reading and spelling tests and tasks. Not surprisingly, the dyslexic children had lower scores than the normal readers on all the reading and spelling tests and tasks. Within the normal readers, there were no significant differences between the ELL and L1 groups, with the exception of the Stanford Reading Comprehension Test in which the ELL students had significantly lower scores. However, it is important to note that in the experimental reading comprehension test, in which background knowledge was controlled, there were no differences between the ELL and the L1 groups in the normal reading groups. It is also important to note that the ELL

TABLE 14.1

Mean Scores of ELL and L1 Children on the Reading and Spelling Tasks in Grade 6

	Normal Readers		Dyslexic	
	English	ELL	English	ELL
WRAT Reading				
M	75.9	76.1	14.4	16.8
SD	16.4	16.4	14.6	15.1
WJ Word Identification				
M	83.2	81.2	19.4	28.1
SD	16.9	17.6	11.5	15.4
WJ Attack				
M	85.3	86.6	20.2	30.9
SD	16.6	15.1	12.7	18.2
Word Fluency				
M	26.9	26.9	14.3	16.1
SD	4.9	4.8	2.9	3.9
Nonword Fluency				
M	37.6	37.6	18.2	23.6
SD	4.1	4.2	7.1	6.4
Reading Comprehension				
M	61.9	57.3	18.6	19.0
SD	23.3	26.1	17.6	16.9
Experimental Reading Comprehension				
M	9.5	9.2	5.9	5.7
SD	2.1	2.1	2.2	2.1

dyslexics had significantly higher scores than the dyslexic L1 group on word identification, word attack, and nonword reading fluency.

Table 14.2 shows the scores on the spelling, arithmetic, and working memory for numbers tasks. The ELL and L1 normal readers did not differ on any of these tasks except arithmetic, in which the ELL had higher scores. However, the dyslexic ELL students had significantly higher scores on the word and pseudoword spelling tasks and the arithmetic tasks than the L1 students.

Table 14.3 shows the scores on a variety of cognitive processing tasks. In the normal reader group, the ELL and the L1 students did not differ on tasks involving syntactic awareness, rapid naming, and phonological awareness. However, within the dyslexic groups, the dyslexic ELL had significantly higher scores on the phonological awareness task than the L1 dyslexics.

TABLE 14.2

Scores of the Dyslexics and Normal Readers on the Spelling and Arithmetic Tasks in Grade 6

	Normal Readers		Dyslexic	
	English L1	ELL	English L1	ELL
	WRAT Spelling			
M	75.1	78.5	15.5	36.33
SD	19.6	20.1	12.0	24.9
	PW Spelling			
M	72.0	67.4	26.73	59.67
SD	19.7	23.2	17.80	26.16
	WRAT Arithmetic			
M	58.3	64.9	18.18	61.67
SD	23.3	25.3	15.88	39.17
	WM Numbers			
M	8.4	8.1	6.45	5.67
SD	2.3	2.2	2.81	1.53

These results are not due to socioeconomic status differences, as we have found with this sample that the relationship between reading and language tasks and socioeconomic status, although initially high, decreases with increased educational opportunities (D'Angiulli & Siegel, 2004; D'Angiulli, Siegel, & Maggi, 2004).

DISCUSSION

The data from this study presents a serious challenge to the wait-until-they-fail traditional approach. In kindergarten, 44% of the children with English as a first language and 54% of the children with English as a second language were at risk for reading difficulties. At the end of grade 6, 1.9% of the children who had English as a first language and 2.3% of the children who had English as a second language were showing dyslexia. It is important to note that the sample included all the children in the district, not a selected sample. Therefore, it seems clear that most children with reading difficulties can be helped early in their school career providing that they are assessed to determine whether they are at risk and if they are at risk, they receive appropriate classroom instruction and, when necessary, some type of resource help.

Several features of the early identification program are worth noting. First, the procedure was simple and took about 20 minutes per child. Our battery was very inclusive. Based on our results, it appears that some of the tasks could be eliminated and the procedure could be as short as 15 minutes. Second, although

TABLE 14.3

Scores of the Dyslexic and Normal Readers on the Language, Memory, and Rapid Naming Tasks

	Normal Readers		Dyslexic	
	English L1	ELL	English L1	ELL
		Oral Cloze		
M	16.1	15.6	11.6	14.0
SD	2.4	2.7	3.7	1.0
		Morphological Words		
M	9.4	9.5	5.6	7.3
SD	1.1	1.0	2.9	2.1
		Nonwords		
M	7.5	7.5	4.6	2.7
SD	2.2	2.2	2.1	2.1
		Working Memory Words		
M	5.7	5.5	3.3	3.7
SD	2.1	1.7	2.1	2.1
		RAN		
M	8.6	8.3	12.2	13.7
SD	1.8	1.8	4.3	5.0
		Phonological Awareness		
M	19.1	19.0	8.6	17.3
SD	5.6	5.3	3.8	4.7

trained graduate students conducted the testing in our study, the teachers can be easily trained to conduct the identification procedures. Third, the teachers were informed of the children's performance on the measures, compared to district (in the case of experimental measures) and national norms (in the case of standardized measures). There was no stigma attached to identification of the child at risk; the teachers merely used the information to provide the necessary help to the child.

Several features of the intervention program are worth noting. It occurred in the context of a balanced literacy program. The children received training in phonological awareness and were encouraged to participate in a variety of activities related to literacy. They were encouraged to read books and there was no specific series of readers that was used. Games and activities were encouraged. Specialist teachers were sometimes able to work with individual students who were having difficulty, although these teachers were not always available.

The ELL dyslexics had significantly higher scores than the English L1 dyslexics on some reading, spelling, and phonological awareness tasks, indicating that bilingualism is not necessarily a problem for dyslexics and may actually be an advantage.

These results are not easily attributable to the socioeconomic level in the district. In fact, the families in the district represent a wide variation of socioeconomic levels. When the children started school, there was a strong relationship between socioeconomic level and language, phonological awareness, and letter identification. This relationship decreased significantly after the children had been in school for one year, indicating that with appropriate educational intervention it is possible to reduce socioeconomic differences (D'Angiulli & Siegel, 2004; D'Angiulli et al., 2004).

This research suggests that the RTI model is feasible and successful. It is possible to identify children at risk for reading difficulties when they are 5 years old and before they have started reading instruction. This identification can be done easily by teachers or other school personnel. It is possible to use classroom-based instruction techniques to develop reading skills, at both the decoding and comprehension level. Early intervention identification for potential reading difficulties can be successful, efficient, and cost effective. Bilingualism is not an impediment to the development of literacy skills and in some cases may be an advantage.

SUMMARY

This chapter describes a simple system for identifying children at risk for reading difficulties and a classroom-based intervention program for them, and the results of an evaluation of the effectiveness of both.

The participants in this study were 792 children from a school district in the metropolitan area of Vancouver, Canada. Approximately 20% of the children had English as a second language; the most common first languages were Cantonese and Persian, although there were 36 other languages spoken by the children in this study. The screening battery consisted of a variety of tasks, specifically, phonological awareness tests (including rhyme detection, and syllable and phoneme identification); a letter-identification task that required the child to identify the name, not the sound, of lowercase letters; and a sentence repetition task in which the child had to repeat verbatim sentences that he or she heard. We also used an oral cloze task in which the child had to fill in the missing word in a sentence heard aurally, and a printing task in which the child was asked to write his or her name and some simple words.

The district used a phonological awareness program called Firm Foundations in addition to a rich language environment in the classroom. The Firm Foundations program was primarily a classroom-based instructional strategy that included the use of activities and games to stress phonological awareness and vocabulary skills. Starting in grade 2, a reading comprehension program called Reading 44 was used. This program stressed reading comprehension strategies.

In kindergarten, 44% of the children with English as a first language were at significant risk for reading difficulties and 54% of the children with English as a second language were at risk for reading difficulties. At the end of grade 6, 1.9 % of the children who had English as a first language and 2.3% of the children who had English as a second language were showing dyslexia. It is important to note that the sample included all the children in the district, not a selected sample.

When the children started school there was a strong relationship between socioeconomic level and language, phonological awareness, and letter identification. This relationship decreased significantly after the children had been in school for one year, indicating that with appropriate educational intervention, it is possible to reduce socioeconomic differences.

It is possible to identify children at risk for reading difficulties when they are 5 years old and before they have started reading instruction. This identification can be done easily by teachers or other school personnel. It is possible to use classroom-based instruction techniques to develop reading skills, at both the decoding and comprehension level. Early intervention identification for potential reading difficulties can be successful, efficient, and cost effective. In addition, the ELL dyslexics had higher scores than the English L1 dyslexics on phonological awareness and spelling tasks. Bilingualism is not an impediment to the development of literacy skills, and in some cases may be an advantage.

ACKNOWLEDGMENTS

The author wishes to thank the teachers, students, and administrators of the North Vancouver School District for their gracious cooperation. This research was supported by grants from the Natural Sciences and Engineering Research Council of Canada, and the Canadian Language and Literacy Research Network.

REFERENCES

Barwick, M. A., & Siegel, L. S. (1996). Learning difficulties in adolescent clients of a shelter for runaway and homeless street youths. *Journal of Research on Adolescence, 6*, 649–670.

Beitchman, J. H., Wilson, B., Douglas, L., Young, A., & Adlaf, E. (2001). Substance use disorders in young adults with and without LD: Predictive and concurrent relationships. *Journal of Learning Disabilities, 34*, 317–333.

Bennett, L., & Ottley, P. (2000). Launch into reading success through phonological awareness training. Austin, TX: PRO-ED.

Blachman, B. A. (1996). Preventing early reading failure. In S. C. Cramer & W. Ellis (Eds.), *Learning disabilities: Lifelong issues* (pp. 65–70). Baltimore: P. H. Brookes.

Boetsch, E. A., Green, P. A., & Pennington, B. F. (1996). Psychosocial correlates of dyslexia across the life span. *Development and Psychopathy, 8*, 539 –562.

Chapman, J. W. (1988). Cognitive motivational characteristics and academic achievement of learning disabled children: A longitudinal study. *Journal of Educational Psychology, 80*, 357–365.

D'Angiulli, A., & Siegel, L. S. (2004). Schooling, socioeconomic context and literacy development. *Educational Psychology, 24*, 867–883.

D'Angiulli, A., Siegel, L. S., & Maggi, S. (2004). Literacy instruction, SES, and word-reading achievement in English-language learners and children with English as a first language: A longitudinal study. *Learning Disabilities Research & Practice, 19*, 202–213.

Denckla, M., & Rudel, R. G. (1976). Rapid "automatized" naming (R.A.N.): Dyslexia differentiated from other learning disabilities. *Neuropsychologia, 14*, 471–479.

Fletcher, J. M., & Foorman, B. R. (1994). Issues in the definition and measurement of learning disabilities: The need for early intervention. In G. R. Lyon (Ed.), Frames of reference for the assessment of learning disabilities: New views on measurement issues (pp. 185–202). Baltimore: Paul H. Brookes.

Francis, D. J., Shaywitz, S. E., Stuebing, K. K., Shaywitz, B. A., & Fletcher, J. M. (1996). Developmental lag versus deficit models of reading disability: A longitudinal, individual growth curves analysis. *Journal of Educational Psychology, 88*, 3–17.

Goldman, R., Fristoe, M., & Woodcock, R. (1974). Goldman-Fristoe Woodcock Auditory Skills Test Battery. Circle Pines, MN: American Guidance Service.

Gregg, N., Hoy, C., King, M., Moreland, C., & Jagota, M. (1992). The MMPI-2 profile of adults with learning disabilities in university and rehabilitation settings. *Journal of Learning Disabilities, 25*, 386–395.

Karlsen, B., & Gardner, E. (1994). Stanford Diagnostic Reading Test. San Francisco: Harcourt Brace.

Lichtenstein, S., & Zantol-Wiener, K. (1988). Special education dropouts. Reston, VA: ERIC Clearinghouse on Handicapped and Gifted Children.

Lyon, G. R. (1995). Research initiatives in learning disabilities: Contributions from scientists supported by the National Institute of Child Health and Human Development. *Journal of Child Neurology, 10*, 120–126.

McBride, H. E., & Siegel, L . S. (1997). Learning disabilities and adolescent suicide. *Journal of Learning Disabilities, 30*, 652–659.

McLeskey, L., & Grizzle, K. L. (1992). Grade retention rates among students with learning disabilities. *Exceptional Children, 58*, 548–554.

Muter, V., Hulme, C., & Snowling, M. (1997). The Phonological Abilities Test. London: Psychological Corporation.

National Center for Education Statistics, (1999). *Digest of education statistics*. Washington, DC: U.S. Department of Education.

North Vancouver School District. (1999). *Reading 44: A core reading framework*. North Vancouver, BC: School District No. 44.

Rosner, J., & Simon, P. D. (1971). The Auditory Analysis Test: An initial report. *Journal of Learning Disabilities, 4*, 384–392.

Sabornie, E. J. (1994). Social-affective characteristics in early adolescents identified as learning disabled and nondisabled. *Learning Disability Quarterly, 17*, 268–279.

Siegel, L. S., & Ryan, E. B. (1989). Subtypes of developmental dyslexia: The influence of definitional variables. *Reading and Writing: An Interdisciplinary Journal, 1*, 257–287.

Snow, C. E., Burns, M. S., & Griffin, P. (1998). Preventing reading difficulties in young children. Washington, DC: National Academies Press.

Stanovich, K. E. (1986). Cognitive processes and the reading problems of learning-disabled children: Evaluating the assumption of specificity. In J. K. Torgesen & B. Y. L. Wong (Eds.), Psychological and educational perspectives on learning disabilities (pp. 87–131). New York: Academic Press.

Thorndike, R. L., Hagen, E. P., & Sattler, J. M. (1986) The Stanford Binet Intelligence Scale: Fourth Edition. Chicago: Riverside.

Wiener, J., & Schneider, B. H. (2002). A multisource exploration of the friendship patterns of children with and without learning disabilities. *Journal of Abnormal Child
Psychology, 30*, 127–141

Wilkinson, G. S. (1993). *The Wide Range Achievement Test 3*. Wilmington, DE: Jastak
Associates.

Willows, D. M., & Ryan, E. B. (1981). Differential utilization of syntactic and semantic
information by skilled and less skilled readers in the intermediate grades. *Journal of
Educational Psychology, 73*, 607–615.

Woodcock, R. (1987). *Woodcock Reading Mastery Test–Revised*. Circle Pines, MN:
American Guidance Service.

15 How the Origins of the Reading Brain Instruct Our Knowledge of Reading Intervention

Maryanne Wolf, Stephanie Gottwald, Wendy Galante, Elizabeth Norton, and Lynne Miller

Human beings come into the world programmed by our genes to interact immediately with our environment. On this basis we are able to see, hear, taste, and touch almost from the moment of birth. And, we are poised to *learn* multiple skills that contribute to human existence and ensure our survival. The full panoply of our genetic capacities represents the legacy of our species' long evolution, memorably summarized by Charles Darwin at the end of *On the Origin of Species*: "From so simple a beginning endless forms most beautiful and most wonderful have been, and are being evolved" (as quoted in Carroll, 2005). Within such a view of our evolution, what are the origins of a totally cultural invention like reading? How did humans ever learn to read? How might an evolutionary view of reading inform modern reading interventions for children who do not learn to read easily or well?

Our first observation is as simple as it is important for all that follows. No genes specific only to reading ever dictated the development of reading in any child. Put another way, human beings have neither brain structures nor genes that are specifically programmed solely for the purpose of reading. Rather, reading is an evolutionary surprise—an outcome of the brain's capacity to rearrange itself to learn something new. Reading, which human beings *invented* only five and a half thousand years ago, is built up of structures for seeing and speaking and thinking which have long existed and are genetically programmed (Dehaene et al., 2002). With the invention of reading, the human species began to use a different organization of the brain; furthermore, each type of writing system involved a somewhat different organization of the brain's structures, with some universal and some particular variations (Bolger et al., 2005). Thus, with the invention of the Chinese writing system, the brain was required to employ more visual cortex, whereas with the invention of syllabaries and an alphabetic system, more temporal, language-involved areas were recruited.

An evolutionary view of reading has unexpectedly radical implications for how we view the development of reading, its various disorders, and the teaching of reading to children with and without reading disorders. For, if the brain can be structured in different ways to learn to read different writing systems, it means that individual children can learn to read in different ways as well. And, with only a small synaptic leap of thought, it also means that if reading does not unfold from some tidy genetic program, then teaching matters a great deal. In this chapter we will briefly describe how the knowledge of reading's origins can help us reconceptualize both the acquisition of reading in the child and also what our teaching and intervention must include for the development of fluent comprehension—the long-term goal of all our efforts. Based on this reconceptualization of reading development, an intervention for children with dyslexia will be described that addresses the principal structures and processes that the brain adapted and rearranged to read. Results from a large randomized control study will be summarized and used as the springboard for a final discussion of how the development of the reading brain informs intervention research on fluency and comprehension.

THE ORIGINS OF THE READING BRAIN

The invention of reading may be a cultural phenomenon, but it could only come about because of the human brain's original plasticity. This almost miraculous feature of our design allows the brain to make new connections among older, already existing structures whenever it learns something new. It is the first and potentially the most basic of three principles of brain organization that allowed our brain to read the first time: plasticity, automaticity, and specialization. Because each of these principles plays a prominent role in the design of the RAVE-O (Retrieval, Automaticity, Vocabulary, Engagement with Language, and Orthography) reading intervention, they will be briefly elaborated here.

The first principle stems from the brain's protean capacity to make novel connections among structures and circuits originally devoted to other and more basic older processes, like vision and spoken language. Unlike vision and speech, reading is not passed on to future generations via DNA, which means that all the parts of the reading circuit must learn how to form the necessary pathways anew every time an individual brain learns to read. This is what makes reading different from other processes, and why it does not come "naturally" to children, like oral language. It is always learned afresh with each new reader. Furthermore, this circuit can only become proficient with massive use, which permits the building and strengthening of connections and ultimately, automatization, the second principle.

In this second principle of brain organization that is exploited by reading, specialized neuronal circuits learn to become virtually automatic. Automaticity, however, does not happen overnight, and it is not a characteristic of the young, novice reader. The brain's circuits and pathways for reading become automatic only through hundreds and, in the case of some children with reading disabilities like dyslexia, thousands of exposures to letters and words. The neuronal pathways for recognizing letters, letter patterns, and words are forged and strengthened with continuous use so that they learn to fire automatically. Thus, these pathways become automatic through pure and simple practice. This principle is of utmost importance in interventions, which involve the development of fluency.

But fluency does not involve only one kind of practice, like seeing letters and letter patterns over and over, however important that also is. Our learned ability to recognize letters and words involves a set of capacities that allows "specialization within a specialization" for many kinds of information, not only visual but also what we hear in the smallest speech sounds, called phonemes, and what we learn words mean and how they can function. Our capacity to make areas of the brain specialists in all these sources of information about words underlies our ability to access, retrieve, and integrate the multiple processes that are activated every time we read a word.

Together, these three principles of the brain's development—plasticity, automaticity, and specialization—permit every new reader's brain to acquire reading. Most pertinent to this chapter's arguments, these principles are imperative not only for understanding reading's development in the species and the child, but they also can help provide a different set of perspectives on reading failure in children with dyslexia and on intervention.

THE DEVELOPMENT OF READING IN THE CHILD

An evolutionary view of the reading brain presents several insights for the development of reading. First, if there are no reading-specific genes that unfold, reading will never "just happen," despite the way this seems to occur for some fortunate children, like Scout in Harper Lee's *To Kill a Mockingbird*. Rather, reading is the product of thousands of exposures to multiple sounds; spoken words; printed letters, and words, concepts, and experiences, each involving specialization in particular cortical regions. Each new reader must learn to recruit and connect these multiple, specialized regions in order to read symbolic characters and know what they mean. Novice readers around the globe must learn, therefore, how to connect an extraordinary panoply of perceptual, cognitive, phonological, semantic, syntactic, orthographic, morphological, pragmatic, conceptual, social, affective, and motor systems that all contribute to learning to read. In other words, learning to read involves the development of an ensemble of processes that depend on older brain structures that need to be both connected rapidly and synchronously coordinated. These latter two features—rapid connections and synchronicity—will be highlighted in the intervention section.

The second implication of such a view is developmental and educational: Each of these systems require explicit learning and explicit teaching, all in a relatively brief period of time for them to become specialized and automatic. Our teachers need to understand and address each of the component systems of reading, and to evaluate whether any system needs extra attention and development. The more that teachers know about all of those parts, the more likely that their students will be able to read with fluent comprehension. Furthermore, as reading develops, each of these abilities is reciprocally facilitated by further reading experience.

Two examples—one well known and one less understood—exemplify the reciprocal relationship between reading and the development of different processes. Extensively documented, children's phonological systems help them to develop an awareness of the phonemes or sounds inside a word that helps them learn letter–sound rules, which helps them learn to read more easily (Adams, 1990; Shaywitz, 2003). As children begin to read, they become ever more exquisitely attuned to the phonological aspects of words, which makes reading easier. This well-studied dynamic goes in both directions (Bradley & Bryant, 1985). Similarly, but less documented in the literature and less familiar to teachers, this facilitation phenomenon occurs for semantic development as well. Children whose semantic systems are well developed know the meanings of more words, which makes them able to decode already known words faster; adds to their written-word repertoire; fosters their oral vocabulary; prepares them to read ever more sophisticated stories; and increases their knowledge of grammar, morphology, and the relationships among words. As the biblical evangelist Matthew and the reading expert Stanovich (1986) both recorded, "The rich get richer and the poor get poorer."

This great, developmental dynamic exists between and among all the underlying component systems of reading development and forms the basis for the achievement of fluency and comprehension in later reading. Each component part aids fluency and comprehension. Such an observation needs underscoring. Twentieth-century research emphasized decoding and phonological skills, but sometimes at the unintended neglect of the needed coemphases on other systems like semantics, syntax, orthography, and morphology. Juel stresses that one of the biggest errors in reading instruction is the notion that after children decode a word, they know the meaning of what they are reading (Juel, 2005). In our 21st-century classrooms, filled with both English-language learners and English-speaking children with impoverished vocabularies, this assumption is misplaced. Semantic, syntactic, orthographic, and morphological knowledge bases are important in and of themselves for children's language development, but they are profoundly important in the development of fluent word-recognition skills and the comprehension of increasingly sophisticated texts by grades 3 and 4.

In other words, all the underlying systems must become specialized in representing their particular form of information (phoneme representations, semantic representations, etc.). Further, the systems need to become both increasingly automatic and coordinated in time. Learning to become automatic within each process and coordinated across all the various linguistic processes requires explicit teaching just as decoding does. For the child to make a great transition from "learning to read" to "reading to learn," by grade 4, all the underlying systems need to be operating effectively and efficiently. This is the basis for our conceptualization of reading fluency (see Wolf & Katzir-Cohen, 2001). This view, however, represents a figure-ground shift from most views of fluency, which tend to view it as the by-product of successful decoding. Indeed most interventions for fluency are based on such a notion and, therefore, are often restricted to activities like "repeated reading," which emphasize largely decoding processes. We see fluency as a developmental set of processes, not an outcome of only decoding skills.

More important, we conceptualize fluency as the platform for children's dawning ability to go beyond the text, to form new thoughts, and to become autonomous learners. Toward that end, the development of each underlying linguistic process—from basic phonological and decoding skills to more sophisticated semantic and morphological knowledge—are all important contributors.

Within this view, fluency allows each new reader the critical time necessary for prediction, comparison, inference, questioning, and for thinking more deeply and more independently, that is, comprehension processes. But these skills too need explicit teaching, particularly in a digital epoch where shortcuts to the formation of knowledge, provided with such immediacy in a Googled universe, are omnipresent. Our children must learn to use the precious, newly earned milliseconds after automatic decoding to think, to analyze, to criticize, and to form inferences and insights. The ultimate maturation of fluent comprehension makes young readers autonomous in their access to knowledge. This is the achievement of the evolved reading brain, and it needs to be the goal of our teaching with the formation of young readers.

EVOLUTIONARY IMPLICATIONS FOR THEORIES OF READING INTERVENTION

There are several insights from the evolutionary and developmental perspective just proposed that are the basis for our intervention for children who can't learn to read in typical fashion. First, if there are no genes or brain structures that are specific only to reading, then there is no one reading center whose demise could cause dyslexia. Rather, within this view, reading failure can result from an impediment in one or more of several possible sources: (a) in any of the older structures recruited for reading; (b) in the connections among the structures; (c) in the rapidity within specialized groups or across the connections in the circuit; and (d) in a different circuit altogether from the conventional one, resulting in imprecision, lack of fluent processing, or both.

In turn, the two most important implications of this broader conceptualization of reading failure are: (a) that reading can break down in different ways in our children; and (b) that intervention must address each of the recruited older structures, their connections to one another, and their capacity for automaticity. Such a statement brings us full circle to the original design principles in the human brain that allowed us to read: the plasticity in rearranging and connecting pre-existing structures; the capacity for automaticity; and the capacity for specialization. In this view of how the brain learned to read, it follows that if there is difficulty learning to read, then we must look to each of these design principles in our intervention.

There is a gap of logic here. If we know there will be multiple types of breakdown, why must intervention go after all these structures with their various representations, connections, and their automaticity? Our answer is both simple and imperfect. At this moment in our field's own development, we are not sufficiently precise at differentiating the exact area(s) of breakdown. Until we are, the most parsimonious solution is the least parsimonious and most comprehensive approach.

Our own efforts to create an intervention program are based on the collective developmental and design principles presented here. Created 10 years ago under the auspices of a grant from the National Institutes of Health, RAVE-O (Wolf, Miller, & Donnelly, 2000) is an intervention designed to provide explicit instruction (a) in the development of representations in each of reading's contributing processes—visual, orthographic, phonological, semantic, syntactic, morphological, and conceptual comprehension; (b) in the multiple connections among these interacting processes; (c) in the automatic access, retrieval, and integration of these processes; and (d) in eliciting the power of the affective systems.

Principles elucidated in a reconceptualized view of the components underlying fluency and comprehension (see Wolf & Katzir-Cohen, 2001) provide the theoretical scaffolding for the RAVE-O program. For example, all levels of reading fluency at the letter, orthographic pattern, word, and connected text levels are systematically addressed, along with the linguistic components that contribute to each level. Thus, fluency at the word level is affected not only by phonological and orthographic knowledge (Posner & McCandliss, 1999), but also by semantic, syntactic, and morphological knowledge (Berninger & Richards, 2002; Henry, 2003; Juel, 2005; Moats, 2000). Fluency and comprehension at the connected text level depend on the amalgamation of all these components and also on critical comprehension processes (e.g., inferential skills and self-monitoring; see Just & Carpenter, 1987: Kintsch & Greene, 1978) and world knowledge. The basic premise of the RAVE-O program is that the more one knows about a word (i.e., its phonemes, orthographic patterns, semantic meanings, syntactic uses, and morphological roots and affixes), the faster the word is decoded, retrieved, and comprehended. Enriched word recognition, in turn, contributes to more fluent comprehension. (See the linguistic and neurological evidence for this view in Wolf, 2007.)

More specifically, the RAVE-O program provides explicit instruction to guide the development of each linguistic component used in reading in daily lessons that introduce and connect the various component areas. In this way instruction helps to simulate the way the brain connects the various high-quality representations of knowledge when it reads. A small set of words, chosen for their ability to represent key aspects of each linguistic component, serve as the platform for teaching the multifaceted content of every word. Very importantly, this approach serves simultaneously to help develop in our children an understanding of the way language works.

For example, establishing semantic representations—comprehending the meaning of words—is accomplished with a series of vocabulary learning activities that go far beyond the mastery of dictionary definitions. As each word is pulled from a treasure chest (a symbol of all the "wealth" students will discover about each core word), students engage in a discussion about all the meanings of the word that they know collectively. Before the session closes, the multiple interesting meanings (MIMs) of their new words become both apparent and fun.

All core words in the program are polysemous and often capable of different syntactic functions: examples like "jam" and "ram" quickly establish a mindset toward both the multiple meanings of words, and also their multiple associations and grammatical functions. Children begin to learn the critical role that syntactic structure plays in connected text, and they gain a new appreciation for the need to think about what words do.

All teaching materials in the program are intended to provide multiple modalities for learning (storing), for remembering, and for retrieving different aspects about words. Intentionally diverse and whimsical, the materials are designed to engage the affective system of learner and teacher alike. Thus in the teaching of MIM words, image cards with drawings that illustrate each possible meaning involve visual imagery in the service of learning and memory. Large, laminated word webs that the children build up show how all the meanings and associations around a word can be visually depicted. The word web helps students quite literally make a network for a word's individual meanings, as well as to realize overlaps and distinctions between meanings, contrast their use in various grammatical functions, and develop the ability to categorize other words similarly. Students regularly begin identifying other multiple meaning words in the rest of their lives and become increasingly less disenfranchised from their own language in the process.

A myriad of tried-and-true games like bingo, crossword puzzles, and letter dice provide practice in a variety of modes for learning the various linguistic dimensions of words. Matching games using word or sentence level materials with image cards and specific vocabulary retrieval strategies develop accuracy of semantic representation, and then, by imposing time limits, encourage speed for fast, automatic recall. Brief short stories called minute stories have been created with only the core words of the program in order to challenge students' recognition of the core words, and their various meanings and functions in the context of connected text. Wherever possible, all the meanings and syntactic functions of the polysemous core words appear in the stories. Specific comprehension strategies encourage not only prediction and recall of story parts, but also the individual insights of children that go beyond the text. In addition, various games for sentence combining and writing activities give students power over their own use of words to increase their abilities to express their own thoughts.

RAVE-O provides a similar developmental trajectory in all the linguistic systems for each core word, thereby enhancing and compounding the impact of each. For example, in orthography, words are first analyzed by individual phoneme, drawing on knowledge established in other phonology programs that students are receiving in the rest of their school day. By examining pairs of words sharing a frequent letter pattern, students learn the "system" of sublexical units through which the English language builds even the simplest words. Development of orthographic representations at the subword level is an essential component for flexible and fluent word identification, and is often missing in the development of struggling young readers. Much time and careful sequencing is expended to build accurate recognition of these orthographic patterns so that they are perceived as units or visual chunks. After these chunks are accurately learned for the most common patterns in English, they are then "speeded," to ensure more automatic reading at both the sublexical and lexical levels. As described for the semantic component, a variety of activities and games are used to engage affect through various modalities. For example, a set of spelling-pattern cards provides a first level, hands-on manipulable material for exploration of sound–symbol relationships at the sublexical level. A set of computer games was designed to provide the "hundreds of exposures" often needed to develop automatic orthographic skills in students with severe reading disabilities. The extent of practice is controlled for individual students by the teacher, whose task it is to guide a careful mix of both adequate practice activities and success experiences to each child.

Along similar lines, knowledge of the morphological component is integrated with orthographic and semantic activities. Students learn almost immediately the role and power of suffixes (called *ender benders*, a metacognitive strategy for remembering what suffixes do) and prefixes, their uses in different parts of speech (grammatical functions), and how knowing them helps to speed up the recognition of a word. Compound and other morphemically combined words (called *fat rats*) are learned as a combination of known orthographic units. This strategy helps children read longer words that are often perceived to be too difficult to read.

Through all these combined emphases, the RAVE-O program's goals are for struggling readers to acquire the ability to integrate their knowledge about words into more accurate and more fluent reading at every level—from better word recognition to more fluent reading comprehension of text. How much any one component is especially emphasized depends on the particular deficits or weaknesses in the individual child. The success of the program's implementation is particularly dependent on teachers, for it requires their specific knowledge of what to look for in the child's developing language and reading systems.

Reported elsewhere in more detail, the results of a large, NICHD-funded study amply support the multidimensional emphases within RAVE-O and another multidimensional program, PHAST (see Lovett, 2000) in several ways. These findings emerge from a large, randomized treatment-control study (Morris et al., 2007) of approximately 300 children in three cities. In this study, alongside a control condition, three treatment conditions were studied: the RAVE-O program; PHAST, which emphasizes metacognitive word-identification strategies, orthography, and morphology; and a phonological program (SRA Reading Mastery). The children in the control condition received a study skills and mathematics intervention the first year and one of the multidimensional treatments after the study ended. The multidimensional design of both the RAVE-O and PHAST programs proved effective in achieving significantly superior gains in every reading-related measure at every level, from letter recognition to text fluency and comprehension. These included spelling, word attack, word identification, fluency for words (trained and generalization to untrained) and nonwords, and silent and oral reading comprehension.

Although students in the two multicomponential programs overwhelmingly outperformed the group who had equal time in purely phonological training, RAVE-O showed additional advantages over PHAST in semantic areas and fluent comprehension. Both multicomponential programs produced superior outcomes on nonword reading measures (Woodcock Word Attack and TOWRE Nonword Reading Efficiency) as compared to the phonology-only control group. At follow-up testing one year later, RAVE-O students demonstrated significant continued linear growth over other students.

RAVE-O and PHAST students performed comparably on single-word decoding tasks (Woodcock Word ID, WRAT Reading, TOWRE Word Reading Efficiency), with both conditions significantly outperforming phonological and control groups. RAVE-O students showed greater growth than any other group on the PIAT spelling measure, which relies on orthographic knowledge. In semantic knowledge and semantic flexibility, measured by the ability to provide multiple meanings of an untrained word, RAVE-O proved significantly more effective than all other treatment conditions in improving multiple definition task scores on the standardized WORD-R and experimental RAVE-O word measures, both after training and beyond the scope of the study into the following year (see Barzillai, Wolf, Lovett, & Morris, 2009). Students in the RAVE-O intervention also significantly outperformed children in other interventions in the word recognition of both trained and untrained polysemous words. These results indicate that the semantic focus of RAVE-O was not only instrumental in increasing the semantic flexibility for trained words, but was also able to help children in their ability to find multiple meanings for words that were not trained in the program. This increased semantic flexibility was further associated with increases in the accuracy of reading words with multiple meanings, indicating the influence of semantic knowledge on single-word reading.

The most important findings concerned the relative changes in fluent comprehension. Both multidimensional programs showed significant gains and outcomes in Gray Oral Reading Test (GORT) accuracy and rate. The RAVE-O students demonstrated greater growth and superior outcomes in fluency and comprehension as compared to all other programs.

These data support the major premise of the RAVE-O program, that is, the more a new reader *knows* about a word, the better and faster the child reads and comprehends it. The data also demonstrate that despite the fact that the RAVE-O program expends more time teaching the words' multiple meanings and uses (and, therefore, less time on phonological and decoding processes), the results in Word Attack and Word Identification are equal to or superior to more purely phonological analysis and blending programs that spend proportionately more time on decoding skills (see Norton, Wolf, Lovett, & Morris, 2009).

The experimental RAVE-O program is evolving with every new study of its implementations in different school settings, including in-school time, after school (Pierce, Katzir, Wolf & Noam, in press), and summer school, as well as in small groups and whole-class groupings. In addition, we are currently studying the effectiveness of RAVE-O with different populations (English-language learners, children using African American Vernacular English), and at different ages (first grade, second and third grades, fourth grade). With each study we are changing the way we teach RAVE-O to more effectively reflect the underlying principles, and the needs of children and teachers.

In summary, we conceptualize the RAVE-O intervention as a program with an *open architecture* that addresses many of the major components and design principles in the reading brain itself, including the capacities to make areas of specialization increasingly automatic. The results to date are extremely supportive. Our ultimate goal is to create an intervention program that explicitly addresses what the brain does when it reads a single word—in all its richness, complexity, and evocativeness so that more children can learn to read.

REFERENCES

Adams, M. (1990). *Beginning to read*. Cambridge, MA: MIT Press.

Barzillai, M., Wolf, M., Lovett, M., & Morris, R. (2009). *Semantic knowledge and the reading process*. Manuscript in preparation.

Berninger, V., & Richards, T. (2002). *Brain literacy for educators and psychologists*. San Diego, CA: Academic Press.

Bolger, D., Perfetti, C., & Schneider, W. (2005). Cross-cultural effect on the brain revisited: Universal structures plus writing system variation. *Human Brain Mapping, 25*, 92–104.

Bradley, L., & Bryant, P. E. (1985). *Rhyme and reason in reading and spelling*. Ann Arbor, MI: University of Michigan Press.

Carroll, S. (2005). *Endless forms most beautiful*. New York: Norton.

Dehaene, S. (2005). Evolution of human cortical circuits for reading and arithmetic: The neuronal recycling hypothesis. In S. Dehaene, J.-R. Duhamel, M. D. Hauser, & G. Rizzolatti (Eds.), *From monkey brain to human brain* (pp. 133–157). Cambridge, MA: MIT Press.

Dehaene, S., & Cohen, L. (2007). Cultural recycling of cortical maps. *Neuron, 56*, 384–398.

Dehaene, S., LeClec'H, G., Poline, J., LeBihan, D., & Cohen, L. (2002). The visual work form area: A prelexical representation of visual words in the fusiform gyrus. *NeuroReport, 13*(3), 321–325.

Henry, M. (2003). *Unlocking literacy: Effective decoding and spelling instruction*. Baltimore: Brookes Publishing.

Juel, C. (2005). The impact of early school experiences on initial reading. In D. Dickinson & S. Neuman (Eds.), *Handbook of early literacy research* (Vol. 2, pp. 410–426). New York: Guilford Press.

Just, M. A., & Carpenter, P. A. (Eds.). (1987). *The psychology of reading and language comprehension*. Newton, MA: Allyn & Bacon.

Just, M. A., Carpenter, P. A., Keller, T. A., Eddy, W. F., & Thulborn, K. R. (1996). Brain activation modulated by sentence comprehension. *Science, 274*(5284), 912–913.

Kintsch, W., & Greene, E. (1978). The role of culture-specific schemata in the comprehension and recall of stories. *Discourse Processes, 1*(1), 1–13.

Lovett, M. (2000). Remediating the core deficits of developmental reading disability: A double-deficit perspective. *Journal of Learning Disabilities, 33*(4), 334–358.

Lovett, M., Borden, S. L., DeLuca, T., Lacerenza, L., Benson, N. J., & Brackstone, D. (1994). Treating the core deficits of developmental dyslexia: Evidence of transfer-of-learning following phonologically-and-strategy-based reading training programs. *Developmental Psychology, 30*(6), 805–822.

Moats, L. C. (2000). *Speech to print: Language essentials for teachers*. Baltimore: Paul H. Brookes.

Morris, R., Lovett, M., Wolf, M., Sevcik, R., Steinbach, K., Frijters, J., et al. (2007). *The importance of multiple-component remediation in developmental reading disabilities*. Manuscript submitted for publication.

Norton, E., Wolf, M., Lovett, M., & Morris, R. (2009). *The effects of intervention across levels of reading fluency*. Manuscript in preparation.

Pierce, M., Katzir, T., Wolf, M., & Noam, G. (in press). Assessing and reading skill among urban children at risk for reading failure. *Reading and Writing*.

Posner, M. I., & McCandliss, B. D (1999). Brain circuitry during reading. In R. M. Klein & P. A. McMullen (Eds.), *Converging methods for understanding reading and dyslexia* (pp. 305–337). Cambridge, MA: MIT Press.

Shaywitz, S. (2003). *Overcoming dyslexia*. New York: Random House.

Stanovich, K. (1986). Matthew effects in reading: Some consequences of individual differences in the acquisition of literacy. *Reading Research Quarterly, 21*(4), 360–407.

Wolf, M. (2007). *Proust and the squid: The story and science of the reading brain*. New York: HarperCollins.

Wolf, M., & Katzir-Cohen, T. (2001). Reading fluency and its intervention. *Scientific Studies of Reading, 5,* 211–238.

Wolf, M., Miller, L., & Donnelly, K. (2000). RAVE-O: A comprehensive fluency-based reading intervention program. *Journal of Reading Disabilities, 33,* 375–386.

Conclusion: Integration of Methodologies in Cognitive Neuroscience—Research, Planning, and Policy

Kenneth R. Pugh and Peggy McCardle

As noted at the outset of this book, in recent years, research on assessment and treatment of specific reading disability (dyslexia) has become a magnet for the application of new techniques and technologies from genetics, neuroscience, cognitive psychology, and cognitive neuroscience. This interdisciplinary trend has yielded numerous and diverse findings regarding the brain and cognitive bases of this syndrome, but work aimed at integrating these findings from very different levels of analysis is just beginning (and was a key motivating factor in the choices we made regarding themes and participants at the symposium from which this book arose). At the level of genetics, a number of candidate genes have been proposed, but this work is just beginning. At the level of brain systems, neurobiological anomalies at key left hemisphere (LH) posterior regions have been observed with surprising consistency in different languages and across different developmental stages, and links between individual differences in brain circuits and behavioral profiles of strengths and weaknesses have been reported. Moreover, several recent studies have demonstrated that intensive remediation/intervention can be associated with increased response of these LH posterior systems, suggesting some degree, at least, of latent functionality in these circuits. These seminal findings on brain plasticity in dyslexia are highly promising but need to be expanded to include a deeper focus on individual differences, differential profiles in distinct written languages, and greater integration across levels of analysis.

This symposium brought together leading researchers from a range of disciplines and several countries to address crucial, cutting-edge, and interrelated topics on the cognitive, neurobiological, and genetic bases of reading disability. We chose to focus on a wide range of topics rather than a singular theme to identify gaps in current knowledge, methodology, and theoretical frameworks that will merit higher research priority in the coming years. We asked the participants to begin with a presentation on the state of the science in their particular field of study, with presentations ranging from genetics through remediation. After the

presentations, we engaged in a 2-day session to identify next steps and implications for research design, policy, and planning across the various disciplines
and scientific areas. The presentations and discussions (and thus the chapters in
this volume) were stimulating and challenging. There were many points of agreement among participants regarding next steps, along with important disagreements. In broad terms we discussed (a) new research directions and priorities and
(b) the methodological developments necessary to support them; (c) how best to
extend research to new and diverse languages, populations, and ages; (d) ways to
strengthen links between research and practice (the presence of several school
directors at the meeting triggered important discussions on translational research
and curriculum development); and (e) implications for policy and funding priorities. We begin our conclusion for this volume with a summary of the major
themes raised across the chapters, and follow this with a set of key recommendations reflecting the full input of the symposium participants on necessary next
steps in dyslexia research.

SUMMARY OF MAJOR THEMES RAISED BY PRESENTATIONS

One focus of this volume is to examine recent findings at multiple levels of analysis: genetics, brain structure and function, and cognitive phenotype. Progress in
the field depends, in part, on developing the means to allow these distinct levels
of analysis to inform and constrain one another in moving toward a neurobiologically grounded account of dyslexia.

Three chapters focus on genetic investigations. Rosen, Wang, Fiondella, and
LoTurco (Chapter 2) discuss three candidate genes in dyslexia (*Dcdc2*, *Kiaa0319*,
and *Dyx1c1*) and new techniques aimed at determining the role these genes play
in typical or atypical brain development (including contributions from animal
models). Early findings from this group have revealed a preponderance of mild
cortical malformations known as ectopias (reflecting anomalous neuronal migration) in postmortem analyses of dyslexic brains. Thus Rosen's group targets genes
that might be associated with atypical neurogenesis; their ongoing work with
gene-disruption models in rats aims to make this crucial link. Although some of
the work is in early stages, the integrated use of genetic analysis, animal models,
and human phenotype studies promises to fill in important gaps in the extant
knowledge. Grigorenko and Naples (Chapter 7) provide a critical review of the
state of candidate genes for dyslexia, and their review suggests notable limitations on replicability (across studies) at present for key candidate genes. Striking a
cautionary note, they make the case for both larger scale epidemiological studies
in the next phase and a more cognitive view of reading and its component processes, which might encourage increased focus on complex genetic interactions in
dyslexia research. Olson, Byrne, and Sameulsson (Chapter 11) provide us with an
update on cross-linguistic longitudinal twin studies, which suggest a high degree
of heritability for reading readiness and early formal literacy skills that appear to
be similar in different languages and cultures. They raise a challenge from some
of their data suggesting quite limited effects of instruction relative to heritability

weighting. This notion raises to the forefront ongoing questions regarding the relative weight of nature versus nurture and poses a challenge to the discussion on optimal instruction and remediation. We suspect that this dynamic will motivate new research questions and will figure prominently in next-phase remediation educational investigations.

All three of these chapters encourage gene–brain–behavior linkage research, but also reinforce the need for crucial developments in cognitive neuroscience to understand the phenotype more precisely. Clearly the next phase of research will need to attend to how we can make use of integrated brain–behavior measures to mediate the link between genetic variability and atypical reading behavior.

On the brain–behavior front, several chapters deal with current findings in cognitive neuroscience (with particular emphasis on powerful tools for structural and function brain imaging in humans). S. Frost et al. (Chapter 1) presented an update of recent functional magnetic resonance imaging (fMRI) findings: converging evidence from functional neuroimaging studies indicates that a key neurobiological marker of dyslexia is reduced activation of LH posterior regions relative to activation levels for nonimpaired readers during tasks that make demands on language and printed-word processing. However, it is interesting that recent evidence from intervention studies suggests that compromised LH systems appear to be responsive to intensive training in young reading disabled (RD) populations (Meyler, Keller, Cherkassy, Gabrieli, & Just, 2008; Meyler et al., 2007; Shaywitz et al. 2004; Simos et al., 2002; Temple et al. 2003). That is, many LH regions that are critically involved in reading and are not activated during reading tasks in young RD readers prior to an intervention period show increased activation after intervention. This reinforces the notion that these LH systems are poorly tuned but not fundamentally disrupted, opening the "for which children" question for the next-phase research—that is, which approaches to treatment will work for a given neurocognitive profile. Although some fairly consistent group differences are found in neurocircuits for reading and these are evident in different languages and with different imaging modalities (see Cornelissen, Chapter 9, for magnetoencephalography findings), functional mapping data largely describe a neurophenotype but do not provide information on the neurodevelopmental mechanisms responsible for the altered circuits. Frost et al. discuss these limits of functional neuroimaging and the need to broaden the investigation of neurobiological underpinnings in dyslexia. This broadening, they argue, should include increased focus on structural brain development and the neurochemistry of brain learning and plasticity, which they illustrate with preliminary findings from a longitudinal study that tracks at-risk children from 7 to 9 years of age with genetics, structural imaging, magnet resonance spectroscopy focused on measuring important neurochemicals and neurotransmitters, functional imaging, and cognitive testing. Ultimately, the aim of their work is to develop a multilevel, brain-based phenotype for genetic candidate analyses.

With a clear agreement across chapters on the need to use multimodal brain imaging techniques to gain a fuller account of both typical and atypical development, Mencl, Frost, and Pugh (Chapter 5) focus on the difficult but critical task of using integrated neuroimaging designs (e.g., combined fMRI, event-related potential [ERP] measures to more fully reveal spatiotemporal patterns in reading) in developmental research. Clearly, the development of integrated imaging techniques and a new generation of multivariate analyses for these complex data will be a crucial target in the next phase of research.

Much of the symposium discussion focused on powerful tools for handling the sorts of data likely to emerge in next-steps research. Rueckl and Seidenberg (Chapter 6) provide a systematic account of computational models (with special focus on parallel distributed processing architectures) in reading and language. They propose that neural network classes of models could be employed to (a) develop a better understanding of complex neural dynamics in reading and language processing observed with functional neuroimaging studies, and (b) provide a means of capturing important differences from one language to another and across the developmental span associated with reading acquisition. They assert that computational models must provide a means of capturing learning, not just static performance levels.

With regard to new analytic tools, Francis (Chapter 4) provides an overview of powerful multivariate statistical methods that are relevant to the goal of multimodal data integration in cognitive neuroscience and to different definitional accounts of dyslexia. Francis particularly addresses whether dyslexia is best viewed as a continuous or discrete syndrome, and whether there may be legitimate subgroups in this population with distinct brain–behavior etiology. This emphasis on statistical methods for dealing with complex data sets will be crucial for meeting the research goals that call for larger scale, next-generation studies discussed later in this chapter.

Cognitive-behavioral profiles have a relatively longer history of empirical research than do genetics and neurobiology in the investigation of reading and reading disability. Therefore, there is sometimes a tendency to assume greater consensus on the phenotype than might be warranted by the state of current theory. Indeed, while most discussions on this topic reinforced the importance of phonological deficits that are uncontroversially implicated in dyslexia, a few major gaps in current cognitive accounts were discussed at the symposium.

Several symposium participants noted that the phenotypes present in variable forms across development, from preschool risk profiles where phonologically analytic processing deficits are pronounced to adolescence where comprehension difficulties play an increasing role. For instance, in Chapter 8, Ramus and Szenkovits acknowledge phonological deficits but report on a line of studies that did not indicate basic spoken-language processing difficulties in young adult dyslexics, although such difficulties would be anticipated by several prominent theories. Cutting, Eason, Young, and Alberstadt (Chapter 10) identify an important but understudied issue: whether deficits in comprehension might emerge as stumbling blocks in older struggling readers, even where phonologically analytic skills and basic word decoding that depends on these skills are within normal limits. Wolf, Gottwald, Galante, Norton, and Miller (Chapter 15) taking up these gaps, argue that reading is a highly integrated set of cognitive operations and that deficits in any part or parts will retard development of fluency and comprehension. R. Frost (Chapter 12), presenting studies contrasting reading in Hebrew and English, argues that cognitive accounts may need to be adjusted to account for linguistic differences in different languages.

Much lively debate arose in the symposium sessions where these ideas were discussed, and these issues are touched upon in the preceding chapters. The key take-home message for next steps in dyslexia/reading disability research is simply that we cannot become too comfortable with general notions of phonological deficits; rather, we must continue to probe cognitive mechanisms with new research tools and we must do so considering developmental trajectories. Indeed, several symposium participants called for renewed focus on whether dyslexia in its behavioral manifestation is better viewed as continuous (the lower end of a normal distribution of language-related cognitive skills) or discrete. This is an old question, and given that it can still be legitimately debated suggests that phenotypic research needs are still acute.

We also have tried to bring renewed focus on language differences: to the degree that developmental dyslexia is gene based, we anticipate its presence in vastly different written languages. The cross-linguistic discussions at the symposium fueled enthusiasm for new research that will include systematic cross-language comparisons, as well as studies of individuals learning to speak and read more than one language. Such studies will allow us to identify both language invariant and idiosyncratic profiles in dyslexia and will promote better theory in the estimation of these participants.

Siegel (Chapter 14), Sherman and Cowen (Chapter 3), and Foorman and Al Otaiba (Chapter 13) provide stirring updates on intervention and instructional research that in broad terms are asking how we can best shape the learning environment to maximize outcomes for children with these distinctive brain–behavior profiles. Siegel notes that systematic remediation along the lines promoted in response-to-intervention (RTI) approaches can dramatically reduce the numbers of high-risk children (identified in first grade) by sixth grade. Moreover, this benefit was seen in her studies equivalently for bilingual and monolingual children. Foorman and Al Otaiba discuss current views on best practice in remediation and curriculum development, with a focus on the importance of monitoring student progress adequately and structuring remediation to the complex classroom environment. Wolf et al. (Chapter 15) explicitly discuss the need for treatments that can flexibly address component skills that are poorly realized in an individual and focus on strengthening complex brain circuits for reading. Sherman and Cowen discuss the need to understand strengths and talents in dyslexia and utilize this in differentiating instruction. They also raise the important issue of how literacy might be changing in this digital age, calling for this to be considered by educators in working with struggling readers.

Symposium participants agreed that treatment must be tailored to the individual. Even the best evidence-based practices will not impact some children. New advances in brain–behavior phenotype research hold promise of providing a more sensitive account of individual differences. As this phenotype is developed, we will be better able to assess "what works for whom." Participants also acknowledge within this the need for preschool (school readiness) instruction as a crucial need in the field, to not only prevent reading difficulties for many children but also to enable us to better understand early brain–behavior risk markers. This should be a high priority in next-phase studies.

NEXT STEPS: A SUMMARY

With the symposium's discussions and debates as well as the updated presentations that have become the chapters of this volume in mind, we offer the resulting recommendations for next steps in research, policy, and practice. Symposium discussions were wide ranging and participants were initially encouraged to generate their wish lists for next steps. Some themes came through with high frequency:

- There is a need for a new generation of epidemiological studies with integrated genetics–brain–behavior designs, and with age ranges from pre-readers through older adolescent samples to assess age-appropriate skill sets.
- New and better tools are needed, particularly computational approaches for multimodal neuroimaging and cross-language comparative studies.
- There should be a renewed focus on definitions (e.g., continuous vs. discrete, subtypes, comorbidities, RTI, and what constitutes nonresponse).
- Work in the classroom and laboratory must be better integrated to improve delivery of reading instruction (e.g., cognitively informed, optimal-learning research; large-scale, school-based research projects; and a deeper focus on brain-based, individually tailored treatment research).

Each of these general targets will demand genuinely interdisciplinary teamwork and the development of a common language, multisite cooperation, and appropriate commitments from funding agencies and foundations. We discuss some of these in greater detail next.

New Generation of Epidemiological Studies With Integrated Genetics–Brain–Behavior Designs Across Age Ranges

The many intriguing findings from genetics through brain circuitry discussed at the symposium, and in this volume, are at present still largely descriptive (e.g., good readers and poor readers differ on some biologic index but we have limited information on cause versus consequence) and findings are still somewhat unconnected across levels of analysis and across age ranges. To generate a more integrated brain-based phenotype for dyslexia, the group unanimously called for a new generation of epidemiological studies using integrated neuroscience measures in conjunction with state-of-the-art behavioral testing to address key gaps in knowledge with sufficient power and a clear developmental focus. Indeed, studies of this sort will demand large and representative samples of at-risk children and would perhaps be feasible only via a multisite collaboration.

Neuroscience measures would include state-of-the-art genetics with continued exploration of candidate genes, measures of the neurochemistry of learning and plasticity (with techniques like spectroscopy this can be done in vivo), structural neuroimaging (including morphometry and diffusion weighted tensor imaging), integrated multimodal functional neuroimaging (yoked electrophysiological and hemodynamic measures will allow more precise specification of the spatiotemporal organization for language and reading at different stages), and a renewed consideration of postmortem histological data to explicate links to animal models of dyslexia. The previous generation of large-scale epidemiological studies have been of great importance in establishing, longitudinally, the behavioral phenotype and developmental trajectories in high-risk populations, but given the explosion of findings in neuroscience, it seems rather clear that a next generation of large-scale longitudinal studies will need to examine the potential causal roles played by individual differences in these neurobiological factors in long-term reading outcomes.

At the behavioral level, renewed attention to the cognitive primitives underlying phonological processing deficits demands cognitively sophisticated paradigms that have not been the focus of previous large-scale studies using primarily standardized assessments. In addition, a new emphasis on reading comprehension and other postcode learning skills in older cohorts will be important in establishing age-appropriate expectations and in determining how higher level skills relate to basic phonological and language issues. Indeed, given the long-term limitations of conventional interventions, a deeper understanding of how decoding feeds into higher level comprehension mechanisms is clearly needed. By targeting toddlers and preschoolers, we can examine early speech perception/production trajectories in relation to later preliteracy skills and enable the targeting of genetic and neurobiological markers of risk. In short, by proposing a new generation of longitudinal studies with many of the tools discussed in this volume, a more integrated understanding of the brain–behavior bases of dyslexia is hoped for.

Of course, it is unsurprising that a group of researchers such as those participating in this symposium would call for new and larger scaled epidemiological longitudinal studies, given the intriguing findings at multiple levels of analysis available that nonetheless make evident such large gaps. However, this group suggested something more. It noted a need for integration across laboratories and research teams and projects, resulting in the use of common core sets of measures, analyses, and sampling decisions; in this way data acquired at different sites, and with different cohorts, might be cumulative in some very substantial manner. This suggestion begins to make sense when considering the value of extremely large samples for gene/phenotype studies. Without common standards, it would be difficult to aggregate data across labs.

RENEWED FOCUS ON DEFINITIONS

Definitional criteria for diagnosis of dyslexia are still subject to debate, confusion, and disagreement. This lack of consensus on defining characteristics can result in different researchers obtaining samples that are not comparable to one another, which muddies the waters when trying to assess why some findings fail to replicate across samples. This becomes even more acute when trying to examine dyslexia across different languages and orthographies, where again criteria are variable. As an example, in English, disabled readers are both error prone and dysfluent in word decoding, but in a very regular orthography like Finnish (where each grapheme maps to only one phoneme and vice versa), dysfluency is similarly seen but errors do not appear to be phenotypic in that language; however, diagnostic criteria are nonuniform across languages. This reinforces the need for ongoing research aimed at classification. It was generally agreed that brain–behavior methodologies have real promise in sharpening our classification and further research on biomarkers is recommended.

At present some researchers continue to employ a discrepancy criterion, where the discrepancy between IQ and some achievement measure is considered diagnostic of a learning disability, at least in terms of legally qualifying that student for special education services. Others simply use low achievement in reading as the inclusion or selection criterion for studies of reading difficulty/disability. However, recent work noting problems with the discrepancy criterion suggests that RTI is a potentially more useful approach (Department of Education Office of Special Education and Rehabilitation Services, 2002). In fact, based on the large body of research cited by the President's Commission on Special Education, the 2004 reauthorization of the Individuals with Disabilities Education Improvement Act (IDEIA, 2004) now allows states an alternative for identifying students with learning disabilities for special services. That alternative is RTI (Fletcher, Lyon, Fuchs, & Barnes, 2006; Haager, Klingner, & Vaughn, 2007): If a child fails to respond to increasingly intensive instructional interventions, then he or she is targeted for special, individualized educational services. RTI has great intuitive appeal, but validation studies will be crucial in order to set standards that will allow age, language, and cross-cultural comparative studies to be on a common footing. Thus, classification research for reading disability should be a continuing priority.

Even with fairly neutral criteria, such as achievement-based statistical diagnosis or promising uses of RTI, our ability to disentangle congenital from environmental factors is difficult because of the heterogeneity seen both in behavioral profiles and brain activation patterns within any cohort with reading difficulties. Fundamental questions like whether dyslexia represents the lower end of a normal distribution or a discrete typology await further research with some of the new statistical and neuroscience tools discussed earlier. However, it remains that there are large individual differences in any cohort of struggling or impaired readers, and even with similar reading deficits, it is hard to predict which children will be treatment responders or resistors to standard interventions. It was suggested by several participants at this symposium that additional gene–brain–behavioral research be focused on parsing this heterogeneity by examining with neurocognitive tools whether there are legitimate subtype dimensions in those with reading problems, particularly in those with comorbidities (e.g., attention deficit/hyperactivity disorder [ADHD], math disability, general cognitive deficits). Although previous behavioral studies have been hard pressed, with conventional testing, to identify robust differences across these potential subtypes, it may be that conventional accuracy or latency measures lack the sensitivity needed. This matters because if dyslexia does not represent a uniform syndrome but rather a condition with many distinct neurobiological pathways with a common end-state (poor phonological and reading skills), this will have profound implications for theory, genetic mapping, and tailoring treatment. Many of the necessary tools are in place, so the potential for real momentum in classification and subtyping work is high.

Cross-linguistic research will benefit from classification work. With comparable neurocognitive measures, and agreed upon sampling criteria, we can begin to examine whether there are core language-invariant features of reading difficulty. There has been some speculation that the sets of deficits needed to produce reading failure in distinct languages and orthographies, varying in orthographic to phonologic regularity, might be partially nonoverlapping. At present, dyslexia research on brain bases or candidate genes is often done in different languages, but this is rarely considered as a potential complication by those researchers. Much more work on language-invariant markers versus language dependencies will be needed to bring this growing body of international research into alignment. Integrated cross-language collaborations are needed to generate a more nuanced understanding of reading difficulties.

INTEGRATION OF LABORATORY RESEARCH AND CLASSROOM INSTRUCTION

A good deal of emphasis was placed on learning, plasticity, and optimal treatment at this meeting. Moreover, the dialogue between researchers and school directors at the meeting brought the questions of what works for whom into central focus. Again, given the early findings that brain imaging can be sensitive to treatment responses, there was a good consensus on the potential value of further neurocognitive plasticity studies. Brain–behavior profiles can reveal important individual differences not always evident in performance on standardized assessments. A next generation of studies looking at pretreatment subtypes by treatment interactions may be able to begin to deliver on the promise of brain-based learning. Again, such work would benefit from multisite collaborations. One tangible outcome from this discussion was a plan to bring research into schools more fully. Independent dyslexia school directors have organized a consortium of educational leaders and researchers to identify designs and plans for school-based research, potentially facilitating the use of schools as research laboratories in a mutually beneficial partnership. For multisite collaborations, it will be crucial to ensure common outcome measures across sites, carefully gathered demographic and cognitive data, state-of-the-art measures (both brain and behavior), and data quality control.

An important question to be addressed through such large-scale networks is which treatments work for whom. However, a high level of enthusiasm was seen in the discussion for a next generation of studies that will systematically vary learning protocols based on cognitive principles. For instance, if a treatment must include A, B, and C, is there a theory-driven "best way" to sequence and weigh these necessary elements (and does this optimal approach vary in different ages, subtypes, languages, or brain phenotypes)? Indeed, Pugh and colleagues reported on a new study reinforcing latent plasticity in older poor readers at the level of brain circuitry, but suggested that learning may not become well consolidated in many dyslexics. Can the treatment be tailored to reflect principles of learning and memory that are well established in humans and animals so as to enhance gains? Of course, the question is whether a more developmentally broad focus will lead us to think somewhat differentially about optimal learning strategies in older and younger cohorts, and how instruction in decoding can be built upon to include higher level language operations relevant to comprehension.

Finally, with respect to optimal instruction, several participants from both the research and school communities pointed to an acute need to better understand talents and strengths in dyslexia to optimize learning environment (see Sherman & Cowen, Chapter 3, this volume). School-based research, while challenging, has already shown great promise to allow a richer and larger scale approach to optimal instruction. Access to concentrated groups of students with reading difficulties may enable even more rapid progress in some areas of investigation. Thus, strengthening partnerships with schools to promote innovative instructional research, development of better gene–brain–behavior models, statistical methods to assess heterogeneity and subgrouping, cognitively motivated work with optimal instruction, and cross-linguistic comparative studies were all topics of high interest in our discussion of next steps in remediation and optimal instruction.

In conclusion, as we consider the wealth of new information presented by the authors in this volume, and as a group their recommendations for how to go about improving our current understanding with new epidemiological studies that are gene–brain–behavior based, renewed focus on definitions with these new tools, and more integrated and cognitively grounded treatment research (supported by strong school–researcher partnerships), we are enthusiastic about these next steps. We hope that the development of new measures, the launching of new neurobiological longitudinal studies, and school–research cooperation will facilitate putting ideas raised in the chapters in this book into action.

REFERENCES

Department of Education Office of Special Education and Rehabilitation Services. (2002). *A new era: Revitalizing special education for children and their families.* Washington, DC: Author.

Fletcher, J. M., Lyon, G. R., Fuchs, L. S., & Barnes, M. A. (2006). *Learning disabilities: From identification to intervention.* New York: Guilford Press.

Haager, D., Klingner, J., & Vaughn, S. (2007). *Evidence-based reading practices for response to intervention.* Baltimore: Paul H. Brookes.

Individuals with Disabilities Education Improvement Act of 2004 (IDEIA), 20 U.S.C. 1414 (2004). Retrieved November 5, 2007, from http://www.nichcy.org/reauth/PL108-446.pdf

Meyler, A., Keller, T. A., Cherkassy, V. L., Gabrieli, J. D. E., & Just, M. A. (2008). Modifying the brain activation of poor readers during sentence comprehension with extended remedial instruction: A longitudinal study of neuroplasticity. *Neuropsychologia, 46*(10), 2580–2592.

Meyler, A., Keller, T. A., Cherkassy, V. L., Lee, D., Hoeft, F., Whitfield-Gabrieli, S., et al. (2007). Brain activation during sentence comprehension among good and poor readers. *Cerebral Cortex, 17*(12), 2780–2787.

Pugh, K. R., Frost, S. J., Sandak, R., Landi, N., Rueckl, J. G., Constable, R. T., et al. (2008). Effects of stimulus difficulty and repetition on printed word identification: An fMRI comparison of non-impaired and reading disabled adolescent cohorts. *Journal of Cognitive Neuroscience, 20,* 1146–1160.

Shaywitz, B. A., Shaywitz, S. E., Blachman, B., Pugh, K. R., Fulbright, R., Skudlarski, P., et al. (2004). Development of left occipito-temporal systems for skilled reading following a phonologically-based intervention in children. *Biological Psychiatry, 55,* 926–933.

Simos, P. G., Fletcher, J. M., Bergman, E., Breier, J. I., Foorman, B. R., Castillo, E. M., et al. (2002). Dyslexia-specific brain activation profile becomes normal following successful remedial training. *Neurology, 58,* 1203–1213.

Temple, E., Deutsch, G. K., Poldrack, R. A., Miller, S. L., Tallal, P., Merzenich, M. M., et al. (2003). Neural deficits in children with dyslexia ameliorated by behavioral remediation: Evidence from functional MRI. *Proceedings of the National Academy of Sciences, 100,* 2860–2865.

Author Index

Subject Index

A

Activation supramarginal gyrus, 9
Adaptive learning, 8–9
ADD. *see* Attention deficit disorder (ADD)
ADHD. *see* Attention deficit/hyperactivity
    disorder (ADHD)
Adolescents, 202
AG. *see* Angular gyrus (AG)
Alphabetic orthographies
    English and Hebrew, 236
    lexical organization and processing, 235
    recognition processes, 249
American education, 57
Anatomic connectivity, 92
    multimodal imaging tools, 92–98
Androgen testosterone, 24
Angular gyrus (AG), 6, 113
Animal models, 23–24
    brain and developmental dyslexia
        experimental tests, 26–34
Anisotropy, 93
Anterior inferior frontal gyrus phonological
    circuits, 114
Anterior system reading acquisition, 7
Arithmetic tasks, 283
Articulatory-phonological form of inferior
    frontal gyrus, 188
Artificial lexicon studies, 126
Assets School in Honolulu, Hawaii, 57
Attention deficit disorder (ADD), 261
Attention deficit/hyperactivity disorder
    (ADHD), 48, 145, 309
    RD, 219
Auditory disorders, 21

B

Baker, William H., xiii
Basic reading skills for children, 275
Behavioral abnormalities, 25
Behavioral-cognitive skills, 14
Behavioral phenotype, 50
Behavioral results, 104
Behavioral symptoms, 21
Beth Israel Hospital, xiii
Bilingualism, 286
Blood-oxygen level dependent (BOLD)
    response, 90

BOLD. *see* Blood-oxygen level dependent
    (BOLD) response
Brain
    animal models, 23–24
    based learning, 309
    behavior profiles, 309
    candidate dyslexia susceptibility genes, 26
    central visual fields, 53
    circuity, 306
    Dcdc2, 33
    development, 291
    developmental dyslexia, 21–36
    Dyx1c1, 28–32
    ectopias dysplasias, 22
    enigmas, 55
    experimental tests in rodents, 26–34
    genetics, 25–33
    good readers, 306
    Kiaa0319, 33
    laminar dysplasias, 22
    LH posterior regions, 301
    neocortical migration, 26
    peripheral visual fields, 53
    poor readers, 306
    postmortem, 22, 140
    SRD, 140
Broca's area, 98
    activation, 180–181
    developmental dyslexia MEG, 182–184, 185
    inferior frontal gyrus, 110

C

Cardiff samples, 139
Carroll School in Lincoln, Massachusetts, 57
Categorical latent variables, 68
CBF. *see* Cerebral blood flow (CBF)
CD. *see* Cerebrodiversity (CD) model
Central visual fields, 53
Cerebral blood flow (CBF), 95
Cerebral cortex malformations, 23
Cerebrodiversity (CD) model, 44, 47–52
    byproducts, 52
    dyslexia, 55
    dyslexia byproduct, 49–50
    evolutionary lens, 50
    gene-brain-environment dynamic, 51
    LD, 49, 51
    microscopic lens, 50